History's Masterminds

3500 B.C. - A.D. 2012
Teacher's Manual & Answer Key

with Orientation, Research Guide, Literature Helps,
Extended Reading List, Timelines, Lesson Plans & Keys

By Sally Barnard
& Linda Thornhill

Self-published by
TRISMS
1203 S. Delaware Place
Tulsa, OK 74104-4129

TRISMS
CURRICULUM

First Place winner of the Practical Homeschooling Reader's Award in the Middle School Curriculum category.

Other titles by *TRISMS*, Inc.

TRISMS High School
Discovering the Ancient World   Prehistory – 500 BC
Expansion of Civilization 500 BC – AD 1500
Rise of Nations 1440 - 1860
Age of Revolution 1850 – 2012

It's About Time (timeline book)
Reading Through the Ages (reading resource)
American History Based Source Texts
World History Based Source Texts

Current listing and prices are available from *TRISMS*, Inc.

Phone: 918-585-2778
Fax: 918-585-2778
Web site: www.trisms.com
Email: Linda@trisms.com

Self-published by *TRISMS*, Inc.
1203 S. Delaware Place
Tulsa, OK 74104-4129

Cover design: Rachel Floyd, 2012
Research Development and Engineering Command   http://www.flickr.com/photos/rdecom/4343923438/

Mastermind: person who originates or is primarily responsible for the execution of a particular idea or project.

Printed in the USA   ISBN 0-9677387-3-3   ISBN 978-0-9677387-3-1   Teacher's Key
                                            ISBN 978-0-9677387-7-2   Student Book
                                            ISBN 978-0-9677387-8-9   Student Pack

To Phillip Barnard and Don Thornhill who had faith in us and our little idea. Our thanks to them for their computer expertise and countless hours of work and encouragement to bring this volume to you.

This new edition and format comes to you with the help of Cheryl Horton and Candy Matheny. They have interviewed parents and students, studied feedback and test groups, and spent countless hours working and encouraging me to finish. Thanks to Nathan Horton for taking on the task of retyping the lesson plans, and to Rachel Floyd for unifying the maps and designing our new cover. Many thanks for a job well done!

History's Masterminds
Teacher's Manual & Answer Key

Table of Contents

Orientation: This section gives an introduction and instructions for History's Masterminds.

Research Guide: A short lesson to help prepare and develop student research skills for each questionnaire.

Literature Helps: This section includes terms and story elements the student will encounter in the Language Assignments.

Extended Reading List: This section contains additional reading selections not listed on the lesson plan. These are categorized by reading level and number of pages in order to facilitate in selecting appropriate books for the student.

Timelines: For further study, timelines are included for women in history, black scientists, inventors, explorers, and an overview of History's Masterminds and church history.

Lesson Plans: The lesson at-a-glance guide for the student and teacher with daily assignment keys following each lesson are:

    Research questionnaires: Scientists, Inventors, and Explorers

    Science Assignments: Keys for those following lesson plan.
    Student assignments for Science are in the Student Book only.

    Language: Keys for Language worksheets follow the lesson plan.
    Student assignments for Language Arts are in the Student Book only.
    Worksheets are located in the Student Pack.

    Quiz and Test Keys

Orientation

This section gives an introduction and instructions for TRISMS History's Masterminds. It defines how students and teachers will use the curriculum.

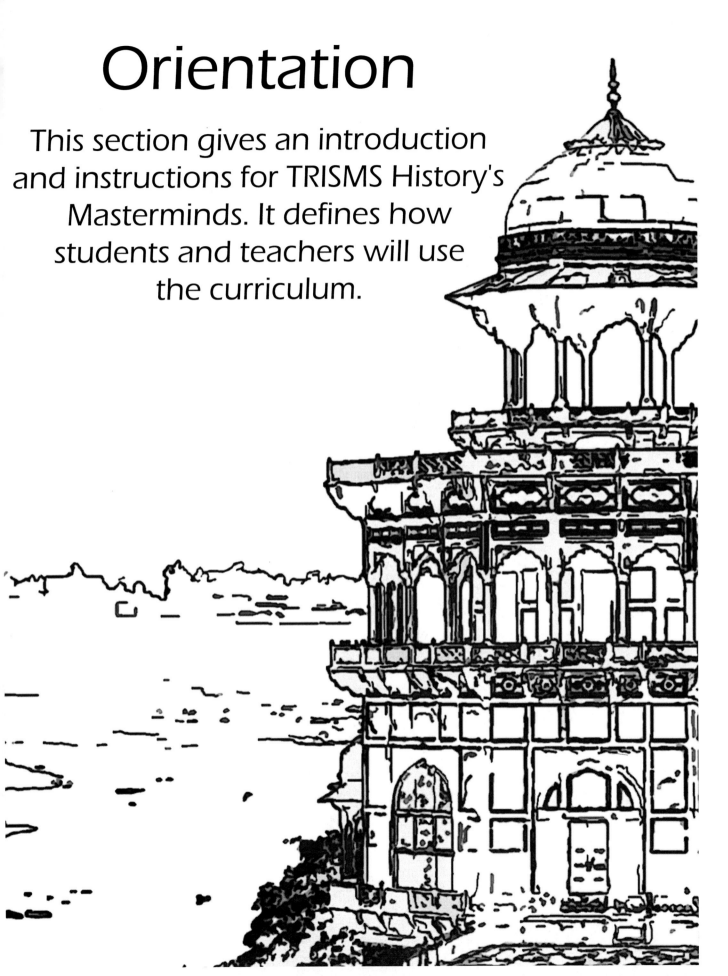

Teacher's Notes

_____

_____

_____

_____

_____

_____

_____

_____

_____

_____

_____

_____

_____

_____

_____

_____

_____

_____

_____

_____

_____

ORIENTATION

This section will introduce and explain the components of the History's Masterminds curriculum. Here you will learn how to use the lesson plans, make a timeline, build coursebooks, and tie everything together. You will also learn what additional resources will help to make full use of this course of study.

Components
History's Masterminds has three basic components:
- Teacher's Manual & Answer Key – includes the orientation, research guide, literature helps, extended reading list, research timelines, lesson plans, answer keys for research questionnaires, science assignments, worksheets, quizzes and tests. **Note: Answers in the key are posted by topic column rather than by daily assignments.**

- Student Assignment Book – includes the research guide, literature helps, research timelines, lesson plans, science assignments, language assignments, poetry selections and IEW assignments.

- Student Pack/Test Packet – includes all research questionnaires, worksheets and maps necessary to complete the assignments in the lesson plans. The test packet contains all quizzes and tests.

Objectives and Overview
The *TRISMS* curriculum is designed to impart a chronological survey and geographical progression of discovery over time. In order to stimulate the child's interest, History's Masterminds focuses on the people involved in important historical events and discoveries rather than just focusing on events or dates. By including the personalities, a context is given that makes the information being learned more meaningful. Throughout the year, the student will read biographies, historical fiction, cultural studies, and most varieties of reference materials. Some students find the subject matter especially interesting and want to spend more time than
the lesson plan presents. With History's Masterminds you can set the pace, choosing to cover the entire course in one year or, more comfortably, in two. In addition, History's Masterminds is easily adapted to a multi-level setting.

Central to the curriculum is the lesson plan. The lesson plan is organized in a weekly format with daily activities. Scientists, Inventions, and Explorers are covered in chronological order from the beginning of recorded history until 2012. The Language Arts and IEW assignments are integrated into this chronology by using materials pertinent to the theme being studied.

The lesson plan also provides a recommended reading list, items of historical significance not covered by daily assignments, additional subjects of interest for more motivated students, and accomplishments in math for the time being studied.

As the student works through the lesson plan, he or she will construct a timeline which chronologically lists the people and events being studied. The timeline provides an overview and reference that cultivates a broad understanding of history.

The student will create a coursebook which will contain the research questionnaires that the student has completed and provide an organized reference for the subjects studied. Also included will be drawings, articles, and pictures the student gathers during the course of study, the language arts and IEW assignments, and completed quizzes and tests.

The following sections explain how each part of History's Masterminds is used:

History's Masterminds Lesson Plan "Explanation Page"

Day	SCIENTISTS	INVENTIONS	EXPLORERS
Mon			

These headings will tell the student which questionnaire to use. They include **Scientist Q**, **Inventions Q**, and **Explorers Q**.

The assignments in each subject column changes from time to time but the questions on the questionnaires remain the same.

334 - 326 BC Alexander the Great expanded his empire from Greece to India

When working on the **Explorer Q.** a picture can be added for enhancement.

Tue

Science Vocabulary
Circumference
Radius
Diameter
Sphere
Hemisphere
Gnomonics

Vocabulary words are to be listed on a sheet of paper and placed in the coursebook for each lesson.

Mark Map 2

Map numbers indicate what map to use for marking the explorer's travels.

Wed 287 – 192 BC Eratosthenes measured the circumference of the Earth.

Use a Scientist Questionnaire

Vocabulary words should include pronunciation, definition and a sentence pertaining to the lesson.

Vocabulary
Emperor
Republic
Universal law

221 BC Magnetic Compass

Thurs 200 BC Archimedes used experiments to discover volume, buoyancy, and simple machines.

200 BC Archimedes' Screw

Draw a Roman army uniform.
Draw a Macedonian army uniform.
How does strategy differ?

Each scientist has a specific achievement that the student will research using their questionnaire.

Lessons often ask the student to transfer information through art. This encourages attention to details and critical thinking.

Vocabulary
Volume
Concave lens
Buoyancy

The **Invention Questionnaires** ask the student to add an illustration along with answering specific questions on the research questionnaire.

Map Vocabulary
Chart
Continent
Equator
Circumnavigate
Geographical map

S-3

"S" stands for a **Science assignment** and #3 is the lesson number. You will find the "S" assignments following the lesson. The assignment correlates with the scientist being studied and may provide a hands-on activity.

200 BC Wheelbarrow

The student will compile their completed questionnaires, maps, and worksheets to form a coursebook which becomes their school portfolio.

Read a background on the Romans.

Select a resource of your choice.

Assignments are divided into days. Each lesson is designed for 1 week unless you choose to do History's Masterminds in 2

Students will use reference materials such as encyclopedias, books, and maps to fill out questionnaires.

LANGUAGE ARTS	READING SELECTIONS
L-3a Oral Book Report	Historical Fiction (read one per lesson)
Write a rough draft on last week's book.	Detectives in Togas – Henry Winterfeld
	The Shadow of Vesuvius – Ellis Dillon
IEW Banned Words	The Eagles Have Flown – J. Williamson
	Yesterday's Daughter – Helen Daringer
	The Young Carthaginian – G. A. Henty
	For the Temple – G. A. Henty
	Mystery of the Roman Ransom - Winterfeld
L-3b Edit and copy	Biographies (an alternate for a historical fiction)
	Archimedes and the Door of Science – Bendick
IEW Dress-ups	Alexander the boy Soldier Who
View IEW DVD 2 and p. 18 in Syllabus	Conquered the World by Simon Adams
L-3c Give oral report	Other Books for Research
	Caesar's Gallic War – Olivia Coolidge
Review p. 8 in the IEW Syllabus	The Librarian Who Measured the World
	In the Shadow of Olympus – Eugene Borza
IEW Dress-ups review the 'because' clause	The World in the Time of Alexander the Great – Macdonald
	Ancient Science – Jim Wiese
L-3d Book jacket review	The Roman World – Michael Vickers
	Spend a Day in Ancient Rome – Linda Honan
	Historical Events for Timeline
	336 BC Alexander sets out to conquer the world
	336 BC King Darius III of Persia
	321-250 BC Seleucids rule Iran and Palestine
	215 BC Great Wall of China begun
	143-63 BC Hebrew Kingdom
	146 AD Carthage destroyed
	146 AD Greece taken by Rome
L-3e Write a book jacket on this lesson's	Other Areas of Interest during this Lesson
selection.	Constantine
	Titus (79-81 AD)
Movie: Spartacus	Julius Caesar
	Hannibal
Write your mini	Gladiators
book report	Cleopatra
	Punic Wars
3 Week Quiz	Accomplishments in Math during this Lesson
	160 AD Hipparchus Nicaea invented trigonometry

"L" denotes a language assignment followed by the lesson number. The assignments follow the lesson plan.

The student selects one book to read each lesson and will write a mini book report on the book. Selections may be made from each lesson's list or other sources, but must deal with the time

Timeline Events
Events can be plotted on a timeline. Timelines can be a continuous sheet or individual lesson timelines.

Movies are encouraged (but not required) for a better understanding of the time period.

Topics for expanded research or reports.

There are quizzes for the student to take throughout the course to teach testing skills and to evaluate retention of subject material.

History's Masterminds - *TRISMS©*

Setting the Pace

Many home educators find History's Masterminds more enjoyable when extended over a two year period. This can be done by spending two weeks on each lesson or more interestingly, by spending more time on subjects especially fascinating. Slow down the beginning to allow the student time to learn to research.

Lesson Plans

Lesson Plans are set up in week-at-a-glance format with daily activities in categories for Scientists, Inventions, Explorers, and Language Arts. Reading selections are provided to serve as a form of immersion in the period. Students should select **one** book per lesson to read or substitute with an audio book or film.

Daily Assignments

Daily assignments are given in the lesson plan. For Scientists, Inventions, and Explorers, research questionnaires are provided in the Student Pack. The student will use reference materials such as encyclopedias, reference books, and maps to fill out the questionnaires. Vocabulary words are also listed for these subjects. The student will come across these words in their reading and study of the subject. The student will create a glossary listing the words, pronunciation, and definition. The student will be quizzed every three lessons and selected words will be on the quarterly test. Additional assignments in Science are referenced in the lesson plan with an **S** and explained in the Science Assignments which follow each lesson. Language and IEW assignments are referenced in the lesson plan with an **L** and are explained in the pages following each lesson.

- Scientists 🖋

Each scientist has a specific achievement noted on the lesson plan to help direct the student's research. These achievements will also appear on the quizzes and tests. Science assignments are cross referenced and included in the Student Assignment Book.

- Inventions 🛠

The student will discover the original form of the invention as well as see the effect these inventions had on society.

- Explorers 🌐

Each explorer has a specific achievement noted on the lesson plan that will be covered on the quizzes and tests. A map is provided for each explorer so the student can mark the route of his exploration as well as continents, oceans, and any other details the teacher wishes the student to study. The maps are numbered and the lesson plan notes which map should be used with each explorer. The maps are located in the Student Pack. The asterisk (*) identifies the destination of the explorer to be used for the lower portion of the research questionnaire. Students should answer these questions for the time period being studied.

- Language 📚

Language and IEW assignments are located directly following the lesson in the Student Assignment Book. This complete Language Arts program includes reading, writing, poetry, speech, listening skills, the eight parts of speech and a complete grammar course.

Ψ *The Institute for Excellence in Writing* Teaching Writing Structure and Style program is used to develop structure and style as the student completes the language arts assignments. Structure refers to the outlines that define an essay, report, research paper, critique, sentence, and paragraph structure. Styles are taught to incorporate descriptive language, figures of speech, repetition and rhythm. IEW is included in assignments and in source text provided. IEW is not required to complete the assignments, but highly recommended.

You will also note questions or assignments in the columns for Scientists, Inventions and Explorers. Examples which include:

📖 Read a background on Egypt. This can be a junior level book on Egypt. Its purpose is to help the student quickly familiarize himself with the time period and region.

✏️ Draw or write a description of an Egyptian. This will go in the coursebook. The assignment gives the student an opportunity to add illustrations to their coursebook. Encourage students to add other drawings or information they find interesting.

🏳️ When a flag is assigned to be drawn or researched, the student should find the flag as it was during the time period being studied because flags represent people, countries, ideas or skills. The symbols and colors represent a people group and give students a better understanding of the culture and time period.

🕐 There are several timelines provided before the lesson plans. Timelines included are women in history, black scientists, inventors and explorers, Bible and church history. They provide more ideas for historical study.

WEEKLY ACTIVITIES
The student will be reading a historical fiction or biography each lesson as a form of immersion in the time period being studied. The student will select **one** book from the reading list to read each lesson. Other historical fiction or biographies can be substituted as long as they fit the time period. Each book on the Reading Selections list has been reviewed. We realize, however, that sensitivity levels vary. Therefore, we recommend parents preview the books their children select. *Reading Through the Ages* is a useful tool that lists books by time period and reading level. It is available individually or as part of the *TRISMS* Starter Set at www.trisms.com.

Mini Book Reports
The student will make mini book reports on all historical fiction and biographies read during the year. These reports should be made on 3x5 or 4x6 index cards and kept in a card file box. The format is as follows:
   ❶ Place the title of the book on the top line
   ❷ Capitalize the first, last and all important words in the title of the book
   ❸ Underline the title
   ❹ On the next line write the name of the author of the book
   ❺ Skip a line and write a few sentences about the story.
      Try to make it interesting without giving away the ending.
   ❻ In the bottom, left-hand corner record the number of pages in the book.
   ❼ In the bottom right corner write your initials.

---

❶❷❸<u>Detectives in Togas</u>
❹By Henry Winterfeld

❺The Xanthos School has been robbed and the teacher injured. School break is declared but there is no time for fun. The mystery must be solved to free a fellow student from prison and certain death.

❻205 pages   ❼LT

Reading Selections

The books listed on the lesson plan are at the junior high school reading level.

The <u>Reading Selections</u> column is divided into the following sections.

- Historical Fiction
- Biographies
- Other Books
- Historical Events
- Other Areas of Interest
- Accomplishments in Math

The Historical Fiction and Biography sub-headings provide lists of books recommended for reading during the lesson. The student is to read **one** of these books or another book from the time period being studied. A historical fiction may appeal to your student because in most cases the main character is the age of the reader. The biography selections will provide much more in-depth treatment of the personalities being studied and may be preferred over encyclopedias as study material.

The Other Books sub-heading provides a list of helpful books which provide additional background to help both the teacher and the student. The Historical Events sub-heading gives dates and events for the student to add to the timeline. Other Areas of Interest gives ideas for further study, and Accomplishments in Math lists contributions in mathematics for each time period.

MONTHLY ACTIVITIES

Oral Reading

Oral reading can be done by the teacher or in a round robin fashion with everyone taking a turn. The following stories are recommended but can be exchanged for others from the time period. This is an easy way for Dad to get involved.

- Sept   *Beowulf* by Robert Nye or Rosemary Sutcliff
- Oct   *Merry Adventures of Robin Hood* by Howard Pyle
- Nov   *The Prince and the Pauper* by Mark Twain
- Dec   *Robinson Crusoe* by Daniel DeFoe
- Jan   *The Count of Monte Cristo* by Alexander Dumas
- Feb   *Little Lord Fauntleroy* by Frances Burnett
- Mar   *Five Little Peppers and How They Grew* by M. Sidney
- Apr   *Call of the Wild* by Jack London
- May   *The Railway Children* by Edith Nesbit

Movies

🎥 Movies can be used to further immerse the student in the time period. Films illustrate costume, customs, social structure, architecture and often language forms. Some recommended titles are:

- Sept   *Jason and the Argonauts (old version)*
- Oct   *Black Arrow*
- Nov   *Ivanhoe*
- Dec   *The Three Musketeers (1948 version)*
- Jan   *The Scarlet Pimpernel*
- Feb   *Oliver Twist*
- Mar   *Spirit of St. Louis*
- Apr   *A Tree Grows in Brooklyn*
- May   *Charlotte's Web*

The books, films, and other resources listed in the lesson plan may be available from a public library.

Timeline

A timeline is a long strip of paper on which a series of dates is printed at specific intervals, creating a visual graph of consecutive events. This gives the visual learner the "big picture" of what is happening. The student will record all the scientists, inventions, and explorers studied on a timeline. They are encouraged to add other persons, inventions, and historical events to their timeline.

BC (BCE) & AD (CE)

In using a timeline, you must know how to read dates and understand their meaning. Time is counted backward and forward from the day Christ was born. The years before those dates are numbered backward, and each year is followed by the letters B.C., meaning "before Christ.", or BCE, meaning "Before Common Era". The years after Christ's birth are numbered forward and are preceded by the letters A.D., which represent "anno Domini (in the year of our Lord)", or CE, which represent "Common Era".

An event that took place in 10 B.C. happened ten years before Christ was born. Something that occurred in the year A.D. 100 took place 100 years after Christ's birth. Usually only the letters B.C. are used. Dates without letters are assumed to be anno Domini.
A century is one hundred years. Therefore, the date 25 B.C. is in the first one hundred years B.C., or the first century before Christ was born. An event in 170 B.C. happened in the second one hundred years, or the second century. An event in A.D. 350 was in the fourth one hundred years, or the fourth century.

- *TRISMS* offers *It's About Time* (a blank timeline book) for those who have limited wall space or take part in mobile classrooms.

Constructing the Timeline

Your timeline begins with prehistory in 5000 B.C. Divide the timeline according to the intervals given below. Each division should be at least an inch. The spread of each interval is shown in the table below. Divide the intervals prior to 3500 B.C. into five hundred year intervals. Between 3500 B.C. and zero, divide the timeline into 100 year intervals, etc.

From		To		Division (Yrs)
Prehistory	B.C.	3500	B.C.	500
3500	B.C.	0		100
0		1400		50
1400		1800		20
1800		1900		10
1900		Now		5

Across the top of the timeline the Ages should be shown. The following chart shows the different Age divisions. Note that some of these overlap.

Age Divisions	From		To	
Prehistory	Prehistory	B.C.	3500	B.C.
Ancient	3500	B.C.	500	B.C.
Classical	500	B.C.	475	A.D.
Dark Ages	475		1000	
Middle Ages	1000		1500	
Renaissance	1300		1550	
Age of Discovery	1500		1800	
Industrial Age	1700	A.D.	1960	A.D.
Technological	1950		Now	

The following is an example of a segment of the timeline. The subjects covered are listed in the far left column.

Time Divisions	Prehistory				Ancient	
Dates		5000	4500	4000	3500	3000
Scientists						
Inventions		Ark		Plow		Wheel
Explorers						
Bible (optional)	Creation	Noah				
Math		Base 60		Base10		
Civilizations	Eden	Middle East	Egypt	China	Chaldean	Aegean

For studying your state's history, simply insert it into the proper time period. It is also fun to add your family history to the timeline.

Coursebooks

The student will create coursebooks for scientists, inventions, and explorers which contain all research questionnaires, maps, and any other interesting information on the subject. Alternatively, students may combine all their work into one coursebook divided by lesson. Allow the student to discover the best organization style for their work. Start each coursebook with an identifying title page and a table of contents. Language Arts, grammar, and IEW assignments may also be added to the coursebook.

Research Questionnaires

Research questionnaires are provided in the Student Pack for Scientists, Inventions, and Explorers. The student will fill these out as each person or topic is studied. A Research Guide to get you started follows the Orientation.

Special Interest Coursebook

Students may want to develop a special interest coursebook. Whatever the student is interested in is the topic. Examples include: sports, boats, the wheel, flags, weapons and military strategy, fashion, wigs and hats, shoes and purses, fabric and fasteners, cooking and cookbooks, beverages and drinking containers, entertainment, dance, music and instruments, medicine, animal husbandry, farming, myths and folklore. The special interest may also be added to the timeline. The student can design a unique questionnaire for their special interest topic and add completed questionnaires to each lesson.

Quizzes and Tests

All quizzes and tests are located in the Student Pack/Test Packet. Quizzes are given every three lessons and should be used as study guides for the quarterly tests, which are given four times throughout the course. It is a good idea for the teacher to look over the quiz before the student begins the three lesson period to make sure the student covers everything that is presented on the quiz.

Necessary Additional Resources

A historical atlas, globe, world map, encyclopedia set, thesaurus, dictionary, and access to a public library.
A world map - It is essential to examine the extent of exploration and vital to understand the origins of civilizations and their expansion.
3-ring binders for coursebooks
1 - 3x5 or 4x6 card file box for mini book reports
1 - set of ruled 3x5 or 4x6 index cards
1 - set of colored pencils and/or markers for maps
Cardstock or tabbed dividers for coursebook title pages

American History Survey

History's Masterminds presents a survey of world history. To add additional focus on American history, students may select a reading book on an American history topic found under Historical Events and Other Areas of Interest on the lesson plan. Students may also include the stories and assignments in the IEW U. S. History-Based Source Texts available as a download. A line can be added to the timeline that reflects events in American history.

Using History's Masterminds for Multi-level Teaching

History's Masterminds was designed with the middle school student in mind. If you desire to adapt the curriculum for younger students you will need to simplify the research questionnaires, eliminating questions requiring abstract reasoning.

What Next?

After completing History's Masterminds, students are ready for *TRISMS* high school volumes. Middle School and even upper elementary students who have been through the History's Masterminds program can begin the high school volumes using the suggestions for adaptation provided in the orientation of Discovering the Ancient World.

TRISMS High School

Discovering the Ancient World Prehistory through 500 B.C.
Discover ancient civilizations through their contributions. Investigate the mysteries and wonders of the ancient world. From the birthplace of civilizations to the Amazon women of the Steppes, experience how people lived before electricity and cell phones. Discover ancient civilizations through their art, music, architecture, science, literature, history and geography in this fully integrated curriculum designed for high school students. Composition assignments include IEW TWSS 2-D instruction. Includes User's Manual, Answer Keys, and notebook ready Student Pack/Test packet. (18 units). 1 year program – 8^(th) or 9^(th)

Expansion of Civilization 500 B.C. to A.D. 1500
Explore the beginnings of Western civilization and its progress. Watch the world develop through the golden age of Greece and Rome, knights and castles. Read some of the greatest literature ever written and study the beginnings of philosophy through the words of Plato and St. Augustine. Examine governments and religions still alive in our culture today. Study the art, music, history, architecture, geography, rhetoric, philosophy, and literature of each civilization. Composition assignments include IEW TWSS 2-D instruction.
Includes Teacher's Manual & Answer Keys, Student Assignment Book, and notebook ready Student Pack/Test Packet. (18 units) 1 year program

Rise of Nations 1440 to 1860
Investigate the birth of the nations of the world through the early Renaissance, Reformation, and Enlightenment. Meet Leonardo da Vinci, Michelangelo, Mozart, and many more great men. See the great cathedrals, palaces, Taj Mahal, and many more architectural wonders. Read the words of Shakespeare, Martin Luther, and René Descartes. Includes cultures from Africa, Asia, Europe, Middle East, North America and South America. Experience the art, music, history, architecture, geography and literature in this fully integrated curriculum. Composition assignments include IEW TWSS 2-D instructions.
Includes Teacher's Manual & Answer Keys, Student Assignment Book, and notebook ready Student Pack/Test Packet. (18 units) 1 year program

Age of Revolution 1850 – 2013
American and modern world history integrated into the people and events of our times from 1850 to 2013. Meet 40 plus authors from around the world review our American presidents, key world leaders, wars, Nobel Prize winners, artists, musicians, architects, and the people who made America what it is today. A balance of World History with American History integrated into the events of this exciting time period with art, music, history, architecture, geography, political science, rhetoric, philosophy, and literature studied in context. Composition assignments include IEW TWSS 2-D instructions.
Includes Teacher's Manual & Answer Keys, Student Assignment Book, notebook ready Student Pack/Test Packet. (18 units) 1 to 2 year program   Printed by semester

Make this your best homeschooling year ever!

Note to Parents and Teachers:

Using the History's Masterminds Answer Keys

TRISMS is research based. There is no one book that has all the answers for the questionnaires, nor do all books have the same facts, dates, or information regarding a particular subject. Please use this answer key as a guideline, not as the "only answer".

1. Learning is not in knowing the answer. It's in the PROCESS of finding the answer.
2. Learning is not in writing the answer you found but in ANALYZING the answer.
3. Learning is not WHAT the answer is but WHY is this the answer.
4. Learning is not realizing you got the wrong answer but in understanding why your answer is wrong.
5. Learning is more about knowing WHERE and HOW to find the answer than in finding the answer itself.
6. Learning is being able to formulate an opinion and back up your opinion with evidence.
7. Learning is about analyzing the source of information as much as the information.
   This definition for learning comes from Karen Caroe.

History is the vehicle *TRISMS* uses to attain the mastery of skills. If the student has checked three sources and can't locate the "answer" then use the answer key as a source and move on. Students should document their search. Even then, keep in mind that history is rather fluid based on new evidence discovered and sources you find. Finding every answer is not the goal.

Furthermore, it is important to realize that your student will look at the information and discoveries (as given in chronological context throughout history) differently than you as a parent. Questions of significance and ethical consequences may be difficult for the student due to their limited life experience. Here is where the parent, as teacher, can aid the student through discussion to work out their logic from the evidence gathered. The scientists can be especially difficult due to the complicated nature of their work and discovery. Extra information is provided on the keys to help the parent with these discussions.

It is important for the student to realize the role of cause and effect, limited communication and transportation at different times, as well as the invention of tools, as methods leading to research development. Discuss the concept that scientific knowledge is neither good nor evil but rather, it is the use of that knowledge that can be ethical or immoral.

Using this as a guideline, students will learn to observe cause and effect, consequences for decisions, and the realization that one person can make a difference.

Learning a new way to think is difficult at first but attainable. *TRISMS* is a proven approach to education – so persevere. Think of it like the experience of learning to drive a car. There are many different tasks we must learn but when they all come together you are driving. Students will advance to this new level by practicing critical thinking and abstract reasoning.

SIXTH GRADE

The sixth grade student should study the listed achievements associated with each person in the lesson plans. Sixth graders may skip lesson plan items listed under **Historical Events**. The sixth grade student can do the language assignments given in the first three quarters. In the fourth quarter the student should do only the assignments that are listed in the following guide.

Lesson 28
Sentences
Endings
Subjects and Predicates
Nouns
Kinds of nouns (abstract and concrete)

Lesson 29
Plural nouns
Possessive
Differences
Verbs and Nouns

Lesson 30
Identifying Verbs
Action and Linking verbs
Verb Phrases
Principal parts of verbs
Transitive and Intransitive verbs

Lesson 31
Adjective
Adverbs
Comparative forms
Using Suffixes

Lesson 32
Personal pronouns
Antecedents

Lesson 33
Prepositions and phrases
Prepositions and Adverbs
Conjunctions – coordinating
Conjunctions – correlative
Interjections

Lesson 34
Direct objects
Indirect objects
Appositives
Negatives
Using this, that, these, and those

Lesson 35
Sentence punctuation and capitalization
Commas
Semicolons and Colons
Apostrophes and Quotation Marks
Underlining, Hyphen and Dash

Lesson 36
Abbreviations
Homonyms
Synonyms and Antonyms

SEVENTH Grade

The seventh grade student should study the listed achievements associated with each person in the lesson plans. The language assignments given fulfill standard seventh grade requirements. In slowing down the pace you could fill in the timeline with the items listed under **Historical Events** in the lesson plans. Discuss the impact of these events on the people studied. Plan and produce a dramatization of one of these events.

EIGHTH Grade

The eighth grade student should follow the given information for each person in the lesson plans. In addition, he or she should include the following Language subjects in the last quarter:

- Study of infinitives, gerunds, predicate nominatives and predicate adjectives.
- Creative drama

There are many books on Grammar and Language Arts available for more practice.

INFINITIVES

Infinitives are the *to*-forms of verbs: to write, to talk. Infinitives can take the place of nouns.
Ex. His answer was a <u>smile</u>. smile in this sentence is a noun
His answer was <u>to smile</u>. to smile is an infinitive
Infinitives are often confused with prepositions.
Remember: to + a noun = preposition
                    to + a verb = infinitive
In today's reading identify 5 or 10 infinitives.

PREDICATE NOMINATIVES

A predicate nominative is a noun or pronoun that renames the subject.
Ex.   My dad is mayor of our town. The noun mayor renames the subject Dad.
To check invert the sentence.
Ex.   The mayor of our town is my dad.
Note where the predicate nominative is now located. Sometimes a form of "to be" is not the linking verb in the sentence. Replace the linking verb with a form of "to be" then invert.
Ex.   <u>Luke</u> <u>became</u> the star player.
                                                 PN
        Luke <u>was</u> the star player.
                                     PN
        The star player was Luke.

Sometimes a sentence will have a compound predicate nominative.
                              PN   PN
Ex.   My favorite sports are soccer and baseball.
        Soccer and baseball are my favorite sports.

Predicate nominative can be hard to find in interrogative sentences. To find the predicate nominative turn the question into a statement then mark the subject verb, and predicate nominative. Invert the statement to check.
                              PN
Ex.   Is Sarah the girl at the end of the line?
                           PN
        Sarah is the girl at the end of the line.
        The girl at the end of the line is Sarah.

<u>Remember</u>: You might have to use the present forms of "to be" (is, am, are) to check for predicate nominative.

- Write five sentences using a predicate nominative. Next, change these five sentences into questions. Note where the predicate nominative is now located.

GERUNDS

Gerunds are used as nouns. Gerunds are formed by adding "ing" to the plain form of verbs. (writing, talking, reading)
Ex.   Aaron enjoyed the <u>walk</u>.
              in this sentence *walk* is a noun
        Aaron enjoyed <u>walking</u>.
              walking is a gerund.

- In today's reading select five sentences that you can change the noun to a gerund.

PREDICATE ADJECTIVES

A predicate adjective is the adjective that follows the linking verb and goes back to describe the subject. The sentence must have a linking verb.
Ex.   My state's flag is blue.
        Flag is the subject noun. The linking verb is "is ".
        Blue is the adjective that describes the flag.

In the sentence, "Jesse wore the blue jacket.", *blue* is <u>not</u> a predicate adjective. The verb "wore" is not a linking verb. *Blue* describes the jacket not the subject, Jesse.

Write five sentences that use a predicate adjective.
Ex.   My country's flag is red, white, and blue.
        This is an example of a compound predicate adjective.

Write five sentences that use a compound predicate adjective.

<u>Remember</u>: to determine if a verb is linking see if you can insert a form of "to be" for the verb.
Ex.   Daniel <u>felt</u> tired.   Daniel <u>was</u> tired.

Creative Drama

These are compositions that tell a story and are written to be performed on a stage.

- Choose a children's book and rewrite it as a play or try your hand at creating a short play.

Teacher's Notes

_____

_____

_____

_____

_____

_____

_____

_____

_____

_____

_____

_____

_____

_____

_____

_____

_____

_____

_____

_____

_____

_____

Research Guide

A short tutorial for the questionnaires to help prepare and develop student research skills.

RESEARCH GUIDE

One of the goals of *TRISMS* is to teach research skills and to empower the student to become an independent learner. This is accomplished by using directed study as a framework and coursebook development as an end product. The Resource and Reading Section lists books we have found helpful in answering the questionnaires. However, your library may not carry these titles. The encyclopedia is always a good place to start.

 You may start with a specific search, such as Transcontinental Railroad. If the subject is not found you may have to broaden the search to include the geography or time frame studied such as Central Pacific Railroad of 1862. As you read, keep in mind the questions you are trying to answer. When using the encyclopedia, be aware of cross-references. These provide the reader with more information on the topic. Readers are directed to other articles by the words *see*, *see also*, or *see under* followed by the subject heading. The abbreviation (q.v.) stands for the Latin words "quod vide", meaning "which see". When this abbreviation follows a word or name, it signals that the word itself is the title of a separate article in the encyclopedia. The supplementary bibliography at the end of the article lists other sources outside of the encyclopedia.

It is unlikely that one book will have all the answers needed to complete a questionnaire or worksheet. Evaluate books by scanning the table of contents or index. If the table of contents does not list your subject it is unlikely to be in the book. You can look up keywords in the index to see if there is any helpful information within the book on your topic. The bibliography may direct you to other books on your topic.

 The Internet can be a valuable research tool. Homework Helps lists sites discovered by families using History Makers that they have found helpful. REMEMBER: Just because it's on the Internet doesn't mean it's true, so double check your sources and document all your research by writing the sources at the bottom of the research questionnaire.

REFERENCE AND RESEARCH HELPS LISTED

• Library	• Reference Books	• Card Catalog (computer or microfiche)
• Internet	• Fiction	• Dewey Decimal system
• Atlas	• Nonfiction	• Current Biography Yearbook
• Library of Congress	• Biography	• Reader's Guide to Periodical Literature
• Almanac	• Bibliography	• Index or glossary
• Call Numbers	• Directory	• Table of Contents
• Dictionary	• Thesaurus	• Periodicals
• Expository Dictionary	• Encyclopedia	• TRISMS Homework Helps

Science Questionnaire Research Guide

This short article was found on the Internet using the search engine, Google.

Hippocrates was a Greek physician born in 460 BC on the island of Cos, Greece. He became known as the founder of medicine and was regarded as the greatest physician of his time. He based his medical practice on observations and on the study of the human body. He held the belief that illness had a physical and a rational explanation. He rejected the views of his time that considered illness to be caused by superstitions and by possession of evil spirits and disfavor of the gods.

Hippocrates held the belief that the body must be treated as a whole and not just a series of parts. He accurately described disease symptoms and was the first physician to accurately describe the symptoms of pneumonia, as well as epilepsy in children. He believed in the natural healing process of rest, a good diet, fresh air and cleanliness. He noted that there were individual differences in the severity of disease symptoms and that some individuals were better able to cope with their disease and illness than others. He was also the first physician that held the belief that thoughts, ideas, and feelings come from the brain and not the heart as others of him time believed.

Hippocrates traveled throughout Greece practicing his medicine. He founded a medical school on the island of Cos, Greece and began teaching his ideas. He soon developed an Oath of Medical Ethics for physicians to follow. This Oath is taken by physicians today as they begin their medical practice. He died in 377 BC. Today Hippocrates is known as the "Father of Medicine".

Designed by: Josephine Delvey

Asimov, I., (1982). *Asimov's Biographical Encyclopedia of Science and Technology* (2nd Revised Edition). Garden City, New York: Doubleday.

Collier, P.F., *Oath and Law of Hippocrates* (1910). Harvard Classics Volume 38 (Online) gopher..//ftp.std.com//00/obi/book/Hippocrates/Hippocratic.Oath (November 11, 1997).

Debus, A.G., (1968) *World Who's Who In Science: A Biographical Dictionary of Notable Scientists from Antiquity to the Present.* Chicago: Marquis

Hippocrates. Encyclopedia Britannica (Online) http://www.eb.com/Hippocrates (November 12, 1997).

Hippocrates Web Page. Asclepeion Hospital - Athens (Online) http://www/forthnet.gr.asclepeion/hippo/htm (November 11, 1997).

Hippocrates: The "Greek Miracle" in Medicine. *Ancient Medicine* (Online) http://web1.ea.pvt.K12.pa.us/medant/hippint.htm#history (November 12, 1997).

Porter, R., (1994). *The Biographical Dictionary of Scientists.* Second Edition. New York: Oxford University Press.

Penfield, W., *The Mystery of the Mind* (1978). Princeton: Princeton University Press.

What clues do we find in this short article to answer the Scientist Questionnaire?

1. Identify the scientist by name. Hippocrates

2. Nationality of scientist. Greek

3. What was the scientist's life span? 460 – 377 BC He lived 83 years.

4. What was the span of research? none found It is difficult to find specific details with these early records. Further research may locate this information.

5. What were the Biblical events? Not found in article. Use the Timelines following the Orientation.

6. What is the scientist's most noted achievement? Medicine through observation and the study of the human body.

7. What is the scientist's secondary achievement? He believed in the natural healing process of rest, a good diet, fresh air and cleanliness. What we call, preventive medicine.

8. What was the scientist's motivation? He rejected the views of his time that considered illness to be caused by superstitions and by possession of evil spirits and disfavor of the gods. If that wasn't the cause, what was?

9. Significance of discovery? This discovery changed the health and lifespan of the Greek people.

10. How was this discovery helpful or harmful to society? This was a most beneficial help to society and individuals.

11. New word: symptom – something showing that something else exists. (Spots on the skin may be a symptom of measles.)

12. What questions came to mind? What caused Hippocrates to think so differently? What gave him the boldness to go against what society believed?

13. Trivia: Hippocrates is known as the "Father of Medicine".

One of the goals of *TRISMS* is to teach research skills; to empower the student to become an independent learner. This is accomplished by using directed study as a framework and coursebook development as an end product.

As an example, we will look at our first invention, the Wheel. We will use the Inventions Questionnaire to direct our research. As you read, keep in mind the questions you are trying to answer. An encyclopedia and a world map are a good place to begin.
- When using your encyclopedia be aware of cross-references. These provide the reader with more information on the topic. Readers are directed to other articles by the words *see*, *see also*, or *see under* followed by the subject heading.
- The abbreviation (q.v.) stands for the Latin words "quod vide", meaning *which see*. When this abbreviation follows a word or name, it signals that the word itself is the title of a separate article in the encyclopedia.
- The index helps you determine if there is information on your subject included within the text.
- The supplementary bibliography lists other sources outside of the encyclopedia.

<u>Webster's New World Dictionary</u>, Page 243
  Ethical: having to do with right and wrong according to some system of morals or behavior.

<u>Funk & Wagnall's New Encyclopedia</u>, Vol. 22, page 87
  Wheel, circular frame or disk, constructed to revolve on a central axis, and constituting an integral feature of most ground conveyances. The earliest known wheels, constructed in ancient Mesopotamia (q.v.), date from about 3500 to 3000 B.C.: see Archeology: *Current Research: The Urban Revolution*. Wheeled vehicles are believed to have appeared after the invention of the potter's wheel (see Pottery), and the wheeled cart soon replaced the sledge as a means of transportation (q.v.). In its most primitive form, the wheel was a solid wooden disk mounted on a round axle, to which it was secured by wooden pins. Eventually sections were carved out of the disk to reduce the weight, and radial spokes were devised about 2000 B.C. The invention of the wheel was a major turning point in the advance of human civilization. The wheel led to better utilization of animals, particularly oxen and horses, for agricultural and other work, and became an invaluable mechanical means for man to control the flow and direction of power or force. The applications of the wheel in modern life and technology are virtually infinite.

In this small selection we found several answers and clues.
We can now answer the questions concerning –
1. **What invention:** wheel (wheel is given in the lesson plan)
2. **When:** 3500 B.C.
3. **Who is the inventor:** ancient Mesopotamia
4. **Motivation:** transportation improvement
5. **How did this invention change life as it was then?**
   Travel and cartage was vastly improved.
6. **What have been the ethical consequences?** The wheel is a versatile invention for good and evil. Early use made life easier. The applications of the wheel are virtually infinite.
Diagram the original invention.

One of the goals of *TRISMS* is to teach research skills; to empower the student to become an independent learner. This is accomplished by using directed study as a framework and coursebook development as an end product.

As an example, we will look at our first explorer, Hanno. We will use the Explorer Questionnaire to direct our research. As you read, keep in mind the questions you are trying to answer. An encyclopedia and a world map are a good place to begin.

- When using your encyclopedia be aware of cross-references. These provide the reader with more information on the topic. Readers are directed to other articles by the words *see*, *see also*, or *see under* followed by the subject heading.
- The abbreviation (q.v.) stands for the Latin words "quod vide", meaning *which see*. When this abbreviation follows a word or name, it signals that the word itself is the title of a separate article in the encyclopedia.
- The index helps you determine if there is information on your subject included within the text.
- The supplementary bibliography lists other sources outside of the encyclopedia.

Funk & Wagnall's New Encyclopedia, Vol. 12, page 178

> Hanno, 5th century B. C., Carthaginian navigator who undertook a voyage of exploration along the west coast of Africa. He probably sailed as far as present-day Sierra Leone. When he retuned to Carthage, he inscribed an account of his travels on a tablet which he deposited in the temple of the Phoenician god Moloch. The original narrative was composed in the Phoenician language; a translation exists, written in Greek and entitled *Periplus (Voyage).*

In this small selection we found several answers and clues. We found that Hanno was an explorer, a Phoenician navigator from Carthage. He sailed along the west coast of Africa to present day Sierra Leone in the 5th century B.C.

We can now answer the questions concerning—
    1. Name: Hanno   (Hanno is a given, since he is the subject of our research.)
    2. Nationality: Carthaginian
    3. When: 5th century B.C.
    4. Point of Departure: Carthage
    7. What was discovered or explored: West coast of Africa to Sierra Leone
Our clues: 5th century B.C. denotes the ancient time period, navigator, explorer, Sierra Leone, and Phoenician.

Using the clue, Phoenician, more information can be obtained on Hanno and his culture. The following book was located at the library to aid our search.

The Phoenicians by Pamela Odijk (Ancient World series) pgs 44-45
> Hanno was a Carthaginian who led an expedition by sea to northwest Africa in about 425 B.C. He set sail with 60 ships and 30,000 people, and founded Thymiaterion and built a temple at Soloeis. He founded five other cities including Carian Fortress, Acra, and Cerne. He reached

the coast of present day Gambia, and it is thought he also reached the Cameroons. Hanno was searching for gold along the African coast.

An account of his voyage was written on a stele in the temple of Baal Hammon, at Carthage. Our knowledge of his voyage is based on a Greek version of Hanno's account in a manuscript called *The Periplus of Hanno*.

Carthage, founded by the Phoenicians of Tyre in 814 B.C. on the north coast of Africa, was built on a triangular peninsula with the Lake of Tunis providing safe anchorage. The peninsula was joined to the mainland by a narrow neck of land, thereby making it easy to defend. The ancient citadel, the Byrsa, was located in Carthage. Tombs have been found, together with cremated remains of children, who were sacrificed to the Carthaginian fertility goddess Tanit.

Carthage gained much of its wealth from agriculture and trade. The city came into conflict with Rome from 300 to 200 B.C., and fell to the Romans in 146 B.C. The city was then plundered and razed to the ground, but was later rebuilt by the Romans.

In this selection we find more answers and clues. We find that the voyage took place about 425 B.C., including 60 ships and 30,000 people. He founded cities and searched for gold. We find that Carthage was founded by Phoenicians from Tyre.

We can now answer the questions concerning—
3. When: 425 B.C., this is more specific than our earlier date
4. Sponsoring Country: Phoenicia
5. Was this place the explorer's home country? (his point of departure) yes
5. Explain: (if necessary) Phoenicia existed in two regions, the Tyre area (eastern Phoenicia) and Carthage (western Phoenicia).
8. How: expedition of 60 ships
9. What was their motivation? searching for gold and to establish cities
Our clues: ancient, wealthy city, and expedition

Using the clue ancient explorer, from our first article, we located a book on this topic.

<u>The World's Great Explorers</u> (Explorers of the Ancient World) by Charnan Simon, pages 7, 8, 10-17

The day dawned fair and bright in Carthage. The blue Mediterranean Sea sparkled in the sunlight, and a brisk breeze blew up from the harbor. Outside the walls of this prosperous North African city, slaves were busy tending the wheat fields owned by their Phoenician masters. Within the city walls, craftsmen were busy, too. Weavers, glassmakers, perfume makers, potters, jewelers, and ivory carvers – all were hard at work fashioning the items for which they were famous throughout the world.

History's Masterminds - *TRISMS*©

In 500 B.C., the "world" did not extend very far. Almost all that the Phoenicians knew of the world were the lands around the Mediterranean Sea. The outer limits of that world were the Pillars of Hercules to the west, the Red Sea to the south, and the Black Sea to the north, and a glimpse of Arabia and Persia to the east. Even at that, the Phoenicians knew more than most of their neighbors did, for they were traders and sailors. Phoenician merchant ships had explored virtually every corner of the Mediterranean. Their goods were prized in cities from Spain to Persia.

For years the Phoenicians had been the undisputed masters of the Mediterranean. Now, however, Greeks were crowding in on Phoenician territory. Greek traders were competing with Phoenician merchants. The Mediterranean was getting too small for the people of Carthage.

The Phoenicians living in Carthage decided to move on. If there was too much competition in the old markets, they would find new markets. They would outwit the Greeks by going beyond the Mediterranean. They would establish new trading centers where the Greeks would never dare to follow.

Around 500 B.C., the Phoenicians outfitted two expeditions. One of them, led by a man named Himilco, sailed west through the Pillars of Hercules (today's Strait of Gibraltar) and north into the Atlantic Ocean . . . it appears that Himilco set out with a fleet of as many as sixty ships. He cruised in the Atlantic for four months, exploring the coasts of Spain and France, possibly even reaching Britain. But he was never able to establish colonies or trading centers.

The second expedition from Carthage was more fortunate. It was led by a man named Hanno, who was said to be Himilco's brother. Instead of going north into the Atlantic, Hanno headed south after passing the Pillars of Hercules. When he returned home to Carthage, he had the story of his voyage carved on a stone tablet. The tablet itself has long since been lost, but a Greek translation of the story has survived.

Hanno's story begins simply enough. One fine morning in Carthage some 2,500 years ago, "It pleased the Carthaginians to commission Hanno to go seafaring beyond the Pillars of Hercules and there to found Libyo-Phoenician settlements."

But the scene at the Carthage harbor was probably not as simple. Some sixty ships were outfitted for the trip. The ships were huge, with curved wooden keels and large, square sails dyed the famous Tyrian purple. Each ship was manned by fifty oarsmen and had a hold big enough to carry provisions for the journey, as well as for establishing permanent colonies along the route. All in all, there were said to be some 30,000 men and women on board the fleet.

At last the word came to set sail. Farmers, carpenters, craftsmen, and sailors crowded the decks as the sails caught the wind. Slowly, surely, the great fleet headed westward out of the Carthage harbor.

Once the ships passed beyond the Pillars of Hercules, things changed. Throughout history, this was as far as ancient peoples had dared to sail . . . . Hanno and his sailors nevertheless traveled on into the uncharted Atlantic. They had no compasses to guide them— Nothing, in fact except the sun, the stars, and their own instincts. Hugging the West African coastline, they took to their oars when the wind was against them and unfurled the sails when the wind came up from behind.

Two days past the Pillars of Hercules, the fleet put to shore. There they founded their first colony, "which we named Thymaterium" (now Kenitra, Morocco). Leaving behind a group of settlers, along with provisions and one or two boats, the rest of the fleet pushed on. Their next stop was in a heavily forested area. No colony would be established here, but workers were left to erect a temple to the sea god, Poseidon.

The ships continued their southward way. Other colonies were founded, "called Cariconticos and Gyette, Acra and Melita, and Arambys." At one point the fleet put to shore and found friendly shepherds tending their flocks. Called Lixites, these shepherds told Hanno of the "inhospitable Ethiopians" who lived farther on. Their mountains were filled with wild beasts, and with "a freakish race of men who run faster than horses." When Hanno set sail again, several of the Lixite shepherds came with him to serve as interpreters. On they pushed, past two days of "desolate desert" land (the Sahara), to a small island where they founded a colony called Cerne. It is believed that Cerne was off the coast of present-day Western Sahara.

Cerne was to be the last of the Carthaginian colonies. From there on, Hanno's voyage became a nightmare. For years, Phoenician sailors had spread misleading and frightening tales to discourage other sailors from exploring their trade routes. Muddy seas, sharp rocks, and swirling whirlpools, bloodthirsty sea serpents, skydiving dragons—no detail was too horrible for the Phoenicians to include. Now, it was as if some of their own horror stories were coming true to haunt them.

First there were the mountains, "Peopled by swarms of wild men dressed in wild beasts' skins, who drove us off with stones and would not let us land". Sailing on, Hanno's ships next came to a river "large and broad, which was infested with crocodiles and river-horses (hippopotami)." It is now believed that this was the Senegal River. For twelve more days the

History's Masterminds - *TRISMS©*

Carthaginians headed south. The only inhabitants they met were Ethiopians "who would not wait our approval, but fled from us." (At that time, natives of central Africa were referred to as Ethiopians.) They sailed on past a sweet-smelling forest, and a low-lying plain, where the travelers could see "fires flaring up by night in every quarter."

Finally Hanno reached a large bay, in the middle which lay a large island. There was a great salt lake in the middle of the island—and in the middle of the lake was yet another, smaller island. There the travelers put ashore for fresh food and water. (Historians believe this island is in Bijagos Bay in today's Guinea-Bissau.)

They did not stay long. In the middle of the night they were awakened to find fires burning and chaos raging everywhere. According to Hanno's account, "We heard the noise of pipes and cymbals and the din of tom-toms and confused shouts. We were seized with a great fear, and our interpreters told us to abandon the island."

Even more terrors lay ahead of them: "We passed a country burning with fires and perfumes and streams of fire supplied from it fell into the sea. The country was impassable from the heat. So we sailed away in terror, and passing on for four days, we discovered at night a country full of fire. In the center a leaping blaze towered above the others and appeared to reach the stars. This was the highest mountain which we saw: it was called the "Chariot of the Gods.""

By now Hanno and his sailors were getting discouraged. Still, they pushed onward until they reached another large bay, now thought to be off the coast of Sierra Leone. Again there was an island in this bay—again the ships put to shore—and again they had an unpleasant surprise. As Hanno put it, "The island was filled with wild people. By far the greater number were women with hairy bodies. Our interpreters called them Gorillas. We gave chase but could not catch any of the men, for they all escaped up steep rocks and pelted us with stones. Three women were taken, but they attacked their captors with their teeth and hands, and could not be prevailed upon to accompany us." Not knowing what else to do, the Carthaginians killed and skinned these "women".

So Hanno returned to Carthage. It had been a remarkable voyage. Most historians agree that Hanno traveled as far as Sierra Leone. This means he covered some 3,000 miles. Without maps or motors or compasses—just a single sail and fifty able seamen per boat—Hanno's fleet had gone from the Mediterranean to within ten compass degrees of the equator.

Nothing really came of Hanno's discoveries. Carthaginian merchants did begin trading with the new cities just beyond the Pillars. Probably they traded as far south as Hanno's colony of Cerne.

From this out of print book we learned many new facts and expanded information.

3. Date: The date given differs greatly with the previous sources. On further searching, the 500 B.C. date is confirmed to be more accurate.

7. What was explored? We are given a detailed list of places explored and how they were reached.

9. Motivation: This expanded to include a commissioned expedition to colonize and develop a new trade route.

15. Trivia: The trivia question can be easily answered from the plentiful information found. After all it depends on what you the reader found intriguing.

Our clues to answer the Questionnaire: Cerne (or Sierra Leone) was the location of the last colony, the last place Hanno visited.

To locate information on geography facts, a history atlas is a valuable resource.
Read carefully. Present day exports and crops may vary from those of ancient times.
The Carthaginians did not utilize these resources but we will record them as part of our research.
Note which ones the Carthaginians did utilize.

Answers taken from the National Geographic Picture Atlas of Our World on page 186.

10. Topography: coastal belt of beaches and swampland to the inland forests, plains, and mountains.

12. Natural Resources: diamonds, rutile (titanium), chrome, bauxite, and fishing

13. Crops: rice, cassava, cacao, ginger, palm kernels, kola nuts, and piassava (palm fibers)

Climate was not a part of the information given in this Atlas. Another source must be consulted to complete the Questionnaire.

Funk & Wagnalls Encyclopedia, Vol. 21, pages 361 & 362, topic—Sierra Leone

11. Climate: tropical climate with an annual temperature of 80 degrees Fahrenheit

Most Bibles include a timeline or you can consult the timeline provided in the Teacher's Manual.

6. Biblical personality of the time: King Darius of Persia

15. Trivia: This can be anything you found interesting or humorous.

Using just a few of our clues, we have completed the Questionnaire for the Explorer Hanno. We have learned the essentials and some extras about him and his expedition. Further research would reveal even more exciting details. Perhaps we could locate a translation of his own descriptions of his journey. Although, we did learn that Carthaginians were inclined to exaggerate.

☑ Note to teacher: Not all questions can be answered. For example, during the Space Race, students will not be able to answer all the questions on the Explorer questionnaire. Consult the Teacher's Manual Answer Keys to be certain.

Teacher's Notes

_____

_____

_____

_____

_____

_____

_____

_____

_____

_____

_____

_____

_____

_____

_____

_____

_____

_____

_____

_____

_____

_____

_____

_____

Literature Helps

This section includes terms
and story elements the student
will encounter in the
Language Assignments.

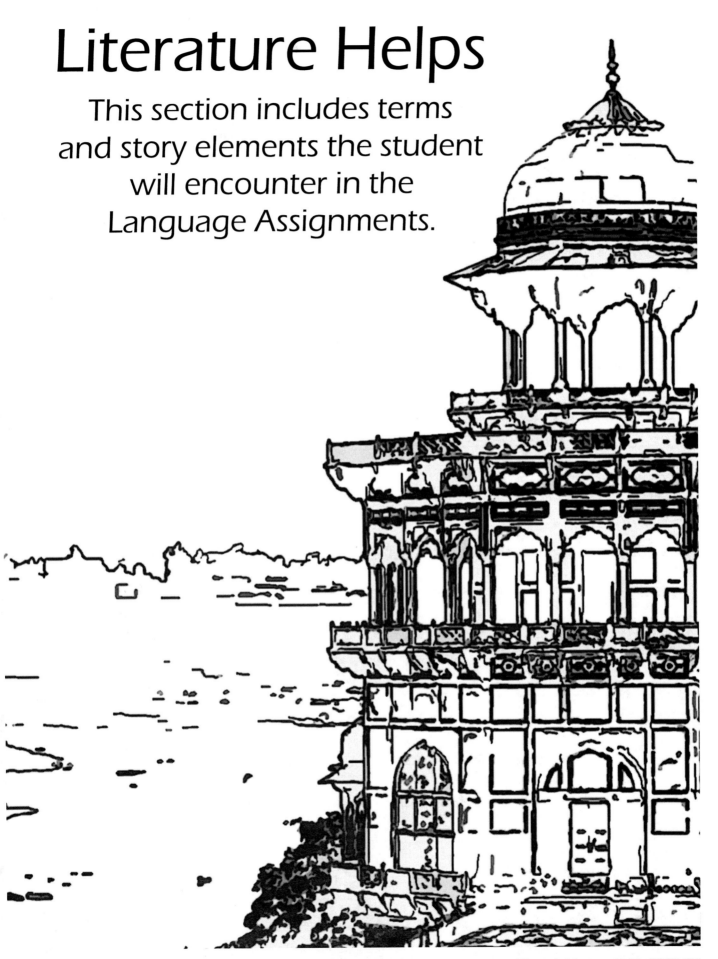

LITERATURE HELPS

This is a section of helpful definitions for assignments in Language.

SELECTING A BOOK

Dewey Decimal System: library book classification and arrangement with ten main subject classes

Fiction: Literature works based on imaginative narration; made-up stories

Nonfiction: genre of literature or film telling a story that takes place in the past around historical events or persons

Biography: written account of another person's life

Autobiography: history of a person's life written or told by that person

READING TECHNIQUES

Skimming: to glance over rapidly to get a quick idea of the general content of the selection

Scanning: searching for specific answers to questions

STORY ELEMENTS

Theme: The *theme* is the message that the author is communicating, the topic.

Plot: The *plot* is the plan or action in a story.

Episodic Plot: An *episodic plot* is several short adventures or episodes within one long story.

Climax: The *climax* is the highest point of action and interest in a story. It is also the turning point where the story begins to resolve.

Mood: The *mood* is the "feeling" of a story created by the use of powerful words.

Conflict: A story usually shows one of two kinds of conflict. A story may have more than one conflict.

Internal: This shows the main character having a struggle within himself.

External: This shows the main character having a struggle with someone or something other than himself - man against nature, man against man, man against society.

Conclusion: an overall statement that can be drawn from facts that you read or conversations you hear. Your conclusion must be supported by facts.

FIGURES OF SPEECH

<u>Personification</u>: This is the figurative language that gives human characteristics to an object.
Ex. "The leaves of the trees clap their hands."

<u>Simile</u>: compares one thing to a different thing using *like* or *as*.
Ex. "He sang as a bird in spring."

<u>Metaphor</u>: compares one thing with a different thing without using *like* or *as*.
Ex. "You're a barrel of laughs."

<u>Imagery</u>: words and phrases used to help the reader imagine each of the senses: sight, small, taste, touch, and hearing
Ex. He reeked of skunk.

<u>Irony</u>: a literary expression in which the intended meaning of the words are opposite their usual sense. To state something as fact that turns out not to be true is one example of irony. Irony can also occur in a story when something is obvious to the reader but not to the characters. Another way is when the author uses words that are too weak (understatement) that play down, or too strong (overstatement) that exaggerate the situation. Irony also takes place when the characters say or do something that they think is normal, but you, the reader, know is not quite the way it should be. Sarcasm is another form of irony that says exactly the opposite of what is meant. A good reader will be able to recognize that the author's words and intentions are not necessarily the same.

<u>Malapropism</u>: a funny misuse of one word for a similar one.
Ex"I just ate a gigantic hamburglar for lunch."

<u>Analogy</u>: comparing things, such as two pairs of words. The word pairs should be related in the same manner. Analogies can be stated two different ways.
Ex. Hammer is to nail as screwdriver is to screw.
Hammer:nail::screwdriver:screw
One colon stands for "is to" and two colons stand for "as".

<u>Idiom</u>: an expression that has a special meaning which is different from the usual meaning of the individual words.
Ex."David drew a blank on the last question of his science quiz."

The following are possible interpretations.
a. He drew an empty box.
b. He couldn't remember the answer.
c. He erased the last question.

LEVELS OF ARGUMENT SOUNDNESS

Fact: something that is known to be true.

Opinion: something that is thought to be true; someone's personal views about the facts.

Allegation: a stated assertion, especially without proof.

Biased Information: information that is told from only one point of view

Propaganda: allegations, facts, opinions, biased information and the like presented with the intention of making you believe a certain way.

Examples include:
Name Calling: The use of labels to arouse hatred or disgust for a person, group, or idea.
Glittering Generalities: The use of phrases such as "wonderful", "the best", "the world's best".
Testimonials: Having someone who allegedly has experience with a product or idea speak on its behalf.
Bandwagon: Phrases such as "everybody's doing it" to convince you that you need to do it too.
Superstition: Using people's fears to persuade them to act or think in a certain way.

POINT OF VIEW

First person: A story that is told by one character and uses the word "I".

Third person: A story told by one character using pronouns such as *he* or *they*.

Three types of third person stories:
1. Omniscient: This tells the thoughts, ideas, and feelings of any or all the characters.

2. Limited Omniscient: This sees the action through the eyes of usually just one character.

3. Objective: This does not enter into the mind of the character. The story is told through the actions.

WRITING STYLES

Formal: This sounds old-fashioned. It is usually precise and descriptive.

Informal: This is more modern, it sounds as if someone were talking to you

Informational: This will be concise, any description it gives is factual

Extended Reading List

This section contains additional reading selections not listed on the lesson plan. These are categorized by reading level and number of pages in order to facilitate in selecting appropriate books for the student.

The Extended Reading List in the Orientation uses the Tulsa Public Library system of identification.

- A - Adult; this indicates that the author wrote about adult topics.
- Y - Young adult; generally high school reading level. These books should challenge the reader with their varied plots, vocabulary, and character development.
- J - Junior; generally covers ages nine to thirteen and has varied characters and a more complex plot.
- E – Easy reader; six to nine-year-old range or second and third grades. These books have large print, photos or pictures, and short chapters. This list also includes picture books.

* Please note that if you have a ten-year-old who reads at the young adult or adult level the themes in the book may not be suitable material for his age level, even if he understands the vocabulary.

A letter "B" following the reading level indicates a biography (the story of an individual's life).

All other listings are historical fiction (An event in history that generally incorporates both real and fictitious characters.)

Extended Reading List – Historical Fiction and various level Biographies

4000 – 500 BC Prehistory (up to 3500) and Ancient (3500 - 500)

A   235   Meadowcroft, Enid LaMonte. *The Gift of the River*. NY: Crowell Co., 2000.
                A story of Egypt
                ISBN: 0690330472

A   185   Rivers, Francine. *Unshaken*. IL: Tyndale House, 2001.
                Story of Ruth from the Bible, 1135.
                ISBN: 0842335978

Y   279   McGraw, Eloise. *Mara, Daughter of the Nile*. NY: Puffin Books, 1985.
                A slave girl must find a way to serve two masters.
                ISBN: 0140319298

Y   176   Beechick, Ruth. *Adam and His Kin: The Lost History of Their Lives and Times*.
                UT: Arrow Press, 1990.
                An overview of the book of Genesis from the Bible
                ISBN: 0940319071

J   267   Levitin, Sonia. *Escape from Egypt*. MA: Little, Brown & Co., 1994.
                Moses leads the Israelites to the Promised Land.
                ISBN: 0316522732

J   212   Williamson, Joanne. *God King*. PA: Bethlehem Books, 2002.
                A story of the days of King Hezekiah. 750 BC Egypt and Judea
                ISBN: 1883937736

J   182   Williamson, Joanne. *Victory on the Walls*. PA: Bethlehem Books, 2002.
                A story of Nehemiah from the Bible, 445 BC in Judea
                ISBN: 1883937965

J   86   Rubalcaba, Jill. *A Place in the Sun*. NY: Puffin Books; Reprint edition, 1998.
                Senmut, the gifted son of a sculptor is taken into slavery but his talent rescues him.
                13th century BC
                ISBN: 0141301236

E   24   Zeman, Ludmila. *Gilgamesh the King*. NY: Tundra Books, 1992.
                Ancient story of the god-man Gilgamesh of ancient Mesopotamia, 6000 BC
                ISBN: 0887762832

E   24   Zeman, Ludmila. *The Revenge of Ishtar*. NY: Tundra Books, 1993.
                6000 BC the Epic of Gilgamesh tells much about the people of Sumer and what they
                believe.
                ISBN: 0887763154

500 BC – 300 BC Classical (500 BC – AD 500)

A 363 Fast, Howard. *Spartacus*. ME: Sharpe, 1996.
71 BC Revolutionaries in the Servile Wars
ISBN: 156324599X

Y 460 Davis, William. *A Victor of Salamis*. MT: Kessinger Publishing, 2005.
Persian Wars, 480 BC
ISBN: 1419175424

J 190 Trease, Geoffrey. *Web of Traitors*. NY: Vanguard, 2000.
Socrates and ancient Athens
ISBN: 0814904335

E 63 Snedeker, Caroline Dale. *Lysis Goes to the Play*. NY: William Morrow, 2000.
A brother and sister in ancient Athens
ISBN: 0688410472

300 BC – AD

J/B 47 Lasky, Kathryn. *The Librarian Who Measured the Earth*. MA: Little, Brown & Co.,
1994. Greek geographer and astronomer Eratosthenes, 276 - 196
This book shows how Eratosthenes measured the circumference of the earth.
ISBN: 0316515264

Anno Domini - AD 500

A 280 Wise, Robert. *The Fall of Jerusalem*. NY: Thomas Nelson Inc., 1994.
Early Christian history
ISBN: 0840731612

A 255 Henderson, Lois T. *Lydia*. NY: Harper Collins, 1991.
A story of Lydia from the Bible
ISBN: 0060638621

The following three books are now published as a trilogy called the *Three Legions*:
Y 216 Sutcliff, Rosemary. *The Eagle of the Ninth*. NY: Farrar, Straus, & Giroux, 1993.
Life under Roman occupation in Britain
ISBN: 0374419302

Y 225 Sutcliff, Rosemary. *The Lantern Bearers*. NY: Farrar, Straus, & Giroux, 1994.
The last Roman auxiliaries are setting sail to leave Britain forever, AD 450.
ISBN: 0374443025

Y 179 Sutcliff, Rosemary. *The Silver Branch*. NY: Farrar, Straus, & Giroux, 1993.
This story picks up in 480
ISBN: 0844667803

Y 167 Ray, Mary. *Beyond the Desert Gate*. PA: Bethlehem Books, 2001.
Palestine in the first century, the Jews have revolted against the Roman occupation.
ISBN: 188393754X

Y 165 Ray, Mary. *The Ides of April*. PA: Bethlehem Books, 1999.
62 AD When their master is murdered, the household slaves fear imprisonment.
ISBN: 1883937434

J 238 Johnston, Annie. *Joel, A Boy of Galilee*. CA: Foundation for Amer Christian, 1992.
A crippled boy follows Jesus and his life is transformed.
ISBN: 0912498110

J 224 St. John, Patricia. *Twice Freed*. Scotland: Christian Focus Pub., 2002.
Story taken from the book of Philemon in the Bible
ISBN: 1857924894

J 152 Lawrence, Caroline. *The Thieves of Ostia*. CT: Roaring Brook Press, 2002.
AD 79 Flavia Gemina, a Roman sea captain's daughter tries to solve the theft of her
father's ring.   Book 1 of the Roman Mysteries
ISBN: 0761315829

J 152 Bendick, Jeanne. *Galen and Gateway to Medicine*. PA: Bethlehem Books, 2002.
AD 129 Roman doctor to the gladiators, the royal family, and the Roman Army.
ISBN: 1883937752

E/B 27 Sabuda, Robert. *Saint Valentine*. NY: Aladdin Paperbacks, 1999.
The Roman doctor and Christian martyr 3rd century.
ISBN: 0689824297

AD 500 – 1000   Dark Ages (410 – 1000)

Y 192 Rosen, Sidney and Dorothy. *The Baghdad Mission*. MN: Carolrhoda Books, 1994.
Alan travels from the Frankish kingdom to Baghdad and back.
ISBN: 0876148283

Y 184 Willard, Barbara. *Augustine Came to Kent*. PA: Bethlehem Books, 1996.
597 England   A captured and taken to Rome but freed by Pope Gregory to return home.
ISBN: 1883937213

J 208 Willard, Barbara. *Son of Charlemagne*. PA: Bethlehem Books 1998.
Get to know Charlemagne through the eyes of his son Carl. 700 Europe
ISBN: 1883937302

J 48 Heide, Florence Parry, and Gilland, Judith Heide. *The House of Wisdom*. NY: DK Inc.,
1999. The son of the chief translator travels the world in search of precious books and
manuscripts.
ISBN: 0789425629

E 32 Christopher, Manson. *Two Travelers*. NY: Henry Holt & Co, 1990.
Haroun-al-Rachid sends a gift to Charlemagne.
ISBN: 0805012141

1000 – 1400   Middle Ages (500 – 1500)

A 503 Porter, Jane. *Scottish Chiefs*. NY: Scribner, 1991.
Scottish rebellion against King Edward of England in 1296 – 1305
ISBN: 068419340

Y 340 Jewett, Eleanore. *The Hidden Treasure of Glaston*. PA: Bethlehem Books, 2000.
Lame Hugh is left at a monastery when his father is forced into exile from England. 1171
ISBN: 1883937485

Y   324   Henty, G. A. *Winning His Spurs*. PA: Preston-Speed Publications, 1997.
A tale of the Crusades, 1190
ISBN: 1887159134

Y   304   Henty, G. A. *Wulf the Saxon*. CA: Indy Publishing Company, 2004.
A young thane wins the favor of Earl Harold and becomes one of his retinue.
ISBN: 1414224540

Y   288   Chaikin, Linda. *Swords and Scimitars*. MN: Bethany House Publishers, 1996.
Peasant Crusade led by Peter the Hermit, 1096
ISBN: 1556618816

Y   272   Goodman, Joan Elizabeth. *The Winter Hare*. NY: Houghton Mifflin, 1996.
1140, Will Belet finds himself enmeshed in England's Civil War.
ISBN: 0395785693

Y   256   Hunter, Mollie. *The King's Swift Rider*. NY: HarperCollins Publishers, 1998.
Hunter (the Knight of the Golden Plain series) visits the 14th-c against the English.
ISBN: 0060271868

Y   226   McGraw, Eloise. *The Striped Ships*. NY: Maxwell Macmillan, 1991.
Saxon side of the Norman invasion in 1066 and the making of the Bayeux Tapestry.
ISBN: 0689505329

Y   195   Bradford, Karleen. *There Will Be Wolves*. NY: Lodestar Books Dutton, 1996.
A young girl, her father, and friend, join the crusades.
ISBN: 0525675396

Y   174   Polland, Madeleine. *The Queen's Blessing*. NY: Henry Holt & Company, 2000.
War-torn Scotland in the 11th century
ISBN: 003045235X

Y   150   Temple, Frances. *The Bedouins' Gazelle*. NY: Orchard Books, 1996.
Life among the Bedouins in 1302
ISBN: 0531095193

J   604   Conscience, Hendrik. *The Lion of Flanders*. NY: Fredonia Books, 2003.
Guilds and medieval life, 1298 - 1305
ISBN: 1410103927

J   320   French, Allen. *The Lost Baron: A Story of England in the Year 1200*.
PA: Bethlehem Books, 2001.
Martin's first day as page and squire to Baron Eric is also his last in Cornwall, England.
ISBN: 1883937531

J   232   Snyder, Zilpha Keatley. *Song of the Gargoyle*. NY: Bantam Doubleday Dell, 1994.
Court Life (mystery)
ISBN: 0440408989

J   230   Jewitt, Eleanore. *Big John's Secret*. PA: Bethlehem Books, 2004.
12-year-old serf, John, goes on the 5th Crusade to the Holy Land as a squire.   1280
ISBN: 1883937892

J   198   Konigsburg, E. L. *A Proud Taste for Scarlet and Miniver*. NY: Aladdin, 2001.
            Eleanor of Aquitaine, 1122 - 1204, Queen of France and England
            ISBN: 068984624X

J   190   Willard, Barbara. *If All the Swords in England*. PA: Bethlehem Books, 2000.
            Story of St. Thomas à Becket, Archbishop of Canterbury   d. 1170
            ISBN: 1883937493

J   178   Pyle, Howard. *Men of Iron*. NY: Dover Publications, 2003.
            The days of King Henry the IV of England, 1399 - 1413
            ISBN: 0486428419

J   169   Cushman, Karen. *Catherine, Called Birdy*. NY: Clarion Books, 1994.
            Diary of a teenager in the Middle Ages
            ISBN: 0395681863

J   155   Rosen, Sidney and Dorothy. *The Magician's Apprentice*. MN: Lerner Publishing, 1994.
            1264, Jean is sent to Oxford to spy on Roger Bacon.
            ISBN: 0876148097

J   128   Branford, Henrietta. *Fire, Bed, and Bone*. MA: Candlewick, 1998.
            A fictional tale set in 1381 during a peasant's rebellion in England, told from a dog's
            point of view.
            ISBN: 0763603384

E   32   Aliki. *Medieval Feast*. NY: Harper Collins, 1986.
            The many preparations made for the king's visit.
            ISBN: 0064460509

E   30   Cullen, Lynn. *The Mightiest Heart*. NY: Dial Books for Young Readers, 1998.
            The Welsh legend of Prince Llywelyn and his loyal dog, Gelert
            ISBN: 0803722923

1400 – 1490   Renaissance (1300 – 1550)

Y   358   Voight, Cynthia. *Jackaroo*. NY: Simon Pulse, 2003.
            The innkeeper's daughter discovers a bandit's costume.
            ISBN: 0689864353

Y   255   Stevenson, Robert Louis. *The Black Arrow*. RI: North Books, 2002.
            The reign of King Henry VI, near the end of the War of the Roses between the houses of
            York and Lancaster in England
            ISBN: 1582871949

Y   255   Levathes, Louise. *When China Ruled the Sea: The Treasure Fleet of the Dragon
            Throne 1405-1433*. NY: Simon & Schuster, 1994.
            ISBN: 0671701584

J   34   Fradin, Dennis. *Hiawatha – Messenger of Peace*. NY: M. K. McElderry Books, 1992.
            Iroquois Indian who brought the five tribes together to form the Iroquois Federation.
            ISBN: 0689505191

E/B   28   Fisher, Leonard Everett. *Gutenberg*. NY: Macmillan Publishing Company, 1993.
German printer, Johann Gutenberg, 1398 – 1468
ISBN: 0027352382

1490 – 1500   Age of Discovery (1400 - 1800)

A   379   Plaidy, Jean. *The Queen's Secret*. NY: Fawcett, 1992.
The story of Queen Katherine of England 1520 - 1542
ISBN: 0449220087

Y   190   Dillon, Elis. *The Cruise of the Santa Maria*. Ireland: O'Brien Press Limited, 1997.
One of the three ships to sail with Columbus in 1492
ISBN: 0862782635

Y   180   Miklowitz, Gloria D. *Secrets in the House of Delgado*. MI: Eerdmans Books, 2002.
In 1492, the Jews, Moors, and anyone sympathetic are being evicted from Spain.
ISBN: 0802852106

Y   160   Grant, George. *Last Crusader – The Untold Story of Christopher Columbus*.
IL: Crossway Books, 1992.
This event seen through the worldview of late 1400's Europe.
ISBN: 0891076905

J   408   Foster, Genevieve. *The World of Columbus and Sons*. CA: Beautiful Feet Books, 1998.
This book tells the story of the world during the Renaissance and the Reformation.
ISBN: 0964380382

J   304   Jones, Terry. *The Lady and the Squire*. London: Pavilion Books, 2000.
Sequel to *The Knight and the Squire*
ISBN: 1862054177

J/B   96   McLanathan, Richard. *Leonardo da Vinci*. NY: H. N. Abrams, 1990.
Renaissance painter, scientist, and inventor, 1452 - 1519
ISBN: 0810412562

J   80   Conrad, Pam. *Pedro's Journal*. PA: Caroline House, 1991.
Journal of the cabin boy aboard the Santa Maria
ISBN: 1878093177

J   80   Dorris, Michael. *Morning Girl*. NY: Hyperion, 1999.
An Indian girl witnesses the arrival of the first Europeans.
ISBN: 078681358X

J/B   63   Burch, Joann. *Isabella of Castile*. NY: Franklin Watts, 1991.
Queen of Spain, 1451 – 1504, who sponsored Columbus
ISBN: 0531200337

1500 – 1520

Y   221   Haugaard, Erik Christian. *The Boy and the Samurai*. MA: Houghton Mifflin, 1991.
A street urchin and an old warrior must prevail against a warlord.
ISBN: 0395563984

J 143 Catherall, Arthur. *Camel Caravan*. NY: Houghton Mifflin Co., 2000.
Two children accompany their uncle's caravan across the desert.
ISBN: 0395288517

J/B 136 Vernon, Louise. *Thunderstorm in Church*. PA: Herald Press, 2002.
Martin Luther, Father of the Protestant Reformation, 1483 - 1546
ISBN: 0836117409

J/B 120 Jackson, Dave and Neta. *The Queen's Smuggler*. MN: Bethany House Publishers, 1991.
The story of William Tyndale, 1497 - 1536
ISBN: 1556612214

J/B 95 McNeer, May and Lyn Ward. *Martin Luther*. NY: Abingdon Press, 2000.
Father of the Reformation
ISBN: 0687236541

1520 – 1540

Y 252 Namioka, Lensey. *Valley of the Broken Cherry Trees*. VT: Tuttle Publishing, 2005.
Japanese history – Samurai
ISBN: 0804836108

Y 216 Namioka, Lensey. *Den of the White Fox*. CA: Harcourt Brace & Co., 1997.
Medieval Japan
ISBN: 0152012834

J 202 Meyer, Carolyn. *Isabel – Jewel of Castilla – Spain, 1466*. NY: Scholastic Inc., 2000.
The Royal Diary Series
ISBN: 0439078059

J/B 47 Brandt, Keith. *Cabeza de Vaca – New World Explorer*. NJ: Troll Associates, 1993.
Spanish explorer who traveled from Florida to Mexico City 1490 – 1556
ISBN: 0816728305

J 32 Kimmel, Eric A. *Montezuma and the Fall of the Aztecs*. NY: Holiday House, 2000.
Recounting of the Aztec nation's demise in 1520
ISBN: 0823414523

1540 – 1600

Y 218 Siegel, Deborah Spector. *The Cross by Day, the Mezuzah by Night*.
PA: Jewish Publication Society of America, 2000.
Isabel/Ruth must flee Spain or face burning at the stake.
ISBN: 0827607377

Y 183 Horowitz, Anthony. *The Devil and His Boy*. NY: Philomel Books, 1998.
Read the Afterword first to better understand the historical background to this tale of
intrigue.
ISBN: 0399234322

J 250 Whitesel, Cheryl Aylward. *Blue Fingers: A Ninja's Tale*. NY: Clarion Books, 2004.
Koji is a child of destiny but he is confused about his part in it all.
ISBN: 0618381392

J   202   Reilly, Robert T. ***Red Hugh, Prince of Donegal.*** PA: Bethlehem Books, 1997.
1587 Ireland, young Hugh is kidnapped by the English and must find a way to escape.
ISBN: 1883937221

E   32   Stanley, Diane and Peter Vennema. ***Good Queen Bess – Elizabeth I of England***.
NY: Harper Collins, 2001.
The story of Elizabeth the first, the last of the Tudor line, 1533 - 1603
ISBN: 0060296186

1600 – 1620

A   331   Morris, Gilbert. ***The Honorable Imposter.*** MA: G. K. Hall, 1995.
With the sailing of the Mayflower a course was set for one man, his family and a whole nation. This is the first book in the House of Winslow series
ISBN: 0816156727

E   93   Bulla, Clyde Robert. ***Charlie's House***. NY: Knopf, 1993.
Indentured servants
ISBN: 0679838414

E/B   46   Fisher, Leonard Everett. ***Galileo***. NY: Maxwell Macmillan International, 1992.
Italian astronomer and physicist, 1564 - 1642
ISBN: 0027352358

1630 -1680

Y   373   Henty, G. A. ***Won by the Sword: A Tale of the Thirty Years' War.***
PA: Preston-Speed Publications, 2000.
France during the latter part of the Thirty Years' War.
ISBN: 1887159444

Y   192   Haugaard, Erick Christian. ***Cromwell's Boy***. NY: Houghton Mifflin Company, 1990.
English Civil War, 1642 - 1651
ISBN: 0395549752

Y   186   Lasky, Kathryn. ***Jahanara – Princess of Princesses***. NY: Scholastic Inc., 2002.
17th century India during the Moghul Dynasty
ISBN: 0439223504

Y   165   Forrester, Sandra. ***Wheel of the Moon***. NY: Harper Collins, 2000.
Pen Downing with other children, were involuntarily transported to the New World.
ISBN: 0688171494

J   277   Bond, Douglas. ***Duncan's War***. MA: P & R Pub., 2002.
1666, Presbyterian Scotts fight against supporters of England's King Charles ll.
ISBN: 0875527426

J   215   Bond, Douglas. ***King's Arrow***. MA: P & R Pub., 2003.
Scottish Covenanters face the Highlanders at the Battle of Drumclog.
ISBN: 0875527434

J   167   Kelley, Nancy. ***The Whispering Rod – A Tale of Old Massachusetts***.
PA: White Mane Kids, 2001.
In 1659, fourteen-year-old Hannah Pryor is troubled by the persecution of Quakers.
ISBN: 1572492481

J 144 Jackson, Dave and Neta. ***Traitor in the Tower***. MN: Bethany House Publishers, 1997. Puritan preacher John Bunyan, author of *Pilgrim's Progress*. 1628 - 1688
ISBN: 1556617410

J 141 Friedman, Michael Jan. ***The Mutt in the Iron Muzzle***. TX: Big Red Chair Books, 1997. Inspired by *The Man in the Iron Mask* by Alexander Dumas.
ISBN: 1570642745

J 130 Wise, William. ***Nell of Branford Hall***. NY: Dial Books, 1999.
The Great London Plague of 1665
ISBN: 0803723938

J 128 De Trevino, Elizabeth Borton. ***Nacar the White Deer***. PA: Bethlehem Books, 2005.
1630 Mexico
ISBN: 1883937914

E 38 Grifalconi, Ann. ***The Village that Vanished***. NY: Dial Books for Young Readers, 2002. The Yao people find a way to escape the slave traders.
ISBN: 0803726236

E 32 Armstrong, Jennifer. ***Little Salt Lick and the Sun King***. NY: Knopf Books, 1994. The many details of seventeenth-century chateau life will intrigue young readers.
ISBN: 0517596210

E 28 Spivak, Dawnine. ***Grass Sandals – The Travels of Basho***. NY: Atheneum Books, 1997. The Japanese poet, Basho crossed his island home observing and writing, Haiku verse.
ISBN: 0689807767

1680 – 1750   1700 Industrial Age Begins

Y 240 Haugaard, Erik Christian. ***The Revenge of the Forty-Seven Samurai***. MA: Houghton Mifflin, 1995. A servant in 18th century Japan relates the revenge for his master.
ISBN: 0395708095

Y 68 Henty, G. A. ***Among Malay Pirates: A Tale of Adventures and Peril***. VT: Quiet Vision Pub, 2004.
ISBN: 1576468828

J 215 Tomasma, Kenneth. ***Om-kas-toe – Blackfeet Twin Captures an Elkdog***. WY: Grandview Publishing Company, 2000.
Account of the Blackfeet "dog days" - Amazing Indian Children series
ISBN: 1880114054

J 144 Jackson, Dave and Neta. ***Hostage on the Nighthawk***. MN: Bethany House, 2000.
William Penn, 1644 - 1718
ISBN: 0764222651

J 143 Avi. ***Night Journey***. NY: Morrow Junior Books, 1994.
Life of indentured servants in Pennsylvania
ISBN: 0688052983

J   92   de Angeli, Marguerite. *Skippack School*. PA: Herald Press, 1999.
           12-year-old Eli Shrawder comes from Germany with his family to live in the Mennonite
           settlement in Pennsylvania.
           ISBN: 0836191242

J   88   Rhoads, Dorothy. *The Corn Grows Ripe*. NY: Puffin Books, 1993.
           Life in a Mayan village after the arrival of the Spanish.
           ISBN: 0140363130

J/B 48   Whiting, Jim. *Junipero Jose Serra*. DE: Mitchell Lane Publishers, 2004.
           Spanish missionary and explorer who traveled to Mexico and then CA building missions.
           ISBN: 1584151870

E   64   Dalgliesh, Alice. *Courage of Sarah Noble*. NY: Aladdin, 1991.
           A little girl accompanies her father to Connecticut as settlers.
           ISBN: 0689715404

E   63   Rappaport, Doreen. *The Boston Coffee Party*. NY: Harper Trophy, 1990.
           Greedy merchants hoard coffee during the Revolution.
           ISBN: 0064441415

E   32   Stanley, Diane. *Peter the Great*. NY: Harper Collins, 1999.
           Emperor of Russia 1672 - 1725
           ISBN: 068816708X

1750 – 1780

Y   408   Henty, G. A. *The Seven Year's War*. OR: Robinson Books, 2002.
           Frederick the Great
           ISBN: 1590871782

Y   322   Altsheler, Joseph. *The Rulers of the Lakes*. NY: Fredonia Books, 2003.
           George and Champlain during the French and Indian War in upstate New York.
           ISBN: 1410103013

Y   275   Speare, Elizabeth George. *Calico Captive*. NY: Houghton Mifflin, 1985.
           French and Indian War, 1755 - 1763
           ISBN: 0618150765

Y   256   Forbes, Ester. *Johnny Tremain*. MA: Houghton Mifflin Co., 1998.
           Boston Tea Party, Dec. 17, 1773
           ISBN: 0395900115

Y   214   Walter, Mildred P. *Second Daughter–The Story of a Slave Girl*. NY: Scholastic, 1996.
           Taken from the 1781 case of Mum Bett. A slave girl who sued her owner for her
           freedom under the Massachusetts Constitution.
           ISBN: 0590482823

Y   117   Henty, G.A. *Redskin and Colonist: A Boy's Adventures in the Early Days of Virginia*.
           PA: Preston Press Pub., 2004.
           French and Indian War
           ASIN: B0008606KG

J 180 Dubois, Muriel L. ***Abenaki Captive***. MN: Carolrhoda Books, 1994.
Abenaki warrior is present when a band of his people captures an English trapper.
ISBN: 0876146019

J 147 Wyeth, Sharon Dennis. ***Once on this River***. NY: Alfred A. Knopf, 1998.
On a trip from Madagascar to New York, Monday learns about slavery.
ISBN: 0679883509

J 141 Jackson, Dave and Neta. ***The Runaway's Revenge***. MN: Bethany House, 1995.
John Newton and slavery in the British Colonies
ISBN: 1556614713

J 96 Reit, Seymour. ***Guns for General Washington***. CA: Harcourt, 2001.
The Knox brothers move cannons from Fort Ticonderoga to Boston, MA.
ISBN: 0152164359

J/B 72 Sherrow, Victoria. ***Phillis Wheatley – Poet***. NY: Chelsea Juniors, 1992.
The Mother of Black Poetry, 1753 – 1784
ISBN: 0791017532

J 69 Tripp, Valerie. ***Meet Felicity***. (Book 1) WI: Pleasant Co., 2000.
Growing up in colonial Williamsburg, Virginia

J/B 51 Barton, David. ***The Bulletproof George Washington***. TX: Wallbuilders Press, 2003.
God's miraculous protection during the French and Indian War, 1755
ISBN: 1932225005

E 30 Winnick, Karen B. ***Sybil's Night Ride***. PA: Boyds Mills Press, Inc., 2000.
1777, 16-year-old Sybil sounds the alarm throughout the country side.
ISBN: 1563976978

1780 – 1790

J 181 Willis, Patricia. ***Danger Along the Ohio***. NY: Clarion Books, 1997.
Three children struggle on alone after they are separated from their father during an Indian raid.
ISBN: 0380731517

J 154 Denenberg, Barry. ***My Name is America: The Journal of William Thomas Emerson – A Revolutionary War Patriot***. NY: Scholastic Inc., 1998.
Twelve-year-old William tells his experiences in Pre-Revolutionary War.
Dear America Book
ISBN: 0590313509

E 43 Gauch, Patricia Lee. ***This Time, Tempe Wick?*** PA: Boyds Mills Press, 2003.
Mutiny at Jockey Hollow
ISBN: 1590781856

1790 – 1800

Y/B 213 Benge, Janet and Geoff. ***William Cary: Obliged to Go***. WA: YWAM Pub., 1998.
William goes to India.
Lifetime 1761 – 1834
ISBN: 1576581470

J	177	Steele, William. ***The Buffalo Knife***. FL: Harcourt, 2004. Frontier Tennessee ISBN: 0152052151
J	160	Barkan, Joanne. ***Tale of Two Sitters***. TX: Big Red Chair Books, 1998. Wishbone imagines himself as a young Frenchman who returns to France during the Revolution. ISBN: 157064277X
E/B	48	Fritz, Jean. ***George Washington's Mother***. NY: Grosset & Dunlap, 1992. Describes the life of Mary Ball, the mother of the first president. All Aboard Reading Book Level 3 ISBN: 0758712081

1800 – 1820

A	327	Austen, Jane. ***Pride and Prejudice***. NY: Alfred A. Knopf, 1991. A comedy of manners in Regency English ISBN: 0679405429
Y	183	Wibberley, Leonard. ***Red Pawns***. MA: Peter Smith, 1991. Sequel to *Leopard's Prey* Treegate story The United States is on the verge of a second war with England in 1811. ISBN: 0844665584
J/B	192	Seymour, Flora. ***Sacagawea – American Pathfinder***. NY: Aladdin, 1991. Shoshone Indian guide who led the Lewis and Clark expedition, 1804 - 1806 ISBN: 0689714823
J	161	Yates, Elizabeth. ***The Journeyman***. SC: BJU Press, 1990. Originally titled *Patterns on the Wall* Jared is apprenticed to a stencil painter and grows in skill and manhood as they travel. ISBN: 0890845352
J/B	67	Birch, Beverly. ***Louis Braille: Bringer of Hope to the Blind***. WI: Gareth Stevens Publication, 1991. Inventor of a reading and writing system for the blind, 1809 – 1852 ISBN: 0836804546
J/B	60	Quiri, Patricia Ryon. ***Dolley Madison***. NY: Franklin Watts, 1993. The 4th Lady Presidentress, 1768 - 1849 ISBN: 0531266973
E/B	72	Barrett, Marvin. ***Meet Thomas Jefferson***. NY: Random House, 2001, 1995. The statesman and 3rd President of the United States, 1743 - 1826 ISBN: 0375812113
E	58	Roop, Peter and Connie. ***Ahyoka and the Talking Leaves***. NY: Harper Trophy, 1994. Sequoyah's Cherokee language alphabet, 1825 ISBN: 0688130828
E	48	Greeson, Janet. ***An American Army of Two***. MN: Carolrhoda Books, 1992. Rebecca and Abigail Bates save the town's ships by playing the armies marching music, 1814. ISBN: 0876145470

History's Masterminds - *TRISMS*©

| E/B | 31 | Kent, Zachary. *Tecumseh*. IL: Childrens Press, 1992.
Shawnee Chief who united a confederacy of Indians, 1768 - 1813
ISBN: 0516066609 |

| E/B | 28 | Adler, David A. *Simon Bolivar*. NY: Holiday House, 1992.
South America's patriot and liberator of many countries from Spain, 1783 – 1830
ISBN: 0823409279 |

| E/B | 24 | Anholt, Laurence. *Stone Girl, Bone Girl*. NY: Orchard Books, 1998.
Mary Anning discovers an ichthyosaur skeleton in 1811 and continued her interest in curiosities.
ISBN: 0531301486 |

1820 – 1840

| J | 182 | Yates, Elizabeth. *Hue and Cry*. SC: BJU Press, 1991.
As a member of the mutual protection society, Jared must find a way to temper justice with mercy.
ISBN: 0890845360 |

| J | 160 | Crofford, Emily. *Born in the Year of Courage*. MN: Carolrhoda Books, 1991.
Japanese Manjiro is shipwrecked and rescued by Americans. He works to open up Japan for foreign trade.
ISBN: 0876146795 |

| J | 139 | Crider, Bill. *Muttketeer!* TX: Big Red Chair Books, 1997.
Wishbone tale inspired by *The Three Musketeers* written by Alexander Dumas.
ISBN: 1570642729 |

| J | 132 | O'Harrell, Beatrice. *Longwalker's Journey*. NY: Dial Books, 1999.
1831 Choctaw Trail of Tears The government removal of the Choctaw from MS to OK.
ISBN: 0803723806 |

| J | 110 | Banks, Sara. *Remember My Name*. CO: Roberts Rinehart Pub.
In Cooperation with Council for Indian Education, 1993.
Trail of Tears, the Cherokee removal from Georgia in 1838
ISBN: 1879373386 |

| J | 99 | Myers, Walter Dean. *Amistad – A Long Road to Freedom*. NY: Puffin Books, 2001.
Historic story of the Amistad's black captives return to their homeland in Africa.
ISBN: 0141300043 |

| J/B | 48 | Lyons, Mary E. *Master of Mahogany – Tom Day, Free Black Cabinetmaker*.
NY: Atheneum, 1994.
Tom was living free in North Carolina during the slavery years of America.
Lifetime 1801 – 1861
ISBN: 0684196751 |

| E/B | 47 | Sabin, Louis. *Jim Beckwourth – Adventures of a Mountain Man*. NJ: Troll, 1993.
The life of a hunter, trapper, and trader, 1798 - 1866
ISBN: 0816728194 |

1850 - 1859

A   410   Pella, Judith. *The Crown and the Crucible*. MN: Bethany House, 1991.
A peasant girl goes to work in Alexander II's palace in 1855.
The Russians series
ISBN: 1556611722

A   297   Cather, Willa. *Death Comes for the Archbishop*. NY: Vintage Books, 1990.
Father Jean Marie Latour comes as Apostolic Vicar to New Mexico, a land American by
law but Mexican and Indian in custom and belief.
ISBN: 0679728899

Y   402   Henty, G. A. *Through the Sikh War*. Canada: Althouse Press, 2002.
A tale of the conquest of the Punjab, 1845 - 46
ISBN: 1590871561

Y   380   Avi. *Lord Kirkles's Money*. NY: Orchard Books, 1996.
Maura and Patrick leave Ireland to be with their father in America.
Book 2 Beyond the Western Sea
ISBN: 0531095207

Y   338   Henty, G. A. *Jack Archer*. Canada: Althouse Press, 2002.
A tale of the Crimean War, 1854 - 1856
ISBN: 1590870808

Y   237   Pearshall, Shelley. *Trouble Don't Last*. NY: Alfred A. Knopf, 2002.
A boy and an elderly slave try to escape to Canada with the help of the Underground
Railroad.
ISBN: 0375814906

Y   197   Demas, Corinne. *If I Ever Return Again*. NY: HarperCollins, 2000.
12-year-old Celia goes on a whaling expedition with her parents on her father's ship.
ISBN: 0060287179

Y   148   Giff, Patricia Reilly. *Nory Ryan's Song*. NY: Delacorte Press, 2000.
When the potato blight causes famine in Ireland, Nory helps her family and neighbors.
ISBN: 0385321414

J   167   Van Leeuwen, Jean. *Bound for Oregon*. NY: Dial Books for Young Readers, 1994.
A true story of a young girl's journey to the West.
ISBN: 0803715269

J   148   Nixon, Joan Lowery. *A Dangerous Promise*. (Book 1) NY: Delacorte Press, 1994.
Mike Kelley runs away to join the Union Army.
The Orphan Train Adventures
ISBN: 0440219655

J   147   Denenberg, Barry. *Elisabeth – The Princess Bride*. NY: Scholastic, 2003.
Her engagement and marriage to her cousin, Franz Joseph l, Emperor of Austria.
ISBN: 0439266440

J   144   Jackson, Dave and Neta. ***The Drummer Boy's Battle***. MN: Bethany House, 1997.
Florence Nightingale   Trailblazer Books
ISBN: 1556617402

J   140   Jackson, Dave and Neta. ***Listen for the Whippoorwill***. MN: Bethany House, 1993.
Story of Harriet Tubman and the Underground Railroad, 1815 – 1913
ISBN: 1556612729

J/B   140   Jackson, Dave and Neta. ***Shanghaied to China***. MN: Bethany House, 1993.
Hudson Taylor missionary to China, 1832 - 1905
ISBN: 1556612710

J/B   138   Jackson, Dave and Neta. ***Escape from the Slave Traders***. MN: Bethany House, 1992.
David Livingstone and his work in Africa. 1813 - 1873
ISBN: 155661263X

J/B   127   Sullivan, George. ***Mathew Brady – His Life and Photographs***. NY: Cobblehill, 1994.
A historian with a camera, 1823 – 1896
ISBN: 0525651861

J   119   Woodruff, Elvira. ***Dear Levi – Letters from the Overland Trail***. NY: Knopf, 1994.
Twelve-year-old Austin writes letters to his younger brother in Pennsylvania as they
travel to Oregon in 1851.
ISBN: 0679946411

J   74   Hopkinson, Deborah. ***Pioneer Summer***. NY: Aladdin, 2002.
Eli Thayer, New England Emigrant Aid Co. recruits families to move to Kansas.
Book 1 of the Prairie Skies Series. Ready for Chapters Book
ISBN: 068984350X

J/B   64   Dunlap, Julie. ***Parks for the People***. MN: Carolrhoda, 1994.
A story about Frederick Law Olmsted, landscape architect, 1822 – 1903
ISBN: 0876148240

J   59   Dickens, Charles. ***David Copperfield***. NY: Michael Neugebauer Book, 1995.
Abridged for public reading by Charles Dickens and Illustrated by Alan Marks.
ISBN: 1558584536

J   55   Hooper, Dorothy and Thomas. ***Treasure in the Stream***. NJ: Silver Burdett Press, 1991.
Amy and her family are overrun by the discovery of gold and the miners that follow.
ISBN: 0382241517

E   39   Glass, Andrew. ***The Sweetwater Run: The Story of Buffalo Bill Cody and the Pony Express***. NY: Doubleday, 1996.
ISBN: 0385322208

E/B   37   Stanley, Diane. ***The True Adventure of Daniel Hall***. NY: Dial Books, 1995.
Adapted from his book: *Arctic Rovings*
ISBN: 0803714688

E   30   Ransom, Candice. *Liberty Street*. NY: Walker & Co., 2003.
Young Kezia finds her way to Canada from Fredericksburg, VA. using the secret system.
ISBN: 0802788718

E   30   Altman, Linda Jacobs. *The Legend of Freedom Hill*. NY: Lee & Low Books, 2000.
During the California Gold Rush, two girls buy freedom with their treasure.
ISBN: 1584300035

E   28   Hopkinson, Deborah. *Maria's Comet*. NY: Atheneum Books, 1999.
Maria (ma-RYE-ah) Mitchell, America's first woman astronomer
ISBN: 0689815018

E   26   Blumberg, Rhonda. *Bloomers*. NY: Maxwell Macmillan International, 1993.
Amelia Bloomer and the Women's Rights Movement.
ISBN: 0027116840

1860 - 1870

A   333   Morris, Gilbert. *The Last Confederate*. MN: Bethany House, 1990.
April 1860, the Winslow family in the South
House of Winslow series
ISBN: 1556611099

A   271   Aldrich, Bess Streeter. *The Lieutenant's Lady*. ME: G. K. Hall & Co., 2001.
In the wake of the Civil War, Linnie comes from back East to becomes an army wife on
the frontier. Based on the diary of an actual army wife.
ISBN: 0783893663

Y   561   Alcott, Louisa May. *Little Women*. NY: J. Messner, 1982.
The effects of the Civil War on a Northern family
ISBN: 0671456512

Y   474   Henty, G. A. *The March to Coomassie*. Canada: Althouse Press, 2002.
Ashanti War in West Africa, 1873 - 1874
ISBN: 1590871286

Y   440   Henty, G. A. *The March to Magdala*. Canada: Althouse Press, 2002.
The British Abyssinian Campaign, 1867 – 1868
ISBN: 1590871308

Y   372   Henty, G. A. *Out With Garibaldi*. Canada: Althouse Press, 2002.
A story of the liberation of Italy by the "red shirts".
ISBN: 1590870964

Y   371   Alcott, Louisa May. *An Old-Fashioned Girl*. MS: Little, Brown, and Co., 1997.
Country cousin Polly comes to visit her city relations.
ISBN: 0316038091

Y   340   Henty, G. A. *The Young Franc-Tireurs*. Canada: Althouse Press, 2002.
Three adventurers in the Franco – Prussian War.
ISBN: 1590871480

Y   337   Henty, G. A. ***With Lee in Virginia***. PA: Preston Speed Publications, 1997.
                A story of the American Civil War.
                ISBN: 1887159320

Y   320   Henty, G. A. ***For Name and Fame***. Canada: Althouse Press, 2002.
                The Second Afghan War with General Roberts, 1873 - 1874
                ISBN: 1590870565

Y   273   Yep, Laurence. ***Dragon's Gate***. NY: HarperCollins, 1993.
                After he is banished, a Chinese boy is sent to America.
                ISBN: 0060229713

Y   208   Brenaman, Miriam. ***Evvy's Civil War***. NY: Putnam's Sons, 2002.
                Evelyn comes of age but resents the restrictions Southern society puts on women and
                slaves.
                ISBN: 0399237135

Y   199   Karr, Kathleen. ***The Great Turkey Walk***. NY: Farrar, Straus & Giroux, 1998.
                A young man attempts to herd 1,000 turkeys from MO to Denver, Co in hopes of making
                a profit.
                ISBN: 0374327734

Y   184   Forrester, Sandra. ***Sound the Jubilee***. NY: Lodestar Books, 1995.
                Roanoke Island self-freed slave community in North Carolina in 1861.
                ISBN: 0140379304

Y   170   Rinaldi, Ann. ***Numbering All the Bones***. NY: Hyperion Books, 2002.
                13,000 Union soldiers died at Andersonville Prisoner-of-War Prison in Georgia.
                ISBN: 0786805331

Y   152   Crane, Stephan. ***Red Badge of Courage***. NY: Prestwick House, 2004.
                A soldier's experiences during the American Civil War at the 1863 Battle of
                Chancellorsville.
                ISBN: 1580495869

J   191   Steele, William. ***Perilous Road***. NY: Harcourt, 1958, 2004.
                Tennessee mountain farm family during the Civil War
                ISBN: 0152052046

J   176   Wisler, G. Clifton. ***Red Cap***. NY: Puffin Books, 1994.
                A young boy enlists as a drummer boy in the Union Army.
                ISBN: 0140369368

J   167   Cox, Clinton. ***Undying Glory***. NY: Scholastic, 1991.
                Massachusetts 54th Regiment, the first black regiment in the Union Army
                ISBN: 0590441701

J   151   Matas, Carol. ***The War Within***. NY: Simon and Schuster, 2001.
                Union forces expel Hannah's family from Mississippi because they are Jewish.
                ISBN: 0689829353

J/B 138 Jackson, Dave and Neta. *Kidnapped by River Rats*. MN: Bethany House, 1991.
Story of William and Catherine Booth and the founding of the Salvation Army.
Trailblazer Books
ISBN: 1556612206

J 137 Calvert, Patricia. *Bigger*. NY: Maxwell Macmillan International, 1994.
The Civil War is over but some men refuse to surrender. Tyler decides to find his father and bring him home.
ISBN: 0684196859

J 88 Banks, Sara. *Abraham's Battle – A Novel of Gettysburg*. NY: Atheneum Books, 1999.
A freed slave joins the ambulance corps of the Union Army.
ISBN: 0689817797

J 69 Porter, Connie. *Meet Addy: An American Girl*. (Book 1) WI: Pleasant Co., 1993.
Escaping North meant leaving family and slavery behind.
ISBN: 1562470760

J 55 Karr, Kathleen. *Spy in the Sky – A Story of the Civil War*. NY: Hyperion Books, 1997.
An aeronaut from the North, Thaddeus Lowe convinces President Lincoln that a Balloon Corps could provide vital information for the Union Army.
ISBN: 078681165X

J 54 Goldin, Barbara Diamond. *Red Means Good Fortune – A Story of San Francisco's Chinatown*. NY: Viking, 1994.
The Chinese Exclusion Act encouraged the illegal importing and sale of slave girls from China. It kept Chinese men from bringing their families to join them in the U.S.
ISBN: 0670853526

E 95 Bulla, Clyde Robert. *Riding the Pony Express*. NY: Sonlight Curriculum, 2000.
Life in a Pony Express station in Nebraska
ISBN: 1887840400

E/B 30 Miller, Robert. *Buffalo Soldiers – The Story of Emanuel Stance*. NY: Silver Press, 1995. 1866, Congress voted to add four all-black infantry regiments to the Army.
ISBN: 0382243919

1870 - 1880

A 350 Pella, Judith. *A House Divided*. MN: Bethany House, 1992.
Battle of the Balkans in 1878
The Russian series
ISBN: 1556611730

A 334 Morris, Gilbert. *The Union Belle*. MN: Bethany House, 1992.
Transcontinental Railroad   House of Winslow series
ISBN: 1556611862

Y 358 Alcott, Louisa May. *Jo's Boys*. NY: Puffin books, 1994.
Post-war home for children
ISBN: 0140367144

Y/B   208   Benge, Janet and Geoff. *Mary Slessor: Forward Into Calabar*. WA: YWAM Pub., 1999. Scottish missionary to Africa,1848 – 1915
ISBN: 1576581489

Y/B   176   Tiner, John H. *Louis Pasteur: Founder of Modern Medicine*. MI: Mott. Media, 1991.
French scientist, 1822 – 1895   Sower series
ISBN: 0880621591

Y   151   Burks, Brian. *Soldier Boy*. NY: Harcourt Brace & Co., 1997.
Johnny has no family and no plans so he joins the Army and finds himself on the frontier.
ISBN: 0152012184

J   140   Myers, Walter. *The Righteous Revenge of Artemis Bonner*. NY: HarperCollins, 1992.
Lad's journey from New York to Tombstone, Arizona with revenge on their minds.
ISBN: 0060208449

J   134   Robinet, Harriette Gillem. *Children of the Fire*. NY: Maxwell Macmillan International, 1991. 1871, dry weather and prairie winds fan the fires that burn Chicago.
ISBN: 0689316550

J   125   Myers, Anna. *Graveyard Girl*. NY: Walker and Company, 1995.
1878, the yellow fever epidemic strikes Memphis, Tennessee leaving many without parents.
ISBN: 0802782604

J   95   Viola, Herman J. *It is a Good Day to Die – Indian Eyewitnesses tell the story of the Battle of the Little Bighorn*. NY: Crown Publishers, 1998.
Sioux and Cheyenne gathered in Montana with Sitting Bull to fight for their lands.
ISBN: 0517709139

E   64   Stevens, Carla. *Lily and Miss Liberty*. NY: Scholastic, 1992.
School children raise money for the pedestal needed for the Statue of Liberty.
ISBN: 0590449192

E   41   Roop, Peter and Connie. *Good-bye for Today*. NY: Atheneum Books, 2000.
A child's life on a whaling ship sailing from Japan to the Arctic Sea.
ISBN: 0689822227

1880 – 1889

A   400   Pella, Judith. *Travail and Triumph*. MN: Bethany House, 1992.
Rebel forces overpower the Tsar   The Russians series
ISBN: 1556611749

Y   406   Henty, G. A. *The Dash for Khartoum*. Canada: Althouse Press, 2002.
A tale of the Nile Expedition, 1884 – 1885
ISBN: 1590871189

Y   300   Henty, G. A. *A Chapter of Adventures*. Canada: Althouse Press, 2002.
The bombardment of Alexandria, Egypt, 1881 – 1882
ISBN: 159087000X

Y   280   Twain, Mark. *The Adventures of Tom Sawyer*. NY: Modern Library, 2001.
              Two friends, Tom Sawyer and Huck Finn, grow up along the Mississippi River in frontier
              America.
              ISBN: 037575681725

J   160   McKissack, Patricia. *Run Away Home*. NY: Scholastic Press, 1997.
              A black family gives refuge to a runaway Apache boy.
              ISBN: 0590467514

J   151   Fleischman, Sid. *Mr. Mysterious and Company*. NY: Greenwillow Books, 1997.
              A traveling magic show
              ISBN: 0688149219

J   142   Robinet, Harriette Gillem. *Missing from Haymarket Square*. NY: Atheneum, 2001.
              Living and working in Chicago and the movement for the 8 hour day.
              ISBN: 0689838956

J   139   Butcher, Nancy. *Lights! Camera! Action Dog!* NY: Gareth Stevens Publications, 2002.
              Wishbone and the famous film making Drake brothers.
              ISBN: 0836826949

J/B   80   Ferris, Jeri. *Native American Doctor*. MN: Carolrhoda Books, 1991.
              Story of Susan Laflesche Picott, young Omaha Indian woman who became the first
              Indian woman to graduate from medical school. 1865 – 1915
              ISBN: 0876144431

J   52   Gross, Virginia T. *The Day It Rained Forever - A Story of the Johnstown Flood*.
              NY: Viking, 1991.
              May 31, 1889 The rains fell, the dam burst, unleashing a wall of water upon South Fork,
              Mineral Point and Johnstown destroying everything in its wake.
              ISBN: 0670835528

J/B   36   Quackenbush, Robert. *Stop the Presses, Nellie's Got a Scoop! A Story of Nellie Bly*.
              NY: Simon & Schuster Books for Young Readers, 1992.
              The crusading reporter, Elizabeth Cochran, 1864 - 1922
              ISBN: 0671760904

J   31   Kent, Deborah. *Jane Addams and Hull House*. IL: Childrens Press, 1992.
              Defender of the oppressed, friend of the homeless, 1860 - 1935
              ISBN: 051604852X

J   28   McCully, Emily Arnold. *The Ballot Box Battle*. NY: Alfred A. Knopf, 1996.
              Elizabeth Cady Stanton attempts to vote in NJ. She worked for Women's Suffrage.
              ISBN: 0679893121

E/B   46   Greene, Carol. *Black Elk – A Man with a Vision*. IL: Childrens Press, 1990.
              Oglala medicine man that had a vision of universal peace, 1863 – 1950.
              Rookie Biography
              ISBN: 0516042130

E 29 Bunting, Eve. *Cheyenne Again*. NY: Clarion Books, 1995.
Indian children were forced to attend off-reservation boarding schools to teach them in white ways.
ISBN: 0396703646

1890 - 1899

A 382 Pella, Judith. *Heirs of the Motherland*. MN: Bethany House, 1993.
Count Remizov returns from exile
The Russians series
ISBN: 155661358X

Y 416 Henty, G. A. *With Kitchener in the Soudan*. Canada: Althouse Press, 2002.
A story of Atbara and Omdurman in Africa.
ISBN: 1590871804

J 144 Jackson, Dave and Neta. *Quest for the Lost Prince*. MN: Bethany House, 1996.
Prince Kaboo/Samuel Morris, first missionary to America. 1872 - 1893
ISBN: 1556614721

J 48 Holmes, Mary Z. *For Bread – 1893*. TX: Raintree Steck-Vaughn, 1992.
Times were hard and everyone in the family must find work just to eat.
ISBN: 0811435016

E/B 48 Saller, Carol. *Florence Kelley*. MN: Carolrhoda Books, 1997.
She worked to pass laws to protect children from danger and sickness on the job.
ISBN: 1575050161

E 30 Brown, Don. *Uncommon Traveler – Mary Kingsley in Africa*. MA: Houghton Mifflin, 2000. British explorer who made trips to west and central Africa. 1862 - 1900
ISBN: 0618002731

E 30 Hopkinson, Deborah. *Fannie in the Kitchen*. NY: Atheneum Book, 2001.
From soup to nuts, how Fannie Farmer invented recipes with precise measurements.
1857 - 1915
ISBN: 068981965X

1900 - 1909

Y 403 Henty, G. A. *With Roberts to Pretoria*. Canada: Althouse Press, 2002.
A tale of the South African War. Anglo-Boer War, Pretoria falls in 1900.
ISBN: 1590871863

Y 302 Henty, G. A. *With the Allies to Peking*. PA: PrestonSpeed, 2003.
A tale of the relief of the Legations during the Boxer Rebellion in China, 1900.
ISBN: 1931587280

Y/B 208 Ruffin, Bernard. *Fanny Crosby – Hymn Writer*. OH: Barbour Publishing, 1995.
American hymn writer and poet, 1870 – 1920 Many of her hymns are still used in churches today.
ISBN: 1557487316

J/B	192	Hammontree, Marie. ***Albert Einstein – Young Thinker***. MN: Sagebrush, 1999. German immigrant and leading American scientist, 1879 – 1955 ISBN: 0808513494
J	184	Hopkinson, Deborah. ***Hear My Sorrow: A Diary of Angela Denoto, a Shirtwaist Worker, New York City, 1909***. NY: Scholastic, 2004. ISBN: 0439221617
J	144	Jackson, Dave and Neta. ***The Forty-Acre Swindle***. MN: Bethany House, 2000. He changed the agriculture of the South. George Washington Carver, 1864 - 1943 "He could have added fortune to fame, but caring for neither, he found happiness and honor in being helpful to the world." - Epitaph on his grave ISBN: 0764222643
J	129	Freedman, Russell. ***The Wright Brothers: How They Invented the Airplane***. NY: Holiday House, 1991. American kite building brothers conquer the air. ISBN: 0823408752
J	121	Myers, Anna. ***Stolen by the Sea***. NY: Walker & Co., 2002. The Galveston hurricane of 1900 brought rich and poor together to fight the storm. ISBN: 0060281537
J	86	Blos, Joan W. ***Brooklyn Doesn't Rhyme***. NY: Charles Scribner's Sons, 1994. Edwina records the people and events in the lives of her Polish immigrant family. ISBN: 0684196948
J/B	73	Dolan, Sean. ***Matthew Henson***. NY: Chelsea Juniors, 1992. Along with the Robert Peary expedition, Henson reached the North Pole, April 1909. Lifetime 1866 – 1955 Junior World Biographies ISBN: 0791015688
J	70	Hyatt, Patricia Rusch. ***Coast to Coast With Alice***. MN: Carolrhoda 1995. The first American women to make a cross-country automobile trip. ISBN: 0876147899
J/B	32	McKissack, Patricia. ***Madame C. J. Walker–Selfmade Millionaire***. NJ: Enslow Publishers, 1992. Wealthy black business woman, philanthropist and inventor. 1867 – 1919. ISBN: 089490311X
E	56	Kudlinski, Kathleen V. ***Earthquake!*** NY: Puffin Books, 1995. San Francisco earthquake in 1906 Once Upon America series ISBN: 0140363904
E/B	31	Anderson, Peter. ***Will Rogers – American Humorist***. IL: Childrens Press, 1992. Oklahoma's own rodeo, radio, and movie star, 1879 - 1935 ISBN: 0516041835

E/B   28   Miller, William. *Zora Hurston and the Chinaberry Tree*. NY: Lee & Low Books, 1994.
Zora is encouraged to be a story teller by her mother. 1891 - 1960
ISBN: 1880000148

1910 – 1919

A   496   Marshall, Catherine. *Christy*. NY: McGraw-Hill, 1967.
Young woman and teacher at a mission in the Appalachian Mountains.
ISBN: 0380001411

A   430   Thoene, Bodie. *In My Father's House*. MN: Bethany House, 1992.
From every culture, men joined together to fight the war to end all wars.
The Shiloh Legacy series
ISBN: 1556611897

A   150   Jones, Mary Harris. *Autobiography of Mother Jones*. NY: Dover Publications, 2004.
Crusader for the American labor movement, 1843 - 1930
ISBN: 0486436454

Y   222   Frank, Rudolf. *No Hero for the Kaiser*. NY: William Morrow & Co., 1986.
Polish boy whose town is invaded in WW l joins a German battalion.
This book was banned and publicly burned by the Third Reich Government of Germany.
ISBN: 0688060935

Y/B   200   Benge, Janet and Geoff. *Lillian Trasher: The Greatest Wonder in Egypt*.
WA: YWAM Pub., 2003.
She built homes for children and widows in Assiout, Egypt. Lifetime 1887 – 1961
ISBN: 1576583058

Y   197   Namioka, Lensey. *An Ocean Apart, A World Away*. NY: Delacorte Press, 2002.
Yanyan, a young woman from a wealthy Chinese family is caught between the old world
of bound feet and silent women to the new world of education and freedom for women.
ISBN: 0385730020

Y   182   Karr, Kathleen. *In the Kaiser's Clutch*. NY: Farrar, Straus, & Giroux, 1995.
The twins are working in a silent anti-German film serial while also solving a mystery.
ISBN: 0374336385

Y   148   Morpurgo, Michael. *War Horse*. NY: Egmont Books Ltd, 2002.
Calvary horse during W W I
ISBN: 0749748508

J   217   Lasky, Kathryn. *A Time for Courage – The Suffragette Diary of Kathleen Bowen*.
NY: Scholastic, 2002.
Washington, D.C., 1917 – Women march for the right to vote.
ISBN: 0590511416

J   197   White, Ellen Emerson. *Voyage on the Great Titanic*. NY: Scholastic, 1998.
The Diary of Margaret Ann Brady.
ISBN: 0590962736

J   153   Head, Judith. *Culebra Cut*. MN: Carolrhoda Books, 1995.
1911, William learns about the construction of the canal and life in Panama.
ISBN: 087614878X

J   144   Jackson, Dave and Neta. *Defeat of the Ghost Riders*. MN: Bethany House, 1997.
Mary McLeod Bethune, 1875 - 1955, black educator and activist
ISBN: 1556617429

J   77   Kinsey-Warnok, Natalie. *The Night the Bells Rang*. NY: Cobblehill Books, 1991.
Life in rural Vermont during WW l.
ISBN: 0525650741

J   73   Kinsey-Warnok, Natalie. *A Doctor Like Papa*. NY: Harper Trophy, 2002.
The epidemic of 1918 challenges Margaret's desire to become a doctor.
ISBN: 0385327889

J   61   Smith, Betsy Covington. *Women Win the Vote*. NJ: Silver Burdett Press, 1989.
Chronicles the struggles and progress of the Suffrage Movement.
ISBN: 0382098374

J   54   Goldin, Barbara Diamond. *Fire! The Beginning of the Labor Movement*. NY: Viking, 1992. Rosie supports unions for better working conditions after the Triangle Shirtwaist factory fire.
ISBN: 0670844756

J   40   Fine, Jil. *The Shackleton Expedition*. NY: Childrens Press, 2002.
1914, Sir Shackleton led a team to cross the Antarctic continent on foot.
ISBN: 051623904X

E   69   Jackson, Robert B. *The Remarkable Ride of the Abernathy Boys*. OK: Levite of Apache, 1993.
1910; True story - two boys, seven and nine years old, drive from NY to OK.
ISBN: 0961863463

E   34   Bildner, Phil. *Shoeless Joe and Black Betsy*. NY: Simon & Schuster, 2002.
Baseball great Joseph Jefferson Jackson and the 1919 World Series scandal.
ISBN: 0689829132

E/B   32   McKissack, Patricia and Fredrick. *Carter G. Woodson – The Father of Black History*. NJ: Enslow Publishers, 2002.
Author, editor, publisher, and historian, 1875 - 1950
ISBN: 0766016986

E   32   Steig, William. *When Everybody Wore a Hat*. NY: Joanna Cotler Books, 2003.
An eight-year-old tells about life in 1916 and how she worked to change fashion.
ISBN: 0060097000

E   30   Skrypuch, Marsha Forchuk. *Silver Threads*. Canada: Fitzhenry & Whiteside, 2004.
The internment of Ukrainian Canadians in concentration camps during World War l in Canada.
ISBN: 155041903X

E/B   30   Cooper, Floyd. ***Coming Home – From the Life of Langston Hughes***. NY: Philomel Books, 1994.
ISBN: 0399226826

E   28   Rabin, Staton. ***Casey Over There***. NY: Harcourt Brace Jovanovich, 1994.
Aubrey's brother Casey has gone overseas to fight in World War I. What can a little brother do?
ISBN: 0152531866

1920 - 1929

A   425   Thoene, Bodie. ***A Thousand Shall Fall***. ME: G. K. Hall, 1992.
After WW I, a promise of peace and prosperity in Arkansas
The Shiloh Legacy series
ISBN: 0816157189

Y/B   131   Collins, David. ***George Washington Carver***. MI: Mott Media, 1981.
The ex-slave that saved the South with agricultural chemistry.
Sower series
ISBN: 0915134993

J   281   Levine, Gail Caron. ***Dave at Night***. NY: HarperCollins, 1999.
11-year-old Dave lives in an orphanage, but finds Harlem night life exciting.
ISBN: 0064407470

J   257   Lewis, Elizabeth Foreman. ***Young Fu of the Upper Yangtze***. NY: Yearling, 1990.
Life in China, 1920's
ISBN: 044049043X

J   160   Hoobler, Dorothy and Tim. ***The 1920's – Luck***. CT: Millbrook Press, 2000.
In 1927, the Dixons move from rural GA to Chicago, where negroes have more opportunities.
ISBN: 0761316027

J   123   Hoobler, Dorothy and Thomas. ***Florence Robinson: The Story of a Jazz Girl***.
NJ: Silver Burnett Press, 1997.
When Florence's father returns to Mississippi after WW l he is a changed man.
Her Story series
ISBN: 0382396448

J   48   Bierman, Carol. ***Journey to Ellis Island***. NY: Hyperion Books, 1998.
Yechuda, his sister and mother escape Russia to come to America.
ISBN: 0786803770

E   52   Weaver, Lydia. ***Child Star - When Talkies Came to Hollywood***. NY: Viking, 1992.
A silent star hopes he can make the change to talkies.
ISBN: 0670840394

E/B   32   Cline-Ransome, Lesa. ***Satchel Paige***. NY: Aladdin Paperbacks, 2003.
First player from the Negro Leagues to be inducted into the Baseball Hall of Fame.
ISBN: 0689856814

E 32 Wells, Rosemary and Tom. ***The House in the Mail***. NY: Viking, 2002.
Emily's pa brings home a house catalog and they order the kit.
ISBN: 0670035459

E 31 Barasch, Lynne. ***Radio Rescue***. NY: Frances Foster Books, 2000.
Morse code and ham radios were the way to communicate in the 1920's.
ISBN: 0374361665

1930 - 1939

A 413 Thoene, Brock and Brodie. ***Danzig Passage***. MN: Bethany House, 1991.
The Nazi terror becomes real to the trapped Jews in 1936.
ISBN: 1556610815

Y 227 Hesse, Karen. ***Out of the Dust***. NY: Scholastic Press, 1997.
Billie Jo tells of the hardships living in OK during the Dust Bowl years.
ISBN: 0590360809

Y 188 Thesman, Jean. ***The Storyteller's Daughter***. MA: Houghton Mifflin, 1996.
1933, Quinn comes from a working class family struggling to make it through the Depression.
ISBN: 0395809789

Y/B 149 Haskins, James. ***Thurgood Marshall - A Life for Justice***. NY: Henry Holt, 1992.
First black judge on the Supreme Court, 1903 – 1993
ISBN: 0805020950

J 276 Taylor, Mildred. ***Roll of Thunder, Hear My Cry***. NY: Puffin Books, 1991.
Young black girl living in Mississippi in 1933.
ISBN: 014034893X

J 182 Ayres, Katherine. ***Macaroni Boy***. NY: Delacorte Press, 2003.
1933, Mike finds that there is more wrong than just the Depression in Pittsburg.
ISBN: 0385730160

J 148 Porter, Tracey. ***Treasures in the Dust***. NY: Harper Trophy, 1999.
The Dust Bowl sends many *Okies* down Rt. 66 to Weed Patch Camp and California.
ISBN: 0064407705

J 144 Jackson, Dave and Neta. ***Flight of the Fugitives***. MN: Bethany House, 1994.
Gladys Aylward helps Chinese orphans escape the war torn region.
ISBN: 1556614667

J 139 Evans, Karen L. B. ***You Must Remember This***. NY: Hyperion Books, 1997.
The treatment of blacks in Hollywood's film industry in 1935.
ISBN: 0786800909

J 139 Denenberg, Barry. ***Mirror, Mirror on the Wall – The Diary of Bess Brennan***.
NY: Scholastic, 2002.
1932 – Perkins School for the Blind in MA.
ISBN: 0439194466

J   107   Myers, Anna. **Red-Dirt Jessie**. NY: Walker, 1992.
Dust Bowl in Oklahoma.
ISBN: 014038734X

J   80   Stanley, Jerry. **Children of the Dustbowl**. NY: Crown, 1992.
A true story of the school at Weed Patch, CA.
ISBN: 0517880946

J   72   Ransom, Candice F. **Fire in the Sky**. MN: Carolrhoda Books, 1997.
Stenny can hardly wait to see the arrival of the Hindenburg.
ISBN: 0876148674

J   72   Ransom, Candice F. **Jimmy Crack Corn**. MN: Carolrhoda Books, 1994.
1932, Jimmy goes with his father and other veterans of the Great War to request bonus money promised to them. President Hoover drives them from the city and burns their camp area.
ISBN: 0876147864

J   56   Ackerman, Karen. **The Night Crossing**. NY: Alfred A. Knopf, 1994.
Persecution of Jews begins in Austria and Clara's family escapes to freedom in Switzerland.
ISBN: 067983169X

E   48   Crofford, Emily. **A Matter of Pride**. MN: Carolrhoda Books, 1981.
How one family adjusts to the Depression.
ISBN: 0876141718

E   31   Moss, Marissa. **Mighty Jackie – The Strike Out Queen**. NY: Paula Wiseman Book, 2004. The young woman who struck out Babe Ruth, Lou Gehrig, and Leo Durocher. She dreamed of playing in the world series but was banned because of her gender.
ISBN: 0689863292

E   30   Miller, William. **Rent Party Jazz**. NY: Lee & Low Books, 2001.
Rent parties originated in the South as fund-raising to help those in financial need.
ISBN: 1584300256

1941 - 1945

A   510   Thoene, Brock and Brodie. **Warsaw Requiem**. MN: Bethany House, 1991.
The Holocaust
Zion Covenant series
ISBN: 1556611889

A   447   Thoene, Brodie. **Say to This Mountain**. MN: Bethany House, 1993.
Arkansas during the Great Depression
The Shiloh Legacy series
ISBN: 1556611919

Y   304   Savery, Constance. **Enemy Brothers**. PA: Bethlehem Books, 2001.
Two brothers, one raised in Germany the other in England.
ISBN: 1883937507

Y   221   Van Stockum, Hilde. ***The Borrowed House***. PA: Bethlehem Books, 2000.
Janna, a German girl joins her parents in occupied Amsterdam.
ISBN: 1883937167

Y   198   Park, Linda Sue. ***When My Name Was Keoko***. NY: Clarion Books, 2002.
Korea under the dominion of Japan.
ISBN: 0618133356

Y   156   Hesse, Karen. ***Aleutian Sparrow***. NY: Margaret K. McElderry Books, 2003.
Removal and interment of the Aluets to "protect" them from the Japanese in 1942.
ISBN: 0689861893

Y   137   Taylor, Theodore. ***The Cay***. NY: Yearling, 2002.
When their freighter is torpedoed Phillip and Timothy find themselves stranded on an island. Sequel to *Timothy of the Cay*
ISBN: 0440416639

J   180   Giff, Patricia Reilly. ***Lily's Crossing***. NY: Delacorte, 1997.
Summer of 1944, Lily befriends Albert, a young Hungarian refugee, causing her to see the war in a different light.
ISBN: 0440414539

J   179   Kehret, Peg. ***Small Steps: The Year I Got Polio***. IL: Albert Whitman, 1996.
12-year-old Peggy describes her battle with polio.
ISBN: 0807574589

J/B 176   Gold, Alison Leslie. ***A Special Fate - Chine Sugihara: Hero of the Holocaust***.
NY: Scholastic, 2000.
ISBN: 0590395254

J   175   Hoobler, Dorothy and Tim. ***The 1940's – Secrets***. CT: Millbrook Press, 2001.
ISBN: 0761316043

J   169   Giff, Patricia Reilly. ***All the Way Home***. NY: Delacorte Press, 2001.
1941, the country is still recovering from the Depression and polio epidemic, while aiding Europe.
ISBN: 0385322097

J   167   Kochenderfer, Lee. ***The Victory Garden***. NY: Delacorte Press, 2002.
Planting a garden in your yard provides more food for the troops.
ISBN: 0385327889

J   161   Taylor, Theodore. ***Timothy of the Cay***. CA: Harcourt Brace, 1993.
Phillip returns to the Cay and recounts the time there with Timothy.
Prequel to *The Cay*
ISBN: 0380725223

J   156   Denenberg, Barry. ***The Journal of Ben Uchida. Citizen 13559, Mirror Lake Internment Camp***. NY: Scholastic, 1999.
12-year-old Ben keeps a journal of his experiences as a prisoner in an internment camp.
ISBN: 0590485318

J   149   Uchinda, Yoshiko. ***Journey to Topaz***. CA: Heyday Books, 2004.
Life is transformed for Japanese-Americans after the attack on Pearl Harbor.
ISBN: 1890771910

J   104   Daly, Maureen. ***The Small War of Sgt. Donkey***. PA: Bethlehem Books, 2000.
A young boy tells of American troops in Italy.
ISBN: 1883937977

J/B   90   Stanley, Jerry. ***I Am An American – A True Story of Japanese Internment***. NY: Crown, 1994. The story of Shiro Nomura and the Japanese internment camps.
ISBN: 0517885514

J   64   Talbott, Hudson. ***Forging Freedom – A True Story of Heroism During the Holocaust***.
NY: Putnam, 2000.
ISBN: 0399234349

E   38   Lee, Milly. ***Nim and the War Effort***. NY: Frances Foster Books, 1997.
Nim's school has a paper drive to help the war effort.
ISBN: 0374355231

E/B   31   Mochizuki, Ken. ***Passage to Freedom – The Sugihara Story***. NY: Lee and Low Books, 1997. Chiune Sugihara was a Japanese diplomat in Lithuania who saved 10,000 Jewish refugees from Hitler's death camps.
ISBN: 1880000490

E/B   30   Adler, David A. ***A Hero and the Holocaust***. NY: Holiday House Book, 2002.
Dr. Janusz Korczak gives his life to the orphans.
ISBN: 0823415481

E   30   Adler, David A. ***Hiding From the Nazis***. NY: Holiday House, 1997.
True story of Lore Baer whose parents hid her with a Christian family in Holland.
ISBN: 0823412881

E   29   Deedy, Carmen Agra. ***The Yellow Star: The legend of King Christian X of Denmark***.
GA: Peachtree, 2000.
King Christian and the Danish resistance to the Nazis during World War ll.
ISBN: 1561452084

E   28   Marx, Trish. ***Hanna's Cold Winter***. MN: Carolrhoda Books, 1993.
During the war, the people of Budapest rally to provide food for the starving hippo's at the zoo.
ISBN: 0876147724

1946 - 1949

Y   230   Wolff, Virginia Euwer. ***Bat 6***. NY: Scholastic Press, 1998.
A small town in post WW ll Oregon.
ISBN: 0590897993

Y   194   Johnston, Julie. ***Hero of Lesser Causes***. Canada: Tundra Books, 2003.
Keeley is devastated when her older brother gets polio.
ISBN: 0887766498

J 88 Douglas, Kirk. *The Broken Mirror*. NY: Simon & Schuster, 1997.
After the war and the destruction of his family, Moishe runs away from home and his faith.
ISBN: 0689814933

J 88 Ada, Alma Flor. *Under the Royal Palms*. NY: Atheneum Books, 1998.
Growing up in Cuba.
ISBN: 0689806310

J/B 52 Adler, David A. *Our Golda – The Story of Golda Meir*. NY: Viking Press, 1984.
Israeli Prime Minister and world leader, 1898 - 1978
ISBN: 0670531073

E/B 46 Greene, Carol. *Albert Schweitzer – Friend of All Life*. IL: Childrens Press, 1993.
Doctor, missionary to Africa, musician, pastor, writer, and teacher, 1875 - 1965
ISBN: 0516042580

E 32 Koestler-Grack, Rachel A. *The Story of Anne Frank*. PA: Chelsea Clubhouse, 2003.
Anne's diary of hiding during Nazi occupied Holland and more details of those who helped.
ISBN: 0791073114

E 30 Adler, David A. *One Yellow Daffodil*. NY: Gulliver Books, 1995.
God sends hope to a boy in Auschwitz.
ISBN: 0152005374

E 30 Evans, Freddi Williams. *A Bus of Our Own*. IL: Albert Whitman & Co., 2001.
Separate but equal was not the case. The black community rallies and got a bus for their children.
ISBN: 0807509701

E 28 Rappaport, Doreen. *Dirt on Their Skirts*. NY: Dial Books, 2000.
The Story of the Young Women Who Won the World Championship.
ISBN: 0803720424

1950 – 1959

A/B 336 Russert, Tim. *Big Russ and Me: Father and Son – Lessons of Life*. NY: Hyperion, 2004. Tim looks back on his South Buffalo neighborhood and the man who taught him his values.
ISBN: 1401352081

Y/B 188 Parks, Rosa. *Rosa Parks: My Story*. NY: Scholastic, 1994.
The "Mother" of the Civil Rights Movement, 1913 - 2005
ISBN: 0590465384

J 160 Hoobler, Dorothy and Tom. *The 1950's Music*. CT: The Millbrook Press, 2001.
Matthew befriends a negro boy who introduces him to a new kind of music.
The Century Kids series
ISBN: 076131606

J 151 Sorensen, Virginia. *The Plain Girl*. CA: Harcourt Brace Jovanovich, 1997.
An Amish girl meets a different world when she must attend public school.
ISBN: 0152047255

J 146 Robinet, Harriette Gillem. *Walking to the Bus-Rider Blues*. NY: Jean Karl Book, 2000.
Black citizens of Montgomery, AL boycott the buses in the summer of 1956.
ISBN: 0689831919

J 121 Myers, Anna. *Rosie's Tiger*. NY: Walker & Co.,1994.
1952, Ronny returns from the war with a new Korean wife and child.
ISBN: 0802783058

J/B 53 Medearis, Angela Shelf. *Dare to Dream*. NY: Lodestar Books, 1994.
Coretta Scott King and the Civil Rights Movement. 1927 - 2006
ISBN: 0525674268

J/B 31 Slater, Jack. *Malcolm X*. IL: Childrens Press, 1993.
The Black Muslin leader that taught self-respect among black Americans. 1925 – 1965.
ISBN: 0516066692

E/B 60 Mohan, Claire Jordon. *The Young Life of Mother Teresa of Calcutta*.
PA: Young Sparrow Press, 1996.
Agnes Gonxha Bojaxhiu 1910 – 1997 Ministers to the dying in Calcutta, India
ISBN: 0943135265

E 34 McKissack, Patricia. *Goin' Someplace Special*. NY: Anne Schwartz Books, 2001.
The public library was one of the few integrated places in the segregated South.
ISBN: 0689818858

1960 - 1969

A/B 205 Taulbert, Clifton L. *The Last Train North*. OK: Council Oaks Books, 1992.
The Southern born and raised Clifton goes north to meet his future in 1963.
ISBN: 0933031629

A/B 103 Saleem, Hiner. *My Father's Rifle: A Childhood in Kurdistan*.
NY: Farrar, Strauss and Giroux, 2005.
Azad grows up in Iraq under Pan-Arabism and Baath nationalism but he remains a Kurd.
ISBN: 0374216932

Y 165 Donahue, John. *Till Tomorrow*. NY: Farrar Straus, & Giroux, 2001.
Adolescence, Army base life, host countries and the Berlin crisis, all in one story.
ISBN: 0374375801

J 163 Murphy, Rita. *Black Angels*. NY: Delacorte Press, 2001.
1961, the Civil Rights Movement comes to Mystic, GA.
ISBN: 0385327765

J/B 120 McKissack, Patricia. *Martin Luther King Jr*. NJ: Enslow Publishers, 2001.
ISBN: 0766016781

J   55   Antle, Nancy. *Tough Choices – A Story of the Vietnam War*. NY: Viking, 1993.
                ISBN: 0670848794

J/B   43   King, Sarah E. *Maya Angelou – Greeting the Morning*. CT: Millbrook Press, 1994.
                A black American poet, writer, and educator   b. 1928
                ISBN: 0785732357

E   52   Gross, Virginia. *The President is Dead*. NY: Viking, 1993.
                The Kennedy assassination in Dallas, 1963.
                ISBN: 0670851566

E   48   Donnelly, Judy. *Moonwalk – The First Trip to the Moon*. NY: Random House, 1989.
                ISBN: 0394824571

E   38   Littlesugar, Amy and Floyd Cooper. *Freedom School, Yes!* NY: Philomel Books, 2001.
                A young white woman comes to Mississippi to teach in the summer.
                ISBN: 0399230068

E/B   37   Krull, Kathleen. *Wilma Unlimited – How Wilma Rudolph Became the World's Fastest
                Runner*. CA: Harcourt Brace, 1996.
                First American woman to win three gold medals in one Olympics, Rome 1960. b. 1940
                ISBN: 0345781205

E   34   Heide, Florence & Heidi Gilliland. *Sami and the Time of the Troubles*. NY: Clarion,
                1992. A Lebanese boy in war torn Beirut.
                ISBN: 0395559642

1970 - 1979

J   48   Beyer, Mark. *Crisis in Space – Apollo 13*. NY: Childrens Press, 2002.
                Recounts the events related to the moon landing mission.
                ISBN: 0516234854

J/B   46   Brill, Marlene Targ. *Journey for Peace*. NY: Lodestar Books, 1996.
                Rigoberta Menchu fights for the right of indigenous people especially the Mayans of
                Guatemala.
                ISBN: 0525675248

1980 - 1989

Y   186   Whelam, Gloria. *Homeless Bird*. NY: HarperTrophy, 2000.
                13-year-old Koly enters the traditional world of marriage and widowhood in India.
                ISBN: 0060284544

J/B   112   Carson, Ben. *Ben Carson*. MI: Zondervan Books, 1991.
                Rising from the bottom of the class to become one of today's heroes. b. 1951
                ISBN: 0310546526

J/B   102   Altman, Linda Jacobs. *The Importance of Simon Wiesenthal*. CA: Lucent Books, 2000.
                Holocaust survivor and Nazi hunter has brought many to account for their role in the
                genocide.
                ISBN: 1560064900

J/B	77	Shaw, Dena. ***Ronald McNair, Challenger Astronaut***. PA: Chelsea House Pub., 1994. Mission specialist and his six crew members died on the space shuttle, Challenger. ISBN: 0791021106

J   64   Schur, Maxine Rose. ***When I Left My Village***. NY: Dial Books, 1996.
Ethiopian Jewish family flees famine and political oppression with the hope of reaching Israel.
ISBN: 0803715617

J   48   Holmes, Mary Z. ***Dust of Life – The 1980's***. TX: Raintree Steck-Vaughn, 1992.
Life is hard in Vietnam after the Americans pull out and the Vietcong take over.
ISBN: 0811435040

E   48   Kilborne, Sarah S. ***Leaving Vietnam – The True Story of Tuan Ngo***.
NY: Simon & Schuster, 1999.
ISBN: 0689807988

1990 - 1999

Y   181   Hahn, Mary Downing. ***December Stillness***. NY: Harper Trophy, 1990.
plight of the homeless
ISBN: 0380707640

J   160   Hoobler, Dorothy and Tom. ***Families***. CT: The Millbrook Press, 2002.
The end of the 20th century finds three families wondering about Y2K.
ISBN: 0761316094

J   150   Skurzynski, Gloria and Alane Ferguson. ***Deadly Waters***.
WA DC: National Geographic Society, 1999.
Something is wrong in the Everglades, endangered species are dying.
ISBN: 0792270371

J   148   George, Jean Craighead. ***The Missing Gator of Gumbo Limbo***. NY: Harper Collins, 1992. Lisa K and five other homeless live in the everglades and want to protect their guardian alligator.
ISBN: 006020396X

J   113   Mead, Alice. ***Girl of Kosovo***. NY: Farrar, Straus & Giroux, 2001.
11-year-old Zana experiences war in her native Kosovo.
ISBN: 0374326207

J   57   Ada, Alma. ***My Name is Maria Isabel***. NY: Maxwell Macmillan International, 1993.
Maria loses her identity in a white school.
ISBN: 0689315171

J/B   42   Bredeson, Carmen. ***Shannon Lucid – Space Ambassador***. CT: Millbrook Press, 1994.
Space shuttle mission specialist who spent six months on the MIR space station.
ISBN: 0761313753

E/B 31 Sakurai, Gail. *Mae Jemison – Space Scientist*. IL: Childrens Press, 1995.
First black American woman in space. b. 1956
ISBN: 0516041940

E/B 31 Jaffe, Elizabeth D. *Ellen Ochoa*. NY: Childrens Press, 2004.
First Hispanic American woman to go into space.
ISBN: 0516258273

E 30 Bunting, Eve. *Your Move*. NY: Harcourt Brace Jovanovich, 1998.
Being a member of a gang sounds cool until James' little brother is endangered.
ISBN: 0152001816

E 30 Altman, Linda Jacobs. *Amelia's Road*. NY: Lee & Low Books Inc., 1993.
The Martinez family are migrant workers and follow the harvests to make a living.
ISBN: 1880000040

E 30 DiSalvo-Ryan, DyAnne. *Uncle Willie and the Soup Kitchen*. NY: Morrow Junior
Books, 1991.
A boy spends a day helping his Uncle Willie at the Soup Kitchen.
ISBN: 0688091652

E 28 Khan, Rukhsana. *The Roses in my Carpets*. NY: Holiday Book, 1998.
Living in the refugee camp to escape war in Afghanistan.
ISBN: 0823413993

2000 to 2005

A 241 Cash, Lt. Carey H. *A Table in the Presence*. TN: W Publishing Group, 2004.
Lt. Cash is a chaplain serving with the U.S. Marines in Iraq.
ISBN: 0849918235

Y 178 Levitin, Sonia. *Dream Freedom*. NY: Harcourt Brace Jovanovich, 2000.
Civil War in the Sudan causes misery for its people.
ISBN: 0152024042

Y 131 Al-Windawi, Thura. *Thura's Diary*. NY: Viking, 2003.
Reporting from inside Iran before and during the invasion of Baghdad.
ISBN: 0670058866

J 147 Alvarez, Julia. *How Tía Lola Came to ~~Visit~~ Stay*. NY: Alfred A. Knopf, 2001.
Tia Lola leaves the Dominican Republic for America to help care for the children.
ISBN: 0375902155

J 134 George, Jean Craighead. *There's an Owl in the Shower*. NY: Harper Collins, 1995.
Endangered Spotted Owls bring the logging community to a halt.
ISBN: 0060248920

J 80 Bruchac, Joseph. *Eagle Song*. NY: Dial Books, 1997.
After moving from the reservation to Brooklyn NY, fourth grader Danny Birdtree faces
stereotypes about his heritage.
ISBN: 0803719191

J	66	Smith, Cynthia Leitich. ***Indian Shoes***. NY: HarperCollins, 2002. Ray Halfmoon tells what it's like to grow up as a Seminole-Cherokee boy. ISBN: 0060295317
J	64	Wheeler, Jill C. ***September 11, 2001 – The Day That Changed America***. MN: Abdo & Daughters, 2002. ISBN: 1577656563
J/B	48	Stone, Tanya Lee. ***Ilan Ramon: Israel's First Astronaut***. CT: The Millbrook Press, Inc., 2003. Member of the Columbia space shuttle crew who died on February 1, 2003 during reentry. ISBN: 0761323767
J	38	Williams, Mary. ***Brothers in Hope***. NY: Lee & Low Books, 2005. The Story of the Lost Boys of Sudan ISBN: 13: 9781584302322
E	30	DiSalvo, DyAnne. ***A Castle on Viola Street***. NY: Harper Collins Publishers, 2001. Habitat for Humanities helps families build houses and help communities. ISBN: 0688176917
E	29	Mitchell, Barbara. ***Red Bird***. NY: Harper Collins, 1996. Visit the annual pow-wow in southern Delaware, where the Nanticoke heritage is celebrated with music, dancing, and special foods. ISBN: 0688108598
E	16	Lindbergh, Reeve. ***My Hippie Grandmother***. MA: Candlewick Press, 2003. A girl describes spending time with her grandmother. ISBN: 0763606715

Timelines

For further study, timelines are included for women in history, black scientists, inventors, explorers, and an overview of History's Masterminds and church history.

Teacher's Notes

LESSON	YEAR	SCIENTISTS, INVENTIONS & EXPLORERS	BIBLE & CHURCH HISTORY
	BC or BCE		
LSN 0	3500	Wheel	
	3200	Hieroglyphics	
	2500	Egyptian sailing ship (Khufu)	
	2348		
	2050		
	2000	Chariot	
	1976		Abraham born
	1876		Isaac born
	1816		Jacob (later named Israel) & Esau born
	1725		Joseph born
	1476		Moses and mass exodus from Egypt
	1040		1436-1040 period of the Judges
	1020		King Saul
	1000		King David
	961		King Solomon & Prophet Elijah
	924		Israel Kingdom divides over taxation
	627 - 570		Prophets Jeremiah, Daniel, and Ezekiel
LSN 1	536		Jews return to Israel (Zerubbabel)
	522 - 486		King Darius of Persia
	500	Hanno explores NW coast of Africa	Prophets Joel & Obadiah
	486-465		King Xerxes of Persia – Queen Esther – Jews under Persian rule
	400	Hippocrates – Father of Medicine	Books of Ezra and Malachi completed – 400 years of silence in Jewish history before birth of Christ
	334	Alexander the Great	Jews under the Alexander the Great
LSN 2	330	Pytheas – Arctic explorer	Jews treated well under Alexander
	310	Aristarchus – estimates sizes and distances between Earth, moon, and sun	Jews under Alexander the Great (Greece)
	300	Euclid – geometry	
	300	Aristotle - classification	
LSN 3	240	Eratosthenes calculates Earth's circumference	Septuagint Translation begun (Greek translation in Alexandria)
	200	Archimedes' Screw	Simon II – The Just is high priest
	200	Wheelbarrow	
	200	Archimedes – volume, buoyancy, simple machines	Hellenistic period – Jews under Egyptian (Ptolemy was Greek) rule
	167		Antiochus IV Epiphanes defiled the temple
LSN 4	**AD or CE**		
	1		Birth of Christ
	33		Resurrection of Christ
	45		Paul's missionary travels
	50		First Council of Apostles
	64		Great Fire of Rome / Flavius Josephus
	70		Titus destroys Jerusalem and the Temple
	85		Gospels of John and Matthew
	100	Ptolemy – maps the stars	Ignatius – Bishop of Antioch (student of the Apostle John) martyred in Coliseum
	313		Edict of Milan
	432		St. Patrick's mission to Ireland
	982	Eric the Red discovers Greenland	984 Antipope Boniface VII murders
			Pope John XIV
	1000	Leif Ericsson discovers Vineland	Iceland converted to the Christian religion
	1000	Gunpowder	1095 Crusades launched by Pope Urban I

LESSON	YEAR	SCIENTISTS, INVENTIONS & EXPLORERS	BIBLE & CHURCH HISTORY
LSN 5	1100		Christians capture Jerusalem in the Crusades
	1208		Francis of Assisi renounces wealth
	1231	Roger Bacon – Observation & Experiment	Pope Gregory IX charters the University of Paris
	1271	Marco Polo – China & Asia	Crusaders take Constantinople
	1273		Thomas Aquinas
	1284	Spectacles	1,500,000 Jews massacred in Europe on
	1350	Cannon	suspicion of having poisoned the springs
	1371	Magnetic compass	
	1378		The Great Schism
	1382		John Wycliffe translates Bible into English
LSN 6	1405		Joan of Arc
	1440	Printing press using movable type in Europe	Bible printed
	1472	Leonardo da Vinci	
	1480		Spanish Inquisition begins
	1483		Martin Luther born
	1488	Bartolomeu Dias – Southern tip of Africa	First complete edition of the Hebrew Bible printed (on a printing press) with the aid of Abraham ben Hayyim dei Tintori
LSN 7	1492	Christopher Columbus – West Indies	Columbus opens new continents to Christianity
	1497	Vasco de Gama – India	Girolamo Savonarola, Dominican priest, orders the Bonfire of the Vanities
	1499	Amerigo Vespucci – South America	Michelangelo completes the Pietà
LSN 8	1500	Musket	
	1508		1508 – 1512 Michelangelo paints the Sistine Chapel ceiling
	1513	Juan Ponce de León – Florida	Leo X becomes Pope and is Pope at the beginning of the Reformation
	1513	Vasco de Balboa – Panama	Thomas Wolsey (later influential Cardinal) rises to power in England and in the Church
	1517		1517 Luther posts 95 Theses – Reformation begins
LSN 9	1519	Hernando Cortés – Mexico	1525 William Tyndale – English Reformation leader
	1519	Ferdinand Magellan circumnavigates the Earth	Erasmus writes *The Freedom of the Will* in contradiction to some of Luther's doctrine
	1525		Anabaptist Movement begins
	1532	Francisco Pizarro – Peru	1526 Tyndale's English New Testament printed
	1536		John Calvin writes *The Institutes of the Christian Religion*
			1536 Jacob Hutter, Anabaptist leader martyred
	1539	Hernando de Soto – SE North America	Thomas Cromwell's *Great Bible* is the first English translation to be authorized for public use in English churches.
LSN 10	1540	Francisco de Coronado – SW North America	
	1543	Nicolaus Copernicus – planets revolve around sun	Parliament of England bans Tyndale's translation as a "crafty, false and untrue translation"
	1545		Council of Trent; Counter Reformation
	1549		Francis Xavier begins mission in Japan
	1558		England a Protestant nation under Elizabeth I
	1577-1580	Sir Francis Drake circumnavigates the earth	1572 John Knox founds the Presbyterian church 1582 Jesuit missionaries in China
	1590	Compound microscope	1587 St. Augustine, first Catholic mission in America founded in Florida
	1598		Edict of Nantes – religious toleration in Europe

LESSON	YEAR	SCIENTISTS, INVENTIONS & EXPLORERS	BIBLE & CHURCH HISTORY
LSN 11	1604	Johannes Kepler – elliptical planetary orbits	1604 Puritans hopes are dashed when they meet King James at Hampton Court
	1606	Samuel de Champlain – east coast of North America	Jacobus Arminius argues that predestination is based on fore-knowledge
	1608	Telescope	
	1609	Henry Hudson – Hudson River	John Smyth founds the Baptist Church
	1610	Galileo Galilei – improved the telescope, phases of Venus, mountains and craters on the moon	1611 King James Bible published
	1616		Christianity suppressed in Japan
	1620		Mayflower Compact – Separatists
LSN 12	1628	William Harvey – blood circulation	Oppression of Puritans in England increases under William Laud, Bishop of London
	1630		1630-1640 Great Migration
	1634		Catholics found St. Mary's City, Maryland
	1636		Puritans found Harvard College
	1660		First Quaker Peace Statement
	1672	Reflecting telescope	
	1673	Louis Joliet & Jacques Marquette – North Mississippi River	John Eliot publishes the Bible in Algonkia (Native American language) and plants 14 Native American Churches
	1677	Sieur de La Salle – Great Lakes	1678 John Bunyan publishes *Pilgrim's Progress*
LSN 13	1685	Sir Isaac Newton – motion and gravity	Edict of Fontainebleau outlaws Protestantism in France and Orthodoxy introduced to Beijing by Russian Orthodox Church
			1695-1703 Madame Guyon imprisoned for loving God
	1728	Vitus Bering – discovered that Asia and America are separate continents	1727 "The Golden Summer" –Revival breaks out among Hussite Moravian refugees and many Moravian missionaries are sent overseas.
	1735		Jonathan Edwards – First Great Awakening
	1738		John Wesley converted – founder of Methodist movement
	1739		George Whitefield joins Edwards – reaches 80% of colonists with the Gospel
	1742		David Brainerd – Missionary to the Indians
	1753	Carolus Linnaeus – classification of life forms	1754 An Historical Account of Two Notable Corruptions of Scripture, by Isaac Newton, published
LSN 14	1764	Spinning Jenny	
	1768	James Cook – South Pacific	Selina Hastings, Countess of Huntingdon brings Methodism to the upper class and founds a Methodist seminary
	1771		Francis Asbury trains circuit-riding preachers
	1779		George Liele is an African American Missionary to Jamaica
	1780		Robert Raikes starts Sunday School movement
	1783	Hot Air Balloon manned flight	

LESSON	YEAR	SCIENTISTS, INVENTIONS & EXPLORERS	BIBLE & CHURCH HISTORY
LSN 15	1789	Antoine LaVaoisier – accurate measurements	1790 Second Great Awakening begins
	1789	Sir Alexander Mackenzie – Western Canada	
	1793	Eli Whitney - Cotton Gin	William Carey (Father of modern missions) sails to India
			Catherine Ferguson - 1st Sunday School in NY
LSN 16	1796	Edward Jenner – smallpox vaccination	Treaty with Tripoli 1796, article 11: "the Government of the United States of America is not, in any sense, founded on the Christian religion"
	1800	Submarine human powered	
	1803	John Dalton – elements	
	1804	Lewis & Clark – explore Louisiana Purchase	Mohawk Indian Joseph Brant speaks for his people and is an Anglican missionary
LSN 17	1805	Zebulon Pike – explore the Midwest & Rocky Mountain region	Samuel J. Mills – haystack prayer meetings
	1807	Robert Fulton - steamboat	Anti-Slavery movement
	1808		1808 The New Testament is published in Hindustani
	1810		Foreign Missions Board founded
	1814	Sewing machines	1813 Adoniram Judson sails to Burma
	1816	Stethoscope	American Bible Society founded
	1821		Lott Carey goes to Liberia
LSN 18	1825	Steam locomotive engine	
	1826		Sunday School Union formed in U.S.
	1830	Auguste Comte – sociology	Charles Finney revivals
		Charles Lyell - geology	William Taylor – world missionary
LSN 19	1831	Michael Faraday converts magnetism to electricity	1832 persecution of Old Lutherans - all Lutheran worship is declared illegal in Prussia in favor of Prussian Union.
	1835	Photography daguerreotype	Dr. Marcus Whitman missionary to Oregon
	1840	Clipper Ship	1844 YMCA founded in London, England
	1846	Anesthetics Morton	Rev. Henry Spaulding – missionary to the Nez Perce Indians
	1849	David Livingstone – Africa	Charles Spurgeon – British preacher
LSN 20	1853		Hudson Taylor – missionary to China
	1857		Livingstone's missionary travels published
	1859	Charles Darwin – evolution theory	Ashbel Green Simonton Missionary, the oldest Brazilian Protestant denomination
	1860	Burke & Wills - Australia	1861-65 D. L. Moody's Civil War outreach
	1862	Louis Pasteur - pasteurization	
LSN 21	1865	Joseph Lister – antiseptic surgery	Civil War revival – civilians & soldiers
	1865	Gregor Mendel – heredity	John Jasper, African American minister to both black and white Baptists
	1867	Typewriter	
	1869	Dmitry Mendeléyev – periodic table	First Vatican Council – asserts the doctrine of Papal Infallibility.

LESSON	YEAR	SCIENTISTS, INVENTIONS & EXPLORERS	BIBLE & CHURCH HISTORY
LSN 22	1871	Sir Henry Stanley – Congo	1875 Joseph Hardy Neesima first Protestant Japanese minister starts Christian school
	1876	Telephone	Evangelical Lutheran Free Church (Germany) founded
	1877	Phonograph	George Muller, Christian evangelist and orphanage director in England
	1879	Incandescent light	William Booth founds the Salvation Army
	1886	Automobile	1879 Moody opens a seminary for women
LSN 23	1895	Wilhelm Roentgen – X-rays	1894 *The Kingdom of God is Within You*, is published by Leo Tolstoy
	1895	X-rays	1896 Billy Sunday revivals
	1895	Radio Telsa	1897 Christian Flag was conceived in
	1896	Motion pictures	Brooklyn, NY
LSN 24	1898	Marie & Pierre Curie isolate radium	
	1899		R.A. Torrey continues Moody's work
	1901	Ivan Pavlov – behaviorism	
	1903	First airplane flight	
LSN 25	1905	Albert Einstein – theory of relativity	Pope Pius XII secretly aids European Jews
			1906 Azusa Street Revivals
	1909	Robert Peary – North Pole with Matthew Henson	Evan Roberts and the Welsh Revival
	1910	Paul Ehrlich – serum therapy	Sir Wilfred Grenfell – medical missionary to the Eskimos
			1910 Mother Teresa is born
LSN 26	1911	Ernest Rutherford – atom	1910 World Mission conference held in Edinburgh
		Roald Amundsen – South Pole	
	1920	Frozen Food	
LSN 27	1920	George Washington Carver – agricultural chemistry	Carver's lab known as "God's Little Workshop"
	1924		Eric Liddell refuses to run on Sunday
	1925	Diesel locomotive	Eric Liddell becomes missionary to China
	1926	Richard Evelyn Byrd – flew over North and South Pole	Father Charles Coughlin's first radio broadcast
LSN 28	1926	Robert Goddard – liquid-fueled rocket	1925 Scope's Monkey Trial
	1928	First TV broadcast Alexander Fleming – penicillin	1929 John Machen founds Westminster Theological Seminary in response to liberalism at Princeton
	1934	William Beebe – bathysphere	1933 Holocaust begins in Europe
LSN 29	1940	Helicopter	
	1942	Enrico Fermi – nuclear chain reaction	Wycliffe Bible Translators founded
	1945	Atomic bomb	Dietrich Bonhoeffer's death
	1947	Thor Heyerdahl – Kon-Tiki	Dead Sea Scrolls found Oral Roberts founded Evangelistic Association
	1948		World Council of Churches formed Israeli War of Independence
LSN 30	1950	Commercial Jet airline service	Mother Teresa begins work in Calcutta
	1951	Jacques Cousteau – ocean exploration Aqua lung	Bill Bright founds Campus Crusade for Christ
	1951	Robert Banks & Paul Hogan	
		Marlex Plastic	

LESSON	YEAR	SCIENTISTS, INVENTIONS & EXPLORERS	BIBLE & CHURCH HISTORY
LSN 31	1953	Sir Edmund Hillary – Mt. Everest Francis Crick & James Watson - DNA	1952 C. S. Lewis' Mere Christianity
	1954	Nuclear submarine	1954 U.S. Pledge of Allegiance modified by act of Congress from "one nation, indivisible" to "one nation under God, indivisible
	1955	Jonas Salk – polio vaccine	Dr. Martin Luther King, Jr. L'Abri Fellowship founded by Francis Schaeffer
	1955		1955 Rev. Schuller begins drive-in church
	1956		1956 "In God We Trust" designated U.S. national motto Jim Elliot & four other missionaries killed by Auca Indians in Ecuador
	1957	Sputnik 1	1958 David Wilkerson goes to NY to reach out
	1958	Explorer 1	to gang members
LSN 32	1961	Yuri Gagarin – first man in space Alan Shepard – first American in space	Religious persecution in Cuba Brother Andrew – Bible smuggler 1960 Loren Cunningham founds YWAM (Youth With A Mission)
	1962	John Glenn orbits the earth	Vatican II
	1963	Valentina Terishkova – 1st woman in space	US Supreme Court rules that Bible reading and prayer in public schools is unconstitutional
LSN 33	1967	Christiaan Barnard – heart transplant	Teen Challenge rehab program founded
	1969	Microprocessor Neil Armstrong – walks on moon	1966 Ralph Carmichael, Father of Contemporary Christian Music
	1973	Cellular Telephone	1970's Jesus Movement
	1975	Digital Camera	
LSN 34	1977	Dr. Edward Stone – Voyager project	1977 Focus on the Family founded by Dr.
		Twin probes	James Dobson
	1978	Robert Edwards & Patrick Steptoe – test tube baby	1978 First non-Italian Pope since 1523 elected Pope John Paul II
	1979	Sony Walkman	1979 Moral Majority Christian political agency formed in America
	1981	Reusable space shuttle	1980 Crystal Cathedral designed by Philip Johnson
		John Young first to fly space shuttle	
LSN 35	1982	Robert Jarvik & William DeVries – artificial heart	The New King James Version is published
	1982	Vinton Gray Cerf & Bob Kahn - Internet	
	1983	Video camera Sally Ride – first woman on space shuttle	International Fellowship of Christians and Jews is founded
	1986	Christa McAuliffe – first civilian in space	Ron Luce founds Teen Mania
	1987		Scandal rocks many mega and TV ministries
LSN 36	1990	Hubble space telescope	Pope John Paul visits Cuba
	1991	Tim Berners-Lee & Robert Cailliau www	1991 Philip Johnson popularizes term
	1991	Sumio Iijima - Nanotubes	"Intelligent Design"
	1991	Wind Farms offshore	
	1992	Palm Pilot	
LSN 37	1994	Global Positioning System	1994 Ken Ham founds "Answers in Genesis"
	1994	Genetically Modified Organisms	1994 "Toronto Blessing" revival begins
	1996	Ian Wilmut – cloning	1996 The Cambridge Declaration
	1997	International Space Station	Mother Teresa dies
	1997	Hybrid car – Toyota Prius	Priests scandal exposes pedophiles
	1998		Women in the Episcopal clergy

Black Scientists, Inventors, and Explorers

Estevan (1501-1539) first explorer in the western region of the United States

Jean Baptiste Pointe DuSable (1745-1818) trapper and trader who founded Chicago

Benjamin Banneker (1731-1806) built the first clock in the New World from wood

York -- (slave of Capt. William Clark) explores from the Mississippi River to the Pacific in 1804-1806

George Peake (1772-1827) invented a stone hand-mill in 1809

Thomas L. Jennings (1791-1859) first to be granted a patent in 1821

James Beckwourth (1798-1866) mountain man who discovered an easier route to the West.

Henry Boyd (1802-1886) designed a stronger bed frame called the "Boyd bed" in 1833

James Forten (1766-1842) invented a sail-handling device for rough waters

Lewis Temple (1800-1854) blacksmith who invented the toggle harpoon and transformed the whaling industry

Norbert Rillieux (1806-1894) invented a sugar-refining process in 1843

John Parker (1827-1900) invented the tobacco screw press in 1854

Harriet Tubman (1820-1913) explored a route to freedom - conductor on the Underground Railroad

Clara Brown (1803-1885) went West and became one of Central Cities leading citizens

Biddy Mason (1820-1903) slave who walked all the way to California with her master and stayed (CA was a free state)

Jan Ernst Matzelinger (1852-1889) invented the shoe-lasting machine in 1882

Elijah McCoy (1859-1929) Canadian inventor of the automatic lubricator for engines in 1882

Granville T. Woods (1856-1910) improved steam boiler furnace and improved telephone transmitter in 1884

Sarah Good -- invented the folding cabinet bed in 1885

Lewis H. Latimer (1848-1928) member of Thomas Edison's research team

Sarah Boothe -- invented the ironing board in 1892

Matthew Henson (1866-1955) first to reach the North Pole in 1909 He was part of the Robert Peary team.

Garret Morgan (1875-1963) developed the automatic street signal & gas mask in 1912

Archie Alexander (1888-1958) engineered bridges, power plants, and major structures across the nation

David Crosthwait (1891-1976) authority on heat transfer, ventilation, and air conditioning

Madame C. J. Walker -- patented her hair products and was America's first female self-made millionaire.

George Washington Carver (1860-1943) agricultural chemistry

Frederick M. Jones (1892-1961) designed the refrigeration system for long-haul trucks

Louis W. Roberts (1913-) physicist, mathematician and electronics specialist

Katherine Johnson (1918-) aerospace technologist / interplanetary trajectories, space navigation, and spacecraft orbits

O. S. Williams (1921-) aeronautical engineer and rocket engine specialist who helped develop first airborne radar beacon

J. Ernest Wilkins, Jr. (1923-) research and development of nuclear power

Rufus Stokes (1924-) developed air filtration equipment

Virgil G. Trice, Jr. (1926-) radioactive waste management of nuclear power generators

Meredith Gourdine (1929-) high-voltage electricity from natural gas

Annie Easley (1932-) computer codes for energy technology

James Harris (1932-) nuclear chemist who discovered two new elements

Caldwell McCoy (1933-) developed long-range submarine systems He now works on energy from magnetic fusion.

Clarence L. Elder (1935-) developed energy saving system

Cordell Reed (1938-) develops more efficient and productive power plants

Donald Cotton (1939-) propellants and nuclear reactors – energy from research in chemistry

Ernest Coleman (1942-) high energy physics research

Mae C. Jemison (1956-) American astronaut, physician, biochemical engineer

Extraordinary Women Timeline

Aspasia 1st C. AD -- Greek obstetrician

Mary the Jewess 1st c. AD -- alchemist

Aglaonike of Thessaly -- Greek astronomer

Fabiola AD 300 -- Roman who founded a hospital

Hypatia (AD 370-415) -- Egyptian scientist

Etherisa(or Egeria) -- nun who traveled to Jerusalem and Egypt in 381-843; she wrote a pilgrim's
    guide to the Holy Land

Trotula 1000 -- Italian gynecologist

Hildegard von Bingen 1100 -- German medicine

Alessandra Giliani 1300 -- Italian anatomist

Sophia Brahe 1543 -- Danish astronomer

Duchess Margaret Cavendish (1623-1673) English, she helped make science fashionable among ladies

Elizabeth Lucas Pinckney (1722-?) agriculturalist, successfully grew indigo in South Carolina,
    providing a new crop

Sybilla Masters -- first American colonist to receive a patent from England in 1715

Catherine Greene (1755-1814) American who worked on the cotton gin with Eli Whitney in 1785

Marie Anne Lavoisier (1758-1836) French writer of a chemistry textbook

Sacagawea -- American Shoshone guided the Lewis and Clark expedition in 1804-06. She is now
    depicted on a U.S. dollar coin for her contributions to the expedition.

Mary Dixon Kies -- first woman to receive an American patent in 1809

Mary Anning (1799-1847) Fossil hunter in England (first find in 1811)

Anne Newport Royall (1769-1854) American widow, wrote travel books about America east of the
    Mississippi River

Ida Pfeiffer (1797-1858) Austrian, journeyed around the world

Maria Mitchell (1818-1889) American astronomer

Lucy Atkinson (1820-1863) English, traveled across the Russian steppes

Elizabeth Blackwell (1821-1910) first woman in America to receive the degree of Doctor
    of Medicine in 1849

Elizabeth Sarah Mazuchelli (1832-1914) English, first European woman to go into the interior
    of the Himalayas

Lady Anne Blunt (1837-1917) English, visited the Bedouin tribes of Arabia and brought back the first Arabian horse

Isabella Bird Bishop (1831-1904) English, world traveler

Alexine Tinne (1835-1869) Dutch explorer in search of the source of the Nile River in 1862

Marianne North (1830-1890) English botanical painter and world traveler

Florence Baker (1841-1916) Transylvanian, searched for the source of the Nile with her husband

Ellen Henrietta Swallow Richards (1842-1911) American chemist & environmental engineer - founder of ecology

Martha Coston (1826-?) American who developed and marketed her husband's idea for the signal flare

Carrie Adell Strahorn (1854-1925) American, wrote stage coach travel books of the American West

Emily Roebling (1843-1903) civil engineering construction of the Brooklyn Bridge

Amanda Jones (1835-1914) American holding patents for preserving food – canning 1873

Sonya Kovalevski (1850-1891) Russian mathematician

Isabella Lucy Bird (Bishop) (1831-1904) English explorer of the Sandwich Islands in 1875

Harriet Hosmer (1830-1908) first American woman sculptor, invented petrified marble in 1880

Lady Florence Dixie (1855-1905) English explorer of Patagonia in 1878 & S. Africa in 1881

Mary Watson Whitney (1847-1920) American astronomer

Nettie Maria Stevens (1861-1912) biologist

Florence Augusta Merriam Bailey (1863-1948) ornithologist in the American West, 1890

May French Sheldon (1847-1936) American led expedition into East Africa in 1891

Alice Eastwood (1859-1953) Canadian botanist

Agnes Smith Lewis (1843-1926) Scottish adventurer in the Sinai

Margaret Smith Gibson (1843-1920) Scottish adventurer in the Sinai

Annie Jump Cannon (1863-1941) American astronomer

Susie Carson Rijnhart (1868-1908) Canadian doctor with her husband pioneered medical missions in China and Tibet

Mary Kingsley (1862-1900) English, exploration of the Ogowe River in Africa

Ella Constance Sykes (18??-1939) First English woman to visit this area of Persia in 1894

Annie Smith Peck (1850-1935) American who climbed the Matterhorn in 1895

Florence Bascom (1862-1945) geologist

Fannie Merritt Farmer (1857-1915) American who wrote the first cookbook with standard measurements

Antonia C. Maury (1866-1952) American astronomer

Marie Sklodowska Curie (1867-1934) Polish nuclear physicist and chemist

Sara Josephine Baker (1873-1945) American doctor devoted to children's health

Fanny Bullock Workman (1859-1925) English, first mountain-climbing record for women in 1899

Harriet Ann Boyd Hawes (1871-1945) American archaeologist

Mary Anderson (1866-1953) American patent for the windshield wiper in 1903

Madame C. J. Walker (1867-1919) developed hair care products and marketed them in 1904.

Osa Leighty Johnson (1894-1953) American photographer and specimen collector in Africa
     and the South Pacific

Delia Denning Akeley (1875-1970) American, first Western woman to cross the African continent

Grace Gallatin Thompson Seton (1872-1952) founded the Campfire Girls in 1910 / reported
     on the status of women

Daisy Bates (1863-1952) Irish amateur anthropologist who studied the Aborigines

Blaire Niles (1880-1959) American writer best known for her travel books

Gertrude Bell (1868-1926) English explorer in the Middle East between 1900-14

Harriet Chalmers Adams (1875-1937) American traveler following the route of Columbus
     and the Conquistadors

Mary Engle Pennington (1872-1952) American chemist who designed industrial
     and household refrigerators

Lillian Moller Gilbreth (1878-1972) industrial engineer

Florence Rena Sabin (1871-1953) anatomist

Emmy Noether (1882-1935) German mathematician

Williamina Paton Stevens Fleming (1857-1911) Scottish astronomer

Judith Graham Pool (1919-1975) American physiologist - Hemophilia research

Edith Clarke (1883-1959) electrical engineer

Anna Johnson Pell Wheeler (1883-1910) American mathematician

Irene Joliet-Curie (1897-1956) French nuclear scientist

Henrietta Swan Leavitt (1868-1921) American astronomer

Marguerite Baker Harrison (1879-1967) American spy / co-founder of the Society
     of Women Geographers

Emma Perry Carr (1880-1972) American physical chemist

Ella Cara Deloria (1889-1971) American anthropologist and linguist

Mildred Cable (1878-1952) English missionary who studied the Gobi Desert - 1920-1930

Evangeline French (1869-1960) English missionary who studied the Gobi Desert - 1920-1930

History's Masterminds - *TRISMS*©

Francesca French (1871-1960) English missionary who studied the Gobi Desert - 1920-1930

Ida Henrietta Hyde (1857-1945) physiologist

Anna Louise Strong (1885-1970) American political journalist

Gerty Radnitz Cori (1896-1957) Czech biochemist who came to America in 1922

Dame Margery Freda Perham (1895-1908) English authority on Africa and British policy

Lucy Evelyn Cheesman (1881-1969) English entomologist who explored SW Pacific Islands looking for insects

Alexandra David-Neel (1868-1969) French, first European woman to reach Lhasa, the capital of Tibet in 1924

Ynes Mexia (1870-1938) American, botanical collecting in Mexico and South America

Violet Cressy-Marcks (1890-1970) traveled around the world eight times

Freya Stark (1893- 1993) French traveler in the Middle East

Louise Boyd (1887-1972) American photographer / oceanographic surveyor, made 7 expeditions into the Arctic

Margaret Mead (1901-1978) American anthropologist

Ella Maillart (1903-?) Swiss journalist who traveled from Peking to Kashmir

Tilly Edinger (1897-1967) German paleontologist 1930; founder of Paleoneurology (fossil brains)

Margaret Bourke-White (1904-1971) American photojournalist; traveled the world recording its notable events

Helen (Battles) Sawyer Hogg (1905-?) American astronomer

Amelia Earhart (1897-1937) America, first woman to fly solo across the Atlantic Ocean in 1932

Ruth Fulton Benedict (1887-1948) American anthropologist

Rita Levi-Montalcini (1909-?) Italian neuroscientist

Rachel Louise Carson (1907-1964) American marine biologist and science writer

Chien-Shiung Wu (1912-) Chinese experimental physicist - 1940 nuclear fission

Lise Meitner (1878-1968) Austrian nuclear physicist - split the atom

Ruth Patrick (1907-) American limnologist - study of diatoms

Hedy Lamarr (1913-2000) Austrian, developed anti-jamming technology in 1942 and cell phone technology

Grace Murray Hopper (1906-1992) American computer scientist and Navy Admiral in 1943

Mary Nicol Leakey (1913-) English anthropologist

Vera Cooper Rubin (1928-) astronomer

Rosalind Elsie Franklin (1920-1958) English x-ray crystallographer and molecular biologist

> uncredited for the discovery of the structure of DNA

Jewel Plummer Cobb (1924-) American cell biologist and educator / skin cancer, 1950

Bessie Bount (Griffin) (1914-) American, patent for portable receptacle support, 1951

Elizabeth Marshall Thomas (1931-) American, studied the Bushmen of the Kalahari Desert, 1951-55

Jane Goodall (1934-) English ethnologist

Grace Murray Hopper (1906-1992) American computer visionary - designed the computer compiler in 1952

Patsy O. Sherman -- accidentally invented Scotchgard fabric protector in 1952

Louise Arner Boyd (1887-1972) American Arctic explorer / first woman to fly over the North Pole, 1955

Ruth Handler (1916-) American who created the Barbie doll in 1956, designed prosthesis for mastectomy patients

Elspeth Josceline Huxley (1907-) English writer who told of the many changes in Africa from 1959-85

Diane Fossey (1932-1985) American zoologist

Bette Nesmith Graham (1924-1980) American secretary invented Liquid Paper in 1960

Dr. Ruth Benerito (1916-) textile chemist created wrinkle-free cotton in 1960

Maria Goeppert Mayer (1906-1972) German theoretical physicist - 1963 Noble Prize in Physics

Valentina V. Tereshkova (1937-) Russian Cosmonaut - first woman to fly in space, 1963

Dervla Murphy (1931-) Irish, rode her bicycle from Ireland to India in 1964

Dorothy Crowfoot Hodgkin (1910-1994) English physical chemist - 1964 Noble Prize for Chemistry

Valentina V. Tereshkova (1937-) Russian cosmonaut, first woman to fly in space, 1963

Stephanie L. Kwolek (1923-) DuPont polymer chemist who invented Kevlar for bullet proof vest in 1966

Jocelyn Bell Burnell (1943-) Irish astronomer and astrophysics

Marika Hanbury-Tenison (1938-1982) English traveler who visited the Stone Age tribes of South America

Yvonne Brill (1924-) Canadian, developed electrical propulsion for rockets

Becky Schroeder (1962-) at age 12 created the Glo-sheet for writing in a dark room

Mildred Davidson Austin Smith (1916-1993) designed a walker attachment (table and carrying pouch) in 1976

Rosalyn Yalow (1921-) Jewish medical physicist - radioisotope research - 1977 Noble Prize in Medicine

Sylvia Earle (1935-) American marine biologist reaches a record diving depth of 1250 feet in 1979

Christina Dodwell (1951-) English explorer of the unmapped areas of Papua New Guinea

Sally Kristen Ride (1951-) American astronaut and astrophysicist

Barbara McClintock (1902-1992) American geneticist - 1983 Nobel Prize winner on instability of genes

Frances Gabe (1915-) American who invented the self-cleaning house

Svetlana Savitskaya (1948-) Soviet, first woman to walk in space in 1984

Nancy Perkins (1949-) American industrial designer invented the Sears Die-Hard battery in 1984

Mae C. Jemison (1956-) American astronaut, physician, and biochemical engineer

Sorrel Wilby -- Australian, treks from Tibet to Lhasa alone in 1985

Judith A. Resnick (1949-1986) American astronaut and electrical engineer - killed in the Challenger explosion

Gertrude Belle Elion (1918-) American biochemist - 1988 Noble Prize for Physiology

Ellen Ochoa (1958-) Hispanic astronaut and electrical engineer

Mildred Dresselhaus (1930-) professor of electrical engineering and physics at MIT

Lesson Plans

This is the teacher/student's guide for the school year. It is a lesson at-a-glance guide with daily assignments.

Teacher's Notes

Lesson 0
Orientation Week
3500 - 540 B.C.

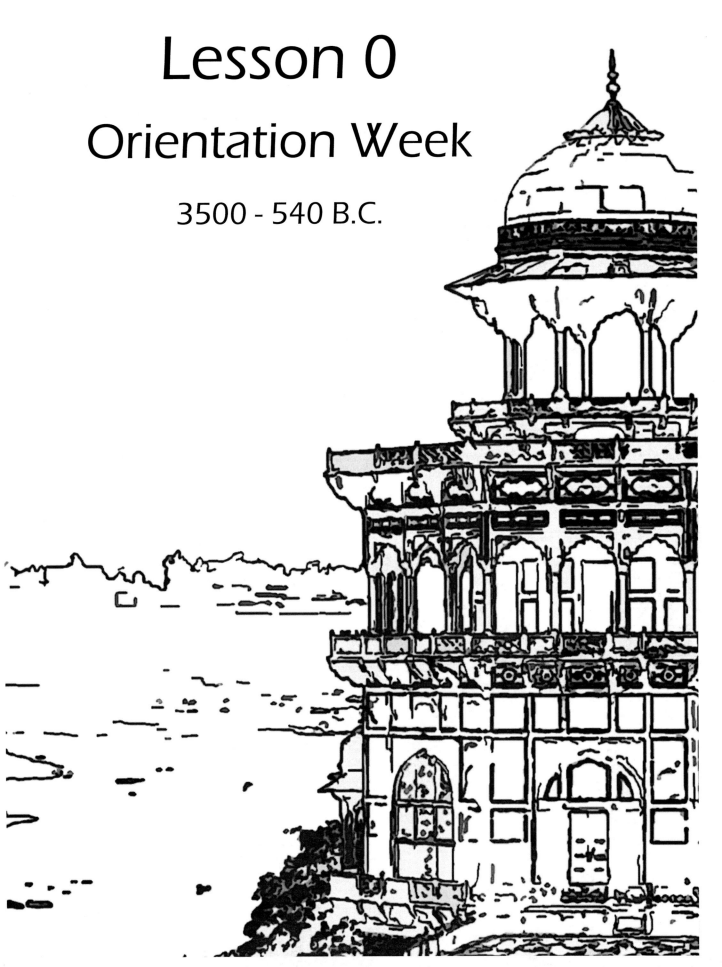

Day	SCIENTISTS	INVENTIONS	EXPLORERS
Mon	**Questionnaire Vocabulary**	**Read background information on**	
	motivation	**Sumer.**	
	topography		
	climate		
	export		
	import		
	achievement		
	consequence		
	ethical		
Tue		3500 BC Wheel	**Map Vocabulary**
		Questionnaire	**horizon**
			landmark
			scale
			direction
			globe
			cartography
Wed		3200 BC Hieroglyphics	**Locate and read background**
		Questionnaire	**information on Egypt.**
			Vocabulary
			civilization
			absolute rule
			pharaoh
			empire
Thu		2500 BC Egyptian Sailing Ship	**Draw or write a description**
		Questionnaire	**of an Egyptian**
		Khufu ship	
			Locate the Nile River & Red Sea
		Draw an Egyptian sailing ship	**on a map**
		for the coursebook	
Fri		2000 BC Chariot	**Geography Vocabulary**
		Questionnaire	delta
			cataract
			sea
			coast
			harbor
			tide

Books listed on the lesson plan are at the junior high reading level.

LANGUAGE ARTS	READING SELECTIONS
Read Orientation (found in Teacher's Manual)	**Historical Fiction (read one per lesson)**
**Set up coursebook as explained in Orientation	Shadow Hawk – Andre Norton
	The Golden Goblet - Eloise McGraw
📖 **Read Research Guide**	Casting the Gods Adrift - Geraldine McCaughrean
Visit your local library	His Majesty, Queen Hatshepsut – Dorothy Sharp Carter
	Hittite Warrior - Joanne Williamson
	God King – Joanne Williamson
	The Cat of Bubastes - G. A. Henty
	Tirzah – Lucille Travis
Read Orientation notes on BC & AD	**Biographies (an alternate for a historical fiction)**
Read Orientaiton notes & set up your timeline	Gods & Pharaohs from Egyptian Mythology – G. Harris
	Angels Sweep the Desert Floor – Miriam Chaikin
	Joshua in the Promised Land – Miriam Chaikin
Vocabulary (See Literature Helps)	**Other Books for Research**
historical fiction	Ancient Mesopotamia – Virginia Schomp
biography	Hieroglyphics from A to Z – Peter Der Manuelian
autobiography	The Sumerians – Pamela Odijk
Dewey Decimal System	The Israelites – Pamela Odijk
	The Indus Valley – Jane Shuter
	Egyptian Boats – Geoffrey Scott
	Valley of the Kings - Stuart Tyson Smith
	Spend the Day in Ancient Egypt - Linda Honan
Dewey Decimal System	**Historical Events for Timeline**
L – 0: Worksheet 1 - located in the Student Pack	Stone Age
	Copper Age
	4000 – 2350 BC Sumerians
	3000 – 1700 BC Indus Valley
	3500 – 1070 BC Egypt
	753 BC Rome founded
	612 BC New Babylon
	559 - 530 BC Cyrus the Great found the Persian Empire
Writing mini book reports	**Other Areas of Interest during this Lesson**
See Orientation	Pyramids of the Aztecs
	Pharaoh's daughter raises Moses
Ψ **IEW Lesson 0**	Knossos in Crete
Taking Notes and Making Outlines	Tower of Babel
View IEW DVD 1 – Structural Unit 1	Exodus from Egypt
Note Making and Outlines	950-710 Libyans rule Egypt
	710-663 Ethiopians rule Egypt
	663-525 Pharaohs rule Egypt
Ψ **IEW Lesson 0**	**Accomplishments in Math**
Make Key Word Outline	5000 BC Sumerian & Chaldean numbering system with 60
Optional - Extra Practice - *Booklice*	as base, multiplication tables up to 59x59
	4000 BC Egyptian numerals with a base of 10
	3000 BC Sumerian numerals based on multiples of 6 & 12
	2000 BC Babylon uses highly developed geometry as basis
Optional Movie: *Prince of Egypt*	for astronomic measurements
	Decimal system used in Crete

Inventions Questionnaire

1. What invention: Wheel (circular object)

2. When: 3000 BC

3. Who is the inventor (person or country): Mesopotamia

4. Motivation: They needed a way to quicken their transportation and ease their work.

5. How did this invention change life as it was then? Wheels made it easier for people to transport or carry heavy or large loads. The mill wheel could grind more meal in less time and human effort. The potter's wheel produced a stronger vessel in less time.

6. What have been the ethical consequences (if any)? Answers will vary. The wheel evolved into many inventions that changed life. For example, the potter's wheel, spinning wheel, water wheel, grinding wheel, astrolabe and cog. Machines can be used for good or evil.

7. Diagram or draw the invention:

Cite your sources:

Inventions Questionnaire

1. What invention: Hieroglyphics

2. When: 2600 BC

3. Who is the inventor (person or country): Egyptians

4. Motivation: They needed a way to record trade, economics, taxes, laws and history.

5. How did this invention change life as it was then? The invention of hieroglyphics made it possible to record their history and transactions.

6. What have been the ethical consequences (if any)? It has taught us about most of Egyptian society and lifestyle. It also let them communicate with each other by writing. Sometimes, written communication can have a negative effect on those to whom it is written, as it can be a more lasting record than the spoken word.

7. Diagram or draw the invention:

Inventions Questionnaire

1. What invention: Egyptian Sailing Ship (Khufu ship)

2. When: 2500 BC (Khufu ship – found in a pit at the foot of the Great Pyramid of Giza)

3. Who is the inventor (person or country): Egyptians

4. Motivation: To create a vessel that could travel on water. The Nile River was a road for the Egyptians.

5. How did this invention change life as it was then? It became the "car" for the Egyptians. It allowed them to travel quicker and trade at farther distances.

6. What have been the ethical consequences (if any)? It greatly increased the economy of the Egyptians by updating their trade and speeding it up. They were able to extend their trade farther. It also allowed them to expand their territory and engage in war at greater distances.

7. Diagram or draw the invention:

Cite your sources:

Inventions Questionnaire

1. What invention: Chariot

2. When: 2000 BC

3. Who is the inventor (person or country): Hyksos

4. Motivation: The invention of the spoke in the wheel made for a stronger, lighter vehicle that could travel faster.

5. How did this invention change life as it was then? The chariot made it possible to hunt and kill food more efficiently. Man could travel with supplies more quickly than with pack animals. It also made a deadly war vehicle. Racing provided a form of entertainment.

6. What have been the ethical consequences (if any)? It made man able to travel faster and be less limited by his own fitness, and more dependent on the fitness of his animal and his chariot. It also made war and conflict easier to enter at greater distances.

7. Diagram or draw the invention:

Cite your sources: Phllips, Robert. ed. *"Chariot."* <u>*Funk & Wagnalls New Encyclopedia*</u> Vol. 5 NY:Funk & Wagnalls, 1975.

No Science assignment in Lesson 0.

Language Worksheet 1

PAGE 2 Practice

1.   b. top left corner
2.   a. where to find the book
3.   c. the book is a biography
4.   b. the book is fiction
5.   c. usually can not be checked out
6.   b. look under the author's last name
7.   a. subject file
8.   b. in biography section under A
9.   a. L
10.   a. reference section

PAGE 3 Practice

1.   a. 200
2.   c. 900
3.   b. 000
4.   b. 400
5.   a. 500

Lesson 1

540 - 330 B.C.

Lesson 1

Day	SCIENTISTS	INVENTIONS	EXPLORERS
Mon			Read background information on the Phoenicians.
			Vocabulary
			cargo
			merchant
			trade
			colony
Tue	Locate and read background information on Ancient Greece.		500 BC Hanno explores the N.W. coast of Africa
	Locate Greece on the globe		Questionnaire
			*Modern Sierra Leone
	Vocabulary		
	city-state		Mark Map 1
	citizens		
	democracy		
	barbarians		
Wed	Draw a Greek person		Ship Vocabulary
	You may draw a man, woman, or child.		forward
			aft
	Vocabulary		hull
	diagnosis		keel
	prognosis		prow
	epidemic		helm
			oar
Thu	400 BC Hippocrates, father of medicine studied diseases and cures		334-326 BC Alexander the Great expanded his empire from Greece to India.
	Questionnaire		Questionnaire
			*Asia
	S-1		
			Mark Map 2
Fri			Vocabulary
			invincible
			strategy
			phalanx
			pillage
			survey
			*indicates present-day location

LANGUAGE ARTS	READING SELECTIONS
Moods in poetry	**Historical Fiction (read one per lesson)**
L-1a	Within the Palace Gates - Anna Siviter
	Singer to the Sea - Vivien Alcock
	Hadassah: The Girl Who Became Queen Esther - Tommy Tenny
	Black Ships Before Troy - Rosemary Sutcliff
	Shadow Spinner - Susan Fletcher
	Escape from Egypt - Sonia Levitin
	Odysseus in the Serpent Maze - Jane Yolen & Robert J. Harris
Poetry without rhyme	**Biographies (an alternate for a historical fiction)**
L-1b	Tales of Greek Heroes - Roger Green
	Alexander: The Boy Soldier Who Conquered the World -
	Simon Adams
Stories in poetry	**Other Books for Research**
L-1c	Aesop's Fables - Saviour Pirotta
	Tales of Ancient Persia - Barbara Picard
	Spend a Day in Ancient Greece - Linda Honan
	Adventures in Ancient Greece - Linda Bailey
	The Phoenicians - Pamela Odijk
	Foods & Feasts in Ancient Greece - Imogen Dawson
	Science in the Ancient Greece - Kathlyn Gay
	The World in the Time of Alexander the Great - F MacDonald
Ideas in poetry	**Historical Events for Timeline**
L-1d	1200 BC Phoenicians
	1100 BC Assyrian Empire
	380 BC Last true Egyptian dynasty
	391 BC Romans defeat Etruscans
	359 BC Philip becomes king of Macedonia
	346 BC Philip of Macedonia forces a treaty with Greece
	336 BC Alexander becomes king
	334 BC Persia defeated by Alexander the Great
People in poetry	**Other Areas of Interest during this Lesson**
L-1e	Surveying
	Irrigation
	Greek Sculpture
Write your mini book report	First coins minted
	Olympic Games begin in 776
	Thales of Miletus
	Arabian Nights
Ψ **IEW Key Word Outline**	**Accomplishments in Math**
Create Outline and Retell Story	1500 BC Mathematical permutations & "magic squares" known in
	Chinese mathematics
	1000 BC Chinese textbook of mathematics includes proportions,
	"rule of 3" arithmetic, geometry, equations with one or more unknown
	quantities, theory of motion

Scientist Questionnaire

1. **Who:** Hippocrates (Father of Modern Medicine)

2. **Nationality:** Greek

3. **Life span:** 460-370 BC

4. **Span of research:** He dedicated his whole life to the study of illness.

5. **Biblical or church history event of the time:** The Jews were under Persian rule and the book of Malachi was written.

6. **Noted achievement & field of interest:** He primarily studied symptoms and their causes and cures.

7. **Secondary achievement & field of interest:** He wrote the Hippocratic Oath and started a medical school.

8. **Motivation:** He wanted to separate myth from medicine. People who were sick should see a doctor instead of seeking out a priest in the temple. Hippocrates noticed the cause and effect of many illnesses and pursued his ideas for the sake of mankind.

9. **Significance of discovery:** It changed the way medicine was approached by including and relying on facts, observation, experimentation, and study.

10. **How was this discovery helpful or harmful to society?** It was helpful because it began the scientific study of medicine and the recording of observations.

11. **New word and meaning:** Answers will vary.

12. **Questions prompted through this study?** Answers will vary.

13. **Interesting bit of trivia:** His teaching included positive encouragement as well as scientific observation and a rational approach to a cure. His favorite medicine was honey.

Cite your sources:

Explorers Questionnaire

1. **Who:** Hanno

2. **Nationality:** Carthaginian

3. **When:** 500 BC

4. **Point of departure:** Carthage
   or
   Sponsoring country: Western Phoenicia

5. **Was this place the explorer's home country?** Yes
   Explain: Phoenicia existed in two regions – Tyre and Carthage in Africa

6. **Biblical or church history personality of the time:** King Darius of Persia

7. **What was discovered or explored?** Present day Sierra Leone

8. **How?** He sailed through the Pillars of Hercules to the Atlantic Ocean. He traveled along the western coast of Africa to present day Sierra Leone.

9. **What was their motivation?** gold, colonization, trade

10. **Topography:** coastal belt of beaches and swampland to the inland forests, plains and mountains

11. **Climate:** tropical; average temperature is 80 degrees

12. **Natural resources:** fish, wild animals

13. **Crops:** rice, cacao, ginger, kola, palm kernels, and fibers

14. **Exports:** Sierra Leone had nothing to trade at this time.
    (Phoenician exports: Purple cloth, Phoenician glass, cheap copies of popular trade items)

15. **Trivia:** Hanno's journals exist in Greek and are entitled, Periplus "The Voyage". Remember, Carthaginians were inclined to exaggerate.

Cite your sources: Simon, Charnan. *Explorers of the Ancient World.* IL: Childrens Press, 1990.

Explorers Questionnaire

1. **Who:** Alexander the Great

2. **Nationality:** Macedonian (He was the king.)

3. **When:** 334 – 326 BC

4. **Point of departure:** Macedonia
   or
   Sponsoring country: Macedonia

5. **Was this place the explorer's home country?** Yes
   Explain: When he became king, he was surrounded by enemies at home and rebellion abroad. He set out with his army to secure his kingdom and expand its boundaries.

6. **Biblical or church history personality of the time:** Zechariah

7. **What was discovered or explored?** He visited and conquered the Greek States, Asia Minor, Syria, Egypt, Part of North Africa, Western India, and Persia.

8. **How?** Over land and boat. He used a traveling army.

9. **What was their motivation?** Conquest. He tried to unite the East and the West into a one world empire. He wanted to establish the Greek culture in his kingdom.

10. **Topography:** Desert, grassland, and woodlands around areas of water.

11. **Climate:** They have hot summers and cool winters.

12. **Natural resources:** mineral deposits

13. **Crops:** wheat and barley

14. **Exports:** textiles, gold, silver, copper, and lead

15. **Trivia:** He destroyed the Persian Empire and introduced the Greek culture. His own people called him Alexander the Invincible. It was the Romans who referred to him as Alexander the Great.

Cite your sources:

S-1
What could have been the specific diseases and the cures that Hippocrates dealt with?
What were the cures or medicines composed of?
Some of the diseases and treatments used included:

Copper for treatment of leg ulcers associated with varicose veins.
Bee honey was an effective medicine for all types of diseases.
Fever could cure the sick by bringing bad humors into balance.
Diseases such as syphilis, tuberculosis, cancer, tumors, and mania were treated by causing fever.
Cauterization the cure for hemorrhoids.
Apples were good for constipation, diabetes, high cholesterol, and colon cancer.
Basil was useful for killing parasites, healing acne and stimulating the immune system.
Bay Leaf Oil was used to topically treat arthritis.
Carrots for the cure of cancerous tumors.
Cannabis as a remedy to treat inflammation, earache, and edema.

Could these work today?
Many herbs are still used today and there has been an avid return to the use of natural herbs and medicines to cure disease in the last 50 to 60 years.

What is the Hippocratic Oath?
The Hippocratic Oath is still used today and is taken by doctors entering the medical field:

Hippocratic Oath
I solemnly pledge myself to consecrate my life to the service of humanity;
I will give my teachers the respect and gratitude which is their due;
I will practice my profession with conscience and dignity;
The health of my patient will be my first consideration;
I will respect the secrets which are confided in me, even after the patient has died;
I will maintain by all the means in my power, the honor and the noble traditions of
the medical professional;
My colleagues will be my brothers;
I will not permit considerations of religion, nationality, race, party politics or social standing to intervene
between my duty and my patient;
I will maintain the utmost respect for human life from the time of conception; even under threat I will
not use my medical knowledge contrary to the laws of humanity.
I make these promises solemnly, freely and upon my honor.

The Hippocratic Collection included 60 papers covering many aspects of medicine. Written between 430 BC and 330 BC, the subjects covered included general pathology, pathology of specific diseases, diagnosis, treatment, physiology, embryology, gynecology, medical ethics, prognosis, surgery and several other subjects. A concern for the patient, as well as a focus on natural cures, were central to the writings.

Teacher's Notes

Lesson 2

330 - 300 B.C.

Day	SCIENTISTS	INVENTIONS	EXPLORERS
Mon	**Vocabulary**		
	inquisitive		
	observation		
	problem		
	investigate		
	discovery		
Tue	310 BC Aristarchus theorized that the		330 BC Pytheas, Arctic explorer
	earth revolves around the sun and		*west coast of Europe to Baltic Sea
	estimated the size of the earth, moon		**Questionnaire**
	and sun.		
	Questionnaire		
			Mark Map 1
Wed	300 BC Euclid - basic principles		**Locate the oceans on a globe or map**
	of geometry		**and memorize them**
	Questionnaire		Arctic Ocean
			Atlantic Ocean
			Pacific Ocean
			Indian Ocean
Thu	Examine "The Elements"		**Geography vocabulary**
	written by Euclid		island
	(reference section of the public library)		peninsula
			ocean
			bay
			strait
			archipelago
Fri	300 BC Aristotle developed a system		**Locate and memorize the seven**
	for classifying and comparing living		**continents**
	organisms.		Europe
	Questionnaire		Africa
			North America
			South America
	S-2		Antarctica
			Australia
			Asia

LANGUAGE ARTS	READING SELECTIONS	
Memorize a poem	**Historical Fiction (read one per lesson)**	
L-2a	The Children's Homer - Padraic Colum	
	Pankration: the Ultimate Game - Dyan Blacklock	
Vocabulary	Victory on the Walls - Joanne Williamson	
nonfiction		
fiction		
Limericks	**Biographies (an alternate for a historical fiction)**	
L-2b	Aristotle: Philosopher, Teacher and Scientist - Sharon Katz Cooper	
Ψ **IEW Lesson 2**		
View IEW DVD 1 – Structural Unit 2		
Read pp. 17 - 29 in Seminar & Practicum Workbook		
Responsive reading	**Other Books for Research**	
L-2c	The Librarian Who Measured the World - Kathryn Lasky	
	Herodotus and the Explorers of the Classical Age - Ann Gaines	
Ψ **IEW Lesson 2**	The Mediterranean - Wilkinson & Dineen	
Make key word outline & retell story	Ancient Rome - Peter Chrisp	
	The Collapse of the Roman Republic - Don Nardo	
	Explorers of the Ancient World - Charnan Simon	
	Foods & Feasts in Ancient Rome - Philip Steele	
	Science in Ancient Rome - Jacqueline Harris	
Descriptive poetry	**Historical Events for Timeline**	
L-2d	500-300 BC Hellenic Period in Greece	
Ψ **IEW Lesson 2**	500-30 BC Roman Republic	
Write story from your key word outline	332 BC Carthage survives in Africa	
	323 BC Death of Alexander	
Movie Reviews	Empire divided between his generals	
L-2e	Candragupta Maurya unites the northern states into first Indian empire	
	321-250 BC Seleucids rule Iran & Palestine	
	Celtic Gauls settled in France and central Europe	
Descriptive poetry		
L-2f	Medicine separated from priesthood	
	Catapults used as weapons	
Write your mini book report	Spartans use chemical warfare	
	Spartacus and the slave rebellion against Roman rule	
	Sappho - Greek female writer, founds school for girls	
Optional Movie: *Hercules* (old version)		
	Accomplishments in Math	
	323 BC Euclid wrote "Elements" a standard work on geometry	

Scientist Questionnaire

1. **Who:** Aristarchus of Samos

2. **Nationality:** Greek

3. **Life span:** 310-250 BC

4. **Span of research:** He studied with Strato in Alexandria shortly after 287 BC.

5. **Biblical or church history event of the time:** The Jews under Persian rule

6. **Noted achievement & field of interest:** He is known for his theory that the earth rotates and revolves around the sun. He proved that we live in a sun-centered universe. He was an astronomer.

7. **Secondary achievement & field of interest:** He estimated the size and distance of the sun and moon from the earth. He was also a mathematician. His geometry was correct, even though he didn't have the tools to make accurate measurements.

8. **Motivation:** He believed Pythagoras's theory (the earth and other planets revolve around the sun) yet strove to learn more in order to further the study of astronomy.

9. **Significance of discovery:** Aristarchus' theories were condemned because of the religious views of his day. His theories were mentioned by other mathematicians and astronomers but the truth of his discovery was lost. Seleucus, a Chaldean, adopted his teaching.

10. **How was this discovery helpful or harmful to society?** Since people did not accept his discovery, it slowed the progress of astronomy for hundreds of years.

11. **New word and meaning:** Answers will vary.

12. **Questions prompted through this study?** Answers will vary.

13. **Interesting bit of trivia:** Aristarchus invented a sundial. Most of the Greeks thought the sun revolved around a flat earth.

Cite your sources:

Scientist Questionnaire

1. **Who:** Euclid of Alexandria

2. **Nationality:** Greek

3. **Life span:** 330-270 BC

4. **Span of research:** Euclid studied in Plato's Academy.

5. **Biblical or church history event of the time:** The Jews were under the rule of Alexander the Great.

6. **Noted achievement & field of interest:** He discovered the basic principles of geometry and wrote *The Elements*.

7. **Secondary achievement & field of interest**: He was the leader of a team of mathematicians who wrote *Complete Works of Euclid*. He was also a teacher at Alexandria.

8. **Motivation:** He wanted to help others to understand math.

9. **Significance of discovery:** His ideas of geometry are still used today.

10. **How was this discovery helpful or harmful to society?**
It advanced the understanding of mathematics.

11. **New word and meaning:** Answers will vary.

12. **Questions prompted through this study?** Answers will vary.

13. **Interesting bit of trivia:** He told the king there was no easier way to do math.

Scientist Questionnaire

1. **Who:** Aristotle   Father of Biology

2. **Nationality:** Greek

3. **Life span:** 384-322 BC

4. **Span of research:** 367-322 BC

5. **Biblical or church history event of the time:** (Alexander the Great) Macedeon conquest of Palestine.

6. **Noted achievement & field of interest:** He developed systems for classifying and comparing living organisms. He also came up with a method of reasoning.

7. **Secondary achievement & field of interest:** He also studied math, astronomy, and medicine. He taught that the earth was the center of the universe.

8. **Motivation:** He said, "Every realm of nature is marvelous so we should venture on the study of every kind of animal without distaste, for each and all will reveal to us something natural and beautiful."

9. **Significance of discovery:** He changed the way people think about science.

10. **How was this discovery helpful or harmful to society?** It helps us organize, classify, and study information.

11. **New word and meaning:** Answers will vary.

12. **Questions prompted through this study?** Answers will vary.

13. **Interesting bit of trivia:** He is recognized as the "Father of Biology". He did not believe we were made of atoms. He was Alexander the Great's tutor.

Cite your sources:

Explorers Questionnaire

1. **Who:** Pytheas

2. **Nationality:** Greek (born in Massilia)

3. **When:** 330 BC   The journey took six years.

4. **Point of departure:** Massilia (France) or
   Sponsoring country: Greece

5. **Was this place the explorer's home country?** yes
   Explain: Massilia was a Greek colony and trade center.

6. **Biblical or church history personality of the time:** Zechariah foretells of Alexander the Great.

7. **What was discovered or explored?** Northern Atlantic route to Tin Islands (up to the tip of Scotland on to Thule, possibly Iceland, Greenland or Scandinavia continuing until drifting ice stopped them) They traveled east to Europa (Germany), seeking amber.

8. **How?** They traveled over seven thousand miles in a 150 foot boat. They sailed through the Carthaginian guard (Pillars of Hercules) and north, following Himilco's path to Cornwall, England and on to the Arctic Ocean and Europe.

9. **What was their motivation?** They sought a sea route instead of paying enormous sums for products to be carried overland from Europa.

10. **Topography:** The Tin Islands have natural harbors. The north and west are mountainous. The east and central region are rolling plains. The south side has chalk hills, barren uplands, and moors.

11. **Climate:** moderate temperature ranging from 40 to 61 degrees. There is thick fog, almost daily rain, and chilly temperatures.

12. **Natural resources:** tin and forest

13. **Crops:** corn and barley

14. **Exports:** tin

15. **Trivia:** Pytheas was a merchant, explorer, scientist, astronomer, and anthropologist. Pytheas took careful notes of the tides in the Atlantic. He was the first to suggest that the moon causes the tides. He determined latitudes of land by figuring the height of the sun by the length of the shadow it casts. This made him the first person to apply astronomy to geography in order to locate a place on earth. This became the basis of accurate mapmaking.
   *He acted as an anthropologist, being the first to record the habits and customs of the people he visited.

Cite your sources: Simon, Charnan. *Explorers of the Ancient World.* IL: Childrens Press, 1990.

S-2

Define *geometry*.

Geometry is a branch of math that deals with the measurement, properties and relationships of points, lines, angles surfaces and solids.

What was Aristotle's system of classification?

Aristotle called the forms of living things "souls," which were of three kinds: vegetative (plants), sensitive (animals) or rational (human beings). Aristotle's classification of animals grouped together animals with similar characteristics into genera (used in a much broader sense than present-day biologists use the term) and then distinguished the species within the genera. He divided the animals into two types: those with blood, and those without blood (or at least without red blood). These distinctions correspond closely to our distinction between vertebrates and invertebrates. The blooded animals, corresponding to the vertebrates, included five genera: viviparous quadrupeds (mammals), birds, oviparous quadrupeds (reptiles and amphibians), fishes, and whales (which Aristotle did not realize were mammals). The bloodless animals were classified as cephalopods (such as the octopus); crustaceans; insects (which included the spiders, scorpions, and centipedes, in addition to what we now define as insects); shelled animals (such as most mollusks and echinoderms); and "zoophytes," or "plant-animals," which supposedly resembled plants in their form -- such as most cnidarians.

No language worksheet with Lesson 2

Lesson 3

250 - 140 B.C.

Day	SCIENTISTS	INVENTIONS	EXPLORERS
Mon	**Science Vocabulary**		
	circumference		
	radius		
	diameter		
	sphere		
	hemisphere		
	gnomonic		
Tue	287-192 BC Eratosthenes measured		
	the circumference of the earth.		
	Questionnaire		
Wed		200 BC Archimedes' Screw	**Read a resource on the Romans for**
		Questionnaire	**background information.**
			Vocabulary
			universal law
			emperor
			republic
Thu	200 BC Archimedes used experiments		Draw a Roman army uniform.
	to discover volume, buoyancy,		Draw a Macedonian army uniform.
	and simple machines.		**Write a paragraph or make a chart**
	Questionnaire		comparing and contrasting them.
			How did their battle strategy change
	Vocabulary		their needs?
	volume		
	concave lens		
	buoyancy		
Fri		200 BC Wheelbarrow	**Map Vocabulary**
	S-3	**Questionnaire**	chart
			continent
			equator
			circumnavigate
			key
			terrain
			*indicates present-day location

LANGUAGE ARTS	READING SELECTIONS
Oral book report	**Historical Fiction (read one per lesson)**
Write rough draft on last lesson's book	The Young Carthaginian - G. A. Henty
L-3a	The Eagles Have Flown - Joanne Williamson
	Yesterday's Daughter - Helen Daringer
Ψ IEW Lesson 3	The Shadow of Vesuvius - Ellis Dillon
View IEW DVD 2 – *Stylistic Techniques: Dress-ups*	For the Temple - G. A. Henty
Read pp. 171-188 IEW Seminar & Practicum Workbook	Detectives in Togas - Henry Winterfeld (series)
Begin Banned Word List	Mystery of the Roman Ransom - Henry Winterfeld (series)
Edit and copy	**Biographies (an alternate for a historical fiction)**
L-3b	Archimedes and the Door of Science - Jeanne Bendick
Ψ IEW Lesson 3 Key Word Outline	
Create a key word outline for *Hannibal*	
Present oral report	**Other Books for Research**
L-3c	Caesar's Gallic War - Olivia Coolidge
Review p. 12 in the IEW Seminar & Practicum Workbook	Augustus Caesar's World - Genevieve Foster
	Ancient Science - Jim Wiese
Ψ IEW Lesson 3 Dress-Ups and Rough Draft	Adventures in Ancient China - Linda Bailey
Review dress-ups and create a rough draft for *Hannibal*	Spend the Day in Ancient Rome - Linda Honan
	I Wonder Why Romans Wore Togas - Fiona MacDonald
	The Roman World - Michael Vickers
	A Roman Fort - Fiona MacDonald
Book jacket review	**Historical Events for Timeline**
L-3d	264-241 BC 1st Punic War
	218-202 BC Hannibal crosses the Alps
Ψ IEW Lesson 3 Final Draft	215 BC Great Wall of China begun
Rewrite *Hannibal* and use a different dress-up in each	164 BC Maccabaeus restore the Temple in Jerusalem
paragraph. Underline the dress-ups.	146 BC Carthage destroyed and Greece taken by Rome
	144 BC Parthians take Babylonia
	143-63 BC Hebrew Kingdom
	141 BC Parthians take Media
Create a book jacket on this lesson's selection	**Other Areas of Interest during this Lesson**
L-3e	Emperor Constantine ruler of Eastern Rome
	Emperor Titus (79-81 AD)
	Julius Caesar, first emperor of Rome
	Hannibal of Carthage
	Gladiators
	Queen Cleopatra of Egypt
Write your mini book report	Punic Wars between Rome and Carthage
3 Week Quiz	**Accomplishments in Math**
	160 AD Hipparchus Nicaea invented trigonometry
Optional Movie: *Spartacus*	

Scientist Questionnaire

1. **Who:** Eratosthenes of Cyrene   Father of Geography

2. **Nationality:** Greek

3. **Life span:** 287-192 BC

4. **Span of research:** He studied at Alexandria and Athens and he became director of the great library in Alexandria in 240 BC.

5. **Biblical or church history event of the time:** The Greek translation of the Old Testament was written.

6. **Noted achievement & field of interest:** He measured the circumference of the earth using geometry. He used a well in Syrene to help estimate the circumference of the earth. He devised a system of latitude and longitude.

7. **Secondary achievement & field of interest:** He also worked with prime numbers and developed the "Seive of Eratosthenes". He was a noted mathematician.

8. **Motivation:** He was known as Beta by his contemporaries because he proved himself second in many fields of study. He worked hard to overcome this name.

9. **Significance of discovery:** He believed that the earth was round, which was not a widely accepted idea.

10. **How was this discovery helpful or harmful to society?** There was no immediate change in society but Columbus believed Eratosthenes and thus sailed west to find India.

11. **New word and meaning:** Answers will vary.

12. **Questions prompted through this study?** Answers will vary.

13. **Interesting bit of trivia:** He was also an astronomer. He compiled a star chart. At the age of 80, blind and worn, he died of voluntary starvation.

Cite your sources:

Scientist Questionnaire

1. **Who:** Archimedes of Syracuse

2. **Nationality:** Greek

3. **Life span:** 287-212 BC

4. **Span of research:** He was curious and loved to solve puzzles. (Formal training unknown)

5. **Biblical or church history event of the time:** The Jews treated well during Hellenistic period.

6. **Noted achievement & field of interest:** Using experiments, he discovered information about volume, buoyancy, and simple machines. His Archimedes' Principle explained buoyancy. He learned that different liquids have different densities.

7. **Secondary achievement & field of interest:** One of the greatest mathematicians of his time. He worked with shapes, including cylinders and spheres, the circle, the cone and its curves, the ellipse, the parabola, and the hyperbola.

8. **Motivation:** King Hieron asked him to find out if his crown was made of solid gold. In doing this, he discovered a way to measure density and volume.

9. **Significance of discovery:** His ideas are still used for testing precious metals. Farmers didn't have to haul water by hand anymore because of the action of the screw to move water from a lower area to a higher area.

10. **How was this discovery helpful or harmful to society?** It was very helpful because metals could now be tested to make sure they are what they appear.

11. **New word and meaning:** Answers will vary.

12. **Questions prompted through this study?** Answers will vary.

13. **Interesting bit of trivia:** Archimedes is said to have created psychological warfare. He invented the screw for moving water. He also worked on hydrostatics and static mechanics. Archimedes used the principle of the lever to design a catapult. Archimedes was killed by an impatient Roman soldier.

Cite your sources: Bendick, Jeanne. *Archimedes and the Door of Science.* ND: Bethlehem Books, 1995.

Inventions Questionnaire

1. What invention: Archimedes' screw

2. When: 200 BC

3. Who is the inventor (person or country): Archimedes of Syracuse is Greek.

4. Motivation: He wanted to simplify and lighten labor using a machine. He wanted to be able to move water in a quicker, more feasible way.

5. How did this invention change life as it was then? It was used to move water from a lower area to a higher area.

6. What have been the ethical consequences (if any)? The ability to move water provided food and hydration for many people. The screw has been applied to many different areas of mechanical engineering, both for use in times of peace and for destruction in times of war.

7. Diagram or draw the invention:

Cite your sources:

Inventions Questionnaire

1. What invention: Wheelbarrow

2. When: Approximately 200 BC

3. Who is the inventor (person or country): It was invented in China.

4. Motivation: They wanted to be able to make things easier to carry.

5. How did this invention change life as it was then? The wheelbarrow greatly eased the life of the laborer who had to carry things on his back or shoulders. It replaced the sledge in narrow conditions as well as the pole with balancing buckets. One person was able to transport more with the wheelbarrow than by just carrying it.

6. What have been the ethical consequences (if any)? The wheelbarrow made the transportation of food and goods easier, and helped the general health of people by taking pressure off of their backs and legs when hauling heavy items. The wheelbarrow is still used today and has been a helpful tool, as well as use for entertainment. Of course, harmful things can be moved in the barrel as well.

7. Diagram or draw the invention:

S-3
Define the three basic concepts of simple machines. Make an example or draw diagrams of each.
See diagrams on the answer key for the first quarter three week quiz.

A simple machine is one designed to accomplish a very specific physical task. The three basic simple machines are the inclined plane, the lever, and the pulley. Also included in simple machines are the wedge, the screw, and the wheel and axle.

No language worksheet with Lesson 3

FIRST QUARTER THREE WEEK QUIZ

MATCH: Match the names on the left with their description on the right by writing the letter of the correct description in the space provided.

D	1.	Alexander the Great	a. classification of living organisms
F	2.	Euclid	b. explored western coast of Europe to Baltic Sea.
G	3.	Hanno	c. calculated the earth's circumference
I	4.	Aristarchus	d. explored while expanding his empire
H	5.	Hippocrates	e. made discoveries about buoyancy and simple machines
A	6.	Aristotle	f. proved basic elements of geometry
B	7.	Pytheas	g. explored the northwest coast of Africa
E	8.	Archimedes	h. father of medicine
C	9.	Eratosthenes	i. estimated size of earth, moon, and sun

TRUE OR FALSE: Mark each statement T for true or F for false in the space provided.

F   1.   Hanno was the very first Egyptian explorer.

T   2.   The "Pillars of Hercules" later became known as the Strait of Gibraltar.

F   3.   Hieroglyphics were used primarily by the Greeks.

F   4.   Pytheas was a scientist.

T   5.   Alexander the Great wanted to rule the known world.

F   6.   All of Alexander's conquests were made on foot.

F   7.   Hippocrates thought all sicknesses were caused by evil spirits.

T   8.   Aristarchus believed the sun was the center of the universe.

F   9.   Euclid wrote a book called "Simple Math".

T   10. Aristotle's system of classifying living organisms was incorrect.

T   11. As a child, Alexander the Great was tutored by Aristotle.

T   12. Aristotle had many interests including science.

T   13. Eratosthenes' measurement of the earth's circumference was fairly accurate.

F   14. Archimedes discoveries were not at all useful.

T   15. Archimedes had a good understanding of simple machines and how they worked.

MATCH: Match the words on the left with their definitions on the right by writing the letter of the correct definition in the space provided.

D	1.	circumnavigate	a. an imaginary circle around the world
E	2.	observation	b. to find out or make known for the first time
A	3.	equator	c. half of a sphere or globe
F	4.	inquisitive	d. to go completely around especially by water
C	5.	hemisphere	e. a noting and recording of facts, as for research
B	6.	discovery	f. inclined to ask many questions, curious

BONUS: Draw and name at least three simple machines.

Possible answers include:

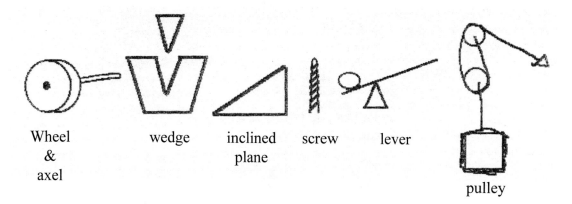

Wheel
&
axel

wedge

inclined
plane

screw

lever

pulley

Lesson 4

A.D. 1 - 1000

Lesson 4

Day	SCIENTISTS	INVENTIONS	EXPLORERS
Mon			**Read a resource on the Vikings for**
			background information.
			Draw a Viking man, woman or child
			Vocabulary
			blood feuds
			migration saga
			chieftain fjord
Tue	100 AD Ptolemy was an astronomer and		**Ship Vocabulary**
	map maker. He established North as the		anchor
	top of the map. He believed that the earth		stern
	was the center of the universe.		mainmast
	Questionnaire		sail
			hold
			bow
	S-4		
			Draw a Viking longboat
Wed		**Read a resource on the Middle Ages**	982 AD Eric the Red sailed from Iceland
		for background information	to Greenland.
			Questionnaire
		Vocabulary	*Greenland
		knights	
		monk	**Mark Map 3**
		peasant	
		feudalism	
Thu	**Vocabulary**	1000 AD Gunpowder	**Mark Viking trade routes using**
	astronomy	**Questionnaire**	the same Map 3
	planet		
	star		
	constellation		
	sun		
	universe		
	alchemy		
Fri			1000 AD Leif Ericsson was the first
			European thought to have reached the
			North American continent
			Questionnaire
			*coast of Newfoundland
			Mark Map 3
			*indicates present-day location

LANGUAGE ARTS	READING SELECTIONS		
Viking Report	**Historical Fiction (read one per lesson)**		
L-4a	The Dawning - Robert Wise		
	Beric the Briton - G. A. Henty		
Gathering notes and information	The King's Shadow - Elizabeth Alder		
L-4b	Augustine Came to Kent - Barbara Willard		
	The Thieves of Ostia - Caroline Lawrence (series)		
	The Wadjet Eye - Jill Rubalcaba		
	Legions - Rosemary Sutcliff		
	The Dragon and the Raven - G. A. Henty		
Work on report	**Biographies (an alternate for a historical fiction)**		
Ψ **IEW** In your Viking report use one dress-up in each	Cleopatra VII, Daughter of the Nile - Kristiana Gregory		
paragraph.	America's Explorers and Pioneers - Just the Facts Goldhill DVD		
Write report	**Other Books for Research**		
	People of Palestine - Olivia Coolidge		
Ψ **IEW Key Word Outline**	Beyond the Desert Gate - Mary Ray		
Make a key word outline from *Knights* source text	The Striped Ships - Eloise McGraw		
	Find the Constellations - H. A. Rey		
	What Do We Know About the Celts? - Hazel Mary Martell		
	The World in the Time of Charlemagne - Fiona Macdonald		
	Foods & Feasts with the Vikings - Hazel Mary Martell		
	The Early Middle Ages - Steck Vaughn Library		
Oral Storytelling	**Historical Events for Timeline**		
L-4c	Birth of Christ in Bethlehem		
	79 AD Pompeii buried by the eruption of Mt. Vesuvius		
Ψ **IEW Rough Draft**	476 AD Fall of Rome		
Write a rough draft on *Knights* from your key word outline	410-1000 AD Dark Ages in Europe		
	479 AD Chi Dynasty in southern China		
	500-1500 Middle Ages in Europe		
	589 AD Queen Theodelinda (Lombards converted to Catholicism)		
	632 Moslems control Mediterranean area		
Listening Skills	**Other Areas of Interest during this Lesson**		
L-4d	Guilds and the rise of a middle class in Europe		
	Alchemy		
Ψ **IEW Final Draft**	Castle architecture		
Use all the dress-ups you have learned and underline them	Saxons		
	King Charlemagne unites Europe		
	Galen, the physician		
Write your mini-report	St. Patrick, English missionary to Ireland		
	Accomplishments in Math		
	250 AD Diophantus - first book on algebra		
Optional Movie: *The Vikings*	595 The first authenticated record of decimal reckoning in India		
	810 Persian mathematician coins the term "algebra"		
	814 Arabs include zero to multiply by 10		
	975 The present mathematical notation was brought to Europe by Arabs		

Scientist Questionnaire

1. **Who:** Ptolemy (Claudius Ptolemaeus)

2. **Nationality:** It is not certain. He was probably born in Egypt and lived in the Hellenistic culture of Roman Egypt. Claudius is a Roman name but Ptolemy is a Greek name.

3. **Life span:** AD 100 -170

4. **Span of research:** He grew up in Alexandria, the educational center of the ancient world. He was surrounded and inspired by the great minds of his day.

5. **Biblical or church history event of the time:** Ignatius became the Bishop of Antioch.

6. **Noted achievement & field of interest:** He established that "North" is at the top of the map. He believed that the earth was the center of the universe and was stationary. Ptolemy believed the planets and sun orbited the Earth in the order Mercury, Venus, Sun, Mars, Jupiter, and Saturn. This system became known as the Ptolemaic system and predicted the positions of the planets quite accurately without the use of a telescope. He was a noted geographer and astronomer.

7. **Secondary achievement & field of interest:** He authored several scientific treatises, three of which continued to have importance to European and Islamic scientists. He wrote on geography, astronomy, astrology, music, and optics.

8. **Motivation:** Unknown.

9. **Significance of discovery:** His positioning of North as the top of the map standardized cartography.

10. **How was this discovery helpful or harmful to society?** North is still the top of the map, making a standard that is useful across cultures and languages.

11. **New word and meaning:** Answers will vary.

12. **Questions prompted through this study?** Answers will vary.

13. **Interesting bit of trivia:** Ptolemy exaggerated the land mass from Spain to China and under-estimated the size of the ocean. This mistake encouraged Christopher Columbus to make his famous voyage in 1492.

Cite your sources:

Inventions Questionnaire

1. What invention: Gunpowder

2. When: 1000 AD

3. Who is the inventor (person or country): The Chinese are given credit for the invention of gunpowder and explosives. German Monk Berthold Schartz and English Monk Roger Bacon are both recognized for their work in the 14th c. Both monks left notes on their experiments to make gunpowder.

4. Motivation: They originally used gunpowder to make firecrackers for celebrations.

5. How did this invention change life as it was then? First firecrackers were invented, then gunpowder was used for mining, and finally for weapons. The gun made it easier for one person to hunt for many.

6. What have been the ethical consequences (if any)? The weapons that use gunpowder have caused the loss of millions of lives and destruction of property. However, it is also a tool for hunting, self-defense, mining, and entertainment.

7. Diagram or draw the invention:

Explorers Questionnaire

1. **Who:** Eric Thorvaldson, nicknamed Eric the Red

2. **Nationality:** Norseman or Viking

3. **When:** 982 AD

4. **Point of departure:** Iceland
   or
   Sponsoring country:

5. **Was this place the explorer's home country?** Yes
   Explain: Eric was exiled from Iceland for three years and spent the time looking for a land that had been sighted earlier. The Norse people needed more land.

6. **Biblical or church history personality of the time:** Pope John XIII was the ruler of the church in Europe.

7. **What was discovered or explored?** Greenland

8. **How?** Sailed the sea by boat and by traversing over land.

9. **What was their motivation?** While in exile, Eric sought the land west of Iceland that had been sighted fifty years earlier by Gunnbjorn Ulfsson. He was looking for additional land for the Norsemen.

10. **Topography:** Largest island is formed by a sheet of ice surrounded by a rim of mountains. There are green fjords and coastal meadows on the southwestern rim.

11. **Climate:** Greenland's summer days are long and light, while its winter days are dark and cold.

12. **Natural resources:** bears, caribou, reindeer, and other wild animals. Fish, including salmon, cod, and halibut are also present.

13. **Crops:** hay, potatoes, and turnips

14. **Exports:** The Norse traded slaves taken in raids for Greek wine. There were no exports from Greenland.

15. **Trivia:** Eric got his nickname from the color of his hair. The Viking longboat is an engineering marvel. In 985, Eric sailed for Greenland with 25 ships of colonists.

Cite your sources:

Explorers Questionnaire

1. **Who:** Leif Ericsson, nicknamed Leif the Lucky

2. **Nationality:** Norseman (Viking)

3. **When:** 1000 AD

4. **Point of departure:** Norway
   or
   Sponsoring country: Norway, King Olaf l

5. **Was this place the explorer's home country?** No, Leif was from Greenland.
   Explain: The king of Norway sent him out to explore and spread Christianity.

6. **Biblical or church history personality of the time:** Leif was sent out as a Christian missionary. This was during the Dark Ages and during a time when monasteries were common.

7. **What was discovered or explored?** Vinland was discovered.

8. **How?** The "Saga of Eric the Red" tells that on the trip back from Norway to Greenland Leif was blown off course and discovered a land of grapes. He then traveled back to Greenland where he successfully introduced Christianity.
   In the "Saga of Olaf" Leif completed King Olaf's commission to Greenland. Eric sent Leif back out to find the land sighted by a trader, Bjarni Herjolfsson, in 985. Leif sailed west from Greenland to Baffin Island (Helluland), south along Labrador (Markland) and finally to the northern tip of Newfoundland (Vinland). He built a small village and wintered there, returning to Greenland in the spring of 1002.

9. **What was their motivation?** He was obeying their king and/or his father.

10. **Topography:** The coastline of Vinland has rolling hills and plains.

11. **Climate:** cool, wet island   The North Atlantic ocean moderates the annual temperatures, keeping it cooler in the summer and warmer in the winter. It is cold and warm randomly, without great variations in temperature.

12. **Natural resources:** tall, thick forests, grassy meadows, fish (salmon) and wild animals, fertile land

13. **Crops:** grapes, self-sown wheat

14. **Exports:** grapes, lumber, fur, and fish   Leif returned to Greenland with timber

15. **Trivia:** "Leif the Lucky", as they called him, got his name for rescuing the drowning crew of a sinking ship. In reward, he received the treasures of the ship.
    Leif inherited his father's position as leader of the Norse colony in Greenland.

Cite your sources: http://historymedren.about.com/od/lwho/p/leif_ericsson.htm 3/16/2012

S-4

Who named the constellations and how did they get their names?

47 of the 88 constellations date back to the time of Ptolemy, who listed them. They were named after Greek and Roman mythological figures and events. Interestingly, the ancient Greeks only named the constellations in the Northern Hemisphere, since those are all they could see from Greece. The Southern constellations were named by the German astronomer Johan Bayer. He continued the tradition of using names from Greek mythology. Later, the French astronomer, La Caille, added the last 13 to fill in the remaining groups and, breaking with tradition, named them after scientific instruments. There are now 88 generally recognized constellations.

Night time activity: Study a star chart, observe and locate five constellations.

L-4a Students select an outline from Worksheet 2 to use for their report.

Lesson 5

1000 - 1400

Lesson 5

Day	SCIENTISTS	INVENTIONS	EXPLORERS
Mon			Read a resource on China for background information
			Vocabulary
			emissary khan
			caravan Steppes
			Silk Road yurt
			pagoda Mongol
			nomad
Tue	**Vocabulary**		1271-1292 Marco Polo traveled throughout China and Asia.
	convex		
	concave		**Questionnaire**
	reflection		*across Asia to China
	refraction		**Mark Map 5**
			Look at Marco's book: "The Travels of Marco Polo"
Wed	1214-1292 Roger Bacon studied alchemy (the beginnings of chemistry) discovering the properties of gun powder	1286 Spectacles **Questionnaire**	Copy some Chinese writing and compare it with English script.
	Questionnaire		**Write a paragraph or diagram the the differences.**
	Roger Bacon believed truth is found by observation and experiment. He disagreed with Aristotle.		
Thu	**S-5 Longitude & Latitude**	1350 Cannon **Questionnaire**	**Draw the Venetian city-state flag**
			Draw a Chinese junk for your coursebook
			Draw China's flag while they were under the rule of the Mongols
Fri		1371 Magnetic compass **Questionnaire**	**Map Vocabulary**
			latitude
			longitude
			meridian
			parallel
			axis
			Find the hemispheres on the globe
			*indicates present-day location

LANGUAGE ARTS	READING SELECTIONS
First and last sentences	**Historical Fiction (read one per lesson)**
L-5a	The Winter Hare - Joan E. Goodman
	The Bedouin's Gazelle - Francis Temple
Ψ **IEW Lesson 5**	Knight of the Golden Plain - Mollie Hunter (series)
Add new words to your collection of replacement words.	Kite Rider - Geraldine McCaughrean
	The Magician's Apprentice - Sidney & Dorothy Rosen
	There Will Be Wolves - Karleen Bradford
	In Freedom's Cause - G. A. Henty
	Plays of Great Achievers - Sylvia Kamerman
Ordering events	**Biographies (an alternate for a historical fiction)**
L-5b	Alfred the Great - Eloise Lownsberry
	Marco Polo and the Wonders of the East - Hal Marcovitz
Ψ **IEW Advanced Dress-ups**	Kublai Khan - Kim Dramer
View IEW DVD 6 - *Stylistic Techniques*	The Look-It-Book of Explorers - Elizabeth Cody Kimmel
See page 171 in Seminar & Practicum Workbook	
Descriptive words	**Other Books for Research**
L-5c	Swords and Scimitars - Linda Chaikin
	The World in the Time of Marco Polo - Fiona Macdonald
Ψ **IEW** *Joan of Arc*	If all the Swords in England - Barbara Willard
Read and make a key word outline for *Joan of Arc*	A Proud Taste for Scarlet and Miniver - E. L. Konigsburg
	Medieval People - Sarah Howarth
	Asia Before Europe - K. N. Chaudhur
	Chinese Writing - Diane Wolff
	Foods & Feasts in the Middle Ages - Imogen Dawson
Thesaurus	**Historical Events for Timeline**
L-5d	1066 William the Conqueror becomes King of England
	1189-1199 King Richard the Lionheart rules England
Ψ **IEW Rough Draft**	1095 Crusades commissioned by the Pope to free the Holy Land
Write a rough draft from your key word outline	1200 Incan Empire in Peru
	1312–1337 Mali Empire reaches its height in Africa
	1337-1453 100 Years' War between England and France
	1346 Black Plague starts in China
	1368 China under the Mongols
Describing people	**Other Areas of Interest during this Lesson**
L-5e	Black Death Plague
	Thomas Aquinas
Ψ **IEW Final draft** *Joan of Arc*	Francis of Assisi leaves behind his wealth to become a monk
Write final using advanced dress-ups	Monasteries flourish in Europe
	Thomas à Becket Archbishop of Canterbury, England
	Eleanor of Aquitaine marries England's King Henry
Write your mini book report	King Arthur of Camelot
	Robin Hood
Optional Movie: *Ivanhoe*	**Accomplishments in Math**
	1202 Leonardo Pisano Fibonacci introduces Arabic numerals
	to Europe

Scientist Questionnaire

1. **Who:** Roger Bacon "the astounding teacher"

2. **Nationality:** He was English.

3. **Life span:** 1214-1294

4. **Span of research:** He was from a wealthy family and was educated early. He was acquainted with the philosophy and science of the Byzantine and Arab worlds. The scientific training Bacon received showed him the defects in existing academic debate. Bacon devoted himself to languages and experimental research.

5. **Biblical or church history event of the time:** 1,500,000 Jews were massacred in Europe on suspicion of having poisoned the springs.

6. **Noted achievement & field of interest:** He studied alchemy (the beginnings of chemistry).

7. **Secondary achievement & field of interest:** He also studied astronomy. He believed that the celestial bodies had an influence on the fate and mind of humans. He challenged the use of the Julian calander.

8. **Motivation:** He believed that truth was found by observation and experimentation. He was not content with merely learning from books. He thought Aristotle's works should be burned so they wouldn't influence others and produce error.

9. **Significance of discovery:** He made gunpowder.

10. **How was this discovery helpful or harmful to society?** Gunpowder weapons replaced all archers in armies, and by the 1500's most armies used firearms.

11. **New word and meaning:** Answers will vary.

12. **Questions prompted through this study?** Answers will vary.

13. **Interesting bit of trivia:** He lectured on Aristotle at Oxford. He became a Franciscan monk in 1253. He was condemned by his order in 1278 suspected of novelties of alchemy and astrology. He wrote a secret book called *Opus Majus (Major Work)* and sent it to the Pope. He later wrote *Opus Minus* and *Opus Tertium.* He wrote "The Mirror of Alchemy" in 1297. In his writings, Bacon called for a reform of theological study encouraging theologians to return to the Bible itself as the center of attention and to thoroughly study the languages in which their original sources were composed.
    He created a simple steam engine. He spent over ten years in jail because of the mysterious work he did in his lab. He worked on optics and the refraction of light through lenses, leading to the development of spectacles. He foretold the invention of the steamship, the locomotive, and the airplane. He died without followers.

Cite your sources:

Inventions Questionnaire

1. What invention: Spectacles

2. When: 1284 AD

3. Who is the inventor (person or country): Italy

4. Motivation: They developed a lens that could enlarge. It made it easier to see print and study the stars.

5. How did this invention change life as it was then? It improved the ability to see and prolonged the usefulness of workers who did hand work such as scribes, poets, painters, and seamstresses.

6. What have been the ethical consequences (if any)? The lens continued to be developed to serve in telescopes, microscopes, binoculars, and gun scopes. Many have benefited from the invention, while others have used it to locate an enemy at great distances. Binoculars can be used to invade another persons' privacy.

7. Diagram or draw the invention:

Inventions Questionnaire

1. What invention: Cannon

2. When: 1350 AD

3. Who is the inventor (person or country): Marco Polo spoke of the cannons used by the Chinese. The cannon first appeared in the early 14th century in Europe.

4. Motivation: To improve warfare and inflict the greatest amount of damage on the enemy at a safe distance. It can blast through walls, ships, horses and riders.

5. How did this invention change life as it was then? It made battles deadlier. No longer were city walls enough protection. Fear of such enemies affected the populations of a region.

6. What have been the ethical consequences (if any)? It made warfare more deadly and cost thousands of lives and destruction of property. Shooting a man out of a cannon is used to entertain in a circus act. Cannons have been used to send a signal of warning or announcement of an event.

7. Diagram or draw the invention:

Cite your sources:

Inventions Questionnaire

1. What invention: magnetic compass (wet compass)

2. When: First recorded use of the compass was Zheng He (1371 -1433) He made seven ocean voyages between 1405 – 1433.
Han dynasty used the "south pointer" spoon shaped pointer
5th c. the compass was used to align construction (geomacy or Feng Shui)
T'ang dynasty magnetized a needle

3. Who is the inventor (person or country): Someone in China realized the lodestone magnetic and pointed out real directions

4. Motivation: unknown Adapted a observation.

5. How did this invention change life as it was then? It improved travel, making navigation safer on the seas and over land

6. What have been the ethical consequences (if any)? The compass changed the world. It allowed people to be more mobile, which over the centuries caused families to be spread further apart, but it also has provided for better and safer exploration.

7. Diagram or draw the invention:
lodestone floated on a stick in the water, aligns itself in the direction of the polestar (north)

Cite your sources:
http://aerospace.wcc.hawaii.edu/compass.html 7/28/2008
www.computersmiths.com/chineseinvention/compass.htm 7/28/2008
www.chaos.umd.edu/history/time_line.html 7/28/2008

Explorers Questionnaire

1. **Who:** Marco Polo

2. **Nationality:** He was Venetian

3. **When:** 1271-1295 AD

4. **Point of departure:** Venice
   or
   Sponsoring country: He was self-sponsored from within his merchant guild.

5. **Was this place the explorer's home country?** Yes. City-state
   Explain: He traveled with his father and uncle across the Silk Road to China to learn the merchant trade.

6. **Biblical or church history personality of the time:** The crusaders take Constantinople. Thomas Aquinas (Catholic priest and medieval theologian and philosopher)

7. **What was discovered or explored?** He went to China and lived there for many years.

8. **How?** by boat and in camel caravans

9. **What was their motivation?** To find a shorter trade route to the East

10. **Topography:** vast Gobi Desert, mountains, tropical forests and grassland
    They crossed most of the land and water areas of the Eastern World.

11. **Climate:** moderate to desert heat
    China has dry, cool weather in the north, and warm, moist weather in the south.

12. **Natural resources:** spices, wood, Mulberry trees, and silk worms

13. **Crops:** rice and wheat

14. **Exports:** silks and spices, jewels, sandalwood, and myrrh

15. **Trivia:** The Chinese ruler asked for Christian missionaries to come, but the few who started out turned back. Marco dictated his travels into a book, *Description of the World*. It was so amazing that no one believed him. The Chinese had many inventions that the Europeans hadn't heard of: eyeglasses, compass, porcelain, fireworks, paper money, and printing blocks.

Cite your sources:

S-5
Does the equator run parallel to the longitude or to the latitude lines?
The equator runs parallel to the latitude lines.

Discuss time zones. Notice that the equator is at 0 parallel.

Do time changes move with the sun from east to west following along the longitude or the latitude lines? Time changes follow the latitude lines, or west and east.

No language worksheet in Lesson 5

Teacher's Notes

_____

_____

_____

_____

_____

_____

_____

_____

_____

_____

_____

_____

_____

_____

_____

_____

_____

_____

_____

_____

_____

_____

Lesson 6

1400 - 1490

Lesson 6

Day	SCIENTISTS	INVENTIONS	EXPLORERS
Mon		1440 Printing with moveable type	**Read a resource on the Renaissance**
		Questionnaire	**for background information.**
			Vocabulary
			guild
			pilgrimage
			apprentice
			mercenary
			crusade
Tue	**Science Vocabulary**		1488 Bartolomeu Dias sailed around the
	hypothesis		southern tip of Africa.
	experiment		**Questionnaire**
	data		*South Africa
	conclusion		
			Mark Map 1
Wed	1472 Leonardo da Vinci investigated		**Locate Portugal on the globe**
	astronomy, botany, engineering, and		
	geology. He drew accurate pictures of		**Draw the Portuguese flag**
	human anatomy.		
	Questionnaire		
	S-6		
Thu	**Locate the Apennine Peninsula on the**		**Ship Vocabulary**
	globe. Many say it's shaped like a boot.		dinghy
			topsail
	Draw the flag of Florence		foresail
			jib
			mainstays
Fri			**Draw a multi-sail ship**
			Identify the parts of the ship
			keel
			bow
			stern
			port
			starboard
			cabin
			mainmast
			mainsail
			rudder
			*indicates present-day location

LANGUAGE ARTS	READING SELECTIONS
Fanciful fiction	**Historical Fiction (read one per lesson)**
L-6a	Jackaroo - Cynthia Voight
Ψ You may want to first view IEW DVD 3	The Midwife's Apprentice - Karen Cushman
and create a story sequence chart for L-6a	The Second Mrs. Giaconda - E. L. Konigsburg
	Dove and Sword: A Novel of Joan of Arc - Nancy Garden
	The Warwick Heiress - Margaret Abbey
	The Lady and the Squire - Terry Jones
Cause & Effect	**Biographies (an alternate for a historical fiction)**
L-6b Worksheet 3	Ink on His Fingers - Louise Vernon
Ψ **IEW Lesson 6**	
View DVD 3 - Retelling Narrative Stories	
View pages 171 and 180 – 183 in the	
IEW Seminar and Practicum Workbook	
Cause & Several Effects	**Other Books for Research**
L-6c	The World in 1492 - Jean Fritz
	When China Ruled the Sea - Louise Levathes
Ψ **IEW Key Word Outline**	Ship - David Macaulay
Make a key word outline for the *Renaissance*	Italian Renaissance - John Clare
	The Hundred Years' War - William Lace
	Amazing Da Vinci Inventions You Can Build Yourself - Anderson
	Medieval Feast - Aliki
	A Day With a Noblewoman - Regine Pérnoud
The Long Voyage	**Historical Events for Timeline**
L-6d	1445-1485 War of the Roses in England
	1453 France establishes a central government
Ψ **IEW Rough Draft**	1453 Turks capture Constantinople
Write a rough draft from your key word outline.	1462 Tsar Ivan III rules Russia (Ivan the Terrible)
	1474 - 1516 Ferdinand & Isabella reigns in Spain
	1476 Chimu civilization in Peru defeated by Inca
	1478 Spanish Inquisition begins to uncover heresy
	1490 Ashikaga Yoshimasa, Japanese shogun
Optional Movie: *Black Arrow*	**Other Areas of Interest during this Lesson**
	Joan of Arc of France
Ψ **IEW Final Draft**	Admiral Cheng Ho of China
Use three openers in each paragraph and mark	Gutenberg Bible published in Germany
appropriately in the margin. Also use two dress-ups	Lancaster and York, Civil War in England
in each paragraph.	Donatello
	Tamerlane defeats the Ottomans
Write your mini book report	Collapse of Khmer Empire
6 Week Quiz	**Accomplishments in Math**

Scientist Questionnaire

1. **Who:** Leonardo da Vinci

2. **Nationality:** Florentine (city-state on the Apennine peninsula – modern day Italy)

3. **Life span:** 1452-1519

4. **Span of research:** He spent his entire life as an artist, scientist, architect and true Renaissance man (a cultured man of the Renaissance who was knowledgeable in a wide range of fields).

5. **Biblical or church history event of the time:** Spanish Inquisition.

6. **Noted achievement & field of interest:** He was an architect, sculptor and painter. He accurately drew human and animal anatomy for the first time.

7. **Secondary achievement & field of interest:** He investigated astronomy, botany, engineering, and geology. He was an inventor. He kept notebooks full of his ideas and observations.

8. **Motivation:** He was curious about everything and always wanted to know more. He looked to the future.

9. **Significance of discovery:** He learned many things in many areas but his most important discoveries were about human anatomy.

10. **How was this discovery helpful or harmful to society?** His anatomical discoveries greatly furthered the science of medicine.

11. **New word and meaning:** Answers will vary.

12. **Questions prompted through this study?** Answers will vary.

13. **Interesting bit of trivia:** He served as the duke's engineer in the military. He was also a civil engineer. He designed roads and bridges and a canal system with locks.

Cite your sources:

Inventions Questionnaire

1. What invention: Printing with movable type

2. When: 1440

3. Who is the inventor (person or country): German Johannes Gutenberg
The Chinese also developed block printing.

4. Motivation: He wanted to be able to publish faster and more productively. He wanted to make the Bible more accessible.

5. How did this invention change life as it was then? It became much faster and easier to make books.

6. What have been the ethical consequences (if any)? It made books affordable and led to a great increase and interest in literacy. Education led to freedom. Printing presses were used to print good as well as evil texts.

7. Diagram or draw the invention:

Explorers Questionnaire

1. **Who:** Bartolomeu Dias

2. **Nationality:** Portuguese

3. **When:** 1487

4. **Point of departure:** Lisbon
   or
   Sponsoring country: Portugal

5. **Was this place the explorer's home country?** Yes
   Explain: Prince Henry the Navigator had an interest in the voyage as well as the trade route.

6. **Biblical or church history personality of the time:** First complete edition of the Hebrew Bible

7. **What was discovered or explored?** Cape of Good Hope and most of South Africa

8. **How?** lateen-rigged caravel

9. **What was their motivation?** Seek out the lands of Pester John, African king of Ethiopia and Christian priest. They wanted to enter into friendly relations. They wanted to find a route to India that avoided the Muslims.

10. **Topography:** hills and prairie grasslands located at the tip of the continent where the Atlantic and Indian Ocean meet.

11. **Climate:** mostly semiarid; subtropical along east coast; sunny days, cool nights

12. **Natural resources:** wild animals

13. **Crops:** corn, wheat, tobacco, and sugar cane

14. **Exports:** wild animals, cattle and sheep

15. **Trivia:** He later sailed with Pedro Cabral and discovered Brazil.

Cite your sources:

S-6
Look at Leonardo da Vinci's sketches and name some modern inventions that resemble them. List some of his many achievements.
Answers will vary as Leonardo sketched many modern-day inventions. Included in his accomplishments were sketches of plans for an alarm clock, a chain-driven pocket watch, a ship's log, a parachute, an airplane, an air conditioner, and even an automobile. He designed paddle-wheel boats, water shoes, tanks, submarines, and a continuous motion lathe. He designed a network of canals that were dug and put into use a full 300 years later.

Leonardo, although best known for painting the *Mona Lisa* and *The Last Supper*, was also an accomplished scientist, engineer, musician, sculptor, and architect – a true Renaissance Man. He wrote notebook entries in mirror (backwards) script, a trick which kept many of his observations from being widely known until decades after his death.

Worksheet 3

Page 1 Practice – Cause and Effect

Draw one line under the cause and two lines under the effect for each sentence or group of sentences.

1. The Vikings ran out of farmland. Therefore **they began raiding surrounding villages**.*

2. Knights of the Middle Ages wore heavy armor so **they could be protected** in battle.

3. As a result of the unsanitary conditions the castles and villages, **many died**.

4. The **alchemists worked long hot hours** in their laboratories hoping to change common metals into gold.

5. **Trade with China began** as a result of Marco Polo's explorations east.

* Answers in bold type reflect student answers for effect.

FIRST QUARTER SIX WEEK QUIZ

MATCH: Match the names on the right with their descriptions on the left by writing the letter of the correct description in the space provided.

C   1.   Eric the Red   a. traveled throughout India & China

E   2.   Leonardo da Vinci   b. explored the Arctic to North America

A   3.   Marco Polo   c. explored Greenland

B   4.   Leif Ericsson   d. rounded the southern tip of Africa

F   5.   Ptolemy   e. artist, scientist, inventor

D   6.   Bartolomeu Dias   f. astronomer and map maker

TRUE OR FALSE: Mark each statement T for true or F for false in the space provided.

F   1.   The Vikings wanted to become a great empire.

T   2.   Leif Ericsson discovered North America because he was blown off course.

F   3.   The Vikings found people already settled in Iceland and Greenland.

F   4.   Marco Polo discovered new lands.

T   5.   Marco Polo went to China and India to trade.

F   6.   Marco Polo traveled all the way to China by ship.

T   7.   Ptolemy believed the earth was the center of the universe.

F   8.   Bartolomeu Dias sailed across the Atlantic to America in 1488.

F   9.   Bartolomeu Dias was Spanish.

F   10. Leonardo da Vinci studied anatomy so he could be a doctor.

MULTIPLE CHOICE: Circle the letter next to the word or phrase that correctly complete the sentence.

1. Greenland's terrain is _____.
   a. mountainous   b. forests and pastureland   <u>c. ice capped</u>

2. Leif Ericsson found Newfoundland (Vinland) to _____.
   <u>a. have lakes & forests</u>   b. be barren   c. have volcanoes

3. China's main crops are _____.
   a. potatoes & berries   b. dairy products   <u>c. tea & rice</u>

4. Bartholomeu Dias traded for _____ at the cape of South Africa.
   a. oil   <u>b. cattle and sheep</u>   c. silks & spices

5. Marco Polo returned from China with _____.
   <u>a. silks & spices</u>   b. tobacco & sugar   c. porcelain

6. The southern tip of Africa is _____.
   <u>a. subtropical</u>   b. rainy   c. mild

7. Iceland and Greenland are in the _____ hemisphere.
   <u>a. northern</u>   b. eastern   c. southern

8. China and India are in the _____ hemisphere.
   a. southern   b. western   <u>c. eastern</u>

9. Africa is in the _____ hemisphere.
   a. northern   <u>b. eastern</u>   c. western

10. The imaginary lines that denote time changes are marked by _____.
   a. latitude   <u>b. longitude</u>   c. equator

MATCH: Match the words on the left with their definitions on the right by writing the letter of the correct definition in the space provided.

C   1.   hypothesis   a. a judgment or opinion formed after thought

D   2.   data   b. the science of stars and other heavenly objects

A   3.   conclusion   c. an unproved theory

B   4.   astronomy   d. facts and figures from which conclusions are drawn

H   5.   constellation   e. a chemist of the Middle Ages that hoped to change base
                                      elements into gold

E   6.   alchemist   f. any heavenly body seen as a small fixed point of light

J   7.   medieval   g. a heavenly body that revolves around the sun

I   8.   renaissance   h. group of fixed stars

G   9.   planet   i. rebirth or revival

F   10. star   j. of the Middle Ages

K   11. longitude   k. imaginary lines running north and south parallel to the meridian

L   12. latitude   l. imaginary lines running parallel to the equator

BONUS: List some ideas Leonardo da Vinci had that have been invented.

helicopter	machine gun	human flight machine
Draw bridge	submarine	Water shoes
tank	parachute	

Teacher's Notes

_____

_____

_____

_____

_____

_____

_____

_____

_____

_____

_____

_____

_____

_____

_____

_____

_____

_____

_____

_____

_____

Lesson 7

1490 - 1500

Day	SCIENTISTS	INVENTIONS	EXPLORERS
Mon			1492-1504 Christopher Columbus discovered the West Indies.
			Questionnaire
			*West Indies
			Mark Map 14
Tue	**Vocabulary for Europe**		**Draw the Spanish flag during the reign of Ferdinand and Isabella**
	heresy		
	Reformation		
	Inquisition		
	excommunication		
			Draw India's flag in 1492
Wed	**Locate Europe on the globe.**		1498 Vasco da Gama sailed from Portugal to India.
			Questionnaire
			*Calicut
			Mark Map 6
Thu			1499-1504 Amerigo Vespucci sailed to the West Indies and South America.
			Questionnaire
			*Brazil
			Mark Map 6
Fri			**Optional Report:** Aztec, Inca or Maya Practice your openers and use one dress-up in each paragraph.
			*indicates present-day location

LANGUAGE ARTS	READING SELECTIONS
Business Letters	**Historical Fiction (read one per lesson)**
L-7a	The Cruise of the Santa Maria - Elis Dillon
	Secrets in the House of Delgado - Gloria Miklowitz
Ψ **IEW Lesson 7**	Last Crusader - George Grant
Continue learning Sentnece Openers	I Sailed with Columbus - Susan Martin
Addressing envelopes	**Biographies (an alternate for a historical fiction)**
L-7b	The Man Who Laid an Egg - Louise Vernon
	Isabella of Castile: Queen on Horseback - Joann Burch
Ψ **IEW Key Word Outline**	
Make a key word outline for *A Pirate in Petticoats*	
Friendly letters	**Other Books for Research**
L-7c	The World of Columbus and Sons - Genevieve Foster
	A Day with a Troubadour - Régine Pernoud
Use Dress-ups and Sentence Openers in your letter	The World's Great Explorers: Henry the Navigator - Charnan Simon
	Foods & Feasts with the Aztecs - Imogen Dawson
	Explorers & Mapmakers - Peter Ryan
Ψ **IEW Rough Draft**	
Write a rough draft for *A Pirate in Petticoats*	
Invitations	**Historical Events for Timeline**
L-7d	King Henry VII rules England
	1492 Moslems driven from Spain (Granada)
Ψ **IEW Final**	1492 Columbus sails west to reach India
Write a final for *A Pirate in Petticoats*	1493 Pope Alexander divides world between Spain and Portugal
Use assigned openers and dress-ups with appropriate	1497 John Cabot discovers North America for England
markings	1498 Portuguese trading centers in India, East Indies, and China
	1498 Columbus makes 3rd voyage
	1500 Treaty of Granada: France & Aragon divide Naples
Postcards	**Other Areas of Interest during this Lesson**
L-7e	Mayans
	Raphael
Thank You Notes	Michelangelo
L-7f	Navigation and ship design improve
	Ferdinand and Isabella of Spain
	John "Giovanni" Cabot
Write your mini book report	Henry the Navigator of Portugal
	Accomplishments in Math
	1505 Scipione de Ferro solves a form of cubic equation
Optional Movie: *Agony and Ecstasy*	

Explorers Questionnaire

1. **Who:** Christopher Columbus

2. **Nationality:** Genoan (city-state on the Apennine peninsula)

3. **When:** 1492-1493

4. **Point of departure:** Port of Palos
   or
   Sponsoring country: Spain

5. **Was this place the explorer's home country?** No
   Explain: His voyage was sponsored by Spain because the king and queen were interested in finding a trade route to Asia.

6. **Biblical or church history personality of the time:** Spain expels all religions that are not Catholic.

7. **What was discovered or explored?** The West Indies – San Salvador, Cuba, and Haiti in the Caribbean Sea.

8. **How?** They sailed three ships; the *Niña* a small caravel, *Pinta* also a caravel, and the *Santa Maria*, a Spanish carrack used for hauling cargo.

9. **What was their motivation?** He wanted to be the first to find a western route to Asia. Queen Isabella wanted to extend Christianity to the East.

10. **Topography:** fertile plains, mountains, and jungle

11. **Climate:** warm in the spring, hot in summer, tropical weather

12. **Natural resources:** trees for lumber, fish, citrus trees

13. **Crops:** indigenous sweet potatoes, cassava, beans, sugar cane, and some tobacco.

14. **Exports:** self-sufficient islands

15. **Trivia:** Columbus traded all his life; even as a young boy he went on trading trips with his father.

Cite your sources:

Explorers Questionnaire

1. **Who:** Vasco da Gama

2. **Nationality:** Portuguese

3. **When:** 1497-1499

4. **Point of departure:** Lisbon, Portugal
   or
   Sponsoring country: Portugal

5. **Was this place the explorer's home country?** Yes
   Explain: Prince Manuel gave Vasco four ships.

6. **Biblical or church history personality of the time:** Pope Alexander VI divided the world between Portugal and Spain.

7. **What was discovered or explored?** They sought an all water route to Calicut, India in the subcontinent.

8. **How?** by ship, all water route

9. **What was their motivation?** He wanted to reach India and establish trade.

10. **Topography:** low lying plains, rivers, and tropical areas

11. **Climate:** monsoon climate, humid in summer and dry in winter

12. **Natural resources:** gold, precious stones, spices, and tea

13. **Crops:** grain, rice, spices, and tea

14. **Exports:** spices, gold, jewels, and jute

15. **Trivia:** He opened trade with India by force.
    King Emmanuel I gave him the title of Dom (Lord) with an annual grant of 300.000 reais, for him and his descendants, and appointed him Admiral of the Indies (January, 1500). In 1519, the Admiral was granted the coveted title of Count of Vidigueira.

Cite your sources: Vasco da Gama: Explorer - EnchantedLearning.com 2/12/2012
www.enchantedlearning.com/explorers/page/d/**dagama**.shtml

Explorers Questionnaire

1. **Who:** Amerigo Vespucci

2. **Nationality:** Florentine (a part of the Apennine peninsula, present day Italy)

3. **When:** 1499-1500

4. **Point of departure:** Cádiz, Spain
   or
   Sponsoring country: Spain

5. **Was this place the explorer's home country?** No
   Explain: He was a Florentine but moved to Spain after going there on a business trip.

6. **Biblical or church history personality of the time:** Priest Girolamo Savonarola orders the Bonfire of the Vanities

7. **What was discovered or explored?** He sailed westward to the east coast of Brazil. He was the first to realize that North and South America were separate continents and not a part of Asia.

8. **How?** Spanish Galleon

9. **What was their motivation?** He was part of the crew that later explored further to try and find China and India.

10. **Topography:** rolling hills, plateaus, and rainforests

11. **Climate:** temperate weather year round

12. **Natural resources:** forests and Brazil wood

13. **Crops:** coffee, sugar cane

14. **Exports:** He took 200 Indians and sold them or kept them as slaves. Brazil wood was used for red dye and coffee.

15. **Trivia:** He studied geography books and maps as a hobby. In 1507, French scholars produced a book on geography and math in which they credited Amerigo with discovering the "New World" and named it America.

Cite your sources:

No science assignments for Lesson 7.

No language assignments for Lesson 7.

Teacher's Notes

Lesson 8

1500 - 1519

Day	SCIENTISTS	INVENTIONS	EXPLORERS
Mon		1500 Musket	
		Questionnaire	
Tue	**S-8**		**Vocabulary**
	Ocean Currents & Trade Winds		Gulf Stream
	Map 6		hurricane
			keys (Florida)
			gulf
			peninsula
Wed			1513 Juan Ponce de León explored
			Florida
			Questionnaire
			*Florida
			Mark Map 9
Thu			**Mark South American Indians**
			on Map 12
			Vocabulary
			isthmus
			subtropical
			Pacific
			scurvy
Fri			1513 Vasco de Balboa crossed Panama
			and sighted the Pacific Ocean
			Questionnaire
			*Panama
			Mark Map 9
			*indicates present-day location

LANGUAGE ARTS	READING SELECTIONS
Hobby clubs	**Historical Fiction (read one per lesson)**
L-8a	Daughter of Venice - Donna Jo Napoli
	The Hawk that Dare Not Hunt by Day - Scott O'Dell
Ψ IEW Key Word Outline	Spy for the Night Riders - Dave & Neta Jackson
Read and make a key word outline for the *Reformation*	
Protocol - rules	**Biographies (an alternate for a historical fiction)**
L-8b Worksheet 4	Vasco Nùñez De Balboa - Maureen Ash
	For Kirk and Covenant - Douglas Wilson
Ψ IEW Rough Draft	Ponce de León - Ann Heinrichs
Write a rough draft from your key word outline	Elizabeth and Her Court - Kathryn Hinds
Making motions	**Other Books for Research**
L-8c	The Boy and the Samurai - Erik Christian Haugaard
	The Early Inventions - Robert Ingpen
Ψ IEW Final	The Castles of Henry VIII - Peter Harrington
Write a final using all of your openers and dress-ups	Build a Better Mouse Trap - Ruth Kassinger
Taking minutes	**Historical Events for Timeline**
L-8d	1474-1516 Ferdinand and Isabella reign in Spain
Ψ Use openers and dress-ups	1509-1547 King Henry VIII rules England
	1516 Charles I becomes Holy Roman Emperor
	1517 Beginning of the Reformation in Germany
	1517 End of Moorish rule in Spain
	1517 Church of England founded by King Henry Vlll
	1517 Turks conquer Cairo
	1517 Portuguese meet with the Chinese
Poem: "When I Heard the Learned Astronomer"	**Other Areas of Interest during this Lesson**
L-8e	Aztecs
	Slave trade brought to the New World
Write your mini book report	King Henry VIII of England defies the Pope
	Medici family
	Catherine of Aragon
	Martin Luther
	John Knox
	Paul Revere and William Dawes
	Accomplishments in Math
	1518 Adam Riese writes book on practical arithmetic

Inventions Questionnaire

1. What invention: Musket

2. When: 1500's

3. Who is the inventor (person or country): First seen around Italy in 1530, it had amour piercing bullets. At that time "Italy" was ruled by Emperor Charles of Spain. They were standardized in England and called Cavaliers.

4. Motivation: To improve the ability to maim and kill the enemy from a safe distance.

5. How did this invention change life as it was then? It was lighter and more accurate than other guns of the time period. They were safer than the Matchlocks.

6. What have been the ethical consequences (if any)? It was used in war to take lives. It was used as a deterrent against thieves and assassinations. One person was able to shoot enough food to feed many. The musket continued to develop into more precise weaponry.

7. Diagram or draw the invention:

Cite your sources:

Explorers Questionnaire

1. **Who:** Juan Ponce de Leon

2. **Nationality:** Spanish

3. **When:** 1513

4. **Point of departure:** Puerto Rico and San Salvador
   or
   Sponsoring country: Spain

5. **Was this place the explorer's home country?** No
   Explain: He was from Spain and Puerto Rico was a newly discovered island.

6. **Biblical or church history personality of the time:** Pope Leo X

7. **What was discovered or explored?** Peninsula of Florida (it was named for the Easter season, the Feast of Flowers, "Florida")

8. **How?** He bought and outfitted three ships to seek out the island called Bimini.

9. **What was their motivation?** He was looking for gold and for the Fountain of Youth. He wanted land for the de Leon family.

10. **Topography:** beaches, rolling hills, lakes, and swamps

11. **Climate:** temperate to subtropical

12. **Natural resources:** fish

13. **Crops:** indigenous sweet potatoes, cassava, beans, corn, citrus fruits, and some tobacco

14. **Exports:** The hostile Indians didn't trade.

15. **Trivia:** He served as a knight and became a soldier. He noted the strange power of the Gulf Stream. He could not identify it however, as the Gulf Stream.

Cite your sources:

Explorers Questionnaire

1. **Who:** Vasco Nuñez de Balboa

2. **Nationality:** Spanish

3. **When:** 1513

4. **Point of departure:** Santo Domingo
   or
   Sponsoring country: Spain

5. **Was this place the explorer's home country?** No
   Explain: He was born in Jerez de los Calballera but traveled to, and lived in, Santo Domingo.

6. **Biblical or church history personality of the time:**

7. **What was discovered or explored?** He realized that the continents separated the two oceans and explored South America. He claimed the Pacific Ocean for Spain.

8. **How?** boat and hiking over land

9. **What was their motivation?** He was running away from debt and also wanted adventure.

10. **Topography:** mountains and thick jungle

11. **Climate:** hot and humid

12. **Natural resources:** animals, forests, and fish

13. **Crops:** cassava, bananas, sugarcane, coffee, corn, and beans

14. **Exports:** unknown

15. **Trivia:** He was falsely accused of treason by a person who was jealous of him. He was beheaded for treason.

Cite your sources: http://allaboutexplorers.com/explorers/balboa/ *3/14/2012*

MAP #0

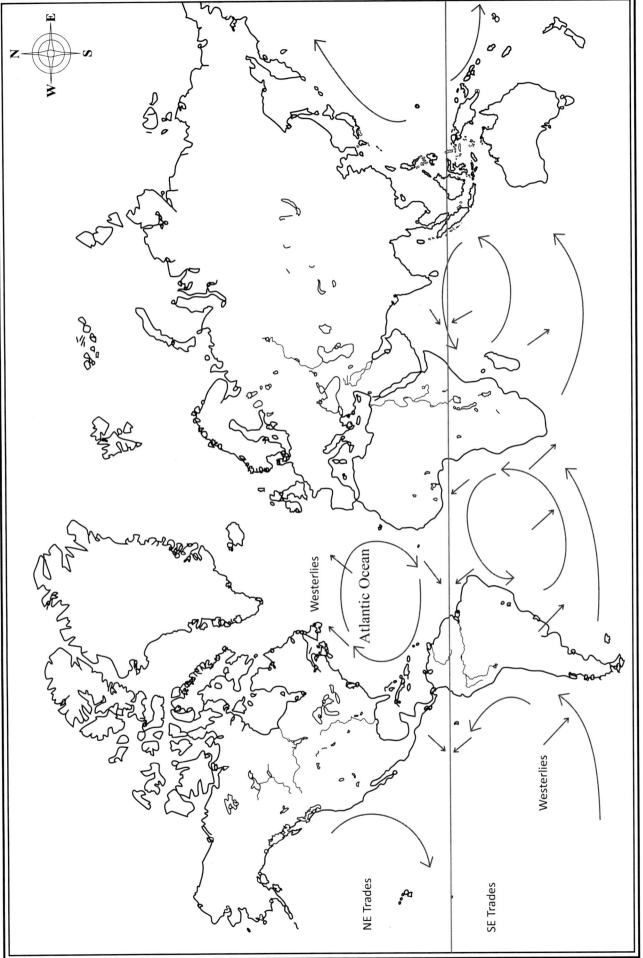

Westerlies

Atlantic Ocean

Westerlies

NE Trades

SE Trades

Equator

→→ Ocean Currents
⇉ Trade Winds

Lesson 8   S-8

Teacher's Notes

Lesson 9

1519 - 1540

Day	SCIENTISTS	INVENTIONS	EXPLORERS
Mon			1519-1521 Hernando Cortés explores
			Mexico, conquers the Aztecs and brings
			horses with him to Mexico.
			Questionnaire
			*Mexico
			Mark Map 9
Tue	**What is the earth's circumference?**		**Draw an Aztec**
			You may draw a man, woman, or child.
			Ship Vocabulary
			cabin
			hatch
			starboard
			port
			winch
Wed			1519-1522 Ferdinand Magellan attempted
			the first voyage around the world.
			Bonus: Did Magellan complete his voyage?
			If not, who did? What happened?
			Questionnaire
			*India
			Mark Map 6
Thu			1531-1535 Francisco Pizarro conquers
			the Incas of Peru.
			Questionnaire
			*Peru
			Mark Map 12
			Draw an Incan warrior
Fri			1539 Hernando de Soto
			First European to explore SE North
			America and crossed the Mississippi
			River
			Questionnaire
			Map 8
			Vocabulary
			expedition
			swamp
			ford
			temperate
			*indicates present-day location

LANGUAGE ARTS	READING SELECTIONS
Preparing for a club meeting	**Historical Fiction (read one per lesson)**
Making calls	Treasure of the Incas - G. A. Henty
L-9a	The Captive - Scott O'Dell
	By Right of Conquest - G. A Henty
Ψ **IEW Lesson 9 - Decorations**	Morning Girl - Michael Dorris
View IEW DVD 4 - *Stylistic Techniques: Decorations*	This was John Calvin - Thea Van Halsema
and Triple Extensions	Dance of the Planets - Nancy Veglahn
Review and study pages 171 and 184-185 in the	
IEW Seminar and Practicum Workbook	
Making Announcements	**Biographies (an alternate for a historical fiction)**
L-9b	*Denotes fictional biography
	*Isabel: Jewel of Castilla, Spain - Carolyn Meyers
IEW Lesson 9	*The Queen's Smuggler - Dave & Neta Jackson
View IEW DVD 4 – *Summarizing a Reference*	*The Betrayer's Fortune - Dave & Neta Jackson
Review pp. 51-52 & following pages in the	
IEW Seminar and Practicum Workbook	Terror on the Amazon - Phil Gates
	Ferdinand Magellan - Milton Meltzer
	Hernando de Soto - Robert Carson
Making Introductions	**Other Books for Research**
L-9c	Valley of the Broken Cherry Trees - Lensey Namioka
	The Inca - Arlette N. Braman
Ψ **IEW Key Word Outline**	Foods & Feasts with the Aztecs - Imogen Dawson
Make a key word outline for the *Aztecs*.	Montezuma and the Fall of the Aztecs - Eric Kimmel
When you are introduced	**Historical Events for Timeline**
L-9d	1516-1556 King Charles I of Spain
	1523 Europeans expelled from China
Ψ **IEW Rough Draft**	1524 Giovanni Verrazano explores coast of N. America
Write a rough draft from your key word outline.	1524 Boer War starts in Germany
	1526 Mogol Emperor Babur founds Mughal Dynasty in Delhi
	1526 Hungary taken by Turks
	1527 Florence becomes a republic
	1534 Cartier explores the coast of Newfoundland
9 Week Quiz	**Other Areas of Interest during this Lesson**
	John Calvin
Write your mini book report	Jesuits
	Counter Reformation
Introducing a speaker	Lady Jane Grey
L-9e	William Tyndale
Ψ **IEW Final**	
Write a final using dress-ups, openers, and decorations	
Use all markings	
Ψ **IEW Bonus:** Psalm 22 uses all the decorations	**Accomplishments in Math**
except one. Can you find them? Which one is missing?	
9 Week Test on Monday	

Explorers Questionnaire

1. **Who:** Ferdinand Magellan

2. **Nationality:** Portuguese

3. **When:** 1519-1522

4. **Point of departure:** Seville, Spain
   or
   Sponsoring country: Spain

5. **Was this place the explorer's home country?** No
   Explain: Magellan renounced his Portuguese nationality and became Spanish because the king did not support his desire to explore a western route to the East.

6. **Biblical or church history personality of the time:** Martin Luther in Germany

7. **What was discovered or explored?** A western sea route around the earth; to Asia and home again.

8. **How?** He sailed west to South America; then south across the Pacific Ocean.

9. **What was their motivation?** He was trying to reach the Spice Islands by a western route.

10. **Topography:** Deccan Plateau of the subcontinent of India

11. **Climate:** Winter is mild to warm days, cool nights. The hot summer is followed by the Monsoon season.

12. **Natural resources:** arable land, and coal

13. **Crops:** tea, rice, cotton, and jute

14. **Exports:** spices, indigo, and textiles

15. **Trivia:** He named the Pacific Ocean for its calmness. He never returned to Spain because he died on the voyage. His ship and remaining crew finished the voyage, successfully circumnavigating the globe.

Cite your sources:

Explorers Questionnaire

1. Who: Hernando Cortés (Hernán Cortéz)

2. Nationality: Spanish

3. When: 1519, the conquest of Mexico

4. Point of departure: Hispaniola, Cuba, the center for Spanish exploration of the New World.
or
Sponsoring country: Spain

5. Was this place the explorer's home country? Yes
Explain: Hispaniola was a Spanish colony in the Spanish Empire.

6. Biblical or church history personality of the time: The Spanish Inquisition was taking place. The bible smuggler, William Tyndale was at work in England.

7. What was discovered or explored? Cortés led an expedition of 600 to Mexico, which was ruled by the Aztecs. He established the colony of Vera Cruz and then conquered Tenochititlán (modern-day Mexico City)

8. How? by ship and over land   He had a few horses. Cortés destroyed his ships to insure that his men would not turn back.

9. What was their motivation? He set out to claim new lands for Spain and to find gold. He wanted more power and conquest.

10. Topography: desert, beaches, and tropical jungles

11. Climate: humid, warm to hot, generally about 60-120 degrees

12. Natural resources: trees, parrots with red feathers, and copper

13. Crops: indigenous sweet potatoes, cassava, beans, corn, and some tobacco

14. Exports: indigenous sweet potatoes, cassava, beans, corn, copper, parrots, and some tobacco

15. Trivia: Cortés studied law but gave that up to go to the New World. First he went to the island of Santo Domingo (now known as the Dominican Republic) in 1504. He was only 19 years old at the time. He stayed there for seven years, and then took part in the Spanish conquest of Cuba in 1511. He became mayor of Santiago de Cuba and stayed there until 1518. He built Mexico City on the Aztec ruins. He became governor of New Spain. In 1524, he explored Honduras. He was called back to Spain in 1528. In 1530, he returned to Mexico. In 1536, he explored the northwest part of Mexico and discovered the Baja California peninsula. He also explored the Pacific side of Mexico. He retired to Seville, Spain in 1539.

Cite your sources: http://www.biography.com/people/hern%C3%A1n-cort%C3%A9s-9258320 4/11/2012

Explorers Questionnaire

1. **Who:** Francisco Pizarro

2. **Nationality:** Spanish

3. **When:** 1531-1535

4. **Point of departure:** Spain to Hispaniola, and Panama
   or
   Sponsoring country: King Charles l of Spain

5. **Was this place the explorer's home country?** Yes
   Explain: Hispaniola was considered part of the Spanish empire.

6. **Biblical or church history personality of the time:** John Calvin

7. **What was discovered or explored?** He explored south of Panama and Peru. He claimed most of South America for Spain.

8. **How?** boat and overland The Spanish had some horses.

9. **What was their motivation?** To explore and conquer territory to the south of Panama. He wanted to rule his own country.

10. **Topography:** Peru has the snow-capped Andean Mountains, plateaus, mountains, hills, valleys, and forests.

11. **Climate:** tropical in the east and dry desert in the west; frigid temperatures in the Andes

12. **Natural resources:** forests, minerals, gold, and silver

13. **Crops:** potatoes, cassava, tomatoes, maize, and coffee

14. **Exports:** potatoes, cassava, tomatoes, maize, lumber, minerals, and coffee

15. **Trivia:** He crossed the Isthmus of Panama with Balboa. He became a citizen of Panama in 1519. He was the conquistador and soldier who led the destruction of the Incan Empire in Peru. The Inca were weakened by inner turmoil in leadership. Pizarro captured the leader, Atahualpa, held him for ransom, and then killed him. He founded Lima as the capital and continued to conquer throughout South America.

Cite your sources:

Explorers Questionnaire

1. **Who:** Hernando de Soto

2. **Nationality:** Spanish

3. **When:** 1539-1542

4. **Point of departure:** Cuba
   or
   Sponsoring country: He paid his own way. He was named governor of Cuba and granted rights to conquer Florida.

5. **Was this place the explorer's home country?** No
   Explain: He was from Spain, but Spain had claim to Cuba.

6. **Biblical or church history personality of the time:** Thomas Cromwell's *Great Bible* is the first English translation to be authorized for public use in English churches.

7. **What was discovered or explored?** He explored Southeast North America from the west coast of Florida. (Present day Florida, North and South Carolina, Alabama, crossed the Mississippi River into Oklahoma, Arkansas and northern Texas.) He spent four years exploring.

8. **How?** ship and over land

9. **What was their motivation?** They were looking for a rich empire to plunder, as well as gold and silver.

10. **Topography:** grasslands, forests, and swamps

11. **Climate:** temperate winters and hot, humid summers

12. **Natural resources:** forests

13. **Crops:** corn, tobacco, beans, and squash

14. **Exports:** The hostile natives did not trade.

15. **Trivia:** He served with Francisco Pizarro in Peru. He died of fever on an expedition in 1542 and was buried by the Mississippi River.

Cite your sources: http://www.newadvent.org/cathen/04753a.htm 4/11/2012

No science assignments for Lesson 9.

No language assignments for Lesson 9.

FIRST QUARTER NINE WEEK QUIZ

MATCH: Match the names on the left with the descriptions on the right. Write the letter of the correct description in the space provided.

C   1.   Juan Ponce de Leon   a. commanded first voyage around the world

E   2.   Christopher Columbus   b. explored across Panama, discovered the Pacific Ocean

A   3.   Ferdinand Magellan   c. explored Florida, searched for the "Fountain of Youth"

F   4.   Vasco da Gama   d. conquered the Inca Empire in Peru

B   5.   Vasco de Balboa   e. discovered the West Indies while looking for China

D   6.   Francisco Pizarro   f. first to sail all the way to India

H   7.   Hernando Cortés   g. explored SE United States and crossed the Mississippi River

I   8.   Amerigo Vespucci   h. explored Mexico, conquered the Aztecs

G   9.   Hernando de Soto   i. explored South America, Americas named after him

MATCH: Match the words on the left with their definitions on the right. Write the letter of the correct definition in the space provided.

C   1.   Trade Winds   a. a religious belief opposed to the doctrine of a church

E   2.   Gulf Stream   b. Spanish conquerors of Central and South America

A   3.   heresy   c. movement of air towards the equator

F   4.   Inquisition   d. the 16th century movement that brought around the formation of Protestant churches

B   5.   conquistador   e. warm ocean current originating in the Gulf of Mexico that follows the east coast

D   6.   Reformation   f. at one time, a tribunal within the church for suppressing heresy

TRUE OR FALSE: Mark each statement T for true or F for false in the space provided.

T   1.   Hernando de Soto was buried by the Mississippi River.

F   2.   Christopher Columbus was Portuguese.

F   3.   Christopher Columbus found the sea route to China.

F   4.   Vasco da Gama found the Cape of Good Hope.

T   5.   America was named after Amerigo Vespucci.

T   6.   Amerigo Vespucci discovered South America was not a part of Asia.

F   7.   Ponce de Leon found the "Fountain of Youth"

T   8.   Vasco de Balboa went across Panama on foot.

T   9.   Vasco de Balboa left for Panama to escape from being put in prison.

F   10.   Hernando Cortés conquered the Maya Indians.

F   11.   Cortés left from Portugal to begin his conquest.

T   12.   The ship Victoria was the only ship of Magellan's to make it back to Spain.

F   13.   Ferdinand Magellan completed his voyage and arrived safely back in Spain.

F   14.   Pizarro treated the Incas better than most of the other conquerors.

T   15.   Pizarro remained the ruler of Peru until his death.

MATCH: Match the location on the left with the discoverer on the right. Write the correct letter in the space provided.

F 1. Panama   a. Magellan

D 2. West Indies   b. Ponce de Leon

G 3. India   c. Vespucci

H 4. Mexico   d. Columbus

E 5. Peru   e. Pizarro

A 6. Voyage around the world   f. Balboa

B 7. Florida   g. Vasco da Gama

C 8. South America   h. Cortés

MULTIPLE CHOICE: Circle the letter of the word or phrase that correctly completes each sentence.

1. The climate of Peru is _____.
   a. cold & wet   b. dry   c. tropical

2. One of Florida's main crops is _____.
   a. tobacco   b. coffee   c. citrus fruit

3. Much of Panama's countryside is covered with _____.
   a. jungle   b. desert   c. canyons

4. The Spanish conquistadors conquered the Indian Empires for their _____.
   a. coffee   b. cocoa   c. gold

5. The Spanish conquerors treatment of the Indians was _____.
   a. helpful   b. cruel & harsh   c. instructional

6. During this time science was hindered by _____.
   a. no new ideas   b. ignorance   c. the Inquisition

7. The Reformation grew out of a desire to _____.
   a. serve God   b. defy the church c. be heretics

BONUS: Match the explorer with the Indians they encountered.

C 1. Columbus   a. Aztec

A 2. Cortés   b. Inca

B 3. Pizarro   c. Maya

Lesson 10

1540 - 1600

Day	SCIENTISTS	INVENTIONS	EXPLORERS
Mon	**9 Week Test**		1540-1542 Francisco de Coronado
			explored and mapped Cibola.
	Science Vocabulary		**Questionnaire**
	star cluster		*northern frontier of New Spain
	nebula		
	galaxy		**Mark Map 8**
	comet		
	asteroid		
	meteor		
Tue	1543 Nicolaus Copernicus showed that		**Vocabulary**
	the earth and other planets revolve		mesa
	around the sun.		canyon
	Questionnaire		butte
			desert
	S-10		
	Look at his book "On the Revolutions		
	of the Heavenly Bodies"		
Wed	**Vocabulary**		1557-1580 Sir Francis Drake - First
	revolve		Englishman to sail around the world
	rotate		**Questionnaire**
			*New Albion - San Francisco area
			Mark Map 6
Thu	**Locate Poland on the globe**	1590 Compound Microscope	**Compare a Spanish Galleon to an**
		Questionnaire	**English Schooner**
	Draw Poland's flag at this time		
			Draw each and label the differences
Fri			**Make a salt map of the known world**
			Salt Dough Recipe
			1/2 cup salt
			1 cup flour
			1/2 cup water
			Mix dry ingredients first, then add
			water as you stir the mixture.
			*indicates present-day location

LANGUAGE ARTS	READING SELECTIONS
Panel discussion	**Historical Fiction (read one per lesson)**
L-10a	Elizabeth l, Red Rose of the House of Tudor - Kathryn Lasky
	By Pike and Dike - G. A. Henty
Ψ IEW Triple Extensions	The Cross by Day, the Mezuzuh by Night - Deborah Siegel
DVD 4 pp.171,176 IEW Seminar & Practicum Workbook	St. Bartholomew's Eve - G. A. Henty
Learn and practice triple extensions	Red Hugh, Prince of Donegal - Robert T. Reilly
	Under Drake's Flag - G. A. Henty
Select topics and questions	**Biographies (an alternate for a historical fiction)**
L-10b	Mary, Queen of Scots, Queen without a Country - Kathryn Lasky
	Mission to Cathay - Madeleine Polland
Ψ IEW Key Word Outline	Johannes Kepler and the New Astronomy - James Voelkel
Make a key word outline for the *Spanish Armada*	Francisco de Coronado - Conrad Stein
The Chairman	**Other Books for Research**
L-10c	Spain in the Age of Exploration - Heather Miller
	One Day in Shakespeare's England - Avis Murton Carter
	Foods & Feasts in Tudor Times - Richard Balkwell
Panel Discussion	
L-10d	
	Historical Events for Timeline
	1558 Queen Elizabeth I rules England
	1565 Spain founds St. Augustine (Florida)
Observation Skills	1566 Netherlands revolt against Spain
L-10e	1571 Venice and Spain defeat the Turks
	1587 England founds Roanoke
Ψ IEW Rough Draft	1588 Spanish Armada defeated by the English
Write a rough draft from your key word outline	1598 King Philip III rules Spain
	1598-1610 King Henry IV of France
	Other Areas of Interest during this Lesson
	Sir Walter Raleigh, England's pirate
	Spanish Armada
Ψ IEW Final	Suleiman the Great
Write final on *Spanish Armada* with dress-ups, openers,	Jesuit Society
and triple extensions.	Protestantism
	Queen Elizabeth I of England
Optional Movie: *Comedy of Errors* or *Merchant of Venice*	Xavier goes to Japan
Write your mini book report	**Accomplishments in Math**
	1550 Rhaeticus writes trigonometric tables
	1576 Francois Viete introduces decimal fractions
	1596 Ludolph van Ceulens gives ratio of the diameter to the
	circumference to twenty places

Scientist Questionnaire

1. **Who:** Nicolaus Copernicus

2. **Nationality:** Polish

3. **Life span:** 1473-1543

4. **Span of research:** The sky was his classroom. He received degrees at several universities and continued research throughout his life.

5. **Biblical or church history event of the time:** John Calvin preaches in France.

6. **Noted achievement & field of interest:** He proposed the heliocentric system of the universe--the sun as the center of the universe. He showed that the earth and other planets revolve and rotate around the sun and that the earth tips on its axis. He was an astronomer and spent his life writing the book, *On the Revolutions of the Heavenly Bodies.*

7. **Secondary achievement & field of interest:** He studied law and medicine. He became a canon of the church and served the people as a doctor. He continued to study the planets and stars.

8. **Motivation:** He wanted to better understand the universe.

9. **Significance of discovery:** It helped others to do further study of the stars and planets.

10. **How was this discovery helpful or harmful to society?** It was helpful because it expanded people's concept of the universe. He made predictions that were proven true with the invention of the telescope.

11. **New word and meaning:** Answers will vary.

12. **Questions prompted through this study?** Answers will vary.

13. **Interesting bit of trivia:** When he died, he did not know how much his discovery changed other people's view of the universe.

Cite your sources:

Inventions Questionnaire

1. **What invention:** Compound Microscope

2. **When:** 1590

3. **Who is the inventor (person or country):** Dutch Zacharias Janssen and his son Hans
   Father of microscopy, Anton van Leeuwenhoek improved magnification and studied bacteria,
   yeast plants, life in a drop of water.
   Englishman Robert Hooke improved on Leeuwenhoek's light microscope and confirmed
   his discoveries.

4. **Motivation:** To be able to see and study microscopic items.

5. **How did this invention change life as it was then?** He became aware that living things are made
   up of cells. People learned how dangerous and unclean things could be. It helped them see health
   aspects they hadn't realized before.

6. **What have been the ethical consequences (if any)?** The ability to see the unseen world made it
   possible to observe and study microorganisms and the effects they have on humans and animals. It
   aided research in the fields of Biology, Botany, and Biochemistry. In some cases, viewing
   previously unseen matter can lead to over-cautiousness about germs and bacteria that can lead to
   over-medication.

7. **Diagram or draw the invention:**

Cite your sources:

Explorers Questionnaire

1. **Who:** Francisco de Coronado

2. **Nationality:** Spanish

3. **When:** 1540-1542

4. **Point of departure:** Comostela, New Spain (modern-day Mexico)
   or
   Sponsoring country: Spain

5. **Was this place the explorer's home country?** No
   Explain: He was a Spanish conquistador.

6. **Biblical or church history personality of the time:** John Calvin

7. **What was discovered or explored?** He explored and mapped the northern frontier of New Spain, (present-day Arizona, New Mexico, California, Oklahoma, Kansas, Texas and Nebraska).

8. **How?** over land, on foot and on horseback They covered over six thousand miles round trip.

9. **What was their motivation?** God, gold, and glory
   Francisco was a younger son and had to find his fortune or work. They were looking for the seven cities of gold. Francisco paid for half of the expedition.

10. **Topography:** deserts, forests, and open plains
    They saw the natural wonders of the Southwest: Grand Canyon, Painted Desert, Great Plains, buffalo herds, Petrified Forest, lava fields, and mud springs.

11. **Climate:** very hot summers and cold winters

12. **Natural resources:** turquoise, silver, cactus, and grasslands

13. **Crops:** corn, beans, and squash

14. **Exports:** self-sufficient villages   turquoise and wool blankets

15. **Trivia:** King Charles I of Spain feared that the conquistadors would create their own empire.

Cite your sources:

Explorers Questionnaire

1. Who: Sir Francis Drake

2. Nationality: English

3. When: 1577-1580

4. Point of departure: Plymouth, England
or
Sponsoring country: England

5. Was this place the explorer's home country? Yes
Explain:

6. Biblical or church history personality of the time: John Knox of Scotland

7. What was discovered or explored? He was the first Englishman to sail around the world. He claimed the San Francisco area for England, naming it New Albion.

8. How? The *Golden Hind* warship galleon and four other vessels, (the *Golden Hind* was the only vessel to return to England).

9. What was their motivation? He tried to find a northern passage between the Pacific and Atlantic Oceans. He was the first Englishman to circumnavigate the globe. He was commissioned by Queen Elizabeth to raid Spanish ships and towns.

10. Topography: hilly

11. Climate: warm winters, and cool summers; cool moist air from the west, dry continental air from the east

12. Natural resources: fish, gold, citrus trees, and forests

13. Crops: citrus fruit, grapes, and sugar beets

14. Exports: fish, gold, citrus fruit, hides, tallow, and wine

15. Trivia: He was a pirate. In 1581, he was knighted by Queen Elizabeth I and became mayor Plymouth. In 1585, he picked up the unsuccessful colonists from Roanoke and returned them to England. He introduced tobacco to England. In 1587, he led the attempt to destroy the Spanish Armada. In 1595, he led a raid against the Spanish West Indies.

Cite your sources: Lathan, Jean Lee. *Drake – The Man They Called a Pirate.* NY: HarperCollins, 1960.

S-10

How did Copernicus show or prove his theory?
Although he was unable to actually prove his theory, it was mathematically strong and in his masterpiece, *On the Revolutions of the Heavenly Spheres* (1543) he demonstrated how the earth's motion could be used to explain the movements of other heavenly bodies. He decided that the simplest and most systematic explanation of heavenly motion required that every planet, including the earth, revolve around the sun. The earth also had to spin around its axis once every day. The earth's motion affects what people see in the heavens, so real motions must be separated from apparent ones.

Draw a diagram of the solar system.   This example is from www.nasa.gov   March 28, 2008

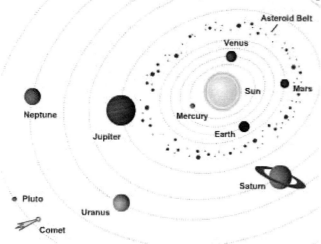

Write their distances from the sun:

Mercury	36 million miles
Venus	67 million miles
Earth	93 million miles
Mars	141.6 million miles
Jupiter	483.3 million miles
Saturn	886.4 million miles
Uranus	1,786 million miles
Neptune	2,794 million miles
Pluto	3,660 million miles Pluto is no longer considered a planet.

What is the difference between astrology and astronomy? Astrology is the study of the effect the stars and their positions have on human affairs, whereas astronomy is the science and study of the heavens and their physical attributes, relative motions, composition, and history.

No language worksheet for Lesson 10

FIRST QUARTER NINE WEEK TEST

MATCH: Match the names on the left with their descriptions on the right. Write the letter of the correct description in the space provided.

C   1. Alexander the Great   a. traveled throughout India & China

E   2. Ptolemy   b. classification of living things

H   3. Hippocrates   c. explored while expanding his empire

A   4. Marco Polo   d. explored Arctic to North America

B   5. Aristotle   e. believed the earth was the center of the universe

D   6. Leif Ericsson   f. explored SE United States and crossed the Mississippi River

J   7. Ferdinand Magellan   g. explored South America

I   8. Francisco Pizarro   h. father of medicine

F   9. Hernando de Soto   i. conquered the Inca Empire in Peru

G   10. Amerigo Vespucci   j. commanded first voyage around the world

gold	sugar	coffee	berries	cattle & sheep
tea & rice	tobacco	silks & spices	Citrus fruit	cocoa

Complete each sentence with a selection from the box above.

1. China's main crops are ___tea & rice.

2. Bartolomeu Dias traded for ___cattle & sheep___ at the cape of South Africa.

3. Marco Polo traded for ___silks & spices___ in China.

4. One of Florida's main crops is ___citrus fruit.___

5. The Indian Empires of the New World were conquered for their ___gold.

TRUE OR FALSE: Write T for true or F for false for each sentence in the space provided.

T   1.   The Strait of Gibraltar was once known as the "Pillars of Hercules".

T   2.   Hieroglyphics were used by the Egyptians.

F   3.   Pytheas was a scientist.

T   4.   Aristarchus believed the sun was the center of the universe.

F   5.   As a child, Alexander the Great was tutored by Euclid.

F   6.   The Vikings wanted to become a great empire.

F   7.   The Vikings found people already settled in Iceland & Greenland.

T   8.   Marco Polo went to China and India to trade.

T   9.   Bartolomeu Dias sailed around the southern tip of Africa.

F   10. Leonardo da Vinci never completed a project because he died.

T   11. The Spanish conquistadors treated the Indians cruelly and harsh.

F   12. Vasco de Balboa went across Panama by ship.

Complete the following exercise:

1. Label the continents and oceans.

2. Draw a line showing the location of the equator.

3. At what two points is it 12 noon at the same time_____?
    a. B & D   b. A & C   c. A & B

4. Label on map using corresponding letter:

E. Spain	K. Italy
F. Portugal	L. Mediterranean Sea
G. West Indies	M. Red Sea
H. China	N. Bering Strait
I. India	O. Great Lakes
J. Egypt	P. England

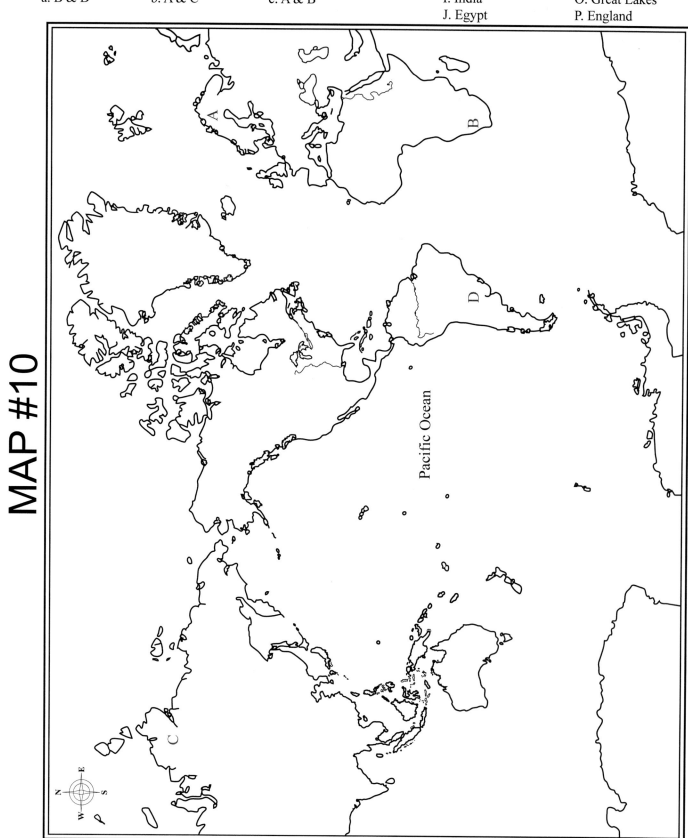

MAP #10

Pacific Ocean

Lesson 11

1600 - 1620

Day	SCIENTISTS	INVENTIONS	EXPLORERS
Mon	**Locate Germany on the globe**	1608 Telescope (magnifying glass)	**Map Vocabulary**
	Germany was made up of several	**Questionnaire**	coordinate
	sovereign states with their own rulers.		degree
	Kepler was born in Swabia in		projection
	SW Germany.		relief map
	Vocabulary		
	orbit		
	ellipse		
Tue	1604 Johannes Kepler discovered the		1609 Samuel de Champlain explored
	distance of the planets from the sun.		the eastern coast of North America to the
	Planets have an elliptical orbit. What		St. Lawrence River
	special instruments did he use for his		**Questionnaire**
	discoveries?		*Lake Champlain area
	Questionnaire		
			Mark Maps 8
	S-11		and **Map 6**
Wed	**Science Vocabulary**		**Locate Lake Champlain and France**
	moon		**on the globe**
	phases		
	waxing		**Vocabulary**
	waning		exploit
	crescent		trapper
	lunar		mutiny
	new moon		river valley
	full moon		
Thu	1610 Galileo Galilei constructs		1609 Henry Hudson explored the NE
	telescopes and explains the phases		coast of North America
	of the moon.		**Questionnaire**
	Questionnaire		*Hudson River Valley (New Amsterdam)
	S-11		**Mark Map 6**
Fri	Galileo wrote the controversial "Dialogue		**Locate England on globe**
	on the Two Great Systems of the World,		
	the Ptolemaic and Copernican".		**Draw the English flag**
			*indicates present-day location

LANGUAGE ARTS	READING SELECTIONS
Root Words	**Historical Fiction (read one per lesson)**
L-11a Worksheet 5	The Corn Raid - James L. Collier
	A Journey to the New World - Kathryn Lasky
Ψ IEW Review your skills	Two Mighty Rivers, Son of Pocahontas - Mari Hanes
Read *The Pilgrims* and create a keyword outline	The Mayflower Secret - Dave and Neta Jackson
Or View DVD 6 & pp 83-108 IEW Seminar &	Our Strange New Land - Patricia Hermes
Practicum Workbook for multiple sources	The Starving Time - Patricia Hermes
	Nzingha, Warrior Queen of Matamba - Patricia McKissack
More Root Words	**Biographies (an alternate for a historical fiction)**
L-11b Worksheet 6	Galileo - Leonard Everett Fisher
	John Smith, English Explorer and Colonist - Tara Baulkusmello
	Galileo: Astronomer and Physicist - Margaret J. Anderson
Prefixes	**Other Books for Research**
L-11c Worksheet 7	Beyond the Sea of Ice: The Voyages of Henry Hudson - Joan Goodman
	Exploration and Empire 1458-1760 - Ann Kramer
Ψ IEW From your outline, write a rough draft	Everyday Life in the Seventeenth Century - Laurence Taylor
	Miles Standish - Susan Martins Miller
Suffixes	**Historical Events for Timeline**
L-11d Worksheet 8	1607 Founding of Jamestown by the English
	1610-1643 King Louis XIII of France
Ψ IEW Write your final using openers,	1618-1648 Thirty Years' War - Spain and Austria defeated
dress-ups & decorations or triple extensions.	1620 Mayflower leaves England with 102 passengers
Use appropriate markings.	1620 Pilgrims found Plymouth
	1620 Kepler's mother arrested for witchcraft
	1620 French Huguenots declare war on King Louis XIII
	1621-1665 King Philip IV of Spain
Compound words	**Other Areas of Interest during this Lesson**
L-11e Worksheet 9	English Captain John Smith
	Pocahontas, Indian Princess
	King James Bible
	Samurai warriors of Japan
	Colonial America
	Mayflower Compact
Write your mini-report	Quakers
	Puritans
Optional Movie: *On the Shoulders of Giants*	**Accomplishments in Math**
	1612 Bartholomew Piticus uses decimal point in his
	trigonometrical tables.
	1620 Edmund Gunter writes treatise on logarithms

Scientist Questionnaire

1. **Who:** Johannes Kepler

2. **Nationality:** German

3. **Life span:** 1571-1630

4. **Span of research:** His whole adult life.

5. **Biblical or church history event of the time:** King James bans the Geneva Bible and its Puritan commentary against the political structure.

6. **Noted achievement & field of interest:** He was an outstanding mathematician. He took over the work of astronomer Tycho Brahe. He discovered the three laws of planetary motion around the sun and completed intensive study of the true orbits of the planets. His last great work was a set of accurate tables of planetary motion.

7. **Secondary achievement & field of interest:** He determined that the moon was responsible for the tides but he did not understand gravity. He continued to study the moon and the comets. He discovered a new star.

8. **Motivation:** He believed in the theory of harmony in geometric figures, numbers, and music and looked for proof for it.

9. **Significance of discovery:** It changed man's view of the sun as the center of our solar system. It put forth ideas of "gravity" and elliptic orbits.

10. **How was this discovery helpful or harmful to society?** It changed the way people viewed the universe. His ideas were proven by Sir Isaac Newton.

11. **New word and meaning:** Answers will vary.

12. **Questions prompted through this study?** Answers will vary.

13. **Interesting bit of trivia:** He was from a poor family and had smallpox when he was three years old. The disease left him with poor eyesight and crippled hands. He began studying for a religious career but the unrest in Germany discouraged him. He studied the works of Copernicus and excelled at astronomy. He became an assistant to Tycho Brahe. Emperor Rudolph II made him the imperial mathematician. In 1610, he received his first telescope. A year later, Rudolph was replaced by his brother Matthias on the Bohemian throne. Kepler was seldom paid on time or in full. He died sick and poor.

Cite your sources:

Scientist Questionnaire

1. **Who:** Galileo Galilei   Father of the Scientific Method

2. **Nationality:** Pisa (Italian)

3. **Life span:** 1564-1642

4. **Span of research:** He studied mathematics and science at the University of Pisa. He continued his research until he died in 1642.

5. **Biblical or church history event of the time:** England became a Protestant nation under Queen Elizabeth I.

6. **Noted achievement & field of interest:** He heard about the invention of the telescope by Hans Lippershey in Holland. Intrigued, he constructed the scientific optical telescope. He made hundreds of telescopes and sent them to scholars all over Europe.

7. **Secondary achievement & field of interest:** He disproved Aristotle's theory of falling bodies. He continued to question Aristotle's other findings. The church put him under house arrest for heresy for the rest of his life because he claimed that Aristotle was wrong about falling objects. He went blind but continued to dictate his scientific thoughts until the end. He, too, spoke of gravity but could not work out the scientific principle behind it.

8. **Motivation:** To convince men of Copernicus' insights.

9. **Significance of discovery:** He used the telescope to observe four of Jupiter's moons and caught a glimpse of the Milky Way. He realized that the Earth and other planets reflect the light of the sun. This explained the different phases of the moon. He described the surface of the moon and identified sunspots.
He proved Copernicus' theory. He saw the planets that Copernicus predicted. Under penalty of death and excommunication, Galileo was forced to deny his findings.

10. **How was this discovery helpful or harmful to society?** It advanced what men knew of the heavens and challenged the beliefs of the church at that time.

11. **New word and meaning:** Answers will vary.

12. **Questions prompted through this study?** Answers will vary.

13. **Interesting bit of trivia:** His work on the motion of bodies opened a new branch of physics known as mechanics.

Cite your sources: http://inventors.about.com/od/gstartinventors/a/Galileo_Galilei.htm *3/7/2012*

Inventions Questionnaire

1. **What invention:** Telescope

2. **When:** 1608

3. **Who is the inventor (person or country):** Hans Lippershey (1570-1619) of Holland is often credited with the invention. However, Italian scientist Galileo Galilei introduced it to astronomy.

4. **Motivation:** To be able to see things far away better, on land and in space. He became the first man to see the craters on the moon, discover sun spots, and see the four large moons of Jupiter, as well as the rings of Saturn.

5. **How did this invention change life as it was then?** They could see the stars and planets better. The phases of the moon were observed and noted.

6. **What have been the ethical consequences (if any)?** Most of the uses of the telescope are positive. We have learned much about the universe and the unseen world. However, it has also been used to spy on others. Most citizens consider this an invasion of privacy.

7. **Diagram or draw the invention:**

Cite your sources:

Explorers Questionnaire

1. **Who:** Samuel de Champlain

2. **Nationality:** French

3. **When:** 1606

4. **Point of departure:** France to Quebec
   or
   Sponsoring country: He was sent by King Henry IV of France.

5. **Was this place the explorer's home country?** Yes
   Explain:

6. **Biblical or church history personality of the time:** Jacobus Arminius argues that predestination is based on fore-knowledge.

7. **What was discovered or explored?** He established Quebec, a settlement on the St. Laurence River, and explored rivers and woods in the northland. He was the first European to see Lake Champlain.

8. **How?** In Canada, they used mostly birch bark canoes and traveled over land. They went south to Lake Champlain.

9. **What was their motivation?** They were still looking for a western route to Asia and France wanted to get their share of the New World. The French king wanted a settlement for French settlers. They were to establish the fur trade and build relationships with the Huron-Algonquin tribes.

10. **Topography:** woodlands and crop land

11. **Climate:** cool summers and very cold winters with lots of snow

12. **Natural resources:** forests, marsh grain, and wild animals

13. **Crops:** marsh grain harvested

14. **Exports:** fur and timber

15. **Trivia:** He is known as the "Father of New France" and he organized the fur trade. He founded Quebec in Canada. He was a geographer and cartographer.
    He was not yet twenty when he made his first voyage with his uncle to Spain and from there to the West Indies and South America. He visited Porto Rico (now Puerto Rico), Mexico, Colombia, the Bermudas and Panama. Between 1603 and 1635, he made 12 trips to North America.

Cite your sources: http://www.thecanadianencyclopedia.com/articles/samuel-de-champlain 3/7/2012

191   History's Masterminds - *TRISMS©*

Explorers Questionnaire

1. **Who:** Henry Hudson

2. **Nationality:** English

3. **When:** 1609

4. **Point of departure:** Dutch island of Texel
   or
   Sponsoring country: Englishman working for the Dutch East India Company

5. **Was this place the explorer's home country?** Yes

6. **Biblical or church history personality of the time:** John Smyth founds the Baptist Church

7. **What was discovered or explored?** He sailed along the northeast coast of America. He followed the waterway 150 miles up the Hudson River and claimed the land as New Amsterdam (present day Albany).

8. **How?** by ship, the *Half Moon*

9. **What was their motivation?** They set out to find a quick way to the Spice Islands by a Northwest Passage, to plunder the Spanish, to set up trade with natives of America, and to find land for settlement.

10. **Topography:** hills and lowlands, river valleys, and forest

11. **Climate:** -32 to 95 degrees

12. **Natural resources:** fish, woodland animals, fresh water, evergreens, sugar maples, and trees for lumber

13. **Crops:** good soil to grow crops, blueberries, cranberries, grapes, grain, and forests

14. **Exports:** Furs that the Indians traded with white explorers.

15. **Trivia:** After returning from his first voyage, the English government seized his ship and required him to work for England. In 1610, he made a second voyage for England sponsored by merchants in search of a Northeast Passage. On his second voyage he and his loyal crew members, including his son, died in the New World. They were abandoned in the Hudson Bay after the rest of the crew mutinied.

Cite your sources:

S-11
What is an elliptical orbit?
An elliptical orbit is oval in shape and is the mathematical shape that all orbiting bodies assume in orbiting around their gravitational partner. It is not circular, and therefore is extremely stable.

On your diagram of the solar system write how many days it takes each planet to rotate and to revolve around the sun:

Time to rotate around the sun in earth days or years

Mercury	88 days
Venus	224.7 days
Earth	365.3 days
Mars	687 days
Jupiter	11.9 years
Saturn	29.5 years
Uranus	84.1 years
Neptune	164.8 years

Discuss how rotation and revolution of the planets determines the lengths of days and years:
Day and night are caused by the earth's rotation, which is counterclockwise. Standing on earth, a person sees the sun rise in the east and set in the west because the earth rotates toward the east, causing it to appear that the sun is moving towards the west. Actually, it is the earth that is moving. For instance, when you are riding on a merry-go-round the people standing on the ground look like they are moving, but it is you that is moving. The earth rotates on its axis once every 24 hours and takes about one year (365 days) to revolve around the sun. The seasons are caused by the earth's revolution around the sun, as well as the tilt of the earth's axis. Revolution refers to the earth's orbit around the sun.

Do these planets follow the same orbital plane?
The planets do not follow the same orbital plane.

Diagram and explain the phases of the moon. In a dark room, do an experiment showing the phases of the moon with a flashlight and a ball or globe.

The phases of the moon are:
Waxing Crescent - The moon appears to be partly illuminated but it is less than half. It is increasing.
First Quarter - One-half of the moon is illuminated. It is increasing
Waxing Gibbous - The moon appears to be more than half but not wholly illuminated. It is increasing.
Full Moon - The moon appears to be fully illuminated.
Waning Gibbous - The moon appears to be more than half but not wholly illuminated. It is decreasing.
Last Quarter - One-half of the moon is illuminated. It is decreasing.

Worksheet 5

Root Words
Using your knowledge of these root words, match the following words with its definition.

Astronomy ---------------the study of the stars

Biology-------------------the study of life

Geography----------------the study of the earth

Mandate------------------hand over authority

Telephone-----------------an instrument used to talk from a distance

Worksheet 6

Root Words
Using your knowledge of these root words, match the following words with their definitions.

Automatic----------------------moves by itself

Benefit-------------------------a favor

Century------------------------a sequence of 100 years

Magnify-----------------------make larger

Sympathy---------------------sameness of feeling

Visible-------------------------able to be seen

Worksheet 7

Prefixes

Each of these words has a prefix. Read the words and match each with its definition.

postpone-----------------------------put off, delay

interact-----------------------------act on each other

compose-----------------------------create, as in music

prepay-----------------------------pay before

transform-----------------------------change form

disobey-----------------------------not obey

protrude-----------------------------thrust forth

supercharge-----------------------------overload

concern-----------------------------sincere interest

nonsense-----------------------------makes no sense

rebound-----------------------------bounce back

submerge-----------------------------place under water

Worksheet 8

Suffixes

A suffix is one or more letters or syllables added to the end of a root word to change its meaning.

Write the root word and suffix for each word below:

	Root word	**Suffix**
comparable	**compare**	**able**
truly	**true**	**ly**
international	**nation**	**al**
artistic	**artist**	**ic**
glamorous	**glamour**	**ous**
difference	**differ**	**ence**
selfish	**self**	**ish**
helpful	**help**	**ful**
playing	**play**	**ing**
excitement	**excite**	**ment**

More practice:
Circle the root words*

invention   **power**ful   **mission**ary   sub**tropics**

founder   un**lock**   non**violent**   semi**circle**

impressionist   **develop**ment   Mid**west**   circum**navigate**

* answers in bold reflect what student should circle

Worksheet 9

Compound Words
Draw a vertical line between the words that make up each compound word below. Write the word in the blank beside its definition.

under\water   self\less   snow\man

earth\quake   bird\house   common\place

1. earthquake

2. selfless

3. birdhouse

4. underwater

5. commonplace

6. snowman

More practice:
Draw a line dividing the compound words into two shorter words. Then draw a line to its meaning.

head\waters-----------------------the source of a stream

time\line--------------------------a graph reflecting dates and events

red\coats--------------------------one wearing a red coat: British soldier

master\piece----------------------anything done with extraordinary skill

over\throw------------------------to cause to fall or fail; defeat

free\hand--------------------------drawn by hand without help of a ruler or guide

Lesson 12

1620 - 1680

Day	SCIENTISTS	INVENTIONS	EXPLORERS
Mon	1628 William Harvey described how blood circulates through the body.		**Locate, name & learn the Great Lakes**
			Lake Erie
	Questionnaire		Lake Ontario
			Lake Michigan
	What do you think about using animals		Lake Superior
	for research?		Lake Huron
Tue	**Diagram how the heart works as a**	1668 Reflecting telescope	**Vocabulary**
	pump	**Questionnaire**	Jesuit
	S-12		Counter Reformation
			shoal
			boundary
			bank (river)
Wed	**Locate major arteries and show how to**		1673 Louis Joliet and Jacques Marquette
	prevent bleeding of an injury by control		explored the northern Mississippi River.
	of circulation.		**Questionnaire**
			*area along the river
			Mark Map 8
Thu	**Vocabulary**		1681-1682 Sieur de La Salle explored the
	pulse		Great Lakes and claimed the Mississippi
	arteries		River valley for France.
	veins		**Questionnaire**
	capillaries		*area along the river
	circulation		
			Mark Map 8
Fri			**Vocabulary**
			savannah
			plain
			valley
			mouth (river)
			*indicates present-day location

LANGUAGE ARTS	READING SELECTIONS
Common and Proper Nouns	**Historical Fiction (read one per lesson)**
L-12a	Won by the Sword - G. A. Henty
	Wheel of the Moon - Sandra Forrester
	Duncan's War - Douglas Bond
	The Whispering Rod - Nancy Kelley
	When London Burned - G. A. Henty
	King's Arrow - Douglas Bond
	Nell of Branford Hall - William Wise
	The Witch of Blackbird Pond - Elizabeth George Speare
Pronouns	**Biographies (an alternate for a historical fiction)**
L-12b	Captain Kidd - Aileen Weintraub
	*Traitor of the Tower - Dave & Neta Jackson
Ψ **IEW Summarizing Narrative Stories**	*Hostage on the Nighthawk - Dave & Neta Jackson
Review IEW DVD 3 - *Retelling Narrative Stories*	William Harvey: Discoverer of How Blood Circulates - M. J. Anderson
Review Seminar & Practicum Workbook pp. 31-50	Benedict Arnold from Patriot to Traitor - Pamela Dell
	*denotes fictional biography
Verbs	**Other Books for Research**
L-12c	Colonial Days - David C. King
	The Man Who Made Time Travel - Kathryn Lasky
Ψ **IEW Story Sequence Chart**	Journal of the Plague Years - Daniel Defoe
Create a keyword outline using the Story Sequence Chart	Jahanara: Princess of Princesses - Kathryn Lasky
(p. 31 IEW Seminar & Practicum Workbook)	Renaissance and Discovery-History of the World - Peter Bedrick Books
	Plays of Great Achievers - Sylvia Kamerman
Adjectives	**Historical Events for Timeline**
L-12d	1625-1649 Charles I reigns in England
	1642-1660 English Civil Wars
Ψ **IEW Summarize your story in three paragraphs**	1643-1715 King Louis XIV of France
This is your rough draft	1660-1685 King Charles II reigns in England
	1664 England takes New York and New Jersey from the Dutch
	1669 Triple alliance against France
	1669 England takes control of Bombay India
	1670 England & France sign anti-Dutch treaty
Adverbs	**Other Areas of Interest during this Lesson**
L-12e	William Penn
	John Winthrop
Ψ **IEW Final Paper**	Roger Williams
Write your final paper with required stylistic techniques.	Mary Rolandson
Don't forget to double space.	King Philip, Indian Chief
	Squanto, friend to the Pilgrims
Write your mini book report	Anne Hutchinson, religious leader
3 Week Quiz	**Accomplishments in Math**
	1629 Brackets and other abbreviations introduced in mathematics
	1631 William Oughtred proposes symbol "x" for multiplication
	1639 Gerard Desargues writes a book on modern geometry

Scientist Questionnaire

1. **Who:** William Harvey

2. **Nationality:** English

3. **Life span:** 1578-1657

4. **Span of research:** He began in his adult life and continued until his death. He became a doctor and served King Charles I.

5. **Biblical or church history event of the time:** Oppression of Puritans in England

6. **Noted achievement & field of interest:** He explained the role of the heart. He dissected animals from the Royal Park and observed that the heart works as a muscle and like a pump. It has valves that prevent the blood from flowing in reverse. He timed the beating and the amount of blood that pumped through the heart.

7. **Secondary achievement & field of interest:** This discovery led him to study the flow of blood. He realized that blood must flow in a circle, starting at the heart and circulating through the body and back to the heart. He observed that blood flows through the veins to the heart, and that the arteries carry the blood away from the heart.

8. **Motivation:** He was a doctor and wanted to continue his education in the study of the body.

9. **Significance of discovery:** Doctors had a better understanding of the heart as a pump.

10. **How was this discovery helpful or harmful to society?** Doctors could better help their patients with heart and circulatory problems.

11. **New word and meaning:** Answers will vary.

12. **Questions prompted through this study?** Answers will vary.

13. **Interesting bit of trivia:** He was elected president of the college of physicians, but declined because of his failing health.

Cite your sources:

Inventions Questionnaire

1. What invention: Reflecting Telescope

2. When: 1672

3. Who is the inventor (person or country): British - Sir Isaac Newton got the idea from a book on optics by James Gregory.

4. Motivation: To improve and build a working telescope. Instead of glass lenses, a curved mirror was used to gather in light and reflect it back to a point of focus.

5. How did this invention change life as it was then? It helped people learn more about space and not just know about it. They could actually see it.

6. What have been the ethical consequences (if any)? The idea has continued to be improved and has been helpful for scientific studies of the Universe. Using a larger mirror multiplies the amount of light that can be reflected.

7. Diagram or draw the invention:

Explorers Questionnaire

1. **Who:** Louis Joliet and Father Jacques Marquette

2. **Nationality:** Canadian trapper and French priest

3. **When:** 1673-1697

4. **Point of departure:** St. Ignace, New France
   or
   Sponsoring country: France

5. **Was this place the explorer's home country?** Yes
   Explain: New France was part of the French Empire

6. **Biblical or church history personality of the time:** John Eliot – Apostle to the Indians

7. **What was discovered or explored?** They went to Quebec, then present-day Michigan and Wisconsin and down 700 miles of the Mississippi River to the Arkansas River. They turned back when friendly Indians let them know they had reached Spanish territory and that the Mississippi emptied into the Gulf of Mexico and not the Pacific Ocean.

8. **How?** They traveled mostly by canoe and portage over land. Five trappers and Father Marquette also made the trip.

9. **What was their motivation?** Their motivation was to convert the Indians to Christianity, and to trade. They were to claim more land for France and ascertain if there was a Northwest Passage along the great river.

10. **Topography:** river valley from (present day Michigan) to within 400 miles of the gulf.

11. **Climate:** -15 degrees to 95 degrees They traveled in spring and summer.

12. **Natural resources:** roots, berries, and marsh grain

13. **Crops:** beans, maize, corn, and grapes

14. **Exports:** lumber, fish, and furs

15. **Trivia:** The return trip to Canada was against the current and very difficult. Father Marquette was a Jesuit priest. He died shortly after his return. The government of New France gave Joliet Anticosti Island in the Gulf of St. Lawrence as a reward for his service.

Cite your sources:

Explorers Questionnaire

1. Who: Robert Sieur de La Salle

2. Nationality: French

3. When: 1679-1682

4. Point departure: Illinois River
or
Sponsoring country: King Louis XlV of France

5. Was this place the explorer's home country? Yes
Explain: New France was a part of the French Empire.

6. Biblical personality of the time: 1678 John Bunyan publishes *Pilgrim's Progress*

7. What was discovered or explored? He explored the Great Lakes in 1679. In 1681, he explored Lake Michigan, the Ohio River, Illinois River, Mississippi River, present-day Louisiana, Texas, and parts of Mexico.

8. How? by the ship, *Le Griffon*, in 1679
In 1681–82, 50 men set out (half French, half Indian) by canoe and portage to explore the waterways to the Gulf of Mexico.

9. What was their motivation? Pioneer a trade route southward across North America, and to claim new lands for France. They named them Louisiana in honor of their king.

10. Topography: thousands of rivers, hills, Allegheny and Rocky Mountains, desert, plains, and savannahs

11. Climate: -25 degrees to 100 degrees

12. Natural resources: wild animals, forest and land

13. Crops: corn, squash, and maize

14. Exports: furs and timber

15. Trivia: His real name was Rene-Robert Cavelier. He took the name La Salle from the name of his family's estate. His final expedition was in 1684. He left Cuba but sailed past the mouth of the Mississippi and became hopelessly lost. By 1687, the men mutinied and shot LaSalle. They deserted him in present-day Texas.

Cite your sources: http://library.thinkquest.org/J002678F/la_salle. Htm 4/11/2012

S-12
What is the function of the heart?
The function of the heart is to move blood, oxygen and nutrients throughout the body.

Diagram how the heart works as a pump. Label its main parts and define their functions.
The following parts of the heart should be defined and labeled:
Diagram provided by http://texasheart.org/HIC/Anatomy/anatomy2.cfm 3/6/2008

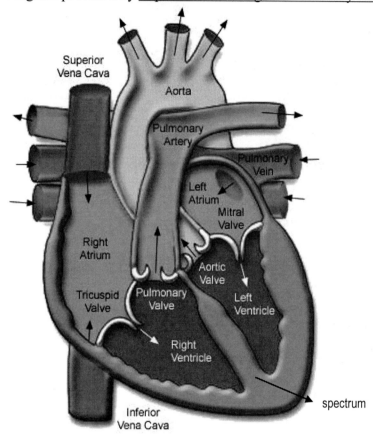

Septum – A wall that separates the right and left sides of the heart.
Left Atrium – Pumps oxygenated blood into the left ventricle
Left Ventricle - It receives oxygenated blood from the left atrium via the mitral valve, and pumps it into the aorta via the aortic valve.
Right Atrium - The thin-walled chamber of the heart which pumps blood into the right ventricle for ejection into pulmonary circulation.
Right Ventricle - It receives de-oxygenated blood from the right atrium via the tricuspid valve, and pumps it into the pulmonary artery via the pulmonary valve.
Aorta - The largest artery in the human body, the aorta originates from the left ventricle of the heart and brings oxygenated blood to all parts of the body in the systemic circulation.
Valve - The heart valves are valves in the heart that maintain the unidirectional flow of blood by opening and closing, depending on the difference in pressure on each side.

No language worksheet with Lesson 12

SECOND QUARTER THREE WEEK QUIZ

MATCH: Match the names on the left with their description on the right. Write the letter of the correct description in the space provided.

E 1. Hernando de Soto

a. discovered planets follow an elliptical orbit

I 2. Henry Hudson

b. discovered the Grand Canyon and explored the SW of North America

H 3. Francis Drake

c. explored along the northern Mississippi River

A 4. Johannes Kepler

d. constructed a telescope, studied phases of the moon

B 5. Coronado

e. explored SE North America looking for gold

C 6. Louis Joliet and Jacques Marquette

f. made discoveries about the heart and circulation

D 7. Galileo

g. explored eastern coast of North America & along the St. Lawrence River

G 8. Champlain

h. first Englishman to sail around the world

J 9. La Salle

i. explored NE coast of North America, many bodies of water named for him

F 10. William Harvey

j. explored the Great Lakes

TRUE OR FALSE: Mark each statement T for true or F for false in the space provided.

T 1. Galileo disproved many of Aristotle's theories.

F 2. Galileo invented the first telescope.

T 3. William Harvey discovered the heart works as a pump.

F 4. William Harvey also made important discoveries about gravity.

T 5. Isaac Newton made improvements on the telescope.

MULTIPLE CHOICE: Circle the letter next to the word or phrase that correctly completes the sentence.

1. The climate of southwest North America is _____.
   a. mild   <u>b. hot</u>   c. cold

2. Fur and timber in North America are abundant in the _____ region.
   a. south western   <u>b. northern</u>   c. central

3. The Mississippi River is a boundary for these present-day states_____.
   <u>a. Missouri, Iowa</u>   b. California, Arizona   <u>c. Mississippi, Alabama</u>

4. The Grand Canyon was discovered by _____.
   a. Francis Drake   <u>b. De Soto</u>   <u>c. Coronado</u>

5. The Grand Canyon is in _____.
   <u>a. Arizona</u>   b. New Mexico   c. Colorado

Label map using the corresponding letters.
A Mississippi River   C *Pikes Peak   E Florida   G Pacific Ocean   I Gulf of Mexico
B Rocky Mountains   D *Grand Canyon   F Atlantic Ocean   H Hudson Bay   J Great Lakes
* general location acceptable

BONUS: Name the Great Lakes.
Lake Ontario   Lake Huron   Lake Michigan   Lake Erie   Lake Superior

Label map using the corresponding letter.

A. Mississippi River
B. Rocky Mountains
C. *Pikes Peak
D. *Grand Canyon
E. Florida
*general location acceptable

F. Atlantic Ocean
G. Pacific Ocean
H. Hudson Bay
I. Gulf of Mexico
J. Great Lakes

Name lakes here:
Lake Ontario
Lake Huron
Lake Michigan
Lake Erie
Lake Superior

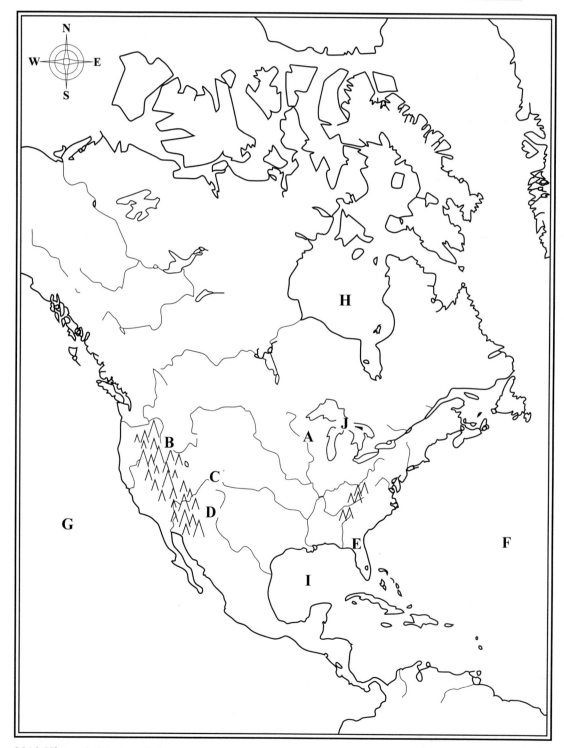

Lesson 13

1680 -1760

Day	SCIENTISTS	INVENTIONS	EXPLORERS
Mon	**Science Vocabulary**		
	motion		
	body		
	outside force		
	action		
	reaction		
	gravity		
	mass		
Tue	1685 Sir Isaac Newton explained motion and gravity mathematically.		**Vocabulary**
			tundra
	Questionnaire		belt
			barren
	S-13		territory
			Navy
Wed			1725 Vitus Bering proved that Asia and North America are separated by water.
			Questionnaire
			Mark Map 4
Thu	1753 Carolus Linnaeus established a system for classifying animals and plants.		**Draw Denmark's flag**
	Questionnaire		**Draw the flag of Vitus Bering's sponsoring country.**
	S-13		
Fri	**Vocabulary**		
	kingdom		
	species		
	phylum		
	protist		
	moneran		
	vertebrate		
	invertebrate		
	exoskelaton		
			*indicates present-day location

LANGUAGE ARTS	READING SELECTIONS
Prepositions	**Historical Fiction (read one per lesson)**
L-13a	Orange and Green - G. A. Henty
	The Ransom of Mercy Carter - Caroline Cooney
Ψ IEW Summarizing Narrative Stories	The Ghost in the Tokaido Inn - Dorothy & Thomas Hoobler
Read *Peter the Great*	Echohawk - Lynda Durrant
Create a key word outline using the Story Sequence Chart	Turtle Clan Journey - Lynda Durrant
(see page 39 in the Seminar & Practicum Workbook)	Saturnalia - Paul Fleischman
	Calico Bush - Rachel Field
	The Chimney Sweep's Ransom - Dave & Neta Jackson
Conjunctions	**Biographies (an alternate for a historical fiction)**
L-13b	Isaac Newton: Discovering Laws that Govern the Universe - M. White
	Ben Franklin - Bruce Fish
IEW Rough Draft	Frederick the Great - Mary Kittredge
Create a rough draft of your story on Peter the Great	Young Man from the Piedmont - Leonard Wibberly
	Isaac Newton: The Greatest Scientist of All Time - Margaret Anderson
	Exploring the Frontier - Carter Smith
Interjections	**Other Books for Research**
L-13c	The Man Who Made Time Travel - Kathryn Lasky
	The Empire of the Czars - Esther Carrion
Ψ IEW Final Give your story a title and clinchers,	Russian Foods and Culture - Jennifer Ferro
openers, 3 dress-ups, and one decoration and	The Longitude Prize - Joan Dash
one triple extension in each paragraph.	Snowflake Bentley - Jacqueline Briggs Martin
Kinds of sentences	**Historical Events for Timeline**
L-13d	1685 All China ports open to foreign trade
	1685-1688 James II reigns in England
	1688 Glorious Revolution William and Mary reign in England
	1715-1774 King Louis XV of France
	1740-1780 Empress Maria Theresa of Austria
	1740-1786 King Frederick the Great of Prussia
	1740-1786 Czar Peter the Great of Russia
	1754-1763 French and Indian War
Grammar notebooks	**Other Areas of Interest during this Lesson**
L-13e	Peter the Great
	Ben Franklin
	Gregorian calendar
	James Watts
Write your mini book report	Sarah Noble
	Jonathan Edwards
	NW Passage
Optional Movie: *The Three Musketeers* (1948 version)	**Accomplishments in Math**
	1715 Brook Taylor invents the calculus of finite differences

Scientist Questionnaire

1. **Who:** Sir Isaac Newton

2. **Nationality:** English

3. **Life span:** 1642-1727

4. **Span of research:** In 1665 he left school and the city because of the plague. He was nagged by the question, "What is it that makes the planets go around the sun"?

5. **Biblical or church history event of the time:** Edict of Nantes is revoked.

6. **Noted achievement & field of interest:** He worked with motion and gravity through mathematics. He developed the Laws of Motion and the Universal Law of Gravitation.

7. **Secondary achievement & field of interest:** He also worked with lenses, prisms, and chemicals. He learned that ordinary white light is made up of all the colors. He used this finding to improve the telescope. He developed the reflecting telescope (1672).

8. **Motivation:** He loved school and was very curious about new things and why they behaved a certain way.

9. **Significance of discovery:** His research made it possible to learn more about the solar system, how gravity works, and other laws that later led to the development of airplanes and other instruments.

10. **How was this discovery helpful or harmful to society?** Newton wasn't interested in publishing his ideas because he didn't like distractions. Edmund Halley finally saw to the publication of Newton's *Principia*. It helped us know more about the world around us. It proved the theories of Copernicus, Galileo, and Kepler.

11. **New word and meaning:** Answers will vary.

12. **Questions prompted through this study?** Answers will vary.

13. **Interesting bit of trivia:** Legends say that he began his studies into gravity after an apple fell on his head. It took him years to formulate the principle of gravity. He also invented calculus.

"If I have seen further than others," Newton once said, "it is only because I have stood on the shoulders of giants who have come before me."

Cite your sources:

Scientist Questionnaire

1. **Who:** Carolus Linnaeus   Father of Taxonomy and modern Ecology

2. **Nationality:** Swedish

3. **Life span:** 1707-1778

4. **Span of research:** He was interested in plants from a young age. He entered university in 1727 to study medicine.

5. **Biblical or church history event of the time:** Isaac Newton writes *An Historical Account of Two Notable Corruptions of Scripture*

6. **Noted achievement & field of interest:** He established a system for naming, ranking, and classifying organisms. In 1735 he published the *Systema Naturae*. Linnaeus simplified naming by designating one Latin name to indicate the genus, and one shortened name for the species. The two names make up the **binomial** ("two names") species name. He continued to develop a convenient way of categorizing the elements of the natural world. It expanded to include animals and minerals.

7. **Secondary achievement & field of interest:** Linnaeus also defined the concept of "race", based on place of origin and skin color. A list of attributes he attached to the races favored Europeans.

8. **Motivation:** He believed the study of nature would reveal the Divine Order of God's creation, and it was the naturalist's task to construct a "natural classification" that would reveal this Order in the universe.

9. **Significance of discovery:** In 1741, he became a professor at Uppsala. He restored the botanical garden and inspired a generation of students. He helped arrange for his students to be sent on trade and exploration voyages to record new findings. He provided them with a method to identify these new discoveries.

10. **How was this discovery helpful or harmful to society?** It provided a simpler way to classify the natural world at a time when exploration and discovery were taking place. Today, much of his work is still used in the biological sciences. His list of racial attributes was biased and harmful to society.

11. **New word and meaning:** Answers will vary.

12. **Questions prompted through this study?** Answers will vary.

13. **Interesting bit of trivia:** At this time, botany was part of a medical degree because doctors had to make their medicines.
    He was one of the pioneers in the field of chronobiology, and created the "Petal Time Clock". His findings found that different species of flowers open at different times during the day.
    He is also the Father of Modern Ecology.

Cite your sources: http://www.academickids.com/encyclopedia/index.php/Carolus_Linnaeus 4/11/2012

Explorers Questionnaire

1. **Who:** Vitus Jonassen Bering

2. **Nationality:** Danish

3. **When:** 1728

4. **Point of departure:** St. Petersburg, Russia
   or
   Sponsoring country: Tsar Peter the Great of Russia

5. **Was this place the explorer's home country?** No
   Explain: Vitus was Danish but was in the Russian Navy.

6. **Biblical or church history personality of the time:** Moravian missionaries

7. **What was discovered or explored?** He proved that Asia and North America are separated by water, making the possibility of a NE Passage to China realistic.

8. **How?** He crossed Russia by land to reach the Kamchatka Peninsula where he built a boat and then traveled through the Bering Strait to prove they were separate continents.

9. **What was their motivation?** He wanted to know if Siberia and North America were connected.

10. **Topography:** Russia, north along the Arctic is barren tundra. Below this is a belt of forests and then the steppe, with a boundary of mountains and deserts.

11. **Climate:** -70 to 75 degrees - short, hot summers and long, and cold winters

12. **Natural resources:** copper, gold, silver, lead, forests, wild animals and fresh water

13. **Crops:** None grow in Siberia

14. **Exports:** They traded gold and furs with China.

15. **Trivia:** During the Great Northern Expedition of 1733-1743, Bering mapped much of the coast of Siberia and Alaska. He spent nearly twenty years exploring the Siberian coast. He died of scurvy while returning home from Alaska. The island he died on was named after him. The first Russian colony in Alaska was settled in 1784.

Cite your sources:

S-13
You can bend light by holding a piece of crystal up to a window so that it reflects the sunlight onto the wall. Or, place a mirror in a glass of water and position the mirror so that it reflects the sunlight onto the wall. Examine the rainbow colors.

Will these colors always be the same? Yes

Will they always be in the same order? Yes

Why? The colors are different wavelength.

What are the colors in their order? red, orange , yellow, green, blue, indigo, violet from longest to shortest wave length.

Describe Linnaeus' system of classification. Linnaeus' system of classification is known as binomial nomenclature. It assigns a two-word Latin name to each individual organism. The first word is the genus and the second is the species name, which is often descriptive. For example, the house cat which is named Felis domesticus versus its relation, the lion, which is Felis leo.

Was he influenced by Aristotle? Yes.

Compare their findings and methods. How are they different?
Linnaeus was influenced by the philosophy of Aristotle, but also by Christian theology. Linnaeus followed a typological (based on a small amount of characteristics) species concept: species were perfect entities, each with a unique "essence", created by God. Within a species, any variation was unimportant.

Is Linnaeus' system still used today? Our modern system has it's roots in Linnaeus' work. Linnaeus is best known for his introduction of the method still used to formulate the <u>scientific name</u> of every species. However, the discovery of the New World and research done by Charles Darwin caused adaptations to be made.

No language worksheet on Lesson 13

Teacher's Notes

Lesson 14

1760 - 1790

Day	SCIENTISTS	INVENTIONS	EXPLORERS
Mon		1764 Spinning Jenny	
		Questionnaire	
Tue			1768-1779 James Cook explored the
			South Pacific. What unusual event did he
			witness?
			Questionnaire
			*Tahiti
			Mark Map 10
Wed			**Vocabulary**
			reef
			monsoon
			squall
			glacier
			floes
			sound
			kayak
Thu		1783 Hot Air Balloon	
		Questionnaire	
Fri			

LANGUAGE ARTS	READING SELECTIONS
Personification	**Historical Fiction (read one per lesson)**
L-14a Worksheet 10	With Clive in India - G. A. Henty
	With Wolfe in Canada - G. A. Henty
	With Pipe, Paddle, and Song - Elizabeth Yates
	The Reb and the Redcoats - Constance Savery
	The Winter People - Joseph Bruchac
	War Comes to Willy Freeman - Christopher & James Collier
Simile	**Biographies (an alternate for a historical fiction)**
L-14b Worksheet 11	Marie Antoinette - Kathryn Lasky
	The Kidnapped Prince - The Life of Olaudah Equiano
Ψ **IEW Narrative Stories**	adapted by Ann Cameron
Continue practicing narrative stories by selecting one of the	Carl Linnaeus: Father of Classification - Margaret J. Anderson
three stories in Lesson 14 and make a key word outline	Thomas Jefferson - Cheryl Harness
using the Story Sequence Chart.	Explorers of the South Pacific - Daniel E. Harmon
	The First Air Voyage in the United States - Alexandra Wallner
Metaphor	**Other Books for Research**
L-14c Worksheet 12	The Colonial Wars - Alden R. Carter
	Revolutionary War Days - David C. King
	Projects About the Woodland Indians - David C. King
Ψ **IEW Rough Draft**	Plays of Great Achievers - Sylvia E. Kamerman
Make a rough draft from your Story Sequence Chart	The Declaration of Independence - Judith Lloyd Yero
	The Young Patriot - Jim Murphy
Analogy	**Historical Events for Timeline**
L-14d Worksheet 13	1762-1796 Empress Catherine the Great of Russia
	1773 Boston Tea Party
Ψ **IEW Final**	1774 First Continental Congress meets in Philadelphia
Write a final with required stylistic techniques	1774-1792 King Louis XVI of France
	1775 Daniel Boone - Wilderness Road
	1776 American Declaration of Independence
	1780-1790 Emperor Joseph II of Austria
	1780 England declares war on the Netherlands
Creative Writing	**Other Areas of Interest during this Lesson**
L-14e	Betsy Ross
	Sign Language
Ψ **IEW apply to L-14e**	Minutemen, citizen militia
Use the Story Sequence Chart to create your outline	European influence on Hawaii
Use all sentence openers, two dress-ups, and one decoration	Sally Townsend
or triple extension.	Anne Bailey
	Lemuel Haynes
Write your mini book report	Crispus Attucks
Optional Movie: *Fiddler on the Roof*	Phillis Wheatley
	Patrick Henrey
	Accomplishments in Math

Inventions Questionnaire

1. What invention: Spinning Jenny (James named his invention for his wife, Jenny.)

2. When: 1764

3. Who is the inventor (person or country): James Hargreaves

4. Motivation: He noticed that more spindles could be added if the wheel lay on its side. One person could now spin yarn onto many spindles instead of just one. This made the process quicker.

5. How did this invention change life as it was then? It made people more efficient at making yarn.

6. What have been the ethical consequences (if any)? Mass production brought down the price and freed the time once needed by individuals to produce the yarn. It provided jobs.

7. Diagram or draw the invention:

Cite your sources:

Inventions Questionnaire

1. What invention: Hot Air Balloon

2. When: 1783

3. Who is the inventor (person or country): French paper-makers Joseph and Etienne Montgolfier

4. Motivation: They were highly educated and read the works of the English scientist, Joseph Priestly. They were very interested in flight. After observing how smoke rises in the fireplace, they decided to experiment themselves. They built a 38 foot in diameter linen bag lined with paper. It rose to an altitude of 6,000 feet and traveled over a mile before landing. Their public demonstartion was a success.

5. How did this invention change life as it was then? The brothers hired a young scientist to continue work on balloons. His name was J. A. C. Charles. Ballooning became a new sport and was also used to spy on enemy forces from the air.

6. What have been the ethical consequences (if any)? The use of the balloon has been further developed with safety features and the use of different gases. Scientists use them to learn more about the atmosphere, to study weather, to map the altitude of clouds, and to map air currents. NASA uses helium balloons to place payloads into a space environment. When used for military purposes, or when people are injured or killed in accidents with balloons, they can lead to a loss of life.

7. Diagram or draw the invention:

Explorers Questionnaire

1. **Who:** Lt. James Cook

2. **Nationality:** English

3. **When:** 1768-71

4. **Point of departure:** Plymouth, England
   or
   Sponsoring country: The British Royal Society persuaded King George III to sponsor the 1769 Venus expedition.

5. **Was this place the explorer's home country?** Yes
   Explain: Yes, he was born in Yorkshire

6. **Biblical or church history personality of the time:** Henry Alline was a missionary to Nova Scotia

7. **What was discovered or explored?** His first voyage lasted two years and eleven months. He wanted to observe Venus passing across the sun from the island of Tahiti. He explored the South Pacific and proved that New Zealand was not a part of a 'southern continent'. He sailed north and sighted the mainland of Australia and Botany Bay. He claimed Australia for Great Britain in 1770. He sailed through the Torres Strait and proved that New Guinea was not a part of Australia. He returned to England by way of the Cape of Good Hope.

8. **How?** He traveled by his ship, the *Endeavour*.

9. **What was their motivation?** He wanted to explore the South Pacific and chart new islands.

10. **Topography:** Tahiti is a volcanic island with a fertile coastline.

11. **Climate:** warm year-round; between 60 to 90 degrees

12. **Natural resources:** fish, tropical fruit: bananas, coconut, vanilla beans, breadfruit

13. **Crops:** sugar cane and tropical fruits

14. **Exports:** tropical fruit, rum, vanilla beans, red parrot feathers, pearls, and fish

15. **Trivia:** Capt. James Cook lacked education and was not a gentleman. However, he was a brilliant navigator, surveyor, and chart maker. He showed intelligence and compassion in his dealings with the seamen and the Pacific Islanders. Cook found that you could prevent scurvy on your ships by feeding the crew fruit.
    Cook made three voyages. On the second voyage he circled Antarctica. On his third voyage he sought a northern sea route between Europe and Asia. He was the first European to reach the Hawaiian Islands. He sailed up the north coast of North America through the Bering Strait to the Arctic Ocean. The ship was blocked by walls of ice so they returned to Hawaii. On February 14, 1779, Cook was killed by natives. The expedition returned to England in October, 1780.

Cite your sources:

No science assignments in Lesson 14

Worksheet 10

Personification
Personification is a figure of speech in which objects, animals, or qualities are given human characteristics.

Underline the personification in each sentence.

1. The <u>sun looked</u> down on me.

2. <u>It touched</u> my face and laughed at me.

3. The <u>wind chased</u> the clouds across the sky.

4. The <u>clouds teased</u> the sun.

5. The <u>sun gobbled</u> up the clouds.

Worksheet 11

Simile
A simile is a statement that tells how one thing is like another and usually uses the words *like* or *as*.

Underline the two things compared.

1. The <u>children</u> acted like <u>jumping jacks</u>.

2. The <u>winner</u> was as proud as a <u>peacock</u>.

3. The <u>castle</u> was like a <u>fortress</u>.

4. <u>Jenny</u> was as cute as a <u>button</u>.

5. The <u>steak</u> was as tough as <u>shoe leather</u>.

Worksheet 12

A metaphor compares one thing to another. It does not use the words *like* or *as*, but implies that one thing is another.

Underline the two things compared.

1. My instructor's <u>heart</u> is pure <u>gold</u>.
2. <u>Gym</u> was an endless <u>torture chamber</u> for Chris.
3. The <u>gym</u> was a <u>jungle</u> full of wild apes.
4. Her <u>room</u> was a heated <u>oven</u>.
5. The <u>pool</u> was an endless <u>ocean</u>.

Worksheet 13

Analogy
Analogies give relationships between words.

Early is to late as:

1. dawn is to *twilight*
2. morning is to *evening*
3. spring is to *fall*
4. day is to *night*

3   century: time = liter: *volume*

1   ruler: measure = scissors: *cut*

2   rain: wetness = lamp: *light*

3   house: building = car: *vehicle*

3   dog: mammal = cricket: *insect*

Lesson 15

1785 - 1795

Day	SCIENTISTS	INVENTIONS	EXPLORERS
Mon	1789 Antoine LaVoisier proved the law of conversion of matter. He emphasized the need for accurate weighing and measuring. **Questionnaire** His name may also be spelled Lavoisier		
Tue	**Vocabulary** combustion		1789-1793 Sir Alexander Mackenzie explored western Canada. **Questionnaire** *NW Territory **Mark Map 8**
Wed		1793 Cotton Gin **Questionnaire**	**Locate Scotland on the globe** **Draw Scotland's flag** **Vocabulary** tributary portage chinook
Thu			**What were explorers looking for when they searched for the Northwest Passage? Who finally discovered it?**
Fri			Bonus: Make a timeline of the different explorers and dates of exploration up until the discovery of the Northwest Passage.
			*indicates present-day location

LANGUAGE ARTS	READING SELECTIONS
Read a biography on Sacagawea	**Historical Fiction (read one per lesson)**
L-15a	Jump Ship to Freedom - Christopher and James Collier
	Cast Two Shadows - Ann Rinaldi
Ψ IEW Lesson 15	Captain Grey - Avi
View IEW DVD 7 - *Inventive Writing*	The Sun, the Rain, and the Apple Seed - Lynda Durrant
Read pp. 109-124 IEW Seminar and Practicum Workbook	
IEW Key Word Outline	**Biographies (an alternate for a historical fiction)**
Create a key word outline on *The Two Revolutions*	Carry On, Mr. Bowditch - Jean Lathan
	Journals of Lewis and Clark - John Bakeless
	Antoine Lavoisier: Founder of Modern Chemistry - Margaret Anderson
	First Across the Continent, Sir Alexander Mackenzie - Barry Gough
	Napoleon - Leslie McGuire
	Robespierre and the French Revolution in World History-Tom McGowen
Ψ IEW Rough Draft	**Other Books for Research**
Write a rough draft from your Key Word Outline	Extraordinary Explorers and Adventurers - Judy Alter
	Life During the French Revolution - Gail B. Stewart
	Animal Tracks of the Pacific Northwest - Karen Pandell
Ψ IEW Final Draft	**Historical Events for Timeline**
Prepare your final with required techniques. Don't forget	1783 Spain recognises US independence
your clinchers, indicators, and double spacing.	1784 US to trade with China
	1789 French Revolution
	1789 Thanksgiving Day established
	1791 War ends between Russia and Turkey
	1794 Telegraph invented
	1795 US and Algiers sign peace treaty
	1795 British capture Capetown South Africa
Write book report on biography	**Other Areas of Interest during this Lesson**
L-15b	Eli Whitney
Use openers/dress-ups with first four questions	Johnny Appleseed
Write paragraphs and use styles as assigned in IEW lesson	Andrew Jackson
	Emperor Napoleon of France
	Lafayette
	Temperance Wick
	William Carey, missionary to India
	Benjamin Banneker
6 Week Quiz	**Accomplishments in Math**
Optional Movie: *A Tale of Two Cities*	

Scientist Questionnaire

1. **Who:** Antoine La Voisier or Lavoisier   Father of Modern Chemistry

2. **Nationality:** French

3. **Life span:** 1743-1794

4. **Span of research:** He excelled at an early age. He pursued many areas of interest. He was beheaded during the French Revolution.

5. **Biblical or church history event of the time:** The Great Awakening began

6. **Noted achievement & field of interest:** He emphasized the need for accurate weighing and measuring. He retested many theories (for example, Priestly and Cavendish) and proved or disproved their findings. However, he often took credit for their discoveries.

7. **Secondary achievement & field of interest:** He invented the system of chemical nomenclature. His *Traité Élémentaire de Chimie (Elementary Treatise of Chemistry,* 1789) was the first modern chemical textbook.

8. **Motivation:** "I have tried. . . to arrive at the truth by linking up facts; to suppress as much as possible the use of reasoning, which is often an unreliable instrument which deceives us, in order to follow as much as possible the torch of observation and of experiment." Antoine Lavoisier

9. **Significance of discovery:** Scientists learned the need to weigh and measure accurately and to test and retest to prove a theory.

10. **How was this discovery helpful or harmful to society?** It was helpful because better calculations were made from more accurate measurements. He set a standard for the study of elements and other scientific discoveries.

11. **New word and meaning:** Answers will vary.

12. **Questions prompted through this study?** Answers will vary.

13. **Interesting bit of trivia:** He married a 13-year-old girl named Anne Marie. She translated English papers to him and illustrated his books. He established the Law of Conservation of Mass. He studied the composition of water. He disproved the phlogiston theory. He showed the role of oxygen in animal and plant respiration. He was also interested in astronomy.

Cite your sources:

Inventions Questionnaire

1. What invention: Cotton Gin

2. When: 1793

3. Who is the inventor (person or country): American Eli Whitney and his friend Phineas Miller

4. Motivation: He wanted to be able to improve on the job of removing cotton seed by developing a machine. His prototype could remove 50 pounds of cotton in a day.

5. How did this invention change life as it was then? Prior to this invention, seeds were removed by hand. It took all day for a worker to remove seeds from one pound of cotton. It made life easier and inspired later inventions.

6. What have been the ethical consequences (if any)? The invention of the cotton gin changed the South. In less than a year after the Cotton Gin was available, cotton sales rose from five to eight million pounds. The benefits of the invention were immediately recognized. Cotton planters copied the idea and built their own. The invention made growing cotton a profitable business and it became an important trade product for America.

7. Diagram or draw the invention:

Cite your sources: http://www.history.com/topics/cotton-gin-and-eli-whitney 4/12/2012

Explorers Questionnaire

1. **Who:** Sir Alexander Mackenzie

2. **Nationality:** Scottish

3. **When:** 1789-1901

4. **Point of departure:** Fort Chipewyan on Lake Athabasca, Canada
   or
   Sponsoring country: British Canada – Northwest Company fur trading firm

5. **Was this place the explorer's home country?** Yes
   Explain: Mackenzie was born in Scotland, immigrated to New York in 1774, and moved to Montreal in 1779.

6. **Biblical or church history personality of the time:** The Great Awakening

7. **What was discovered or explored?** He explored western Canada (NW Territory) across the Great Slave Lake up the Mackenzie River to the Arctic Ocean.

8. **How?** He traveled by ship and canoe, by river and over land. He traveled with five voyagers, two squaws, and a Chippewa guide.

9. **What was their motivation?** They were exploring to find a NW Passage in the NW Territory to expand the fur trade.

10. **Topography:** plains, mountains, rivers and lake systems

11. **Climate:** bitter cold winters and cool temperate summers averaging around 60 degrees

12. **Natural resources:** forest, furs, and fish

13. **Crops:** none in this region

14. **Exports:** furs

15. **Trivia:** Mackenzie was the first man to explore the North American continent north of Mexico on an overland journey. He later published a book about his adventures.

Cite your sources:

No science assignments in Lesson 15

No Language worksheets in Lesson 15

SECOND QUARTER SIX WEEK QUIZ

MATCH: Match the names on the left with their descriptions on the write. Write the letter in the space provided.

C   1.   Carolus Linnaeus   a. laws of motion & gravity

F   2.   Alexander Mackenzie   b. discovered Asia & North America are separated by water

E   3.   Antoine LaVoiser   c. classification of plants & animals

B   4.   Vitus Bering   d. explored the South Pacific Ocean

A   5.   Isaac Newton   e. proved the law of conversion of matter, emphasized the accurate measuring of
         chemicals

D   6.   James Cook   f. explored western Canada

TRUE OR FALSE: Mark each statement T for true or F for false in the space provided.

T   1.   Newton's discoveries proved the theory that the earth rotates.

F   2.   Vitus Bering was an English explorer.

F   3.   Botany is the study of animals.

F   4.   There is a land bridge connecting Asia and North America.

T   5.   Through LaVoiser's efforts, chemistry became considered a science.

F   6.   Sir Alexander Mackenzie was the first English explorer to sail around the world.

F   7.   James Cook's employment was as an astronomer.

T   8.   Summers in the arctic are very short.

F   9.   Sir Alexander Mackenzie discovered the Northwest Passage.

MULTIPLE CHOICE: Circle the letter next to the word or phrase that correctly completes the sentence.

1. The easiest form of transportation in the arctic is _____.
    a. ship   b. car   c. dog sled

2. The arctic is in the _____ hemisphere.
    a. southern   b. western   c. northern

3. These islands are in the South Pacific _____.
    a. Hawaiian   b. Philippines   c. Indies

4. Precise weighing & measuring of chemical products is important _____.
    a. sometimes   b. for safety   c. never

5. Mackenzie had to cross the _____ during his journey to reach the Pacific Ocean.
    a. Bering Strait   b. Rocky Mountains   c. Mississippi River

BONUS: What was the rare event that Captain James Cook witnessed during his South Pacific Voyage?
During his voyage, Captain Cook witnessed the passage of Venus between the earth and the sun.

Lesson 16

1795 - 1805

Day	SCIENTISTS	INVENTIONS	EXPLORERS
Mon	**Science Vocabulary**		
	infectious		
	bacteria		
	vaccine		
	immune		
Tue	1796 Edward Jenner discovered that vaccination created immunity to disease.		**Draw American flag of 1800**
	Questionnaire		
	How does a vaccine work?		
	How is one made?		
	S-16		
Wed	**Science Vocabulary**	1800 Human Powered Submarine	1804 -1806 William Clark & Meriwether
	molecule	**Questionnaire**	Lewis explore the Louisiana Purchase
	atom		for President Thomas Jefferson.
	element		**Questionnaire**
	compound		*area of purchase
	formula		
	ion		**Mark Map 8**
	isotope		
			Sacagawea, Shoshone Indian guide
Thu	1803 John Dalton studied chemical elements, compounds, and molecules.		**Vocabulary**
			squaw
	Questionnaire		keelboat
			piroque
	S-16		estuary
			rapids
			foothills
Fri	**Learn the periodic symbols for:**		
	chlorine silver		
	hydrogen gold		
	sodium iron		
	sulfur copper		
	carbon		
	oxygen		
	nitrogen		
	Learn and write the molecular		
	formula for:		
	ammonia		
	carbon dioxide		
			*indicates present-day location

LANGUAGE ARTS	READING SELECTIONS
Read a fiction about Sacagawea	**Historical Fiction (read one per lesson)**
L-16a	The Tiger of Mysore - G. A. Henty
	Streams to the River, River to the Sea - Scott O'Dell
Ψ IEW Lesson 16	
View IEW DVD 8	
Pay special attention to the TRIAC Model	
Ψ IEW Summarizing Narrative Stories	**Biographies (an alternate for a historical fiction)**
Read the article on *Napoleon*	William Carey: Obliged to Go - Janet and Geoff Benge
Create a Key Word Outline using TRIAC Model	America's Explorers and Pioneers - Just the Facts Goldhill DVD
	The Look-It- Book of Explorers - Elizabeth Cody Kimmel
	Edward Jenner, Conquerer of Smallpox - Ana Maria Rodriguez
	Journal of Lewis & Clark - John Bakeless
Ψ IEW Rough Draft	**Other Books for Research**
Write a rough draft from your outline	How Did We Find Out About Germs? - Isaac Asimov
	Robert Fulton: Steamboat Builder - Joanne Henry
	Lewis and Clark - Andrew Santella
	O, Say Can You See? - Sheila Keenan
	Steam and Stirling-Engines you can Build - William C. Fitt
	The War of 1812 - Alden R. Carter
	120 Great History Projects - Rachel Halstead and Stuan Reid
Book report on fiction	The Story of the Louisiana Purchase - Mary Kay Phelan
L-16b	**Historical Events for Timeline**
Use openers and dress-ups	1796 Treaty of Tripoli
	1796 Last of British troops leave U.S.
Ψ IEW Final Draft	1796 Spain declares war on England
Double space and use all appropriate markings	1804 Mungo Park begins African exploration
Use all openers, two dress-ups, and a decoration	1804 Union of Great Britain and Ireland
or triple extension in each paragraph.	1804 Napoleon crowned emperor of France
	1805 U.S. Marines attack Tripoli
	1805 Battle of Trafalgar England defeats Spain & France at sea
Do compare and contrast	**Other Areas of Interest during this Lesson**
L-16c	Daniel Webster
Use all styles in each paragraph	Thomas Jefferson
	Louisiana Purchase
	Eli Whitney and interchangeable parts
	Sojourner Truth
	Daniel Boone
	Shoshones
	Accomplishments in Math

Scientist Questionnaire

1. **Who:** Edward Jenner

2. **Nationality:** English

3. **Life span:** 1749-1823

4. **Span of research:** He studied nature from his youth. As a country doctor, he listened to the old wives' tales and tried to discern if they contained any truth. He worked twenty years studying records and documented cases before he attempted his bold experiment to intentionally infect a human being.

5. **Biblical or church history event of the time:** The first Sunday Schools were started in New York.

6. **Noted achievement & field of interest:** He pioneered immunology. He discovered that vaccination created immunity to disease.

7. **Secondary achievement & field of interest:** He studied nature. He observed and recorded the behavior of the Cuckoo bird.

8. **Motivation:** To do something to cure and prevent smallpox. Smallpox killed sixty million people in Europe between 1700 and 1800.

9. **Significance of discovery:** The population can be protected from infectious diseases.

10. **How was this discovery helpful or harmful to society?** The idea of vaccination has been applied to other illnesses. It has improved the heath of the population. It is believed by some that vaccines have a negative health affect and can cause autism or other neurological problems.

11. **New word and meaning:** Answers will vary.

12. **Questions prompted through this study?** Answers will vary.

13. **Interesting bit of trivia:** Jenner did not patent his discovery. He felt it would make it too expensive for some. He wanted it to be his gift to the world. Within twelve years of his discovery, the number of deaths decreased by seventy percent. In 1980, the World Health Organization declared that smallpox was extinct throughout the world.

Cite your sources:

Scientist Questionnaire

1. **Who:** John Dalton

2. **Nationality:** English

3. **Life span:** 1766-1844

4. **Span of research:** He was gifted in math and opened his own school at the age of twelve. In 1787 he began the careful recording and study of meteorology. He worked throughout his life, applying mathematics to science.

5. **Biblical or church history event of the time:** Protestants began having tent meetings in Louisiana.

6. **Noted achievement & field of interest:** He combined the fields of physics and chemistry to formulate the atomic theory of matter. He laid the foundation for modern chemistry.

7. **Secondary achievement & field of interest:** He realized that each element has a different weight. He made a list of atomic weights and determined how much of each element was needed to make a chemical compound.

8. **Motivation:** He wanted to know every little detail about matter, down to the atom.

9. **Significance of discovery:** Although foundational, his research was not very accurate and attracted little attention at the time.

10. **How was this discovery helpful or harmful to society?** Dalton's list of elements was not accurate but was helpful as it provided a basis for the modern periodic table of elements.

11. **New word and meaning:** Answers will vary.

12. **Questions prompted through this study?** Answers will vary.

13. **Interesting bit of trivia:** He worked as a teacher. In 1794, he presented his paper on vision and color, which resulted in documentation of the condition known today as color-blind. It was originally named after Dalton, and known as Daltonism. In 1801, he wrote a series of essays that concluded in the Law of Partial Pressures of mixed gases.

Cite your sources: http://www.answers.com/topic/john-dalton 1/4/2012

Inventions Questionnaire

1. **What invention:** Submarine (human powered)

2. **When:** 1800

3. **Who is the inventor (person or country):** Several designs and attempts were made to create a submarine in the 1600's. However, Robert Fulton is noted as its inventor. He designed and built the human powered *Nautilus* for the French.

4. **Motivation:** To be able to travel unseen underwater.

5. **How did this invention change life as it was then?** It was not used much at first, but gradually became an important weapon of war.

6. **What have been the ethical consequences (if any)?** The submarine was created to destroy and kill and has taken many lives. It also patrols our coastlines as protection against invasion by sea. Scientists are able to study the depths of the oceans and its creatures as well as the affects of pressure on human beings. Tourists can view the wonders of the reefs in small submarines.

7. **Diagram or draw the invention:**

Cite your sources:

Explorers Questionnaire

1. **Who:** Capt. William Clark and Capt. Meriwether Lewis

2. **Nationality:** American

3. **When:** 1804-1806

4. **Point of departure:** They started at a camp near St. Louis, MO.
   or
   Sponsoring country: United States

5. **Was this place the explorer's home country?** Yes
   Explain: President Jefferson wanted his new land purchase from France to be explored and hired these men to do so.

6. **Biblical or church history personality of the time:** Elisha Bowman was a Methodist missionary in New Louisiana. Joseph Brant was a minister to the Mohawk Indians.

7. **What was discovered or explored?** They explored the Louisiana Purchase from St. Louis to the Pacific Ocean, over 8,000 miles, following the rivers.

8. **How?** They used several modes of transportation; flatboats, canoes and portage, walking over land. The Shoshones provided them with horses to get over the mountains.

9. **What was their motivation?** It was their job as professional explorers hired by President Jefferson to survey, make maps, report mineral resources and fertile lands, and gather information on the Indians of the Louisiana Purchase area. They also kept detailed records of new animals they encountered.

10. **Topography:** varied topography; mountains, rivers, lakes, marshes, ponds, forests, and deserts

11. **Climate:** varied climate; semi-tropical on the Gulf of Mexico up into the cool weather along the Canadian border

12. **Natural resources:** wild animals and forest

13. **Crops:** wilderness

14. **Exports:** lumber for ships, furs, and minerals

15. **Trivia:** The expedition was made up of 26 soldiers, two interpreters, Clark's servants, and a Shoshone squaw, Sacagawea, and her infant son.

Cite your sources: http://lewisclark.net 1/4/2012

S-16

How do vaccines work?
A vaccine triggers antibody production against a particular disease. Some vaccines are made from the disease-causing bacteria or viruses that have been killed, or from live bacteria or viruses in a weakened form that do not actually cause the disease.

What was the first anesthetic?
The first anesthetic was nitrous oxide. It was not tried until 1844 by an American dentist, Horus Well, on himself, while having a tooth pulled.

Who developed it?
It was developed by Humphrey Davy, a British doctor, in 1799.

What kinds are there today?
Today there are over 14 different types of general anesthetics and four primary local ones.

Draw Dalton's table of elements.

Daltons 1808AD symbols and formulae.

⊙ Hydrogen	⦀ Soda	⊙⦀ Ammonia
⦶ Nitrogen	⦀ Pot Ash	⊙● Olefiant
● Carbon	○ Oxygen	○● Carbonic Oxide
⊕ Sulphur	Ⓒ Copper	○●○ Carbonic Acid
Ⓟ Phosphorus	Ⓛ Lead	Sulphuric Acid
⊙ Alumina	⊙○ Water	

http://www.chemsoc.org/exemplarchem/entries/2001/robson/symbolspart1.htm (5/8/2006)

Does the table of elements used today look like Dalton's? No

Add Copper, Iron, and Chlorine to your list.
Copper – Cu, Iron – FE, Chlorine - Cl
When two or more elements are chemically combined they produce a new substance called *compounds*. The symbols for compounds are called *molecular formulas*.

What are the formulae for water, ammonia, and carbon dioxide?
Water H_2O
Ammonia NH_3
Carbon dioxide CO_2

No language worksheet in Lesson 16

Lesson 17

1805 - 1825

Day	SCIENTISTS	INVENTIONS	EXPLORERS
Mon			1805-1807 Zebulon Pike explores the midwest and Rocky Mountain region.
			Questionnaire
			*present-day Colorado
			Mark Map 8
Tue		1807 Steamboat	**Vocabulary**
		Questionnaire	headwaters
			peak
			timber line
Wed		1814 Sewing machine	
		Questionnaire	
Thu		1816 Stethoscope	
		Questionnaire	
Fri			
			*indicates present-day location

LANGUAGE ARTS	READING SELECTIONS
Skimming and scanning	**Historical Fiction (read one per lesson)**
L-17a	Journey to Nowhere - Genesee Trilogy - Mary Jane Auch
	Washington City is Burning - Harriet Gillem Robinet
Ψ **IEW Lesson 17**	On the Irrawaddy - G. A. Henty
Review IEW DVD 4	The Switherby Pilgrims - Eleanor Spence
Review the stages IEW Seminar & Practicum Workbook p. 52	Imprisoned in the Golden City - Dave and Neta Jackson
	The Boy Who Drew Birds-A Story of James Audubon - J. Davies
Using reference materials	**Biographies (an alternate for a historical fiction)**
L-17b Worksheet 14	Audubon - Jennifer Armstrong
	Sacagawea: American Pathfinder - Flora Seymour
Ψ **IEW Stage One**	Zebulon Pike-Explorer and Soldier - Robin S. Doak
Outline and summarize one topic from one paragraph source	Dickens-His Work and His World - Michael Rosen and Robert Ingpen
Use *Ships at War*	The Atomic Pioneers-From Irish Castle to Manhattan Project -W. Moore
	America's Explorers and Pioneers-Just the Facts - Goldhill DVD
Following directions	**Other Books for Research**
L-17c Worksheet 15	Victorian Days - David C. King
	Usborne Victorians
Ψ **IEW Stage Two**	Art Revolutions "Impressionisms" - Linda Bolton
Outline & summarize one topic from multi-paragraph source	DK Eyewitness Chemistry - Dr. Ann Newmark
Use *Saving St. Michaels*	Colorado - It's My State - Linda Jacobs Altman
Use "topic-clincher"	
Other directions	**Historical Events for Timeline**
L-17d	1805 US Marines attack shores of Tripoli
	1814-1821 King Louis XVIII of France
Ψ **IEW Stage Three**	1814 Washington city is burned
Choose several sources for the *War of 1812*. Follow	1821 Mexico wins independence from Spain
assignment instructions for outlining, rough draft	1824-1830 King Charles X of France
and final paper.	1824 Simon Bolivar named dictator of Peru
	1825 Erie Canal opens
	1825 Malden Island discovered
Forms	**Other Areas of Interest during this Lesson**
L-17e Worksheet 16	Napoleon
	War of 1812
	Estevanico - Mountain man
	Charles Dickens
Optional Movie: *David Copperfield*	Impressionists Movement
	Mary Pickersgill
	Davy Crockett
	Johann Burckhardt

Inventions Questionnaire

1. **What invention:** Steamboat

2. **When:** 1807

3. **Who is the inventor (person or country):** American Robert Fulton

4. **Motivation:** Encouraged by Robert Livingston, he shipped a small steam engine from England and constructed a hull with paddle wheels on either side. He wanted to be able to travel faster both ways on the rivers and realized that steam was more dependable than the wind.

5. **How did this invention change life as it was then?** The steamboat made transportation much more reliable since it was no longer reliant on wind and current. It could also reach the western tributaries. The work was carried on by Henry Miller Shreve.

6. **What have been the ethical consequences (if any)?** Steam power was used to adapt machines and trains. This invention provided a new source of power but also contributed to pollution by the necessary burning to produce heat. Burning coal blackened city walls and trees. Men work underground to remove the coal needed.

7. **Diagram or draw the invention:**

Cite your sources:

Inventions Questionnaire

1. **What invention:** Sewing Machine

2. **When:** 1830 (first functional machines)
   1846 Elias Howe, (powered by hand crank)
   1850's (first commercially successful machine) treadle powered

3. **Who is the inventor (person or country):** French tailor Barthelemy Thimonnier,
   American Elias Howe, and American Isaac Singer

4. **Motivation:** to invent a machine that would speed up sewing and allow for mass production
   of clothing.

5. **How did this invention change life as it was then?** Thimonnier received a patent from the French
   government. He built a factory with 80 machines and made uniforms. It caused a riot among the
   tailors who feared a machine would replace them. They burned down the garment factory, with
   Thimonnier barely escaping.
   A patent war took place between Isaac Singer and Elias Howe. Howe won in 1854.

6. **What have been the ethical consequences (if any)?** It took a time-consuming, laborious task
   and made it faster and more precise. Replacing tailors with machines did cause some people to
   lose their jobs.

7. **Diagram or draw the invention:**

Inventions Questionnaire

1. **What invention:** Stethoscope

2. **When:** 1807

3. **Who is the inventor (person or country):** French; René Théophile Laënnec

4. **Motivation:** He got his idea from some street urchins. They let him hear the scratching of a pin transmitted through the length of a wooden beam. The doctor used the idea to fashion a listening device to be able to hear a heartbeat and other internal sounds better.

5. **How did this invention change life as it was then?** Patients could be diagnosed better for heart difficulties and internal problems.

6. **What have been the ethical consequences (if any)?** Patients can be diagnosed sooner, rather than waiting for other symptoms.

7. **Diagram or draw the invention:**

Explorers Questionnaire

1. **Who:** Zebulon Montgomery Pike

2. **Nationality:** American

3. **When:** 1805-1807

4. **Point of departure:** St. Louis, MO
   or
   Sponsoring country: United States of America

5. **Was this place the explorer's home country?** Yes
   Explain: He was born in New Jersey.

6. **Biblical or church history personality of the time:** Haystack prayer meetings, led by Samuel J. Mills, were popular during this time.

7. **What was discovered or explored?** He explored the upper Mississippi Valley in the Louisiana Territory in present-day Oklahoma, Texas, Colorado, Kansas and the Rocky Mountains. He discovered the peak in Colorado that was later named after him.

8. **How?** He traveled by horseback, traveled by boat on the Arkansas and Rio Grande rivers, and walked.

9. **What was their motivation?** He was an Army officer who was exploring and surveying for President Jefferson.

10. **Topography:** The region has three types of topography; sedimentary plateaus, plains, and mountainous.

11. **Climate:** cold winters and cool summers

12. **Natural resources:** forest and wild animals

13. **Crops:** berries and roots

14. **Exports:** furs and lumber

15. **Trivia:** In 1805, Pike searched for the source of the Mississippi River. He was caught as a spy by the Spanish in 1806. Pike's Peak was named after him. He was killed in the War of 1812.

Cite your sources: http://zebulonpike.org/ and http://www.answers.com/topic/zebulon-pike 2/14/2012

No science assignment in Lesson 17

Worksheet 14

Using Reference Materials

Which of the following types of reference books would you use to answer the question? Some questions could have more than one answer. Write the letters next to the question.

1. C or D   What states border California?
2. A or C   When did the first transcontinental railroad run?
3. F   What is the molecular formula for Ammonia?
4. E   A famous Thomas Jefferson quote.
5. B   Different word forms for the word explore.
6. A C D   Where is Pike's Peak?
7. A C   What is the temperature range in the Rocky Mountains?
8. H   The English meaning for the Spanish word El carro.
9. A   What is an element?
10. F   Who won the Noble Prize for Physics in 1938?
11. G   How were anesthetics first used?

No keys for worksheets 15 & 16

Lesson 18

1825 - 1830

Day	SCIENTISTS	INVENTIONS	EXPLORERS
Mon		1825 Steam Locomotive Engine	
		Questionnaire	
Tue	1830 Auguste Comte founder of sociology		
	Questionnaire		
	Vocabulary		
	sociology		
	philosophy		
	metaphysical		
Wed	1830 Charles Lyell studied the earth's		
	crust. He wrote "Principles of Geology".		
	Questionnaire		
	S-18		
Thu	**Vocabulary**		
	igneous rock		
	sedimentary rock		
	metamorphic rock		
	magma		
	crystalline		
	erosion		
	fossil		
Fri			

LANGUAGE ARTS	READING SELECTIONS
Using Graphic Aids	**Historical Fiction (read one per lesson)**
Timeline	Where the Broken Heart Still Beats - Carolyn Meyer
L-18a Worksheet 17	Piper's Ferry - Clifton Wisler
	Lyddie - Katherine Paterson
Ψ IEW Lesson 18	Hoggee - Anna Myers
Review IEW DVD 6	Hugh Glass, Mountain Man - Robert McClung
Review Unit 6 IEW Seminar and Practicum Workbook	Grace - Jill Paton Walsh
	Victor Lopez at the Alamo - James Rice
	The Voyage of Patience Goodspeed - Heather Vogel Frederick
Street Map	**Biographies (an alternate for a historical fiction)**
L-18b	Bridget "Biddy" Mason - Jean Kinney Williams
Ψ IEW Topic and Key Word Outline	*Attack in the Rye Grass - Dave and Neta Jackson
Use the encyclopedia style article to choose your topics	
and the other articles to create key word outlines on your	
topics.	
Ψ IEW Fused Outline	**Other Books for Research**
Create a fused outline from your key word outlines	Projects About the Spanish West - David C. King
	DK The Visual Dictionary of the Earth
	Make it Work! - Andrew Haslam and Barbara Taylor
	Slavery and the Underground Railroad - Carin T. Ford
	Freedom Roads-Searching for the Underground Railroad -Joyce Hansen
	DK Eyewitness Chemistry - Dr. Ann Newmark
Ψ IEW Rough Draft	**Historical Events for Timeline**
Write your rough draft on the *Erie Canal*	1825 US Congress approves Indian Territory
	1826 End of First Burmese War
	1827 Dutch Trade Company get opium monopoly
	1827 Creek Indians lose all US property
	1828 Russians defeat the Turks
	1830 France captures Algeria
	1830 Richard & John Lander discover the source of the Niger
	1830 Peter II, the last of Vladikas Dynasty
Ψ IEW Write your final paper	**Other Areas of Interest during this Lesson**
Complete your final paper for Lesson 18	Cyrus McCormick, inventor
with all required stylistic techniques.	Henry Martyn, missionary to India
	Nat Turner
	Red Jacket, American Indian leader
Write your mini book report	Edgar Allen Poe
	Elizabeth Barrett Browning
	Jim Bridger, American Fur Trade
	Charles Goodyear
9 Week Quiz	**Accomplishments in Math**
9 Week Test on Monday	

Scientist Questionnaire

1. **Who:** Isidore Auguste Marie François Xavier Comte   Grandfather of Sociology

2. **Nationality:** French

3. **Life span:** 1798-1857

4. **Span of research:** He began his work at the age of 19 at the École Polytechnique.

5. **Biblical or church history event of the time:** Charles Finney revivals in America and England

6. **Noted achievement & field of interest:** He believed that there was one universal law at work in all sciences. He applied this to society as the "Law of Three Phases" (theological, metaphysical, and scientific (positive). These phases take the human mind through the process of thought, reasoning and logic to the understanding of the world.

7. **Secondary achievement & field of interest:** He was the grandfather of sociology. He wanted to bring universal harmony by the political reorganization of society. He opposed individual rights but promoted altruism (a moral obligation to serve others before serving yourself).

8. **Motivation:** He was curious about how science applied to society and social relationships.

9. **Significance of discovery:** His research rejected the metaphysics of the Enlightenment and from his foundation, the field of social research and study was developed.

10. **How was this discovery helpful or harmful to society?** His emphasis on a quantitative (having to do with quantity), logical, and mathematical basis for decision-making remains with us today.

11. **New word and meaning:** Answers will vary.

12. **Questions prompted through this study?** Answers will vary.

13. **Interesting bit of trivia:** Comte was known as an arrogant, violent, and unstable man. He came up with the term sociology to name the new science revealed by Saint-Simon.

Cite your sources:

Scientist Questionnaire

1. Who: Charles Lyell

2. Nationality: Scottish

3. Life span: 1797-1875

4. Span of research: He started studying at Oxford at age 19 and pursued geology after hearing William Buckland lecture.

5. Biblical or church history event of the time: Missionaries were traveling throughout the world teaching, preaching, and helping the needy.

6. Noted achievement & field of interest: He studied geology and wrote the three volumes "Principles of Geology". He thought the actions of observable processes (rain, flooding, volcanoes, earthquakes, etc.) could explain geological history.

7. Secondary achievement & field of interest: He rebelled against the theories of the day based on the interpretation of the book of Genesis. To explain fossil remains, he excluded sudden geological catastrophes.

8. Motivation: He wanted to share his knowledge of geology. He traveled worldwide to conduct his studies.

9. Significance of discovery: He wrote books of his studies and presented a different view of the evidence he saw in geology.

10. How was this discovery helpful or harmful to society? Lyell challenged the ideas of the day about the earth, fossils and creation's timeline. It changed the way scientists looked at the world.

11. New word and meaning: Answers will vary.

12. Questions prompted through this study? Answers will vary.

13. Interesting bit of trivia: His father was an active naturalist. He was knighted in 1848 and became a Baron in 1864. He was a strong supporter and friend of Charles Darwin.

Cite your sources: http://www.victorianweb.org/science/lyell.html 4/12/2012

Inventions Questionnaire

1. What invention: Steam Locomotive Engine

2. When: 1825

3. Who is the inventor (person or country): Englishman George Stephenson, while working for the Liverpool and Manchester Railway, built the first steam train, which was named "Rocket".

4. Motivation: To be able to transport passengers and haul freight more quickly.

5. How did this invention change life as it was then? Transportation was revolutionized, and goods were able to travel further and more quickly. People could travel by train more quickly than on horseback or wagon.

6. What have been the ethical consequences (if any)? Railways can be used during peace time as well as war, and can be used to transport just about anything.

7. Diagram or draw the invention:

Cite your sources:

S-18
Diagram the layers of the earth and label the depth of each layer.
See the illustration in the answer key for the second quarter six week quiz.

The layers of the Earth:

Crust	5 miles
Continental Crust	35 mile and 1112 degrees F
Mantle	100-1899 miles and 6332 degrees F
Outer Core	3100 Miles and 8132 degrees F
Inner Core	3963 Miles and 9032 degrees F

Worksheet 17

Timeline

Use your timeline to answer these questions.

1. In what year did Lewis & Clark make their expedition?   *1804*

2. Which was invented first, the Spinning Jenny or the Cotton Gin?
   Spinning Jenny

3. What happened in 1611? *King James Bible published*

4. What year was the first telescope invented?   *1608*

5. Was the first clipper ship built before or after the first steamboat?   *After the first steamboat.*

6. What two things were invented the same year? *Fulton's steamboat & stethoscope*

7. What year did James Cook go on his voyage?   *1768*

8. What year was Pilgrims Progress written?   *1678*

SECOND QUARTER NINE WEEK QUIZ

MATCH: Match the names on the left with their descriptions on the right. Write the correct letter in the space provided.

C 1. Sacagawea   a. explored territory of the Louisiana Purchase

F 2. Charles Lyell   b. discovered vaccination

E 3. Zebulon Pike   c. guide to Lewis & Clark

A 4. Lewis & Clark   d. studied chemical elements

G 5. Auguste Comte   e. explored Midwest and Rocky Mountain regions

D 6. John Dalton   f. conducted studies of the earth

B 7. Edward Jenner   g. founder of sociology

TRUE OR FALSE: Mark each statement T for true or F for false in the space provided.

T 1. Vaccines are used to induce immunity to a disease.

F 2. Lewis & Clark never made it to the Pacific Ocean.

F 3. Sacagawea and her baby became a burden to Lewis & Clark

T 4. Elements are the simplest form of matter.

T 5. Colorblindness is also known as Daltonism.

T 6. A mountain peak in the Rocky Mountain range is named after Zebulon Pike.

F 7. Sociology is the science of the earth and its development.

F 8. Lyell's theories reflect the creation theory.

MULTIPLE CHOICE: Circle the letter next to the word or phrase that correctly completes the sentence.

1. Jefferson purchased the Louisiana Territory from _____.
    a. England   b. France   c. Spain

2. Pikes Peak is in what present day state?
    a. Colorado   b. New Mexico   c. Wyoming

3. The molecular formula for Carbon Dioxide is _____.
    a. CO_2 b. $C20$ c. CO

4. The element symbol for silver is _____.
    a. Au   b. Cu   c. Ag

5. The Rocky Mountain winters are _____.
    a. mild   b. short   c. harsh

BONUS: diagram the layers of the earth.

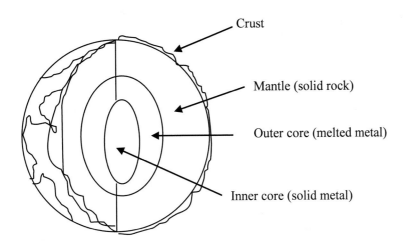

Crust

Mantle (solid rock)

Outer core (melted metal)

Inner core (solid metal)

Teacher's Notes

_____

_____

_____

_____

_____

_____

_____

_____

_____

_____

_____

_____

_____

_____

_____

_____

_____

_____

_____

_____

_____

_____

Lesson 19

1830 - 1850

Day	SCIENTISTS	INVENTIONS	EXPLORERS
Mon	1831 Michael Faraday converted		
	magnetism into electricity.		
	Questionnaire		
	S-19		
Tue	**Vocabulary**	1835 Photography (Daguerreotype)	
	current	**Questionnaire**	
	circuit		
	insulator		
	conductor		
	static		
	spark		
	magnetism		
	electromagnet		
Wed		1840 Clipper Ship	**Vocabulary**
		Questionnaire	abolitionist
			missionary
			drought
			tributary
Thu		1846 Anesthetics	1849-1873 David Livingstone explored
		Questionnaire	the course of the Zambezi River in Africa.
			Questionnaire
			*Zambezi River
			Mark Map 1
Fri			
			*indicates present-day location

LANGUAGE ARTS	READING SELECTIONS
Front page	**Historical Fiction (read one per lesson)**
L-19a	The Pioneers Go West - George Rippey Stewart
	Daughter of Madrugada - Frances M. Wood
9 Week Test	Edge of Two Worlds - Weyman Jones
	Soft Rain - Cornelia Cornelissen
Ψ **IEW Lesson 19 - 5 Paragraph Essay (multiple source)**	The Escape from Home - Avi
Review IEW DVD 6	Mountain Light - Lawrence Yep
Review Unit 6 IEW Seminar and Practicum Workbook	If I Ever Return Again - Corinne Demas
Choose topics & create key word outlines	Day of Tears - Julius Lester
Table of Contents	**Biographies (an alternate for a historical fiction)**
L-19b	David Livingstone: Africa's Trailblazer - Janet & Geoff Benge
	Riding Freedom - Pam Munoz Ryan
Ψ **IEW Fused Outline**	Florence Nightingale - David Collins
Fuse your outlines - p.88 Seminar & Practicum Workbook	George Müller: The Guardian of Bristol's Orphans - J & G Benge
	Thomas "Stonewall" Jackson - Robin S. Doak
	Samuel Morse and the Story of the Telegraph - Susan Zannas
	Michael Faraday and the Discovery of Electromagnetism - Susan Zannas
	Karl Marx - Nigel Hunter
Staff and Jobs	**Other Books for Research**
L-19c	Projects About Pioneer Days - David C. King
	Discovery and Inventions - Geoff Endacott
Ψ **IEW Rough Draft**	A History of Invention-From Stone Axes to Silicon Chips -T. I. Williams
Write your rough draft, including an introduction and	*Drummer's Boy's Battle - Dave & Neta Jackson
conclusion - don't forget clinchers	*Shanghaied to China - Dave & Neta Jackson
	*Listen for the Whippoorwill - Dave & Neta Jackson
	*Abandoned on the Wild Frontier - Dave & Neta Jackson
	Samuel Morse and the Telegraph - David Seidman
News Stories	**Historical Events for Timeline**
L-19d	1831 Separation of Belguim from the Netherlands
*Optional - Write a news story as outlined in Lesson 19	1833 British take control of Falkland Islands
of the IEW assignments	1834 French Foreign Legion founded
	1836 Alamo fought in Texas
	1837-1901 Queen Victoria of England
	1848 February Revolution - Louis overthrown
	1849 California Gold Rush
	1850 First National Women's Rights convention in US
Proofreading rules	**Other Areas of Interest during this Lesson**
L-19e	Karl Marx
	Samuel Morse
Ψ **IEW Write your final draft**	Ireland potato famine
	American Civil War
	Heinrich Geissler, inventor of vacuum tube
Write your mini book report	Clara Barton
	Brönte Sisters
	Hudson Taylor
Optional Movie: *Uncle Tom's Cabin*	

Scientist Questionnaire

1. **Who:** Michael Faraday

2. **Nationality:** English

3. **Life span:** 1791-1867

4. **Span of research:** His interest in science started in 1806 while he was apprenticed as a bookbinder. He attended the lectures of Sir Humphrey Davy, a chemist and inventor and Davy hired Faraday as a lab assistant.

5. **Biblical or church history event of the time:** Jedediah Smith "Knight in Buckskins"

6. **Noted achievement & field of interest:** He studied the relationship between electricity and magnetism. In 1821, he proved that an electric current could produce magnetic effects.

7. **Secondary achievement & field of interest:** He proved that the reverse was true as well. In 1831, he showed that moving a magnet through a coil of copper wire caused an electric current to flow in the wires.

8. **Motivation:** He chose to be a person that constantly seeks to understand the secrets of nature.

9. **Significance of discovery:** Electromagnetism is the foundation of the electric motor. Electromagnetic induction is the foundation of the electric transformer. Power plants use transformers to provide a community with electricity.

10. **How was this discovery helpful or harmful to society?** The Basic Law of Electricity states that all electricity is the same, whether it comes from the atmosphere, the chemicals of batteries, or the bodies of living things (electric eel, torpedo fish and Gymnotus). Faraday's work laid a foundation for the conveniences we enjoy today.

11. **New word and meaning:** Answers will vary.

12. **Questions prompted through this study?** Answers will vary.

13. **Interesting bit of trivia:** He was the son of a blacksmith. In his later years he was sick and began to lose his memory, so he turned his work over to younger men.

Cite your sources:

Inventions Questionnaire

1. What invention: Photography (daguerreotype)

2. When: 1839

3. Who is the inventor (person or country): Louis Daguerre of France

4. Motivation: He wanted to be able to make a permanent picture that could be reproduced exactly.

5. How did this invention change life as it was then? People who did not have artistic talent could make permanent pictures of people and places and the pictures could be completely accurate.

6. What have been the ethical consequences (if any)? Sometimes people's pictures are taken without their knowledge or permission. Also, photography is used in pornography. However, photography is a gift that allows us to preserve memories and record history, as well as aid police in solving criminal activities. In America, there is political debate regarding the use of photography as a form of surveillance.

7. Diagram or draw the invention:

Cite your sources: http://memory.loc.gov/ammem/daghtml/dagdag.html 4/13/2012

Inventions Questionnaire

1. What invention: Clipper Ship

2. When: 1840's

3. Who is the inventor (person or country): The Clipper ships (slang for "clipping along") were primarily an American invention during the 1840's, although some English ships of the era were considered to be "clippers". Donald McKay, an American, invented the American Yankee clipper ships in the 1850's after the dreams of several men (beginning with Nat Palmer) were combined with his building expertise.

4. Motivation: After the War of 1812, many men realized that there was a need for sleeker, faster vessels could carry a light cargo and move quickly

5. How did this invention change life as it was then? It made it faster to move products and transport passengers. It became a reliable, seagoing vessel and was also very popular with smugglers, slavers, and West Indies pirates. Unfortunately, after the opening of the Suez Canal and other routes, it became more economical to use ships that could carry larger cargoes, even though they moved more slowly.

6. What have been the ethical consequences (if any)? The Clipper era of trade was replaced by the seagoing steamships. The Clipper ship was used for good and bad purposes, but has a special place in history as "a dream realized".

7. Diagram or draw the invention:

Cite your sources:

Inventions Questionnaire

1. What invention: Anesthetics

2. When: 1846

3. Who is the inventor (person or country): American dentist William Morton – first to prove its practical use.
English chemist Humphry Davy (1799)
American dentist Horace Wells

4. Motivation: To render the patient unconscious of pain during a tooth extraction or other surgical operation

5. How did this invention change life as it was then? Surgeries were no longer painful and people were more willing to go to the doctor or dentist.

6. What have been the ethical consequences (if any)? Anesthetics are carefully monitored. However, there is always the slim risk of the patient not awakening or some part of their body being damaged. Nonetheless, anesthetics have eased pain and saved the lives of millions of people.

7. Diagram or draw the invention:

Explorers Questionnaire

1. **Who:** David Livingstone

2. **Nationality:** Scottish

3. **When:** 1849-1873

4. **Point of departure:** England
   or
   Sponsoring country: London Missionary Society of England

5. **Was this place the explorer's home country?** Yes
   Explain: Scotland (a part of the United Kingdom)

6. **Biblical or church history personality of the time:** British minister Charles Spurgeon begins preaching. Hudson Taylor goes to China.

7. **What was discovered or explored?** He explored Africa as a British missionary (the first knowledge of Africa's interior). In 1844, he traveled north to regions unseen by Europeans. In 1849, he discovered Lake Ngami. In 1850, he traveled the Zambezi River. In 1855, he looked for a route to the interior from the east or west coast. He went north to Cape Town to the Zambezi and west to Luanda on the Atlantic coast. He retraced his journey to the Zambezi and followed it to the Indian Ocean. He discovered Victoria Falls on his journey. He went on to Quelimane, northeast of the mouth of the river on the African coast. In 1857, he returned to London and in 1858, he became British Consul at Quelimane and commanded an expedition to explore east and central Africa.

8. **How?** He traveled by foot and by river raft.

9. **What was their motivation?** He wanted to look for a route from the east to the west coast in order to bring medical aid to the Africans, and to share Christianity with them.

10. **Topography:** Kalahari Desert, Makgadikgadi Salt Pan, Okovando Basin The basin is swamp, and the plateau is where most of the people live.

11. **Climate:** 54 to 98 degrees, arid and subtropical

12. **Natural resources:** wild game, coal, and salt

13. **Crops:** corn, millet, and beans

14. **Exports:** slaves, salt, and coffee

15. **Trivia:** In 1857, his book *Missionary Travels and Researches in South Africa* made him famous. His exploration caused revisions of all contemporary maps. In 1865, he wrote *Narrative of an Expedition to the Zambezi and its Tributaries* including a condemnation of slave traders and ideas for commercial development of the region. Dr. Livingstone died in a native village in 1873. His followers buried his heart at the tree where he died. His remains were buried at Westminster Abbey in 1874.

Cite your sources:

S-19
Since electricity could produce magnetism, Faraday wondered if the reverse could be true. Is it?
Yes, magnetism produces electricity.

What is this process called? It is called Electromagnetism.

How is it used today? Today it is used to create energy for light, for heat, and for motion of many objects.

No language worksheet in Lesson 19

SECOND QUARTER NINE WEEK TEST

MATCH: Match the names on the left with their descriptions on the right. Write the correct letter in the space provided.

D 1. Henry Hudson   a. explored along the Great Lakes

E 2. Galileo   b. explored western Canada

A 3. La Salle   c. explored the Midwest & Rocky Mountain region

G 4. William Harvey   d. explored the east coast of North America, bodies of water named for him

B 5. Alexander Mackenzie   e. studied phases of the moon, constructed telescopes

I 6. Vitus Bering   f. studied chemical elements

J 7. James Cook   g. made discoveries about the heart and blood circulation

C 8. Zebulon Pike   h. discovered vaccine and the lifesaving effects of vaccination

F 9. John Dalton   i. discovered Asia & North America are separated by water

H 10. Edward Jenner   j. explored the South Pacific Ocean

TRUE OR FALSE: Write T for true or F for false for each sentence in the space provided.

F 1. Francis Drake was the first to sail around the world.

T 2. Kepler discovered planets follow an elliptical orbit.

F 3. Henry Hudson discovered the Grand Canyon.

F 4. Lake Champlain is one of the five Great Lakes.

F 5. Sacagawea traveled with Joliet and Marquette along the Mississippi River.

T 6. Newton proved the theory that the earth rotates.

T 7. Asia and North America are not joined by land.

F 8. Pikes Peak is located in the Appalachian Mountains.

T 9. Auguste Comte has been considered the founder of sociology.

F 10. The element symbol for gold is Ag.

MATCH: Match the words on the left with the definitions on the right. Write the correct letter in the space provided.

E 1. sociology   a. a science dealing with the history of earth

A 2. geology   b. the source of a stream or river

G 3. chemistry   c. the study of the ultimate causes and underlying nature of things

C 4. metaphysics   d. the smallest portion of an element

J 5. elements   e. the study of the development and structure of society

D 6. atom   f. force of attraction between objects

I 7. tributary   g. a science dealing with the composition and structure of substances

B 8. headwaters   h. the process of burning

F 9. gravity   i. flows into a larger stream or lake

H 10. combustion   j. can't be separated into substances different from itself

Number the order of the planets with number one being the closest to the sun.

5_ Jupiter   8_Neptune   2_Venus

4_Mars   3_Earth   7_Uranus

1_Mercury   6_Saturn

Label map using the corresponding letter.

A. Mississippi River
B. Rocky Mountains
C. *Pikes Peak
D. *Grand Canyon
E. Florida
*general location acceptable

F. Atlantic Ocean
G. Pacific Ocean
H. Hudson Bay
I. Gulf of Mexico
J. Great Lakes

Name lakes here:
Lake Superior
Lake Michigan
Lake Huron
Lake Erie
Lake Ontario

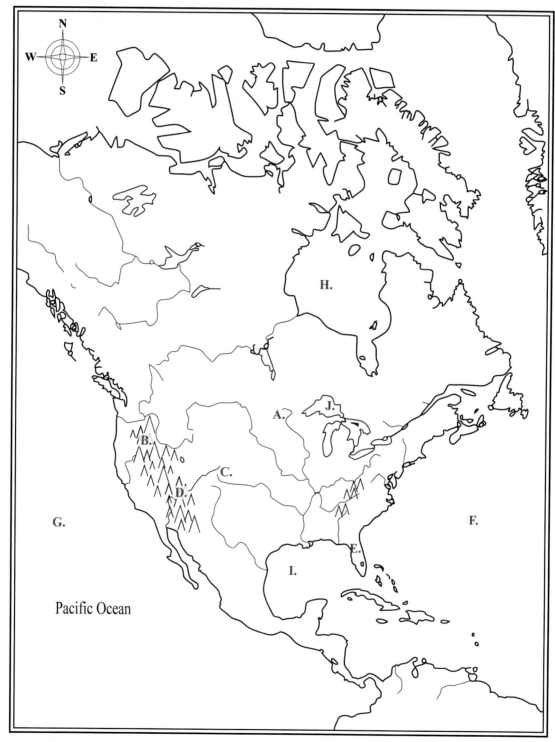

Pacific Ocean

Lesson 20

1850 - 1865

Day	SCIENTISTS	INVENTIONS	EXPLORERS
Mon	**Science Vocabulary**		**Locate and read background**
	theory		**information on Australia.**
	extinct		Locate Australia on the globe
	evolution		
	naturalist		**Vocabulary**
	ecology		Aborigine
	hypothetical		marsupial
	adapt		outback
	habitat		dingo
Tue	1859 Charles Darwin proposed the		**Draw an Aborigine for your**
	theory of evolution of plants and		**coursebook.**
	animals and wrote.		
	"The Origin of Species".		
	Questionnaire		
Wed			1860 Burke & Wills cross Australia
			from south to north.
			Questionnaire
			*Australia
			Melbourne to Gulf of Carpentaria
			Mark Map 15
Thu	**Science Vocabulary**		
	micro-biology		
	pasteurization		
	micro-organism		
	fermentation		
	sterile		
Fri	1876 Louis Pasteur invented		
	pasteurization to kill bacteria that		
	spreads diseases.		
	Questionnaire		
	S-20		
			*indicates present-day location

LANGUAGE ARTS	READING SELECTIONS
Feature story	**Historical Fiction (read one per lesson)**
L-20a	Undying Glory - Clinton Cox
Ψ IEW assignment optional	A Family Apart - Joan Lowery Nixon (Orphan Train Quartet)
Ψ IEW Writing from Pictures	With Lee in Virginia - G. A. Henty
View IEW DVD 5 - *Writing from Pictures*	Evvy's Civil War - Miriam Brenaman
Read pp. 65-81 IEW Seminar & Practicum Workbook	Sound the Jubilee - Sandra Forrester
Read the background story *Pony Express*.	The River Between Us - Richard Peck
	My Brother's Keeper - Nancy Johnson
	Kidnapped by River Rats - Dave & Neta Jackson
Comic Strips	**Biographies (an alternate for a historical fiction)**
L-20b	Mathew Brady, His Life and Photographs - George Sullivan
Ψ IEW assignment optional	Stonewall Jackson: Loved in the South, Admired in the North - Ludwig
	Elizabeth Van Lew, Southern Belle, Union Spy - Karen Zeinert
Ψ IEW Key Word Outline	The Boy's War - Jim Murphy
Use the outline method for Writing from Pictures to	Frederick Douglass - Patricia McKissack
create an outline for the *Pony Express* pictures	D. L. Moody - Bonnie Harvey
	Charles Darwin: Naturalist - Margaret J. Anderson
Want ads	**Other Books for Research**
L-20c	Abe Lincoln Remembers - Ann Turner
Ψ IEW assignment optional	Black Stars of Civil War Times - Jim Haskins
Ψ IEW Rough Draft	Civil War Days - David C. King
Create a rough draft from your outline	Plays of Great Achievers - Sylvia Kamerman
Editorials	**Historical Events for Timeline**
L-20d	1854 Commodore Perry opens trade with Japan
Ψ IEW assignment optional	1854-56 Crimean War
Ψ IEW Final	1858 British proclaim peace in India
Write your final three paragraph story. Don't forget	1858 Prince William of Prussia
clinchers.	1859 France declares war on Austria
	1860 Burke and Wills explore Australia
	1861 Italy proclaimed a kingdom
	1861-1865 Civil War in the United States
Your opinion	**Other Areas of Interest during this Lesson**
L-20e	Chicago destroyed by fire
Ψ IEW assignment optional	John Speke
	Townsend Harris
	Abraham and Mary Todd Lincoln
Optional: write your mini book report	Harriet Tubman
	Mary Patten
Optional Movie: *Red Badge of Courage*	Joseph John Thomson - electrons
	Civil War Revivals

Scientist Questionnaire

1. **Who:** Charles Darwin

2. **Nationality:** English

3. **Life span:** 1804-1882

4. **Span of research:** His hobby became his life's work. At age 22 he joined the crew of the HMS *Beagle* for its five-year voyage around South America.

5. **Biblical or church history event of the time:** Townsend Harris opens Japan to Christian missionaries.

6. **Noted achievement & field of interest:** In 1856, he started writing a book that explained his new theory of evolution, "*On the Origin of Species by Means of Natural Selection*". It was published in 1859 and caused controversy because it appeared to contradict the Bible.

7. **Secondary achievement & field of interest:** In 1871, he expanded his theory and published, "*The Descent of Man*". He believed many animals had a common ancestor. He suggested that man was descended from apes. He pointed to the tail bone as a point of proof of his theory.

8. **Motivation:** Through his wonder of nature, questions arose and he studied to find the answers.

9. **Significance of discovery:** His theory challenged the way people thought about the origin of the earth, humans and animals. It provided an explanation for how animals adapted to their environment.

10. **How was this discovery helpful or harmful to society?** It contradicted the creationist view and caused some to doubt the creation story. It looked at the age and development of the earth and living things in a different way than previous science had. Because Darwin viewed humans as descendants of animals rather than uniquely created beings, the value of the human gradually diminished in the eyes of many in science and society. The debate over evolution has caused those who believe in a literal creation and intelligent design to study and find scientific support for their beliefs.

11. **New word and meaning:** Answers will vary.

12. **Questions prompted through this study?** Answers will vary.

13. **Interesting bit of trivia:** He joined nature clubs. He met Dr. Robert Grant, a marine zoologist and also met a taxidermist. His father wanted him to become a doctor and when that wasn't possible, a minister. At Cambridge he studied theology and met John Henslow, a botanist, and Adam Sedwick, head of geology. He was influenced by "An Essay on the Principles of Population" by Thomas Malthus and "Principles of Geology" by Charles Lyell.

"Darwin saw religion as a strictly personal matter and regarded science as completely separate from religion. In general, he thought that the question of God's existence was outside the scope of scientific inquiry. However, he did think that his theory of evolution was compatible with a belief in God, but did not think that the natural laws of evolution imply a purposeful God created them." (Barlow, Page 94)

Cite your sources:

Scientist Questionnaire

1. Who: Louis Pasteur   Father of Microbiology

2. Nationality: French

3. Life span: 1822-1895

4. Span of research: 1848–1895 His college headmaster recognized his genius.

5. Biblical or church history event of the time: Joseph Hardy Neesima takes the gospel to the interior of Japan.

6. Noted achievement & field of interest: He was a biologist and chemist who invented pasteurization (1865); the process of killing bacteria without changing the composition or flavor of the liquid.

7. Secondary achievement & field of interest: He studied anthrax and rabies, resulting in the prevention and cure of these and many other diseases in men and animals. In science, this field is known as bacteriology. He created a vaccine for "mad dog disease", better known today as rabies. He proved the germ theory of disease and founded the science of immunity. He artificially developed the vaccine rather than using weak bacteria.

8. Motivation: He wanted to help his fellow man. He is known as the Benefactor of Humanity.

"Fortune favors the prepared mind, for the unprepared mind cannot see the outstretched hand of opportunity." Louis Pasteur

9. Significance of discovery: He extended the germ theory to explain that many diseases are caused by germs; one of the greatest scientific contributions of all time. He also disproved the popular theory of spontaneous generation of life.

10. How was this discovery helpful or harmful to society? It was helpful as it kept many from disease and rabies. In time, polio and typhus were eradicated. His study of organic chemistry in 1848 laid the foundation for modern stereo chemistry. As with all developments, overuse or misuse can cause harm, even death.

11. New word and meaning: Answers will vary.

12. Questions prompted through this study? Answers will vary.

13. Interesting bit of trivia: He saved the silkworm industry by discovering a microbe that was attacking the eggs. Eliminating the microbe saved the worms. Pasteur's proofs inspired Edward Jenner's work.

Cite your sources: http://www.notablebiographies.com/Ni-Pe/Pasteur-Louis.html 4/12/2012

Explorers Questionnaire

1. **Who:** (Name) Robert O'Hara Burke and William John Wills (John King the only survivor)

2. **Nationality:** Irish and English

3. **When:** 1860 – 1861

4. **Point of departure:** Melbourne, Australia
   or
   Sponsoring country: Victorian Government sponsored exploration of inland Australia from the south to the north; Melbourne to the Gulf of Carpentaria.

5. **Was this place the explorer's home country?** Yes, by the time of the journey they lived in Australia.
   Explain: Burke had come to Australia to work as a jailer and made it his home.

6. **Biblical personality of the time?**

7. **What was discovered or explored?** No inland sea was discovered. Crossed Australia from south to north

8. **How?** Overland on foot

9. **What was their motivation?** They were the first Europeans to cross the interior of Australia.

10. **Topography:** plains, desert

11. **Climate:** tropical monsoon season and warm, dry season with SE trade winds

12. **Natural resources:** hardwoods, fish

13. **Crops:** grass for animal fodder

14. **Exports:** wool

15. **Trivia:** The first Europeans to live in Australia were British prisoners and their jailers.

Cite your sources:

S-20
What is the process of pasteurization and what is its purpose?
Pasteurization is the process of killing yeasts, molds and disease causing bacteria by heating food at specific temperatures for certain periods of time. Its purpose is to preserve food and prevent disease. It causes certain enzymes naturally present in foods to become inactive.

No language worksheet in Lesson 20

Teacher's Notes

_____

_____

_____

_____

_____

_____

_____

_____

_____

_____

_____

_____

_____

_____

_____

_____

_____

_____

_____

_____

_____

_____

_____

_____

_____

_____

Lesson 21

1865 - 1870

Lesson 21

Day	SCIENTISTS	INVENTIONS	EXPLORERS
Mon	**Science Vocabulary**		
	genetic		
	hybrid		
	inherit		
	heredity		
	botany		
	dominant		
	recessive		
	mutation		
Tue	1865 Gregor Mendel developed the		
	principles of heredity.		
	Questionnaire		
	Draw Austria's flag		
	Locate Austria on the globe		
Wed	**Science Vocabulary**	1867 Typewriter	
	antiseptic	**Questionnaire**	
	gangrene		
	infection		
	contaminate		
Thu	1865 Joseph Lister established the use		
	of antiseptic surgery.		
	Questionnaire		
	S-21		
	Examine the Periodic Table of Elements		
Fri	1869 Dmitri Mendeléyev forms the		
	periodic table of elements.		
	Questionnaire		
	S-21		
	Examine the Periodic Table of Elements		
	Vocabulary		
	periodic		
	atomic number		
	atomic weight		

LANGUAGE ARTS	READING SELECTIONS
Fact	**Historical Fiction (read one per lesson)**
L-21a	Numbering All the Bones - Ann Rinaldi
* Ψ IEW assignment optional	Brady - Jean Fritz
	Clem's Chances - Sonia Levitin
Ψ IEW Writing from Pictures	A Woman of the Commune - G. A. Henty
Read the background story, *Full Steam Ahead and*	Twelve Travelers, Twenty Horses - Harriette Gillem Robinet
make an outline from the pictures provided.	Dragon's Gate - Laurence Yep
	Old Fashioned Girl - Louisa May Alcott
Opinion	**Biographies (an alternate for a historical fiction)**
L-21b	Hudson Taylor: Deep in the Heart of China - Janet & Geoff Benge
* Ψ IEW assignment optional	Window on the West - Laurie Lawlor
	*Round-up of the Street Rovers - Dave & Neta Jackson
Ψ IEW Rough Draft	Gregor Mendel: Father of Genetics - Margaret J. Anderson
Write a rough draft for your story	Alexander Graham Bell and the Telephone - Christine Webster
	Crazy Horse: Sioux Warrior - Brenda Haugen
	Inventors: Nobel Prizes in Chemistry, Physics, and Medicine-N. Aaseng
Biased information	**Other Books for Research**
L-21c	I Could Do That! - Linda Arms White
* Ψ IEW assignment optional	America in the Time of Sitting Bull - Sally Senzell Isaacs
	Science Experiments: Chemicals - John Farndon
Ψ IEW Final	DK Eyewitness Chemistry - Dr. Ann Newmark
Write your final story from pictures with required	DK Eyewitness Visual Dictionary of Chemistry - Jack Challoner
stylistic techniques	
Propaganda	**Historical Events for Timeline**
L-21d	1865 United States Civil War ends
* Ψ IEW assignment optional	Occupation and Reconstruction begin
	1866 Prussian-Italian alliance against Austria
	1866 1st U.S. train robbery
	1867 US takes possession of Alaska
	1868 Revolution in Spain
	1868 Invention of barbed wire changes the West
	1868 Meiji Dynasty (abolished by the Shogunate) is restored
	1870 Franco-Prussian War
Propaganda	**Other Areas of Interest during this Lesson**
L-21e	General George Custer
* Ψ IEW assignment optional	Alexander Graham Bell
	Susan B. Anthony
Write your mini book report	Walter Reed
	Louisa May Alcott
Optional Movie: *Little Women*	Lucretia Mott
	Alfred Nobel
	Charles Loring Brace
3 Week Quiz	

Scientist Questionnaire

1. **Who:** Gregor Johann Mendel

2. **Nationality:** Austrian

3. **Life span:** 1822-1889

4. **Span of research:** He was a brilliant student but his parents couldn't afford higher education so he became an Augustinian monk. His research was based on his love of nature.

5. **Biblical or church history event of the time:** John Jasper becomes a successful black minister who touched the lives of both blacks and whites (predominantly Baptists) during a time when it was illegal for blacks to preach.

6. **Noted achievement & field of interest:** He was very interested in biology and botany and developed the principles of heredity; the transmission of physical characteristics.

7. **Secondary achievement & field of interest:** He experimented with hybridization. *Experiments with Plant Hybrids,* describes how traits are inherited.

8. **Motivation:** He tried an experiment to prove Lamarck's view of the environment's influence on plants. The results disproved the theory but challenged him to answer other questions it raised.

9. **Significance of discovery:** Mendel's work became the foundation for modern genetics.

10. **How was this discovery helpful or harmful to society?** It was helpful as it improved crops and is now helping fight hereditary diseases. As technology advances, there have been some repercussions health wise for the use of genetically modified foods.

11. **New word and meaning:** Answers will vary.

12. **Questions prompted through this study?** Answers will vary.

13. **Interesting bit of trivia:** He was also interested in meteorology and the theories of evolution. It took 34 years for the scientific community to catch up with his discoveries.

Cite your sources: http://www.newworldencyclopedia.org/entry/Gregor_Mendel 4/11/2012

Scientist Questionnaire

1. **Who:** Joseph Lister   Father of Antiseptic Surgery

2. **Nationality:** British

3. **Life span:** 1827-1912

4. **Span of research:** Joseph pursued medicine as a career in 1848.

5. **Biblical or church history event of the time:** Civil War revivals among American civilians and soldiers.

6. **Noted achievement & field of interest:** He was a surgeon and established the use of antiseptic surgery; a chemical means of preventing infection.

7. **Secondary achievement & field of interest:** Lister developed a machine that sprayed carbolic acid into the air around an operation. Preventative medicine saved lives.

8. **Motivation:** To increase the health and lifespan of surgery patients.

9. **Significance of discovery:** His antiseptic surgical discoveries reduced the number of deaths. The death rate of surgery patients went from 45% to 12%.

10. **How was this discovery helpful or harmful to society?** It raised the survival rate of surgery patients and led the way to the discovery of other antiseptics. Misuse or overuse of antiseptics has led, in some cases, to immunity and ineffectiveness.

11. **New word and meaning:** Answers will vary.

12. **Questions prompted through this study?** Answers will vary.

13. **Interesting bit of trivia:** Lister was a shy, unassuming man and was deeply religious. He was firm in his purpose, humbly believing himself to be directed by God. He was uninterested in social success or financial reward. He was influenced by Louis Pasteur (biochemist) and Theodor Schwann (physiologist) and recognized the relationship between their works.
His methods were met with indifference, but by 1870, Germany adopted his methods during the Franco-Prussian War, saving many Prussian soldiers. Lister made tours of the leading surgical centers. England and America did not accept his germ theory. Lister knew he must convince London for his work to be accepted. He got his opportunity in 1877 when he was offered the chair of clinical Surgery at King's College.

Cite your sources:

Scientist Questionnaire

1. **Who:** Dmitri Ivanovich Mendeléyev

2. **Nationality:** Russian

3. **Life span:** 1834-1907

4. **Span of research:** Dmitri spent time at the glass factory with the chemist. His sister's husband also taught him science. It was apparent that Dmitri had exceptional comprehension of complex topics. He entered university in 1850.

5. **Biblical or church history event of the time:** First Vatican Council in 1869

6. **Noted achievement & field of interest:** He developed the Periodic Table of Elements by arranging the elements according to the weights of their atoms. He had to change some of the atomic weights of known elements to fit his table. He published his paper in 1871. In 1879 and 1886, other elements were found to fit his predictions. Time has proven his changes were correct.

7. **Secondary achievement & field of interest:** He also studied astronomy. He accurately predicted the existence of Neptune and three terrestrial planets that have now been found.

8. **Motivation:** He sought to discover a plan of unity among the chemical elements and their compounds.

9. **Significance of discovery:** By using his law, he was able to predict the existence and chemical properties of elements not yet discovered. In 1875, one of the elements was found.

10. **How was this discovery helpful or harmful to society?** It was helpful as it brought organization to the elements and a goal for those to search for the unknown elements to complete his table.

11. **New word and meaning:** Answers will vary.

12. **Questions prompted through this study?** Answers will vary.

13. **Interesting bit of trivia:** He was born in Siberia. Mendeléyev spent much of his time working to improve the technological advances taking place in Russia. Many of his research findings dealt with agricultural chemistry, oil refining, and mineral recovery.

Cite your sources:

Inventions Questionnaire

1. What invention: Typewriter

2. When: 1867

3. Who is the inventor (person or country): The Sholes & Glidden typewriter was built by the gun makers Remington & Sons. American Christopher Latham Sholes spent hours at Kleinsteuber's Machine Shop in Milwaukee, Wisconsin in the year 1868. Carlos Glidden was one of the men at the machine shop. Sholes patented the device but did not have an interest in marketing his invention and sold his rights to James Densmore, an investor who took the machine to Remington.
In 1878, Remington built a second model that fixed the shortcomings of the original design.

4. Motivation: He was a mechanical engineer that liked to tinker and had an idea for speeding up the printing process for individuals and businesses with a smaller machine than a printing press.

5. How did this invention change life as it was then? It found its place in every business. It made it easier and faster to write letters and provided a consistent script that was easier to read. It opened a new job market to trained technicians. The role of women changed as they became secretaries and could do more work in less time.

6. What have been the ethical consequences (if any)? As the years have passed, typing has evolved to computer keyboards and removed the emphasis on the art of handwriting, but the speed and affordability brought by the typewriter increased literacy and provides a great means of communication.

7. Diagram or draw the invention:

S-21

What made Mendeléyev think there were more elements that hadn't been discovered?
Mendeléyev thought there were more elements because in 1869, he and another chemist independently proposed an arrangement of the elements in what is now called the periodic table. Both scientists arranged the elements in order of increasing mass and according to similarity in properties, but found there were gaps where no known element fit in. Based on the table, Mendeléyev predicted the properties of three unknown elements, which were discovered between 1875 and 1886.

Did he discover any new elements? Yes

Which ones? During his lifetime his research led to the discovery of gallium, scandium, and germanium.

No language worksheet in Lesson 21

THIRD QUARTER THREE WEEK QUIZ

MATCH: Match the names on the left with their description on the right by writing the letter of the correct description in the space provided.

E 1. Joseph Lister   a. converted magnetism into electricity

F 2. Dmitri Mendeléyev   b. missionary to Africa's interior

A 3. Michael Faraday   c. developed theory of evolution

B 4. David Livingstone   d. discovered principles of inheritance

C 5. Charles Darwin   e. founder of antiseptic surgery

D 6. Gregor Mendel   f. known for his formulation of periodic laws of elements

TRUE OR FALSE: Mark each statement T for true or F for false in the space provided.

T 1. Michael Faraday's discoveries made way for the invention of the electric motor.

F 2. David Livingstone wanted to become a famous explorer.

F 3. David Livingstone became lost in the jungles of Africa.

T 4. Livingstone became very concerned about the slave trade taking place in Africa.

T 5. Joseph Lister realized the importance of clean surgical areas and tools.

T 6. Joseph Lister was a surgeon.

F 7. The scientific community completely accepts the theory of evolution.

F 8. Evolution has been proven and is based on scientific fact.

T 9. Gregor Mendel made his discoveries through his study of peas and beans.

F 10. Mendel's studies influenced Darwin in his theory of evolution.

T 11. Botany is the science that deals with plants and plant life.

F 12. Dmitri Mendeléyev made discoveries in genetics.

T 13. Dmitri Mendeléyev continued studies begun by Dalton.

MATCH: Match the words on the left with their definition on the right by writing the letter of the correct definition in the space provided.

C 1. ecology   a. to make impure

D 2. hypothesis   b. scientifically acceptable principle offered to explain phenomena

A 3. contaminate   c. study of the relationship between organisms and their environments

B 4. theory   d. an unproved theory tentatively accepted to explain certain facts

F 5. heredity   e. the theory that existing types of living things developed from previously existing living things

E 6. evolution   f. the transmission of characteristics by means of genes

BONUS: Explain what a theory is. Are we to accept someone's theory just because they are famous? Not necessarily. **Why or why not?** Scientists create scientific theories with the scientific method, when they are originally proposed as hypotheses and tested for accuracy through observations and experiments. Once a hypothesis is verified, it becomes a theory.

Teacher's Notes

Lesson 22

1870 - 1889

Lesson 22

Day	SCIENTISTS	INVENTIONS	EXPLORERS
Mon			1871-1888 Sir Henry M. Stanley explored
			the Congo River. He originally went to
			Africa in search of David Livingstone.
			Questionnaire
			*Congo River area
			Mark Map 1
Tue			**Vocabulary**
		1876 Telephone	journalist
		Questionnaire	expedition
			cataracts
			reservoirs
Wed		1877 Phonograph	**Draw the flag of Wales**
		Questionnaire	
Thu		1879 Incandescent light	
		Questionnaire	
Fri		1886 Automobile with four wheels powered	
		by a fuel only engine	
		Questionnaire	
			*indicates present-day location

LANGUAGE ARTS	READING SELECTIONS
Front page	**Historical Fiction (read one per lesson)**
L-22a	Not With Our Blood - Elizabeth Massie
	Bicycle Madness - Jane Kurtz
Ψ IEW Inventive Writing	Soldier Boy - Brian Burks
Review DVD 7 - *Inventive Writing*	The Young Colonists - G. A. Henty
Review Unit 7 in the IEW Seminar and Practicum Workbook	The Forgotten Heroes - Clinton Cox
Read the story on the *Salvation Army* and *William Booth*	The Girl Who Chased Away Sorrow - Ann Turner
and choose three topics. Create an outline using the	Walk Across the Sea - Susan Fletcher
"My Dog" model on p. 109	
Reliable source	**Biographies (an alternate for a historical fiction)**
L-22b	Mary Slessor: Forward into Calabar - Janet & Geoff Benge
	Louis Pasteur: Founder of Modern Medicine - John H. Tiner
Ψ IEW Rough Draft	Princess of the Press - Angela Shelf Medearis
Begin your rough draft today	Always Inventing - Tom L. Matthews
	*The Bandit of Ashley Downs - Dave & Neta Jackson
	Louis Pasteur: Disease Fighter - Magaret Anderson
	Dr. Livingstone-Missionary and Explorer - Sam Wellman
	Henry Ford-The Car Man - Carin T. Ford
Paper sections	**Other Books for Research**
L-22c	Wild West Days-American Kids in History Series - David C. King
	Mark Twain and the Queens of the Mississippi - Cheryl Harness
Ψ IEW Rough Draft	Cowboys! Reflections of a Black Cowboy - Robert Miller
Complete your rough draft, adding your introduction and	Window in the West - Laurie Lawlor
conclusion.	Democratic Republic of the Congo - Terri Willis
	Artisans Around the World-Africa South of the Sahara - Susan Rich
	African Playground - Putumayo Kids CD African Folk Songs
	Through the Grapevine - retold by Martha Hamilton and Mitch Weiss
Ads	**Historical Events for Timeline**
L-22d	1871 Germany united as an empire
*Optional IEW assignment	1874 End of Ashanti War
Ψ IEW Final Draft	1874 Britain annexes the Fiji Islands
Write your final five paragraph paper with required	1875 Rebellion in China
stylistic techniques.	1876 Korea becomes an independent nation
	1876 Battle of the Little Bighorn
	1878 Yellow Fever Epidemic in Tennessee
	1889 Oklahoma Land Run
Writers' terms	**Other Areas of Interest during this Lesson**
L-22e	Belva Lockwood
	George Kodak
	Booker T. Washington
	Thomas Edison
	First Skyscrapers
Write your mini book report	Emily Dickinson
	Fisk Jubilee Singers
	1886 dishwasher invented by Josephine Cochran
Optional Movie: *The Miracle Worker*	

Inventions Questionnaire

1. What invention: Telephone

2. When: 1876

3. Who is the inventor (person or country): Scottish; Alexander Graham Bell

4. Motivation: He wanted to produce a device that would allow more than one message at a time to cross the same wire.

5. How did this invention change life as it was then? The telephone quickly became a part of everyday business and in the household.

6. What have been the ethical consequences (if any)? The phone changed the way we live and relate to each other. The world is now a smaller place, we are a global people. Today you can't go anywhere that there aren't people talking on phones. With the combination of picture phones, the Internet, cell phones, and GPS, it is nearly impossible to have a truly private life. Telephones can be used to convey good news and events, but can also be used for malicious activity and gossip.

7. Diagram or draw the invention:

Cite your sources:

Inventions Questionnaire

1. **What invention:** Phonograph

2. **When:** 1877

3. **Who is the inventor (person or country):** American; Thomas Edison

4. **Motivation:** Result of his work on two other inventions, the telephone and telegraph. Edison was working on a machine that would transcribe telegraphic messages through indentations on paper tape. This led Edison to speculate that a telephone message could also be recorded in a similar way.

5. **How did this invention change life as it was then?** His invention was improved by Alexander Graham Bell and Charles Tainter, who named it a gramophone and received a patent.

6. **What have been the ethical consequences (if any)?** Edison foresaw many uses for his invention; the dictation machine, an answering machine, speaking books for the deaf, and speaking clocks. The phonograph made it possible for everyone to listen to music for enjoyment even if you could not play an instrument or sing well. It could be used for teaching elocution, preserving languages, important records, and family histories. Music boxes and toys were also made. The phonograph brought both good and bad influences in music and the spoken word into the home.

7. **Diagram or draw the invention:**

Cite your sources: http://memory.loc.gov/ammem/edhtml/edcyldr.html 3/8/2012

Explorers Questionnaire

1. **Who:** Sir Henry Morton Stanley (real name John Rowlands)

2. **Nationality:** Welsh

3. **When:** 1871-1888

4. **Point of departure:** New York
   or
   Sponsoring country: United States

5. **Was this place the explorer's home country?** Yes
   Explain: He came to live in the states as a child.

6. **Biblical or church history personality of the time:** Joseph Hardy Neesima takes the Gospel to interior Japan.

7. **What was discovered or explored?** Stanley traveled from Zanzibar to Lake Victoria in 1874 and proved this was the source of the Nile River. He explored west, sailing down the River Lualaba and the Congo River reaching the west coast while searching for David Livingstone. After ten months, he found Dr. Livingstone in the village of Ujiji near Lake Tanganyika.

8. **How?** He traveled with a large expedition; guides and porters. They walked and took boats down river.

9. **What was their motivation?** In 1871, he was sent by the editor of the *New York Herald* to discover what had happened to Dr. David Livingstone.

10. **Topography:** jungle, grasslands, desert, and rivers

11. **Climate:** hot, humid, and tropical

12. **Natural resources:** elephant tusk, coal, uncut diamonds, and salt

13. **Crops:** grain, coffee beans, and vegetables

14. **Exports:** slaves, ivory tusks, and diamonds

15. **Trivia:** He changed his name to honor the man who adopted him. He became famous as a newspaper journalist after he found Dr. Livingstone. He led an expedition in 1887-89 to southern Sudan. Stanley and Livingstone mapped much of the interior of southern Africa over the next thirty years.

Cite your sources:

No science assignments in Lesson 22

No language worksheets in Lesson 22

Teacher's Notes

Lesson 23

1889 - 1898

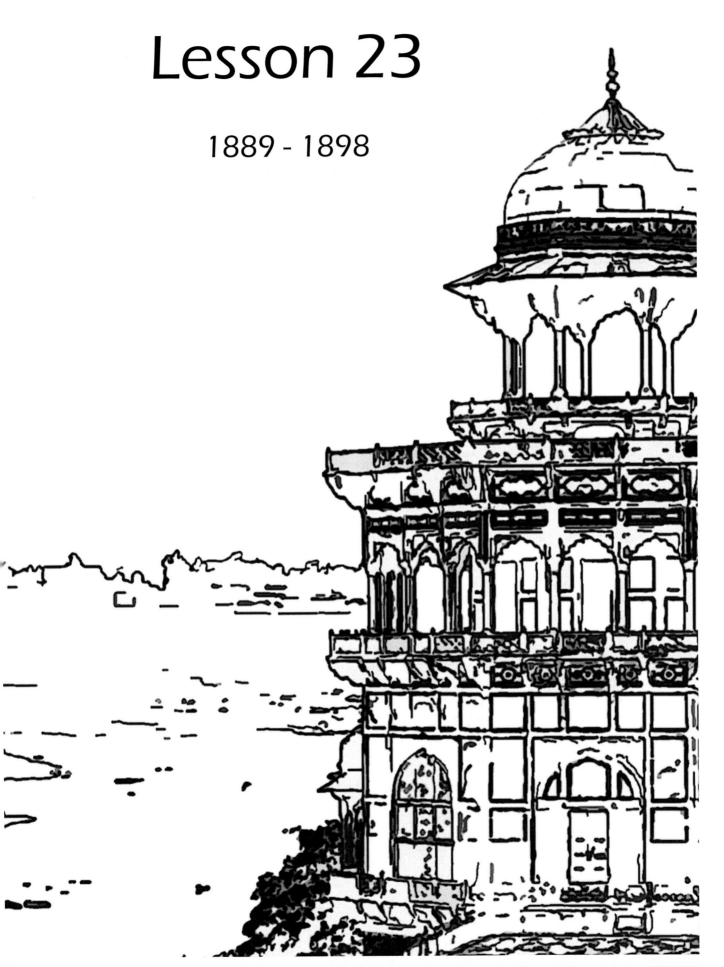

Day	SCIENTISTS	INVENTIONS	EXPLORERS
Mon	**Science Vocabulary**	1895 X-ray	
	radiation	**Questionnaire**	
	x-rays		
		Visit your dentist or doctor and view	
		some x-rays.	
		How do they help?	
Tue	1895 Wilhelm Roentgen discovered		
	x-rays.		
	Questionnaire		
	S-23		
Wed		1895 Radio	
		Questionnaire	
Thu		1896 Motion Pictures	
		Questionnaire	
		Movie: *Singing in the Rain*	
Fri			

LANGUAGE ARTS	READING SELECTIONS
Write a report	**Historical Fiction (read one per lesson)**
L-23a	Curtain Going Up - Dorothy & Tom Hoobler
* Ψ IEW techniques optional	Exploring the Chicago World's Fair - Laurie Lawlor
	Land of Hope - Joan Lowery Nixon
Ψ IEW Inventive Writing	Through Three Campaigns - G. A. Henty
Read the stories about Theodore Roosevelt and	Little Town on the Prairie - Laura Ingalls Wilder
choose three topics and create a key word outline using the	Kaiulani, The People's Princess - Ellen Emerson White
"My Dog"model on p.109 and the outline model on p. 122	Danger on the Flying Trapeze - Dave & Neta Jackson
	Quest for the Last Prince - Dave & Neta Jackson
Continue working on your report	**Biographies (an alternate for a historical fiction)**
	Florence Kelley - Carol Saller
	Marie Curie and Her Daughter Irene - Rosalyn Pflaum
Ψ IEW Rough Draft	*The Gold Miner's Rescue - Dave & Neta Jackson
Write your rough draft on Theodore Roosevelt.	Marie Curie: Discoverer of Radium - Margaret J. Anderson
	Other Books for Research
	Uncle Sam's Little Wars - John P. Langellier
Ψ IEW Final Draft	Plays of Great Achievers - Sylvia E. Kamerman
Begin your final draft	50 American Heroes Every Kid Should Meet - Dennis Denenberg
	A History of Inventions - Trevor I. Williams
	Projects with Nineteenth Century European Immigrants - Barian Broida
Informal Outline	**Historical Events for Timeline**
L-23b	1889 Oklahoma Land Run
	1893 Fridtjof Nansen crosses the Arctic Ocean
	1894 Korea and Japan declare war on China
Ψ IEW Final Draft	1895 Cuba fights Spain for its independence
Complete your final draft with techniques and clinchers	1896 Russia & China sign the Manchurian Convention
	1897 Turkey declares war on Greece
	1898 Battle at Thessalie: Turkish army beats Greece
	1898 Treaty annexing the Republic of Hawaii to the US
Gathering information	**Other Areas of Interest during this Lesson**
L-23c	Mary Kingsley
	Panama Canal
	Theodore Roosevelt
	Billy Sunday
	Jan Ernst Matzeliger
Write your mini book report	Granville T. Woods
	Garrett A. Morgan
	1899 Johan Vaaler invents the paperclip
Optional Movie: *Hidalgo*	

Scientist Questionnaire

1. **Who:** Wilhelm Conrad Rontgen

2. **Nationality:** German

3. **Life span:** 1845-1923

4. **Span of research:** Adult life

5. **Biblical or church history event of the time:** Billy Sunday revivals in America

6. **Noted achievement & field of interest:** He observed that a magnetic field can rotate a plane of vibrating light. While working on electricity flow in a vacuum tube he discovered that "rays" were emitted.

7. **Secondary achievement & field of interest:** He also worked on mechanics, heat, and electricity.

8. **Motivation:** He was following up on Michael Faraday's work.

9. **Significance of discovery:** It made it possible to see solid objects such as bones behind soft tissue, like skin and muscle. Surgery needs can be detected and verified.

10. **How was this discovery helpful or harmful to society?** Doctors are greatly aided by this discovery. It can take most of the guess work out of internal injuries. His discovery aided Henry Mosely in his work of determining atomic number. X-ray, when overused, can cause cancers and other diseases.

11. **New word and meaning:** Answers will vary.

12. **Questions prompted through this study?** Answers will vary.

13. **Interesting bit of trivia:** He was a professor at the University of Wurzburg when he made his famous discovery. He named them X-rays because of their unknown nature.

Cite your sources:

Inventions Questionnaire

1. What invention: X-ray

2. When: 1895

3. Who is the inventor (person or country): Wilhelm Roentgen   He received the first Nobel Prize for Physics in 1901.

4. Motivation: To see through soft tissue to reveal the bone or other foreign objects

5. How did this invention change life as it was then? It has saved many people from harm by being able to see into their soft tissue to discover how to help them medically.

6. What have been the ethical consequences (if any)? Most of its uses are helpful and varied; medical, dental, archaeology, and security. However, extended exposure to radiation is harmful.

7. Diagram or draw the invention:

Cite your sources: http://www.netdoctor.co.uk/health_advice/examinations/x-ray.htm 4/11/2012

Inventions Questionnaire

1. What invention: Radio (radio waves)

2. When: 1895

3. Who is the inventor (person or country): Serbian Nikola Tesla in 1893 and
Italian Marconi Guglielmo took Telsa's idea, tweaked it, and promoted it in London in 1895. Nine
months after Tesla's death in 1943, the Supreme Patent Court of the USA decides that Nikola Tesla
must be considered the father of wireless transmission and radio.

4. Motivation: Nikola was an electrical engineer who loved to invent.
Marconi had achieved his aim of turning Hertz's laboratory demonstration into a practical means
of communication.

5. How did this invention change life as it was then? They were able to convey information quickly
and wirelessly.

6. What have been the ethical consequences (if any)? Marconi received the Nobel Prize in 1911
for wireless telegraphy. Depending on what is being broadcast, it can either be positive or
negative information.
Nikola refused the Nobel Prize.

7. Diagram or draw the invention:

Cite your sources: http://www.pbs.org/tesla/ll/ll_whoradio.html 4/13/2012

Inventions Questionnaire

1. What invention: Motion Pictures

2. When: 1896

3. Who is the inventor (person or country): The Frenchman Louis Lumiere is often credited as inventing the first motion picture camera in 1895.
Edison showed his improved Vitascope projector. It was the first commercially successful projector in the U.S.

4. Motivation: They wanted to record movement on film.

5. How did this invention change life as it was then? It provided a new form of entertainment and information source.

6. What have been the ethical consequences (if any)? A series of developments over time. First the news reel, comic skits, 1900's tourist films, 1920's silent era, 1930's talkies, 1940's the war and film noire, 1950's era of epic films and the threat of television, 1960's era of independent, underground cinema, 1970's advent of the blockbuster film, 1980's the sequel and teen age films, 1990's computer generated films, 2000's age of advanced special effects. Films have become the literature of our day. Film can be misused to produce pornography and sometimes people assume that if something is on film it actually took place or happened the way it is re-enacted, which is not always true.

7. Diagram or draw the invention:

Cite your sources:

S-23

What is the Nobel Prize?

Nobel Prizes are awarded each year to people, regardless of nationality, who have made valuable contributions to the "good of humanity." In his will, the Swedish inventor of dynamite, Alfred Nobel directed that the income from his $9-million estate be used to fund five annual prizes. The awards are given in the fields of physics, chemistry, physiology or medicine, the most distinguished literary work of an idealistic nature, and the most effective work in the interest of international peace.

To who was it first presented, when was it presented, and for what accomplishment was it given?

It was first presented to Emil von Behring in medicine, in 1901, for his discovery of a diphtheria antitoxin.

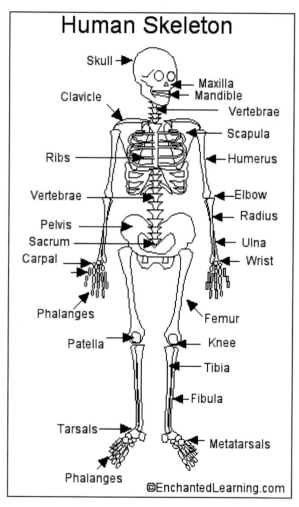

Study the human skeletal structure and learn the major bones in the body.

The bones learned should include (but does not need to be limited to) skull (cranium), jawbone (mandible), shoulder blade (scapula), breastplate (sternum), thigh bone (femur), shin bone (tibia), calf bone (fibula), tarsals (ankle bones), upper arm bone (humerus), hip bones (pelvis), low arm bone thumb side (radius), low arm bone pinky side (ulna), knee cap (patella), finger and toe bones (phalanges), wrist bone (carpal), backbone (spine), back bone disk (vertebrae), and tailbone (coccyx).

Col, Jeananda. Enchanted Learning.
http://www.EnchantedLearning.com 1996

No language worksheet in Lesson 23

Lesson 24

1898 - 1905

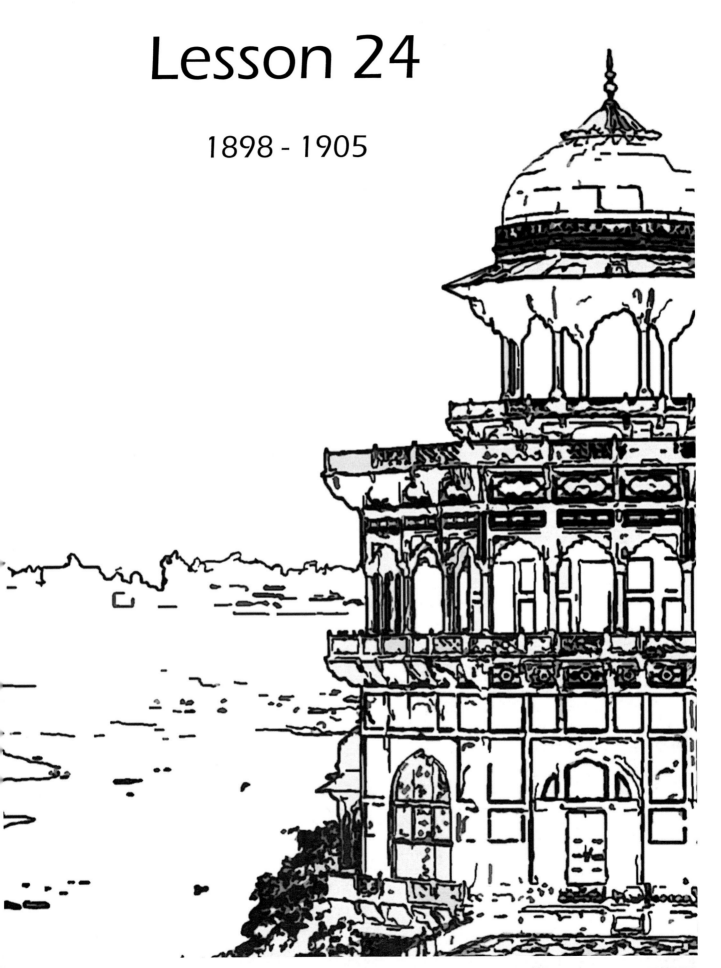

Day	SCIENTISTS	INVENTIONS	EXPLORERS
Mon	1898 Marie & Pierre Curie isolated		
	radium.		
	Questionnaire		
	Vocabulary		
	radiation		
	radium		
	purify		
	leukemia		
Tue	**Science Vocabulary**		
	conditioning		
	reflexes		
	instinct		
	habit		
	behaviorist		
	stimuli		
Wed	1900 Ivan Pavlov worked to better		
	understand human behavior.		
	Questionnaire		
	S-24		
Thu		1903 First Airplane flight	
		Questionnaire	
		Movie: *The Wright Brothers*	
Fri			

LANGUAGE ARTS	READING SELECTIONS
Take notes - use the IEW key word outline method	**Historical Fiction (read one per lesson)**
L-24a	With the Allies to Peking - G. A. Henty
	Stolen by the Sea - Anna Myers
Ψ IEW Personal Letter	Jim Ugly - Jim Fleischman
Five paragraphs with three themes. "My Dog" model p. 109	The Journal of Finn Reardon, Newsie - Susan Campbell Bartoletti
	Mask of the Wolf Boy - Dave & Neta Jackson
	The Hidden Jewel - Dave & Neta Jackson
	Call of the Wild - Jack London
Take notes - use the IEW key word outline method	**Biographies (an alternate for a historical fiction)**
	Helen Keller, Toward the Light - Stewart & Polly Anne Graff
Ψ IEW Personal Letter	Ivan Pavlov: Exploring the Animal Machine - Daniel Todes
Create an outline for your letter	Lenin: Founder of the Soviet Union - Abraham Resnick
Take notes - use the IEW key word outline method	**Other Books for Research**
	Immigrant Kids - Russell Freedman
Optional interview	Kids on Strike - Susan Campbell Bartoletti
L-24b	Far Beyond the Garden Gate - Don Brown
	Discovery and Inventions - Geoff Endacott
Ψ IEW Personal Letter Rough Draft	National Geographic Student Atlas of the World
Create a rough draft from your outline	On Their Toes: A Russian Ballet School - Ann Morris
Outline Fuse Key Word Outlines	**Historical Events for Timeline**
L-24c	1898 US declares war on Spain over Cuba
	1900 US goes on gold standard for currency
Ψ IEW Personal Letter Final Draft	1900 Sire Arthur Evans discovered Knossus
Write your final draft with greeting and closing.	1903 The British take North Nigeria
	1904 Russo-Japanese War
	1904 American occupation of Cuba ended
	1905 Race riots in Atlanta Georgia
	1905 Tsarists troops fire on Bloody Sunday demonstrators
Write rough draft	**Other Areas of Interest during this Lesson**
L-24d	Sigmund Freud
	Rasputin
	Florence Nightingale
	Babe Ruth
	Fanny Crosby
	Andrew Carnegie
Write mini book report	John D. Rockefeller
	1900 German Wilhelm Wien discovered protons
6 Week Quiz	**Accomplishments in Math**
	1900 Max Planck formulates the quantum theory

Scientist Questionnaire

1. **Who:** Pierre and Marie Curie (Manya Sklodowska)

2. **Nationality:** Pierre was French and Marie was Polish

3. **Life span:** Pierre 1859-1906   Marie 1867-1934

4. **Span of research:** Pierre 1899–1906   Marie 1899–1934

5. **Biblical or church history event of the time:** R. A. Torrey continues Moody's work.

6. **Noted achievement & field of interest:** Together they began to investigate the radioactivity of Uranium. It led to the discovery of two elements; polonium or radium F and radium.

7. **Secondary achievement & field of interest:** In 1914, she wrote *Radiology in War*. Marie designed mobile X-ray units. They were called "little Curies". She also set up 200 permanent X-ray units. She educated doctors and others in the field of radiology.

8. **Motivation:** Pierre and Marie decided to pursue Marie's doctoral project. Uranium gave out rays; where did the energy come from and what was it like?

9. **Significance of discovery:** They discovered that radiation helped kill disease cells and helped cure growths, tumors, and some kinds of cancer.

10. **How was this discovery helpful or harmful to society?** In 1902, the Curies decided not to patent their methods of obtaining radium for profit. "It would be contrary to the scientific spirit". They freely shared their knowledge. Their work paved the way for nuclear physics and cancer therapy.

11. **New word and meaning:** Answers will vary.

12. **Questions prompted through this study?** Answers will vary.

13. **Interesting bit of trivia:** In 1929, America collected money to buy Marie a gram of radium so she could continue her work at the laboratory in Warsaw. She won the Nobel Prize for Physics in 1903 and in 1911 for Chemistry for the discovery of two new elements.

Cite your sources:

Scientist Questionnaire

1. **Who:** Ivan Pavlov

2. **Nationality:** Russian

3. **Life span:** 1849-1936

4. **Span of research:** 1884-1936   He studied for the priesthood but chose to pursue science.

5. **Biblical or church history event of the time:** Asuza Street revivals took place in 1906

6. **Noted achievement & field of interest:** In 1889, he demonstrated conditioned and unconditioned reflexes. He influenced the development of physiology oriented behavior theories, "classical conditioning". He used a dog in his experiments to prove the conditioned responses.

7. **Secondary achievement & field of interest:** He pioneered work in the physiology of the heart, nervous system, and digestion.

8. **Motivation:** To better understand the behavior of humans and animals.

9. **Significance of discovery:** He learned about reflex responses. Our reflexes allow us to act quickly in response to danger or pain.

10. **How was this discovery helpful or harmful to society?** It was helpful as people could better understand natural human behavior. Conditioning can help stop bad behavior. He and others looked at environmental causes for behavior. His theories have influenced child psychology. Sometimes people use conditioned response as an excuse for poor behavior.

11. **New word and meaning:** Answers will vary.

12. **Questions prompted through this study?** Answers will vary.

13. **Interesting bit of trivia:** Ivan went to school in Poland. He was a behaviorist. He received the Nobel Prize in 1904 for his work on the physiology of the digestive glands.

Cite your sources: http://www.ivanpavlov.com 4/13/2012

Inventions Questionnaire

1. What invention: Airplane

2. When: 1903

3. Who is the inventor (person or country): American brothers, Orville and Wilbur Wright

4. Motivation: The possibility of a manned flight by creating an engine propelled heavier-than-air craft.

5. How did this invention change life as it was then? The speed of transportation was greatly increased. It has made the world a smaller place.

6. What have been the ethical consequences (if any)? They are used in wartime for delivering troops, weapons, supplies, destructive payload, and aerial surveillance. Other uses include transporting people, mail and packages, and transporting organs quickly. Planes are used to spray pesticides on fields. Airplanes have been deliberately crashed, high-jacked, and used for destructive purposes.

7. Diagram or draw the invention:

Cite your sources:

S-24

State as simply as you can Pavlov's conditioning theory.
Pavlov believed that behavior is related to conditioning from outside stimuli. He found that repeating an artificial stimulus (ringing bell) caused a physiological reaction in dogs, (they began to salivate like they would if they were going to eat) which he called a conditioned reflex. This led him to believe that all acquired habits, even higher mental activity, depends on chains of conditioned reflexes.

Do you agree with his theory? Why? Answers will vary.

No language worksheet in Lesson 24

THIRD QUARTER SIX WEEK QUIZ

MATCH: Match the names on the left with their description on the right by writing the letter of the correct description in the space provided.

A   1.   Marie & Pierre Curie   a. isolated radium used to treat several diseases

C   2.   Henry M. Stanley   b. discovered x-ray

E   3.   Ivan Pavlov   c. sent to central Africa to find Dr. Livingstone

B   4.   Wilhelm Roentgen   d. proved bacteria spreads disease and developed pasteurization

D   5.   Louis Pasteur   e. discovery of the conditioned reflex

TRUE OR FALSE: Mark each statement for T for true or F for false in the space provided.

F   1.   Henry Stanley's primary occupation was that of an explorer.

F   2.   Dr. Livingstone found Stanley lost and confused in Africa's interior.

T   3.   Stanley went on to explore parts of Africa with Dr. Livingstone.

F   4.   Louis Pasteur made only one important contribution to science.

T   5.   Roentgen discovered x-rays by accident.

T   6.   The Curies received two Nobel prizes for their achievements.

F   7.   Marie Curie spent most of her working years in the pursuit of one discovery.

F   8.   Pavlov's theories have influenced child psychology.

MULTIPLE CHOICE: Circle the letter of the word or phrase that correctly completes each sentence.

1. _____ sent Sir Henry Stanley to find Dr. Livingstone.
   a. The missionary organization   b. The New York Herald   c. NBC news

2. Pasteurization kills microscopic organisms in food by a _____ process.
   a. freezing   b. heat   c. chemical

3. _____ developed the treatment for rabies.
   a. Ehrlich   b. Roentgen   c. Pasteur

4. Marie Curie died of _____ .
   a. years of exposure to radiation   b. being hit by a horse drawn cab   c. heart failure

MATCH: Match the names on the left with their description on the right by writing the letter of the correct description in the space provided.

C   1.   stimuli   a. the rays sent out

A   2.   radiation   b. the science dealing with matter and energy

B   3.   physics   c. something that causes a response or action

D   4.   coagulate   d. to cause to become semi-solid; clot

BONUS: Radiation can be both helpful and harmful. Write an essay giving four examples of how it can be helpful and harmful. (4 points) *Possible answers*

X-rays allow doctors to see bones	Long term exposure causes leukemia and other cancers
Used to kill cancer tissue	Radiation poisoning damages human body tissue
Carbon dating helps archaeologists	Cell phones emit radiation
Irradiation kills germs in foods	Atomic bomb releases radiation into the atmosphere that
Nuclear fission creates electricity	gets on farmland and is transferred into the food

Lesson 25

1905 - 1910

Day	SCIENTISTS	INVENTIONS	EXPLORERS
Mon	**Science Vocabulary**		
	inertia		
	velocity		
	relativity		
	emission		
	mass		
	quantum		
Tue	1905 Albert Einstein's theory of relativity		**Vocabulary**
	used mathematical formulas to explain		frostbite
	the laws of the universe.		hypothermia
	Questionnaire		hummocks
	S-25		
Wed			1906-1909 Robert Peary and Matthew Henson
			are the first explorers to reach the North Pole.
			Questionnaire
			*North Pole
			Mark Map 4
Thu	**Science Vocabulary**		
	serum		
	serum therapy		
	chemotherapy		
	coagulation		
	antitoxin		
Fri	1910 Paul Ehrlich developed serum		
	therapy and chemotherapy.		
	Questionnaire		
	Locate Germany on the globe		
	Draw the German flag		
			*indicates present-day location

LANGUAGE ARTS	READING SELECTIONS
Proofread & correct	**Historical Fiction (read one per lesson)**
L-25a	A Sea So Far - Jean Thesman
Ψ IEW Essay Writing	Dragonwings - Laurence Yep
View IEW DVD 8	The Final Freedom - Bill Wallace
Read pp. 125-146 IEW Seminar & Practicum Workbook	Orphan of Ellis Island - Elvire Woodruff
Read about Henry Ford and think three themes	
See the Champlain model on pp. 125, 130	
Write your key word outline	
Begin Writing Final Paper	**Biographies (an alternate for a historical fiction)**
L-25b	Carry a Big Stick - George Grant
	Fanny Crosby, Hymn Writer - Bernard Ruffin
Ψ IEW Rough Draft	Albert Einstein, Young Thinker - Marie Hammontree
Create your rough draft	Albert Einstein: Physicist and Genius - Magaret J. Anderson
Continue work on your final paper	**Other Books for Research**
L-25c	The 1900's - Stephen Feinstein
	Taking Flight - Stephen Krensky
Title page and bibliography	**Historical Events for Timeline**
L-25d	1906 U.S. troops occupy Cuba
	1906 Belgium King Leopold claims Congo as a personal possession
Ψ IEW Final Paper	1907 Maria Montessori opens her first school
Complete your essay on Henry Ford and the automobile.	1907 England and France agree on Siamese independence
Include a final clincher and all required structures	1908 South Africa is established
and styles. Checklist on p. 145 Seminar & Practicum	1909 Civil war in Honduras
Workbook	1910 Japan annexes Korea
	1910 Revolution in Portugal
Put report in binder	**Other Areas of Interest during this Lesson**
L-25e	Santos Dumont Father of Aviation
	Henry Moseley
Creative writing	Panic of 1907
L-25f	Lusitania
* Ψ IEW optional	Halley's comet
	Anglo-Boer War
	1902 Willis Carrier invents the air conditioner
	Mary McLeod Bethune
Write your mini book report	**Accomplishments in Math**
	1905 Einstein formulates the Theory of Relativity and more
Optional Movie: *Spirit of St. Louis*	1908 Hermann Munkowski formulates four-dimensional geometry

Scientist Questionnaire

1. **Who:** Albert Einstein

2. **Nationality:** German Jew He became a Swiss subject in 1901 and a German citizen in 1914, but renounced it in 1933. He became an American citizen in 1940.

3. **Life span:** 1879-1955

4. **Span of research:** 1902-1955

5. **Biblical or church history event of the time:** The Pope works secretly to aid European Jews.

6. **Noted achievement & field of interest:** 1905 Theory of Relativity $E=mc^2$
   This theory shows that matter can be turned into energy and energy into matter.
   E=energy, M=mass, c=velocity of light. He provided the foundation of modern physics.

7. **Secondary achievement & field of interest:** In 1939, Albert wrote to President Roosevelt suggesintg the possibility of the atomic bomb. He was certain Hitler was developing the deadly device. He hoped the bomb would be used as a show of force to bring peace.

8. **Motivation:** "I want to know how God created this world. I am not interested in this or that phenomenon, in the spectrum of this or that element. I want to know His thoughts; the rest are details." -- Albert Einstein

9. **Significance of discovery:** He proved his belief in a well ordered universe in which events may be predicted by laws of cause and effect. He opened the door to the atomic age and the peaceful use of atomic energy.

10. **How was this discovery helpful or harmful to society?**
    Albert changed our concept of the universe.

11. **New word and meaning:** Answers will vary.

12. **Questions prompted through this study?** Answers will vary.

13. **Interesting bit of trivia:** He was such a slow learner that his parents feared he was retarded. But at age 14, he taught himself integral and differential calculus and analytical geometry from textbooks. He worked in the Swiss Patent Office while he went to school. In 1933, Albert was teaching at Princeton. Hitler had come to power and was persecuting the Jews so Albert remained in America. After World War II, Einstein was a leading figure in the World Government Movement, and he was offered the Presidency of the State of Israel, which he declined.

Cite your sources:

Scientist Questionnaire

1. **Who:** Paul Ehrlich   Father of synthetic chemotherapy

2. **Nationality:** He was a German Jew.

3. **Life span:** 1854-1915

4. **Span of research:** 1874 until his death

5. **Biblical or church history event of the time:** Dr. Silfred Grenfull preaches to the Eskimos.

6. **Noted achievement & field of interest:** He developed serum therapy. He discovered that certain dyes were selective. When they were injected they would dye certain organs. By adding a poison to the dye a diseased area could be treated without harming the host. He also discovered alkaline stains for identifying bacteria.

7. **Secondary achievement & field of interest:** In 1909, he discovered the "magic bullet" for syphilis. It was Salvarsan, a chemical used to successfully treat syphilis.

8. **Motivation:** To affect the specific growth of bacteria instead of medicating the entire body. It took 606 tries to find Salvarsan.

9. **Significance of discovery:** It could isolate and treat disease without harming the patient.

10. **How was this discovery helpful or harmful to society?** It was helpful as it healed many people and inspired other scientists to expand on the work.

11. **New word and meaning:** Answers will vary.

12. **Questions prompted through this study?** Answers will vary.

13. **Interesting bit of trivia:** His uncle was the great bacteriologist Karl Weigert. His work on the staining of granules in blood cells laid the foundations of future work on haematology and the staining of tissues. In 1890 Robert Koch, director of the newly established Institute for Infectious Diseases, appointed Ehrlich as one of his assistants and Ehrlich then began the immunological studies. This work and his other immunological studies led Ehrlich to formulate his famous side-chain theory of immunity. During the later years of his life, Ehrlich was concerned with experimental work on tumors.
In 1908, he won the Nobel Prize for Medicine and Physiology.
Paul Ehrlich was credited as founder of synthetic chemotherapy in 1909.

Cite your sources: http://www.jewishvirtuallibrary.org/jsource/biography/Paul_Ehrlich.html *4/11/2012*

Explorers Questionnaire

1. **Who:** Robert Edwin Peary and Matthew Henson

2. **Nationality:** Americans

3. **When:** April 6, 1909

4. **Point of departure:** New York City
   or
   Sponsoring country: United States

5. **Was this place the explorer's home country?** Yes
   Explain:

6. **Biblical or church history personality of the time:** Evan Roberts and the Welsh Revivals

7. **What was discovered or explored?** They were the first to reach the North Pole.

8. **How?** The men used ship, dog sled, skis, and traveled on foot with snow shoes.
   On the first attempt, Matthew Henson was accepted by the Inuit people, learned their language and customs and they taught him how to live in the frozen environment. He learned to drive a dog sled and build an igloo. On the final stretch there were five people; Matthew and four Intuits.

9. **What was their motivation?** They wanted to be the first to reach the North Pole.

10. **Topography:** ice, snow, tundra, and mountains

11. **Climate:** 0 to -70 degrees

12. **Natural resources:** whales, fish, seals and seafood in the surrounding Arctic Ocean

13. **Crops:** none

14. **Exports:** The Inuit are self-sufficient.

15. **Trivia:** Henson explored with Peary, starting in 1888. They made several attempts to reach the North Pole. 756 other men died trying to reach the Pole. It is said that Peary had to rest three miles from the Pole and Henson and four Intuits completed the journey to the top of the world.

    Upon his return Peary wrote: "My life work is accomplished... I have got the North Pole out of my system. After 23 years of effort, hard work, disappointments, hardships, privations, more or less suffering, and some risks, I have won the last great geographical prize."

Cite your sources:

Lesson 26

1910 - 1920

Lesson 26

Day	SCIENTISTS	INVENTIONS	EXPLORERS
Mon	**Science Vocabulary**		**World War I Vocabulary**
	atom		armistice
	neutron		negotiate
	electron		neutrality
	proton		diplomat
	nucleus		
	quark		**Draw a WW I uniform**
			Do World War l Worksheet
Tue	1911 Ernest Rutherford described the inside of the atom.		1910 Roald Amundsen became the first to reach the South Pole.
	Questionnaire		*Antarctica
			Questionnaire
	S-26		
			Mark Map 11
	Diagram an atom		
Wed			**Locate Norway on globe**
			Draw the Norwegian flag
Thu		1920 Frozen Food	
		Questionnaire	
Fri			
			*indicates present-day location

TRISMS© - History's Masterminds   320

LANGUAGE ARTS	READING SELECTIONS
Biography - George Washington Carver	**Historical Fiction (read one per lesson)**
L-26a	Gilbert and Sullivan, Set Me Free - Kathleen Karr
	The Road Home, The Story of an Armenian Girl - David Kherdian
Ψ IEW Persuasive Essay	A Time For Angels - Karen Hesse
Read pp. 139, 140, 141 IEW Seminar & Practicum Workbook	Angel on the Square - Gloria Whelan
Read the information about the *Panama Canal.*	Sacred Shadows - Maxine Rose Schur
Reread the articles on Theodore Roosevelt	A Time for Courage - Kathryn Lasky
	Operation Clean Sweep - Darleen Bailey Beard
	Ambushed in Jaguar Swamp - Dave and Neta Jackson
Ψ IEW Begin research to support your argument	**Biographies (an alternate for a historical fiction)**
Record resources for your bibliography	Lillian Trasher: The Greatest Wonder in Egypt - Janet & Geoff Benge
Remember three themes with the pros and cons	George Washington Carver - David Collins
Write your key word outline	Trial by Ice - K. M. Kostyal
	Tomboy of the Air - Julie Cummins
	*Voyage of the Great Titanic - Ellen Emerson White
	*Defeat of the Ghost Riders - Dave & Neta Jackson
Periodicals	**Other Books for Research**
L-26b	Tin Lizzie - Peter Spier
	The 1910's - Stephen Feinstein
Ψ IEW Rough Draft	The Causes of World War I - Tony Allen
Write your rough draft, including your introduction and	Fire! The Beginning of the Labor Movement - Barbara D. Goldin
conclusion. Be sure to state your question in the introduction	
and your final opinion in the conclusion..	
Ψ IEW Final Paper	**Historical Events for Timeline**
Write a final paper with styles and bibliography.	1911-12 Turk-Italian War
	1911 Revolution in Central China
	1912-13 Balkan War
	1914 Nigeria united
	1914-18 World War I
	1920 End of the Russian Civil War
	1920 League of Nations established
	1920 US declines membership in League of Nations
Book Report on Biography	**Other Areas of Interest during this Lesson**
L-26c	Titanic - Molly Brown
* Optional IEW inclusion	League of Nations
	Jim Thorpe
	Zeppelins
	Francisco "Pancho" Villa
	Panama Canal
	Mary McLeod Bethune
	1913 Henry Ford uses assembly line for mass production of automobiles.
Mini book report optional	**Accomplishments in Math**
	After 1908, we do not see specific accomplishments in mathematics
Optional Movie: *Sgt. York*	but we do recognize that all advances in computer, space technology,
	and physics are directly due to mathematics.

Scientist Questionnaire

1. **Who:** Ernest Rutherford   The first true Alchemist.

2. **Nationality:** English (New Zealander)

3. **Life span:** 1871-1937

4. **Span of research:** He began university in 1889. He worked throughout his adult life.

5. **Biblical or church history event of the time:** Christy Huddleston is a missionary and teacher to the people of the Appalachian Mountains in 1912.

6. **Noted achievement & field of interest:** He was one of the first researchers in the field of nuclear physics. He formulated the idea of a nuclear atom: +alpha nucleus, -beta negatively charged particles, and he predicted the existence of the neutron.

7. **Secondary achievement & field of interest:** He investigated how uranium electrifies the air. He identified the components of radiation; alpha, beta, and gamma rays. His *Theory of Radioactive Transmutation*, describes the radioactive transformation of one element to another.

8. **Motivation:** "I know of no more enthralling adventure than this voyage of discovery into the almost unexplored world of the atomic nucleus." Ernest Rutherford

9. **Significance of discovery:** He showed that an atom's electrons move around a heavy nucleus with positive electric charges. Elements do transmute themselves and can be artificially changed. He gave us a visual of atomic structure.

10. **How was this discovery helpful or harmful to society?** Gamma rays are used to burn off cancer cells. His work brought scientists closer to artificially induced nuclear reaction.

11. **New word and meaning:** Answers will vary.

12. **Questions prompted through this study?** Answers will vary.

13. **Interesting bit of trivia:** He was one of the first people to design highly original experiments with high-frequency, alternating currents. Ernest also discovered the half-life of radioactive elements and applied this to the study of age determination in rocks by measuring the decay period of radium to lead-206.
He received the 1908 Nobel Prize for Chemistry. During WWI, he worked on submarine detection problems. Otto Hahn, who later discovered atomic fission, worked under Rutherford at the Montreal Laboratory in 1905-06.

Cite your sources:

Inventions Questionnaire

1. What invention: Frozen food

2. When: 1920

3. Who is the inventor (person or country): American Clarence Birdseye

4. Motivation: To preserve food better and longer without canning. He found a way to flash-freeze and then deliver food in this form to the public.

5. How did this invention change life as it was then? Food stayed fresher for longer no matter the season.

6. What have been the ethical consequences (if any)? Entire meals are available to meet the demand for quick and easy dining. The freezers that keep the food preserved have emissions that are harmful to the atmosphere and ozone layer. Sometimes frozen food is over or under processed or is not at its ripest state when frozen and loses some of its nutrition because of the state in which it was originally harvested.

7. Diagram or draw the invention:

Cite your sources: http://inventors.about.com/library/inventors/blfrfood.htm 4/11/2012

World War l Worksheet

Read a book on World War I to find the answers to these questions.

1. **Who was the American President at this time?** President Woodrow Wilson

2. **What makes a world war different from other wars?** A world war involves all major governments and nations

3. **When did World War I begin?** July 1917

4. **How did World War I begin?** Austria-Hungary accused Serbia of murdering Archduke Francis Ferdinand, heir to their throne.

5. **What drew the United States into the war and when?** April 6, 1917 Germany's declaration to attack passenger and shipping vessels brought the U.S. into the war. They sank the Lusitanian. The Lusitanian carried American passengers.

6. **What is the famous quote from the speech President Wilson gave to convince Congress to approve our declaration of war?** "The world must be made safe for democracy."

7. **Who were the Allies?** Great Britain, Italy, France, United States

8. **Who were the Central Powers?** Germany, Austria-Hungary, Turkey, Bulgaria

9. **What countries remained neutral?** Netherlands, Switzerland, Spain, Sweden, Norway, Denmark

10. **What were zeppelins?** Zeppelins were rigid airships with a cigar-shaped body supported by internal gas cells.

Explorers Questionnaire

1. **Who:** Roald Gravning Amundsen

2. **Nationality:** Norwegian

3. **When:** 1911

4. **Point of departure:** Norway
   or
   Sponsoring country: Norwegian Navy

5. **Was this place the explorer's home country?** Yes
   Explain:

6. **Biblical or church history personality of the time:** Christy Huddleston begins teaching in Appalachia in the United States.

7. **What was discovered or explored?** South Pole, Antarctica

8. **How?** Several forms of transportation were needed. He used Fridtjof Nansen's ship the *Fram* and the airship *Norge*, designed and built by Italian explorer, Umberto Nobile. Dog sleds were used and he traveled on foot to the Pole.

9. **What was their motivation?** They wanted to be the first to reach the South Pole. He was racing against the British explorer Robert Scott.

10. **Topography:** ice, snow, and mountains   Antarctica is twice as big in the winter.

11. **Climate:** 0 to -70 degrees

12. **Natural resources:** penguins, seals, and seabirds

13. **Crops:** frozen wasteland

14. **Exports:** no inhabitants

15. **Trivia:** Amundsen had originally planned on discovering the North Pole. He was about to leave when he heard that Commander Robert E. Peary, an American explorer, had just reached the pole. Amundsen changed his plans and decided to lead an expedition to the South Pole instead. He became a well-known lecturer and writer. In 1927 he wrote his autobiography, *My Life as an Explorer*.

Cite your sources: http://www.famousnorwegians.com/amundsen-roald 3/14/2012

S-26
What is an atom? Diagram an atom and label the parts.
The atom is one of the basic units of matter. Everything around us is made up of atoms. An atom is incredibly tiny, more than a million times smaller than the thickness of a human hair. The smallest speck that can be seen under an ordinary microscope contains more than 10 billion atoms. The diameter of an atom ranges from about 0.1 to 0.5 nanometers. A nanometer is a billionth of a meter, or about 1/25,400,000 inch. Atoms are the building blocks of chemical elements such as hydrogen and oxygen, each of which consists of one basic kind of atom. Atoms vary in weight, but are about the same size

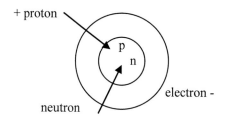

What is a quark?
A quark is a fundamental particle possessing both electric charge and 'strong' charge. They combine in groups of two or three to form composite objects that are held together by a strong force. Protons and neutrons are familiar examples of such composite objects -- both are made up of three quarks.

What happens when an atom is split?
When you split an atom, you are making two new atoms from one. You are actually splitting the nucleus (the central core) of the atom. When the nucleus breaks into two pieces energy is released, usually in the form of heat. These two new atoms can then hit other atoms and continue to break apart - this is called a chain reaction.

No language worksheet in Lesson 26

Lesson 27

1920 - 1926

Day	SCIENTISTS	INVENTIONS	EXPLORERS
Mon	1920 George Washington Carver worked with agricultural chemistry. **Questionnaire** **S-27**		
Tue		1925 Diesel Locomotive **Questionnaire**	
Wed			1926 Richard Evelyn Byrd is first to fly over the North and South Pole. **Questionnaire** *Antarctica
Thu			**Vocabulary** aurora meteorology moraine
Fri			
			*indicates present-day location

LANGUAGE ARTS	READING SELECTIONS
Read a fiction or watch a film about	**Historical Fiction (read one per lesson)**
George Washington Carver	Discovery at Flint Springs - John Erickson
L-27a	After the Dancing Days - Margaret Rostkowski
	The 1920's, Luck - Tim and Dorothy Hoobler
Ψ IEW Persuasive Essay	The Circle Maker - Maxine Rose Schur
Locate and read information about immigrants	Witness - Karen Hesse
	Tulsa Burning - Anna Myers
	Treasures in the Dust - Tracey Porter
	The Forty-Acre Swindle - Dave and Neta Jackson
	Biographies (an alternate for a historical fiction)
Ψ IEW Key Word Outline	Free to Dream - The Making of a Poet - Audrey Osofsky
Create a key word outline	Nora Neale Hurston, Storyteller of the South - Roz Calbert
Remember- three themes with the pros and cons	Benito Mussolini: Fascist Italian Dictator - Brenda Haugen
	Exploring the Polar Regions - Harry S. Anderson
	*Risking the Forbidden Game - Dave and Neta Jackson
Ψ IEW Rough Draft	**Other Books for Research**
Write your rough draft on immigration with an introduction	Women Win the Vote - Betsy Covington Smith
and conclusion	Extraordinary People of the Harlem Renaissance - Stephen Hardy
	The 5,000-Year-Old Puzzle - Claudia Logan
	Black Stars of the Harlem Renaissance - Jim Haskins
	Polar Explorers for Kids - Maxine Snowden
	A History of Invention - Trevor I. Williams
	How to Survive in the Antarctic - Lucy Jane Bledshoe
Write a book report or film review on what you read or	**Historical Events for Timeline**
watched about George Washington Carver.	1921 King Faisall of Iraq
L-27b	1920 American Women win the right to vote
	1922 Britain recognizes the Kingdom of Egypt
Ψ IEW Final Paper	1922 Mussolini forms a Fascist government
Write final draft with techniques, introduction and conclusion	1922 The Soviet states form the USSR
Use a final clincher that reflects the title and introduction	1924 Greece is proclaimed a republic
	1926 Lebanon becomes a republic
Complete a Compare and Contrast worksheet on your	**Other Areas of Interest during this Lesson**
book or film selection.	Ku Klux Klan (KKK)
L-27e	Aeroflot
*Optional IEW inclusion	Prohibition
	Nazi Party
	Mary Cassatt
	Captain Eddie Rickenbacker
Mini book report optional	William Einthoven invents the EKG
	Earl Dickson invents the band-aid
9 Week Quiz	
9 Week Test on Monday	

Scientist Questionnaire

1. **Who:** George Washington Carver

2. **Nationality:** American

3. **Life span:** 1864-1943

4. **Span of research:** From the time he was a boy until his death

5. **Biblical or church history event of the time:** Carver's lab was known as "God's Little Workshop". He was known as the "plant doctor".

6. **Noted achievement & field of interest:** Using his horticulture and chemistry skills, he came up with over 300 products derived from peanuts and over 120 derived from sweet potatoes to help the southern farmers to multiply the uses of a single crop. He also experimented with soy beans. Agricultural Chemistry and Economics were his fields of interest.

7. **Secondary achievement & field of interest:** He developed a hybrid cotton, soil improvement, and crop rotation. In 1896, he was invited to head the Agriculture department at Tuskegee Institute to help prepare future farmers.

8. **Motivation:** He was a devout Christian and wanted to discover the secrets of God's provision.

9. **Significance of discovery:** It revitalized agriculture in the South. It created many new markets to help farmers in selling their products.

10. **How was this discovery helpful or harmful to society?** It was helpful as the land stayed productive and more products could be made from a single crop. Like all crops, those he developed can be misused or overused.

11. **New word and meaning:** Answers will vary.

12. **Questions prompted through this study?** Answers will vary.

13. **Interesting bit of trivia:** He was born of slave parents and eventually raised by the slave owners, the Carvers. He left home at age ten so he could go to school. He gave himself the middle name Washington as a child when his teacher asked him his middle name and he had none. He would have remained a cook if a northern college hadn't taken a chance on a black student. He enjoyed painting and produced all his paints from Alabama soils. During the war, he developed dehydrated foods.
George never failed to have a fresh flower in his lapel. George donated all his savings to establish the Carver Museum and to the George Washington Carver Foundation, which supported young African-Americans engaged in scientific research.

Cite your sources:

Inventions Questionnaire

1. What invention: Diesel Locomotive

2. When: 1925

3. Who is the inventor (person or country): (1917 General Electric produced an experimental engine.)
Mid-20's Baldwin Locomotive Works and Westinghouse Electric.
In 1929, the Canadian National Railway became the first North American railway to use diesels

4. Motivation: To improve on the commercial version that is more efficient than the external combustion steam locomotive.

5. How did this invention change life as it was then? It made it possible for people and products to get places more quickly.

6. What have been the ethical consequences (if any)? Pollution is higher because of the exhaust produced by diesel engines. In America, railroads are no longer used as frequently for passengers, but, trains carry tremendous loads great distances in an inexpensive manner.

7. Diagram or draw the invention:

Cite your sources: http://www.locomotives-and-trains.com/diesel-locomotive-2.html 4/13/2012

Explorers Questionnaire

1. **Who:** Admiral Richard Evelyn Byrd

2. **Nationality:** American

3. **When:** 1926

4. **Point of departure:** Spitzbergen, Norway
   or
   Sponsoring country: United States

5. **Was this place the explorer's home country?** No
   Explain: The location allowed the Fokker tri-motor plane *Josephine Ford* with pilot Floyd Bennett
   to attain the goal.

6. **Biblical or church history personality of the time:** Eric Liddell refused to run in the 1924
   Olympics because it was held on Sunday.

7. **What was discovered or explored?** He was the first to fly over both the North and South Pole.
   He made the first flight over the North Pole in 1926 and in 1929 he flew over the South Pole.
   He made his first land expedition in 1928 establishing Little America on the Bay of Whales, on the
   South Pole.

8. **How?** by airplane

9. **What was their motivation?** They wanted to map Antarctica for scientific research.

10. **Topography:** ice, snow, mountains, and water

11. **Climate:** sub-freezing

12. **Natural resources:** The wildlife of the seas surrounding Antarctica includes: about 100 fish
    species, six seal species, several whale species, including the blue, fin, sei, humpback, sperm and
    right whales, and more than 50 species of birds including seven penguin species.

13. **Crops:** none

14. **Exports:** none

15. **Trivia:** Between 1928 and 1957 he did more than any other person to direct the exploration of the
    bleak, frozen continent of Antarctica. He wrote several books about his adventures; *Skyward* in
    1928, *Little America* in 1930, *Discovery* in 1935, *Exploring with Byrd* in 1938, and *Alone* in 1938.

Cite your sources:

S-27
What were some of the uses Carver created for peanuts and beans? Just a few were peanut butter, paper, ink, and oils. From the sweet potato he came up with a synthetic rubber and material for paving.

Do a study of early black scientists in America. List their names and discoveries or inventions.
(Note: There is an extended list of famous black Americans in the front of your book.)

George Peake 1772-1827	Invented a stone hand-mill in 1809
Norbert Rillieux 1806-1894	Invented a sugar refining process in 1843
Elijah McCoy 1859-1889	Canadian inventor of the automatic lubricator for engines in 1882
Sarah Goode 1855-1905	Invented the folding cabinet bed and was the first black Amercan women to receive a patent in 1885
Archie Alexander 1888-1953	Engineered bridges, power plants and major structures across the nation
Fredrick M. Jones 1892-1961	Designed the refrigeration system for long-hauled trucks
Garrett Morgan 1875-1963	Developed the automatic street signal and the gas mask
Otis Boykin 1920-1982	Electronic devices for heart stimulators and guided missiles
James Harris 1932--	Nuclear chemist who discovered two new elements
Annie Easley 1932-2011	Computer codes for energy technology
Cordell Reed 1938--	Develops more efficient and productive power plants
Mae C. Johnson 1956--	American astronaut, physician, biochemical engineer

No language worksheet in Lesson 27

Teacher's Notes

_____

_____

_____

_____

_____

_____

_____

_____

_____

_____

_____

_____

_____

_____

_____

_____

_____

_____

_____

_____

_____

_____

_____

THIRD QUARTER NINE WEEK QUIZ

MATCH: Match the names on the left with their description on the right by writing the letter of the correction description in the space provided.

C   1.   Ernest Rutherford   a. companion to Peary

G   2.   Robert Peary   b. produced the theory of relativity

E   3.   George Washington Carver   c. described the inside of an atom

A   4.   Matthew Henson   d. flew over the North & South Poles

F   5.   Roald Amundsen   e. conducted research in agriculture & chemistry

B   6.   Albert Einstein   f. first to reach the South Pole

D   7.   Richard Byrd   g. first to reach the North Pole

TRUE OR FALSE: Mark each statement T for true or F for false in the space provided.

T   1.   Albert Einstein used mathematical equations to explain the laws of the universe.

T   2.   Einstein suggested the idea that an atomic bomb could be made.

T   3.   Einstein hoped the bomb would never be used.

F   4.   Einstein's famous mathematical formula is Em+c2.

T   5.   Robert Peary never reached the North Pole, but his team did.

T   6.   Robert Peary lost many men on his final expedition.

T   7.   Matthew Henson was a black American explorer.

F   8.   Robert Amundsen went with Peary to the South Pole.

F   9.   Roald Amundsen and his team never made it back from the South Pole.

T   10.   The atom can be split in two.

F   11.   The protons and neutrons of an atom circle the electrons in the center.

F   12.   George Washington Carver was the first black explorer.

MATCH: Match the names on the left with their description on the right by writing the letter of the correct description in the space provided.

D   1.   velocity   a. the smallest part of an atom

C   2.   inertia   b. dangerously low body temp. caused by prolonged exposure to cold.

B   3.   hypothermia   c. tendency of matter to remain at rest unless affected by an outside force

A   4.   atom   d. rate of motion

E   5.   Botany   e. the science dealing with plants and plant life

BONUS: Diagram the structure of an atom and label the parts. What do the letters in Einstein's famous equation stand for? 6 points

Bonus:

$E=MC^2$
E=energy
M=mass
C=velocity of light

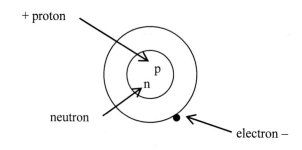

Lesson 28

1926 - 1940

Day	SCIENTISTS	INVENTIONS	EXPLORERS
Mon	**Begin a space age timeline**		
	Science Vocabulary		
	thrust		
	booster		
	altitude		
	recoil		
	exhaust		
Tue	1926 Robert Goddard invented the		
	multi-stage rocket.		
	Questionnaire		
	S-28		
Wed	**Science Vocabulary**	1928 First TV broadcast	
	bacteria	**Questionnaire**	
	virus		
	antibiotic		
Thu	1928 Alexander Fleming discovered		**Vocabulary**
	penicillin.		curator
	Questionnaire		zoology
			orinithology
Fri			1934 William Beebe descended 3,028 feet
			under the ocean in a bathysphere.
			Questionnaire
			*Bermuda
			Mark Map 10
			Draw a bathysphere
			*indicates present-day location

LANGUAGE ARTS	READING SELECTIONS
The sentence	**Historical Fiction (read one per lesson)**
L-28a	Number the Stars - Lois Lowry
	Flying Lessons - Kezi Matthews
9 Week Test	The Storyteller's Daughter - Jean Thesman
	Memories of Clason Point - Kelley Sonnenfeld
Ψ **IEW Basic Essay**	If Wishes Were Horses - Natalie Kinsey-Warnock
Descriptive five or seven paragraph essay	Flight of the Fugitives - Dave & Neta Jackson
pp. 130, 137 Seminar & Practicum Workbook	Dear Papa - Anne Ylvisaker
Read source text and use two additional resources	Song of the Trees - Mildred D. Taylor
Kinds of sentences	**Biographies (an alternate for a historical fiction)**
L-28b	Cameron Townsends Good News in Every Language - J. & G. Benge
	Eric Liddell: Something Greater than Gold - Janet & Geoff Benge
Ψ **IEW Basic Essay**	Thurgood Marshall, A Life for Justice - James Haskins
Create a key word outline for each source.	Eleanor Roosevelt, A Life of Discovering - Russell Freedman
	Dorothea Lange, Life Through the Camera - Milton Meltzer
	Franklin D. Roosevelt - Barbara Silberdick Feinberg
Subjects and predicates	**Other Books for Research**
L-28c	The Great Depression - R. Conrad Stein
	The Night Crossing - Karen Ackerman
Ψ **IEW Fused Outline**	Top Secret - Paul B. Janeczko
Fuse your key word outlines for *The Great Depression.*	The Empire State Building - Gini Holland
	Hitler Invades Poland - John Malam
Nouns	**Historical Events for Timeline**
L-28d	1928 Soviet Union exiles Leon Trotsky
	1928 USSR signs Braind-Kellogg pact
Ψ **IEW Rough Draft**	1929 Vatican City becomes a sovereign state
Write your rough draft from your fused outline.	1933 Nazi Revolution in Germany
	1936-1939 Spanish Civil War
	1938 Hans Albrecht Bethe explains nuclear energy
	1939 Leo Szilard - nuclear chain reaction
	1939-1945 World War II
Kinds of nouns	**Other Areas of Interest during this Lesson**
L-28e Worksheet 18	Stock Market Crash
	Frits Zernike invents the Phase Contrast Microscope
Ψ **IEW Write your final paper**	President Roosevelt
Use required styles. Utilize the checklist on page 145.	Winston Churchill
Add maps and pictures	Holocaust
Write your mini book report	James Chadwick
	Eleanor Roosevelt
Optional Movie: *The Hiding Place*	Big Band Sound

Scientist Questionnaire

1. **Who:** Robert Hutchings Goddard   Father of Modern Rocketry

2. **Nationality:** American

3. **Life span:** 1882-1945

4. **Span of research:** His parents supported and encouraged his experiments. He started at age five. In 1899, while sitting in a tree, he had a daydream about a device that could fly. (This is before the Wright Brothers success)

5. **Biblical or church history event of the time:** Holocaust in Europe

6. **Noted achievement & field of interest:** He launched his first rocket using liquid fuel in 1926. He designed the multi-stage rocket.

7. **Secondary achievement & field of interest:** He wanted to build a rocket that could reach the moon with liquid fuel. Between 1930 and 1935, he developed guidance systems and gyroscopes to keep them headed in the right direction.

8. **Motivation:** He pursued his dream to invent a device that could lift off and zoom into the sky.

9. **Significance of discovery:** It did become possible to reach the moon.

10. **How was this discovery helpful or harmful to society?** He is credited with launching the Space Age. His experiments led to earth satellites, missiles and exploration of space. Rockets can be used for good causes and bad causes.

11. **New word and meaning:** Answers will vary.

12. **Questions prompted through this study?** Answers will vary.

13. **Interesting bit of trivia:** The Smithsonian published his report, *A Method of Reaching Extreme Altitudes* that mentions rockets reaching the moon. A few days later newspaper headlines announced Goddard was working on a moon rocket. He was hounded by reporters.
In WWI, Goddard volunteered to investigate rockets as weapons. He received a government grant to develop long range rockets. He invented the 'bazooka'.
Some of Goddard's designs were used by the Germans in WWII in their V-2 missiles.

Cite your sources:

Scientist Questionnaire

1. **Who:** Alexander Fleming

2. **Nationality:** Scottish

3. **Life span:** 1881-1955

4. **Span of research:** In 1908, he began at the Inoculation Dept. at St. Mary's under Sir Almroth Wright. Wright and Fleming both believed that the body's natural defenses could cure nearly any disease or illness if given a little help.

5. **Biblical or church history event of the time:** The Dead Sea Scrolls are discovered in 1947

6. **Noted achievement & field of interest:** "I didn't do anything, nature makes penicillin; I just found it. . . I can only suppose that God wanted penicillin, and that was his reason for creating Alexander Fleming."
He established a new department of medicine, antibiotics. Fleming could not develop penicillan into a usable form.

7. **Secondary achievement & field of interest:** In 1919, he discovered lysozyme, an antiseptic found in our tears. It kills germs in our respiratory system.

8. **Motivation:** "Most scientists are artists, in a sense. Unless they have vision they can do comparatively little with their formulae." Alexander Fleming

9. **Significance of discovery:** At his funeral it was said, "By his work he has saved more lives and relieved more suffering than any other living man, perhaps more than any man who has ever lived."

10. **How was this discovery helpful or harmful to society?** Antibiotics fight diseases caused by bacteria. As time passed, antibiotics became overused or misused by the patient, which then produced a "super bacteria" that no longer responds to the antibiotic.

11. **New word and meaning:** Answers will vary.

12. **Questions prompted through this study?** Answers will vary.

13. **Interesting bit of trivia:** These were exciting times in medicine.
Louis Pasteur in France
Edward Jenner and Joseph Lister in England
Rober Koch in Germany
In 1937, Australian pathologist Howard Florey and German chemist Dr. Chain studied the chemistry of penicillin. After four years they succeeded in concentrating the drug which we use today. They received a Nobel Prize for their work in 1954.

Cite your sources: http://www.newworldencyclopedia.org/entry/Alexander_Fleming 4/11/2012

Inventions Questionnaire

1. **What invention:** Television

2. **When:** 1928

3. **Who is the inventor (person or country):** Several people are credited with inventing the television. Philo Taylor Farnsworth of the United States was first. He conceived of the principles of electronic television when he was twelve. RCA fought over the patent but Farnsworth won.
   Scottish engineer, John Logie Baird created the mechanical television system first used by the BBC in 1929.

4. **Motivation:** To bring news and pictures to people.

5. **How did this invention change life as it was then?** Radios were for listening but television added another sense to the absorption of information presented. It brought moving pictures and sounds from around the world into millions of homes.

6. **What have been the ethical consequences (if any)?** Television is a source of entertainment and news. People do not communicate like they used to. For example, it is unusual to get a personal letter or to sit outside just to visit. Advertisers entice us to spend money on items we never knew we needed before the commercial. We have become couch potatoes who don't exercise and stay inside our homes.

   "There's nothing on it worthwhile, and we're not going to watch it in this household, and I don't want it in your intellectual diet." - Philo Farnsworth's feelings about watching television.

7. **Diagram or draw the invention:**

Explorers Questionnaire

1. **Who:** Charles William (Will) Beebe

2. **Nationality:** American

3. **When:** 1934

4. **Point of departure:** NY, United States
   or
   Sponsoring country: New York Zoological Society, United States

5. **Was this place the explorer's home country?** Yes
   Explain:

6. **Biblical personality of the time:** German Christians accept Hitler's propaganda.

7. **What was discovered or explored?** 700 new life forms: birds, worms, plants   87 new species of fish
   He led more than 60 scientific parties to all parts of the world.

8. **How?** He descended 3,028 feet (half a mile) into the ocean in a bathysphere built by Otis Barton.

9. **What was their motivation?** As an underwater naturalist he wanted to discover the truth about nature and share these with the world.

10. **Topography:** Nonsuch, Bermuda in the Caribbean. It has low hills with fertile depressions.

11. **Climate:** year-round subtropical, mild temperatures and hurricanes, cooler in winter

12. **Natural resources:** limestone, beautiful beaches, and coral reefs

13. **Crops:** citrus fruit; no permanent crops

14. **Exports:** Tourist trade

15. **Trivia:** He had read Darwin's account of the Galapagos Islands. Nonsuch, Bermuda was loaned to the New York Zoological Society for Beebe and John Tee Van to use as a marine research station. His work off Bermuda was stopped by WWII when America made Bermuda a naval base. He wrote over 300 books about his underwater explorations.

Cite your sources: http://sites.google.com/site/cwilliambeebe/Home 4/13/2012

S-28

What is a multi-stage rocket?
A multistage rocket is one that uses two or more sets of combustion chambers and propellant tanks and is required for longer journeys. The sets are either attached side by side or stacked end to end. When one stage runs out of propellant it is discarded, which makes the rocket lighter and allows the rocket to accelerate more strongly. Rockets have been designed with as many as five stages, but the Space Shuttle only uses two stages.

Are bacteria and viruses useful, harmful, or both? Explain.
The correct answer is both. While some bacteria cause diseases in humans, others prevent the body from getting illnesses. Harmful bacteria prevent the body from functioning properly by destroying healthy cells.
Bacteria that usually live harmlessly in the body may cause infections when a person's resistance to disease is low. For example, if bacteria in the throat reproduce faster than the body can dispose of them, a person may get a sore throat.

Are antibiotics used for viruses or bacterial infections? Antibiotics will effect bacterial infections, but not viruses.

How do they work? Antibiotics kill bacteria by preventing the formation of the stiff cell walls bacteria need to survive.

Can they treat the common cold?
The common cold is a viral disease and can not be cured with antibiotics. In addition, the effectiveness of antibiotics is limited because both pathogenic (causing disease) microbes and cancer cells can become resistant to them.

Worksheet 18

Nouns: Concrete and Abstract

Change the words in parenthesis into abstract nouns by adding one of these suffixes: *ity, ty, ism, dom, ment.*

1. My idea of (content) is a good book on a rainy afternoon. *Contentment*

2. A good play is my idea of (entertain). *Entertainment*

3. (Loyal) is necessary in a relationship between friends. *Loyalty*

4. We show our (human) when we are sensitive to the needs of others. *Humanity*

THIRD QUARTER NINE WEEK TEST

MATCH: Match the names on the left with their description on the right by writing the letter of the correction description in the space provided.

D	1.	Charles Darwin	a. missionary to Africa's interior
A	2.	David Livingstone	b. isolated radium
F	3.	Michael Faraday	c. pasteurization
G	4.	Wilhelm Roentgen	d. theory of evolution
B	5.	The Curies	e. theory of relativity
J	6.	Henry Stanley	f. converted magnetism to electricity
C	7.	Louis Pasteur	g. discovered x-rays
I	8.	Robert Peary	h. companion to Peary
E	9.	Albert Einstein	i. first to reach North Pole
H	10.	Matthew Henson	j. sent to find Dr. Livingstone

TRUE OR FALSE: Mark each statement T for true or F for false in the space provided.

F   1.   David Livingstone became lost in the jungles of Africa.

T   2.   Joseph Lister discovered the importance of clean surgical tools and areas.

T   3.   Henry Stanley worked for the New York Herald.

F   4.   Pasteurization kills microscopic organisms by a freezing process.

F   5.   Pierre Curie died of years of exposure to radiation.

T   6.   Ehrlich's discoveries of serum therapy and chemotherapy are used to fight disease today.

F   7.   Einstein wanted to drop the atomic bomb to end the war.

T   8.   Roald Amundsen was the first to reach the South Pole.

T   9.   George Washington Carver conducted research using peanuts and soy beans.

F   10.   Electrons are the center of the atom.

MULTIPLE CHOICE: Circle the letter of the word or phrase that correctly completes each sentence.

1. Einstein's famous mathematical formula is _____.
   a. E=mc   b. Em=c2   <u>c. E=mc2</u>

2. If an atom is split, it _____.
   <u>a. produces energy</u>   b. falls apart   c. can't be split

3. Richard Bryd flew over _____.
   a. the North Pole   b. the South Pole   <u>c. the North and South pole</u>

4. _____ discovered the treatment for rabies.
   a. Ehrlich   <u>b. Pasteur</u>   c. Roentgen

5. Roentgen's discovery of x-rays _____.
   a. took years of hard work   <u>b. happened by accident</u>   c. was forgotten for years

MATCH: Match the names on the left with their description on the right by writing the letter of the correct description in the space provided.

H   1.   theory   a. something that causes a response or action

E   2.   ecology   b. tendency of matter to remain at rest unless effected by an outside force

B   3.   inertia   c. an unproved theory, tentatively accepted to explain certain facts

I   4.   fact   d. rate of motion

A   5.   stimuli   e. study of the relationship between organisms and their environments

F   6.   compound   f. substance containing two or more elements chemically combined

D   7.   velocity   g. the transmission of characteristics by means of genes

C   8.   hypothesis   h. scientifically accepted principle offered to explain phenomena

L   9.   element   i. something that has happened or is true

N   10. coagulate   j. the rays sent out; nuclear particles

M   11. atom   k. to make impure

O   12. hypothermia   l. any substance that cannot be separated into different substances

G   13. heredity   m. the smallest part of an element

J   14. radiation   n. to cause to become semi-solid

K   15. contaminate   o. dangerously low body temperature caused by prolonged exposure to cold

Lesson 29

1940 - 1950

Day	SCIENTISTS	INVENTIONS	EXPLORERS
Mon		1940 Helicoptor	**World War II Vocabulary**
		Questionnaire	Axis
			Allies
			Isolationist
			genocide
			treaty
			dictator
			-
Tue	1942 Enrico Fermi - first controlled		**Draw a World War II uniform**
	nuclear chain reaction		
	Questionnaire		**Complete World War II Worksheet**
	Vocabulary		
	fusion		
	fission		
	reaction		
	energy		
Wed	**S-29**	1945 Atomic Bomb is created by J. Robert	**Vocabulary**
		Oppenheimer.	balsa
		Questionnaire	anthropologist
			archaeology
Thu			1947 Thor Heyerdahl organized and led
			the voyage from Peru to Polynesia on the
			raft Kon Tiki.
			Questionnaire
			*French Polynesia
			Mark Map 10
Fri			Optional Movie: *Kon Tiki*
			*indicates present-day location

LANGUAGE ARTS	READING SELECTIONS
Plural nouns	**Historical Fiction (read one per lesson)**
L-29a Worksheet 19	Friends and Enemies - Lousann Gaeddert
	Enemy Brothers - Constance Savery
Ψ IEW Basic Essay - Optional*	One Eye Laughing, the Other Weeping - Barry Denenberg
Five-paragraph with three themes	A Call to Honor - Gilbert Morris
Read the article *Gandhi* and do more research.	Torn Thread - Anne Isaacs
	When My Name was Keoko - Linda Sue Park
*Students may refine or complete the essay in Lesson 28 or	Journey to Topaz - Yoshiko Uchida
write a second five-paragraph essay.	When the Soldiers Were Gone - Vera W. Propp
Possessive nouns	**Biographies (an alternate for a historical fiction)**
L-29b Worksheet 20	A Special Fate, Chine Sugihara - Alison Leslie Gold
	Corrie Ten Boom-Heroine of Haarlem - Sam Wellman
Ψ IEW Ghandi Essay - Champlain Model	I Am an American - Jerry Stanley
Create a key word outline as assigned, referencing sources	The Soldier's Voice - Barbara O'Connor
on your individual outlines and then fusing them	Thor Heyerdahl and the Kon Tiki Voyage - Philip Steele
	Harry S. Truman - Jim Hargrove
Differences	**Other Books for Research**
L-29c Worksheet 21	The 40's: From WW II to Jackie Robinson - Stephen Feinstein
	Leaders of WW II - Stewart Ross
Ψ IEW Rough Draft	The Causes of the Cold World - Stewart Ross
Write a rough draft of your essay, including introduction	The Flag with Fifty-six Stars - Susan Goldman Rubin
and conclusion paragraphs.	World War II Days - David C. King
	Going to War in World War ll - Moria Buterfield
	Immigrant Cooking in America - Loretta Frances Ichord
Subject/Verb agreement	**Historical Events for Timeline**
L-29d Worksheet 22	1941 Pearl Harbor bombed
	1941 The United States declares war on Japan
Ψ IEW Final Paper	1945 Atomic bomb dropped
Write your final paper with stylistic techniques and structures.	1945 United Nations formed
	1948 Jewish state of Israel established
	1948 Ghandi assassinated
	1949 Apartheid established in South Africa
	1950 Ho Chi Minh begins offensive against French troops in Indochina
Nouns/Verbs	**Other Areas of Interest during this Lesson**
L-29e	Internment of Japanese, Italian, and German-American citizens
	Mahatma Ghandi
	Lise Meitner - fission
	Harry S. Truman
	Corrie Ten Boom
	Resistance forces
Write your mini book report	Margaret Mead
	Polio epidemic
Optional Movie: *Tora! Tora! Tora!*	

Scientist Questionnaire

1. **Who:** Enrico Fermi   Father of the Atomic Bomb

2. **Nationality:** Italian   He became an American citizen in 1944.

3. **Life span:** 1901-1954

4. **Span of research:** At age 14, Enrico became consumed by the study of physics. His work began in Rome in 1934, and continued until 1945 when the first bomb exploded.

5. **Biblical or church history event of the time:** U.S. National Council of Churches

6. **Noted achievement & field of interest:** Quantum Theory applied to matter. He supervised the construction of the first nuclear reactor, in which uranium fission occurred in a controlled chain reaction. This was the first step in producing the bomb. The Manhattan Project developed the A-bomb.

7. **Secondary achievement & field of interest:** Fermi demonstrated that nuclear transformation occurs in almost every element subjected to neutron bombardment. This work led to the discovery of slow neutrons, which led to the discovery of nuclear fission and the production of elements lying beyond what was, until then, the Periodic Table.

8. **Motivation:** "Nothing should halt the progress of science. Whatever the future holds for mankind, however unpleasant it maybe, we must accept it, for knowledge is always better than ignorance." Enrico Fermi
He wanted to produce the bomb before Germany could. They had a three year head start.

9. **Significance of discovery:** It ended the war with Japan.

10. **How was this discovery helpful or harmful to society?** It was helpful because it ended the killing of the war but was destructive to a large amount of Japan's population and property. Fermi saw unlimited possibilities for atomic energy. Nuclear energy can produce heat and electricity for entire cities.

11. **New word and meaning:** Answers will vary.

12. **Questions prompted through this study?** Answers will vary.

13. **Interesting bit of trivia:** He was the Nobel Prize winner in Physics in 1938. The invitation to Stockholm to receive the prize helped Fermi and his family escape Italy.
In 1946, the Los Alamos group formed the Association of Men of Science to try and prevent the atrocities caused by the bomb. Fermi did not join this group. He saw it as a step toward world government.

Cite your sources:

Inventions Questionnaire

1. **What invention:** helicoptor   "helio" for spiral and "pter" for wings

2. **When:** 1940 (He began work in 1910) Sikorsky's VS-300
   - 1550's Leonardo DaVinci made drawings for an ornithopter flying machine
   - 1784   Launoy and Bienvenue created a toy helicoptor that worked
   - 1863   Ponton D'Amecourt was the first person to use the term "helicoptor"
   - 1907   Paul Cornu invented the first piloted helicoptor
   - 1924   Etienne Oehmichen flew a helicoptor one kilometer
     - The German Focke-Wulf Fw 61 flew, unknown inventor
   - 1940's Sikorsky built the first military model, XR-4
   - 1944   Stanley Hiller, Jr. make the first helicopter with stiff metal blades
   - 1946   Arthur Young adds full bubble canopy to the Bell Model 47
   - 1949   Stanley Hiller, Jr. piloted across the United States with the helicopter named Hiller 360
   - 1958   Sikorsky built the first chopper that could land and take off from water. It could also float.

3. **Who is the inventor:** (person or country) Igor Sikorsky "father of the helicoptor"

4. **Motivation:** to create the first successful helicoptor

5. **How did this invention change life as it was then?** The chopper can land and take off vertically so it does not require a runway. It can move forward, backward and sideways.

6. **What have been the ethical consequences?** (if any) The helicoptor "life flight" can be used to carry accident or wounded victims quickly to the hospital. Helicoptors are used for crop dusting, fire fighting, tourism, and search and rescue missions.
   Since the 1960's military gunships have utilized helicopters. They can carry lateral mounted armaments that fire from the side and deliver troops and supplies to remote areas.

7. **Diagram or draw the invention**

Cite your sources: inventors.about.com *3/20/2012*   www.guncoptor.com

Inventions Questionnaire

1. What invention: Atomic Bomb

2. When: 1945 during World War II

3. Who is the inventor (person or country): J. Robert Oppenheimer of the United States. Scientists who invented the atomic bomb under the Manhattan Project: Robert Oppenheimer, David Bohm, Leo Szilard, Eugene Wigner, Otto Frisch, Rudolf Peierls, Felix Bloch, Niels Bohr, Emilio Segre, James Franck, Enrico Fermi, Klaus Fuchs and Edward Teller

4. Motivation: To win the race for splitting the atom and developing the atomic bomb during World War II. Germany was near accomplishing the building of a bomb.

5. How did this invention change life as it was then? The bomb killed most of the population of Japan's cities, Hiroshima and Nagasaki. The powerful weapon convinced Japan to end the war. The destruction put people into a panic about a nuclear war. It did make America a super-power.

6. What have been the ethical consequences (if any)? More countries have these destructive weapons and can use them against their enemies. The development of atomic power has been useful in generating inexpensive power for many populations.

7. Diagram or draw the invention:

Cite your sources:

World War ll Worksheet

Read a book on World War II to find the answers to these questions.

1. Who were the leaders in World War II?
America – Franklin D. Roosevelt and Harry Truman
Germany – Adoph Hitler   Italy – Benito Mussolini
Japan – Emperor Hirohito   England – Winston Churchill

2. What major countries were Axis powers? Germany, Italy, Japan

3. What major countries were Allies? United States, Britain, Russia, China

4. How did World War II begin? Germany attacked Poland

5. Why did the United States enter the war? Japan bombed Pearl Harbor, HI, Dec. 7, 1941

6. Who attacked Pearl Harbor? Japan

7. Where is Pearl Harbor? Oahu, Hawaii

8. What does Blitzkrieg mean? "lightening war" battle strategy – air raid followed by troops

9. What was D-Day? The day a military attack or important event is to take place. In June, 1944 the allies landed in France.

10. Did the United States lose any battles during this war? Answers will vary.
List them: The Battle of Bataan, 1942, is one battle the U.S. lost during the war.

11. Name two scientists who helped develop the atom bomb? Answers will vary.
What did they contribute?
Example – Enrico Fermi worked on the first nuclear reaction.
Ernest Lawrence improved cyclotron.

12. When were the atom bombs dropped? August 6, 1945 Hiroshima, Japan
August 9, 1945 Nagasaki, Japan

13. When did Germany surrender? May 7, 1947

14. When did Japan surrender? September 2, 1945

15. List any of your family members who served in this war and what they did.

Explorers Questionnaire

1. **Who:** Thor Heyerdahl

2. **Nationality:** Norwegian

3. **When:** 1947

4. **Point of departure:** Peru
   or
   Sponsoring country: The Peruvian government cooperated with Thor.

5. **Was this place the explorer's home country?** No
   Explain: He was from Norway and he sponsored himself.

6. **Biblical personality of the time:** Corrie Ten Boom, a Dutch watchmaker is released from Ravensbruck. She traveled the world telling of her family and their experiences hiding Jews from the Nazis, and the lessons she learned in the concentration camp.

7. **What was discovered or explored?** He traveled all the way to Polynesia, covering 4300 miles of ocean. The Humboldt Current flows westward from Peru and the Trade Winds continue to blow westward, which enabled his expedition.

8. **How?** A balsa raft called the *Kon Tiki* was used. The raft was constructed of balsa logs lashed together with rope, 45 feet long and 22 feet wide. It had two masts with a small open cabin. Six men and a parrot manned the raft.

9. **What was their motivation?** To prove that the Pacific Islands were populated by Indians from South America whose ancestors were probably Phoenician or Cretan.

10. **Topography:** Taumotu Archipelago surrounded by reefs (present-day French Polynesia)

11. **Climate:** tropical - hot, humid, rainy, and sunny

12. **Natural resources:** tropical fruit, bread fruit, coconut and date palms, fish, and seafood

13. **Crops:** tropical fruit

14. **Exports:** Seafood

15. **Trivia:** Thor is a world-renowned scientist, adventurer, and writer. To pay for his trip he traveled and gave lectures. He wrote a book, *Kon Tiki.* It became a bestseller and was made into a film.

Cite your sources:

S-29
What is a nuclear chain reaction?
A nuclear chain reaction occurs when, on average, more than one neutron from a nuclear fission reaction (the splitting of the nuclei of atoms into two fragments of approximately equal mass), causes another fission reaction. Chain reactions can produce an enormous amount of energy.

What does one cause?
With uranium it can produce a steady and enormous supply of energy. Only nuclei that have many more neutrons than protons, such as uranium nuclei, can produce a nuclear chain reaction. In order to slow down a reaction, water, graphite or "heavy water" is used. A nuclear explosion can occur if the chain reaction is not kept under control. The scarce uranium isotope U-235 is the only natural material that nuclear reactors can use to produce a chain reaction.
Some reactors use water as a moderator, while others use graphite or heavy water.
*"heavy water" is water composed of heavy isotopes of hydrogen or oxygen, or of both.

Worksheet 19

Plural Nouns

Write the plural form of each noun below.

child	*children*	book	*books*
man	*men*	sheep	*sheep*
foot	*feet*	sea	*seas*
dictionary	*dictionaries*	story	*stories*
box	*boxes*	half	*halves*

Worksheet 20

Possessive Nouns

Write the singular and plural possessive forms.

	SINGULAR	PLURAL
1. my (teacher) pupil	teacher's	teachers'
2. the (artist) work	artist's	artists'
3. the (writer) books	writer's	writers'
4. your (friend) talent	friend's	friends'
5. the (scientist) experiment	scientist's	scientists'
6. the (soldier) ship	soldier's	soldiers'

L: 29   **Worksheet 21**

Confusing Plurals and Possessives
An apostrophe is used to form the possessive of a noun. It is almost never used to form the plural of a noun.

Read this report about Thomas Edison's inventions. Correct the words that need apostrophes. You will find ten words to correct.

   Thomas Alva **Edison's** first patented invention was an electronic vote recorder. This invention improved the method of totaling **voters'** ballots. Later, Edison improved the financial **world's** communication by designing a better stock ticker. In time, Edison set up this **country's** first industrial research laboratory. Using the **laboratory's** equipment, he developed the **world's** first commercially successful electric light bulb. The **public's** response to his inventions was tremendous. **Edison's** ideas have made possible many electronic devices. When he died, **Edison's** inventions numbered over 1,000. His inventions have affected almost **everyone's** life.

Worksheet 22

Subject – Verb Agreement

Read the paragraph and underline the correct verb for the sentence.

In 1990, Thor Heyerdahl (was, were) digging in a remote area near the coast of Peru. He (had, have) been looking for a civilization older and more advanced than the Incas. He (was, were) exploring the Tucume pyramids. He believes they (was, were) built by ancient seafarers who reached the new world on rafts. He (began, begun) work in 1991. The pyramids (was, were) made of adobe, a material most often used in Mesopotamia, near Iraq. The complex (is, are) linked to the sea by a 12-mile system of canals big enough for rafts like the Kon-Tiki.

In 1947, Heyerdahl (leave, left) on the Kon-Tiki in an attempt to prove his theory that prehistoric civilization reached the Americas from across the Pacific on rafts carried by ocean currents. This discovery (do, does) prove that they were able to successfully sail.

Lesson 30

1950 - 1951

Day	SCIENTISTS	INVENTIONS	EXPLORERS
Mon	**Vocabulary**	1950 Jet airline service	
	oceanographer	**Questionnaire**	
	undersea archaeology		
	the prefix "sub"		
	Write 5 words using the prefix "sub"		
Tue	1951 Jacques Cousteau invented		
	the Aqua Lung.		
	Questionnaire		
Wed	Movie: *Undersea World of Jacques*		1951 Jacques Cousteau explored the
	Cousteau		oceans in his ship *Calypso.*
			Questionnaire
			*oceans of the Earth
			Mark Map 10
Thu	1951 Robert Banks & Paul Hogan		**Visit a scuba shop.**
	discovers plastic. Marlex		
	Questionnaire		
Fri			
			*indicates present-day location

LANGUAGE ARTS	READING SELECTIONS
Action or linking verbs	**Historical Fiction (read one per lesson)**
L-30a Worksheet 23	Hero of Lesser Causes - Julie Johnston
	The Bomb - Theodore Taylor
Optional - Write a report on Jacques Cousteau	Circle of Fire - Evelyn Coleman
	Water Buffalo Days - Quang Nhuong Huynh
	The 1950's Music - Dorothy & Tom Hoobler
Ψ **IEW Expanded Essay**	
*Assignment may require two lessons for completion.	
You will need more resources to complete this essay.	
Verbs that act as action or linking verbs	**Biographies (an alternate for a historical fiction)**
L-30b Worksheet 24	Nate Saint: On a Wing and a Prayer - Janet & Geoff Benge
	Jim Elliot: One Great Purpose - Janet & Geoff Benge
Ψ **IEW Key Word Outlines**	Dwight D. Eisenhower - Wilma Hudson
Gather sources and create key word outlines. You will need	Dare to Dream - Angela Shelf Medearis
five topics for this expanded essay.	Golda Meir - Mollie Keller
	Frank Lloyd Wright for Kids - Kathleen Thorne Thomsen
Verb phrases and auxiliary verbs	**Other Books for Research**
L-30c	The Korean War - R. Conrad Stein
	The 1950's from the Korean War to Elvis - Stephen Feinstein
Ψ **IEW Fused Outline**	Scuba Diving - Sue Vander Hook
Create a fused outline for your expanded essay.	Sunk! Exploring Underwater Archaeology - Runestone Press
	Down Under, Down Under - Ann McGovern
Principle parts	**Historical Events for Timeline**
L-30d Worksheet 25	1950 Britain recognizes Communist China
	1950 Israeli Knesset resolves Jerusalem is capital of Israel
Ψ **IEW Rough Draft**	1950 India becomes a republic free from Britain
Write your rough draft, adding introduction and conclusion.	1950 USSR & Communist China sign peace treaty
	1950-1953 Korean Conflict
	1950 United States signs military assistance pact with Vietnam
	1951-1976 Vietnam Conflict
	1951 Israel demands compensation from Germany
Transitive and intransitive verbs	**Other Areas of Interest during this Lesson**
L-30e Worksheet 26	Jacques Piccard
	Billy Graham
Ψ **IEW Final Paper**	Atomic energy
This may be completed in Lesson 31	Black market
	Golda Meir
	Marian Anderson
Write your mini book report	1952 Joseph Woodland & Bernard Silver invent bar codes
	1956 Noah McVicker invents play dough
3 Week Quiz	
Optional Movie: *October Sky*	

Scientist Questionnaire

1. **Who:** Jacques-Yves Cousteau

2. **Nationality:** French

3. **Life span:** 1910-1997

4. **Span of research:** In 1930, he entered the Naval Academy with plans to be a pilot. A car accident ended his career in aviation.

5. **Biblical or church history event of the time:** Pope John XXIII

6. **Noted achievement & field of interest:** In 1943, he invented the Aqua Lung (Self-Contained Underwater Breathing Apparatus) a cylinder of compressed air connected through a pressure regulating valve to a face mask, which allowed a diver to stay underwater. During WWII he served with the French Resistance. The aqua-lung helped them act as mine sweepers in French harbors.

7. **Secondary achievement & field of interest:** Oceanographer In 1950, Loel Guinness bought the ex-Royal Navy minesweeper *Calypso* and leased it to Jacques. In the *Calypso,* Cousteau visited the most interesting waters of the planet, including some rivers. By the mid-1950s, Cousteau worked with Luis Marden to pioneer the underwater camera. Together with Jean Mollard, he created the SP-350, a two-man submarine that could reach a depth of 350 meters below the ocean's surface. In 1957, Cousteau was made director of the Oceanographic Museum in Monaco, created the Underseas Research Group, and was the leader of the Conshelf Saturation Dive Program (long-term immersion experiments, the first manned undersea colonies).

8. **Motivation:** He was a nature lover, especially fond of the sea. He wanted to learn more about the "blue continent".

9. **Significance of discovery:** Reported the effects of pollution, over-exploitation of resources and coastal development. He made many new underwater discoveries and inventions.

10. **How was this discovery helpful or harmful to society?** Water conservation was encouraged. He founded the international Cousteau Society in 1973 to raise awareness, to provide environmental education, and to keep the oceans alive for future generations.

11. **New word and meaning:** Answers will vary.

12. **Questions prompted through this study?** Answers will vary.

13. **Interesting bit of trivia:** In 1946, the innovative explorer established the Undersea Research Group and became a pioneer inventor of marine devices including the anti-shark cage, special underwater cameras, and the Aqua lung. He was a naval officer, marine explorer and ecologist, pioneer of marine conservation, author, and documentary filmmaker. He had his own TV show during the 60's and 70's entitled *The Underwater World of Jacques Cousteau* that dramatized his underwater adventures. His work allowed people of all continents to visit life under the ocean's surface and explore, through television, the resources of the "blue continent."

Cite your sources:

Scientist Questionnaire

1. **Who:** Robert Banks and Paul Hogan

2. **Nationality:** American

3. **Life span:** 1921-1989   1919-2012

4. **Span of research:** 1951-1957 from theory to product Marlex (plastic)
The toy, hula hoop, made Marlex popular.

5. **Biblical event of the time:** In 1951, Campus Crusade for Christ was founded at UCLA

6. **Noted achievement & field of interest:** Chemistry
Discovery of crystalline polypropylene and high density polyethylene

7. **Secondary achievement & field of interest:** Plastics engineering – development and manufacturing process of Marlex

8. **Motivation:** They were looking for ways to convert the hydrocarbons (ethylene and proplylene) produced when refining natural gas into components for gasoline. In the process, they found the catalyst that would transform the hydrocarbons into solid polymers.

9. **Significance of discovery:** Plastics are in nearly everything we use.

10. **How was this discovery helpful or harmful to society?** Opened the world to a strong, lightweight material useable for everything from wrapping to outdoor furniture. Plastic is not biodegradable.

11. **New word and meaning** Answer will vary
Polymers: substance made up of many molecules all strung together to form long chains

12. **Questions prompted through this study?** Answers will vary

13. **Interesting bit of trivia:** Answers will vary
One of two of the greatest discoveries in the 20th century (penicillan is the other)

Cite your sources: Bartlesville Examiner-Enterprise, Vol. 117, Issue 49 Sunday, Feb. 26, 2012.
"Discovery by Legendary Phillips Chemists Leaves Lasting Legacy – Pioneers of Plastic"

Inventions Questionnaire

1. What invention: Jet Airline Service

2. When: 1952

3. Who is the inventor (person or country): BOAC British Overseas Aircraft Corp. World's first commercial airline service

4. Motivation: Aviation transportation between far distances; transporting mail, cargo, and people. To provide mass air transportation for the average man at rates he can afford to pay.

5. How did this invention change life as it was then? It provided quicker and better transportation. It's used by the military to transport troops, cargo, supplies, drop bombs, and perform surveillance.

6. What have been the ethical consequences (if any)? Although it provided fast transportation, many air tragedies resulted from it. It is still safer than driving.

7. Diagram or draw the invention:

Explorers Questionnaire

1. **Who:** Jacques-Yves Cousteau

2. **Nationality:** French

3. **When:** 1951

4. **Point of departure:**
   or
   Sponsoring country: France

5. **Was this place the explorer's home country?** Yes
   Explain:

6. **Biblical or church history personality of the time:** Billy Graham preaches in America.

7. **What was discovered or explored?** He explored the oceans of the world.

8. **How?** He explored in his ship the *Calypso*

9. **What was their motivation?** They wanted to learn more about ocean life and the possibility of man living under the seas.

10. **Topography:** The ship became home to 28 crewmen, a lab, and a film studio for his TV show.

11. **Climate:** From the warm waters of the Indian Ocean to the ice of Antarctica

12. **Natural resources:** Deep water animals, mammals, fish, Kelp, and sea weed

13. **Crops:** none

14. **Exports:** The sea has many exportable products such as fish, bi-valves, crustaceans, and salt, kelp, coral, shells.

15. **Trivia:** He became the symbol of a world to be explored. He was a messenger of peace and of protecting the water planet for future generations. He founded the Cousteau Society in 1973 to protect ocean life. In 1985, President Reagan gave him the Medal of Freedom.

No science assignment in Lesson 30

Worksheet 23

Identifying Verbs
Pick out the verbs in each sentence. Identify it as either an action verb or linking verb by labeling it with *A* or *L* over the verb.

                               L   A

The diving bell <u>is</u> not a new invention. Alexander the Great <u>may have used</u> one in

the 300's BC. Roger Bacon <u>made</u> (A) a similar device as far back as 1200. But it <u>is</u> (L) only

in this century that diving bells <u>have become</u> (L) real aids to underwater work.

A diving bell <u>was</u> (L) a metal chamber the shape of a bell or sometimes a box , but was without a floor.

It <u>was</u> (L) lowered into the water. Men <u>worked</u> (A) inside the bell for long periods of time. Even though

They <u>stood</u> (A) on the bottom of the sea, they <u>did</u> (L) not <u>get</u> (L) wet and they <u>had</u> (L) plenty of air to breathe.

The diving bell <u>could be used</u> (A) for many things. Usually it <u>provided</u> (A) protection for

men who <u>were laying</u> (A) foundations for bridges or <u>doing</u> (A) underwater cable work.

Telephone and telegraph wires <u>were</u> (L) often <u>strung</u> (A) under rivers and diving bells <u>helped</u> (A) the men do

these jobs. Diving bells <u>are</u> (L) still sometimes used to observe underwater life, although there <u>are</u> (L)

more mobile machines available for this purpose now.

Worksheet 24

Identifying Verbs
Some verbs can be either action or linking verbs. Some of these are: appear, become, feel, grow, look, remain, seem, smell, sound, stay, and taste. The use of a verb in a sentence determines whether it is a linking verb or an action verb.

Rewrite the paragraph. Use a linking verb or an action verb for each blank.

Oceanography, the study of oceans, <u>is</u> a fascinating science. Jacques Cousteau <u>is</u> a famous oceanographer who <u>was</u> born in France in 1910. Cousteau <u>wanted</u> to develop new means of exploring oceans. He <u>is</u> one of the inventors of the Aqua-Lung. With an Aqua-Lung a diver <u>can</u> <u>stay</u> underwater for a long time without surfacing. Cousteau also <u>helped</u> to develop a diving saucer for undersea use.

Jacques Cousteau <u>is</u> a dedicated scientist. He once <u>discovered</u> a plan by France to dump dangerous waste into the sea. Cousteau <u>is</u> also an author and a motion picture producer. His first book <u>was</u> *The Silent World*. It <u>was</u> published in 1953. Cousteau <u>wrote</u> two other books. They <u>are</u> *The Living Sea* and *World Without Sun*. Jacques Cousteau's contributions to oceanography <u>are</u> still used today. Oceanography <u>is</u> an important science.

**Teacher's note: Answers will vary.

Worksheet 25

On your paper, chart these verbs showing the three principle parts.

Present	Past	Past Participle
1. do	*did*	*has, have done*
2. set	*set*	*has, have sat*
3. run	*ran*	*has, have ran*
4. go	*went*	*has, have gone*
5. come	*came*	*has, have come*
6. eat	*ate*	*has, have eaten*
7. give	*gave*	*has, have given*
8. write	*wrote*	*has, have written*
9. teach	*taught*	*has, have taught*
10. learn	*learned*	*has, have learned*
11. know	*knew*	*has, have known*
12. take	*took*	*has, have taken*
13. bring	*brought*	*has, have brought*
14. see	*saw*	*has, have seen*
15. freeze	*froze*	*has, have frozen*
16. swim	*swam*	*has, have swum*
17. steal	*stole*	*has, have stolen*
18. drive	*drove*	*has, have driven*
19. draw	*drew*	*has, have drawn*
20. ride	*rode*	*has, have ridden*
21. choose	*chose*	*has, have chosen*
22. sit	*sat*	*has, have sat*
23. begin	*began*	*has, have begun*
24. drink	*drank*	*has, have drunk*
25. ring	*rang*	*has, have rung*

Worksheet 26

Transitive and Intransitive Verbs

Read the following sentences. Circle the intransitive verbs. Underline the transitive verb.

1. Early explorers <u>sailed</u> across unknown seas.

2. They <u>feared</u> monsters in the oceans.

3. People <u>began to explore</u> the seas in the mid-20th century.

4. Jacques Cousteau *is* a pioneer in oceanography.

5. He <u>developed</u> several inventions for undersea exploration.

6. His research ship *is* the Calypso.

7. He <u>has explored</u> many shipwrecks.

8. He <u>has recorded</u> his discoveries about sea life on film.

9. He <u>was exploring</u> the possibility of humans living under the sea.

10. He <u>has constructed</u> sea houses.

* Bold italics reflects circled answers

Teacher's Notes

_____

_____

_____

_____

_____

_____

_____

_____

_____

_____

_____

_____

_____

_____

_____

_____

_____

_____

_____

_____

_____

_____

_____

_____

FOURTH QUARTER THREE WEEK QUIZ

MATCH: Match the names on the left with their description on the right by writing the letter of the correct description in the space provided.

C   1.   Robert Goddard   a. descended in the ocean in a bathysphere

F   2.   Alexander Fleming   b. sailed from Peru to Polynesia by raft

A   3.   William Beebe   c. invented the multi-stage rocket

D   4.   Enrico Fermi   d. performed the first controlled nuclear chain reaction

B   5.   Thor Heyerdahl   e. ocean explorer

E   6.   Jacques Cousteau   f. discovered penicillin

MULTIPLE CHOICE: Circle the letter of the word or phrase that correctly completes each sentence.

1. Jacque Cousteau invented the _____.
      a. multi-stage rocket   b. aqua lung   c. bathysphere

2. Thor Heyerdahl's raft was called _____.
      a. Riki Tiki Tava   b. Calypso   c. Kon Tiki

3. The name of the famous testing sight for the atom bomb was _____.
      a. Los Almos   b. Los Angeles   c. Las Vegas

4. The name of the famous testing sight for the atom bomb was _____.
      a. New Mexico   b. Arizona   c. Nevada

TRUE OR FALSE: Mark each statement T for true or F for false in the space provided.

F   1.   Robert Goddard's invention opened the door to deep sea exploration.

T   2.   Penicillin is an antibiotic that can weaken or kill bacteria.

F   3.   A virus is a helpful influence needed for fermentation.

T   4.   Enrico Fermi was a part of the team that created the atom bomb.

T   5.   Enrico Fermi worked on the Manhattan Project.

F   6.   Thor Heyerdahl's motive was for fun and sport.

T   7.   Jacques Cousteau is an inventor and an explorer.

F   8.   One of Thor Heyerdahl's men was killed during their voyage.

MATCH: Match the names on the left with their description on the right by writing the letter of the correct description in the space provided.

D   1.   antibiotic   a. disease producing organisms

C   2.   fission   b. one celled living organism that brings fermentation, putrefaction and produce disease

F   3.   oceanography   c. act of splitting into parts by natural division, or in the process of releasing nuclear energy

B   4.   bacteria   d. a substance produced by fungi, which in diluted solution inhibit or destroy bacteria

E   5.   fusion   e. uniting of various elements into a whole as if by melting together

A   6.   virus   f. science dealing with undersea space and the conducting of research in such areas as
                               underwater transportation, communication, geography, and engineering

BONUS: Diagram and label a nuclear chain reaction.

BONUS: Diagram and label a nuclear chain reaction.

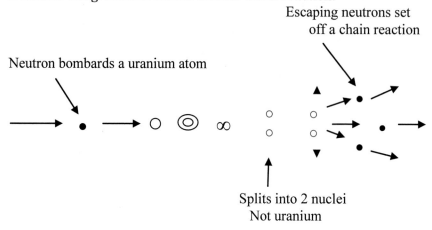

Lesson 31

1951 - 1960

Day	SCIENTISTS	INVENTIONS	EXPLORERS
Mon	**Science Vocabulary**	**Space Vocabulary**	**Vocabulary**
	bio	satellite	summit
	polio	NASA	glacier
	paralysis	outer space	avalanche
	virologist	trajectory	ravine
	biology		crevasse
	biophysicist		
	atrophy		
	Find other words using the prefix "bio"		
Tue	1953 Jonas Salk developed the		1953 Sir Edmund Hillary became the
	anti-polio vaccine.		first person to successfully climb
	Questionnaire		Mount Everest.
			Questionnaire
			*Himalayas
			Mark Map 5
Wed	**Science Vocabulary**	1954 Nuclear Submarine	**What country is Mt. Everest in?**
	helix	U.S.S. Nautilus III	
	DNA	**Questionnaire**	**Draw that country's flag**
	chromosome		
	gene		
	S-31		
Thu	1953 Francis Crick & James Watson	1957 Sputnik I	Optional: National Geographic -
	constructed a model of the DNA molecule	**Questionnaire**	*On the Climbing of Mount Everest*
	the chemical that controls heredity.		
	Questionnaire		
Fri		1958 Explorer I	
		Questionnaire	
			*indicates present-day location

LANGUAGE ARTS	READING SELECTIONS
Adjectives	**Historical Fiction (read one per lesson)**
L-31a	My Name is Sepeetza - Shirley Sterling
	Water Buffalo Days - Quang Nhuong Huynh
Ψ IEW Expanded Essay - Optional	Close to Home - Lydia Weaver
Complete essay from Lesson 30 or begin a new essay.	
Read *Born to Change History* as the basis for your essay.	
You will need more resources for this essay.	
Suffixes	**Biographies (an alternate for a historical fiction)**
L-31b	*The Fate of the Yellow Woodbee - Dave & Neta Jackson
	Dare to Dream - Angela Shelf Medearis
Ψ IEW Key Word Outlines	Malcolm X - Jack Slater
Gather sources and create key word outlines. You will need	Sir Edmund Hillary - Whitney Stewart
five topics for this expanded essay. Record bibliography	
information on each key word outline	
Adverbs	**Other Books for Research**
L-31c	Black Stars of the Civil Rights Movement - Jim Haskin
	America Heroes - Marfe Ferguson Delano
Ψ IEW Fused Outline	The Korean War - Conrad R. Stein
Create a fused outline with introduction and conclusion	Surviving Everest - National Geographic DVD
for your expanded essay.	American Heroes - Marfe Ferguson Delano
	Great People of the 20th Century - Time
	Blood and DNA Evidence Experiments - Kenneth G. Rainis
Comparative forms	**Historical Events for Timeline**
L-31d	1953 Marshal Tito is the president of Yugoslavia
	1953 Modern Egypt is established
Ψ IEW Rough Draft	1955 USSR ends the war with Germany
Write your rough draft.	1956 Sudan becomes independent
and conclusion.	1958 European Common Market established
	1959 Fidel Castro takes leadership of Cuba
	1960 US & Japan sign joint defense treaty
	1960 European Free Trade Association forms in Stockholm
Writing with Adjectives and Adverbs	**Other Areas of Interest during this Lesson**
L-31e	Civil Rights Movement
	Dwight D. Eisenhower
Ψ IEW Final Paper	Martin Luther King
	Segregation
Optional: Write your mini book report.	The Rosenbergs, atomic spies
	1953 RCA designs color television
	Transistor, 1956
	1959 Richard Feynman - Father of Nanoscience

Scientist Questionnaire

1. Who: Jonas Salk

2. Nationality: American

3. Life span: 1941-1995

4. Span of research: He became interested in biology and chemistry and decided to go into research. In 1938, he graduated from medical school. In 1942, he began studies in epidemiology (the study of the causes and control of epidemics). In 1947, he began teaching and researching at the University of Pittsburgh.

5. Biblical event of the time: Archbishop Makarios becomes president of Cyprus in 1959.

6. Noted achievement & field of interest: He developed a vaccine to prevent polio. He was a virologist. Between 1956 and 1958, massive inoculations were given throughout the United States which effectively stopped the crippling virus.

7. Secondary achievement & field of interest: At age 76, he directed the multinational effort to develop an AIDS vaccine. Salk received the approval of the federal Food and Drug Administration to begin large-scale testing of an experimental vaccine.

8. Motivation: He dedicated himself to studying immunology. He wanted to be able to cure those with viral disease. Dr. Salk never patented his polio vaccine but distributed the formula freely so the whole world could benefit from his discovery.

9. Significance of discovery: He eliminated widespread polio with a vaccine.

10. How was this discovery helpful or harmful to society? His vaccine has almost eradicated polio. The Salk Institute continues to research the causes, prevention and cure of diseases such as cancer and AIDS.

11. New word and meaning: Answers will vary.

12. Questions prompted through this study? Answers will vary.

13. Interesting bit of trivia: During WWII Salk aided in the successful development of an influenza vaccine. Daniel O'Connor, director of March of Dimes, challenged Jonas to join the battle against polio. In 1954, the vaccine was developed. Salk immunized his team and their families as proof. Between 1956 and 1958, massive inoculations throughout the United States greatly reduced the crippling virus.

Cite your sources: http://www.achievement.org/autodoc/page/sal0bio-14/14/2012

Scientist Questionnaire

1. **Who:** Francis Harry Compton Crick and James Dewey Watson   Fathers of Molecular Biology

2. **Nationality:** Crick was British and Watson was American

3. **Life span:** 1916-2004 (Crick)   1928- (Watson)

4. **Span of research:** Crick was inquisitive even as a child. His parents bought him an encyclopedia set because he asked so many questions. After the war, he was inspired by a book, *What is Life? The Physical Aspect of the Living Cell* by Erwin Schrodinger. In 1949, he pursued biological research. Watson began university at 15 and had his doctorate at 22. In 1951, Crick (age 35) and Watson (age 22) met and agreed on their own theory of DNA; DNA, not proteins, carry the genetic information.

5. **Biblical event of the time:** The Revised Standard Version of the Bible was published for Protestants.

6. **Noted achievement & field of interest:** Since they disagreed with the theory of the day, they had to gather scientific data and re-evaluate the information. They constructed a model of the DNA molecule, the chemical that controls heredity, and they expanded the fields of Biochemistry and Molecular Genetics. They also published a book entitled *The Double Helix*.

7. **Secondary achievement & field of interest:** In 1966, Dr. Crick began working in embryology, focusing on brain functions, the nature of the consciousness, and dreams.
   Watson continued in the field of genetics. Watson and his team discovered the molecular nature of cancer and identified cancer genes for the first time. Watson headed the Human Genome Project.

8. **Motivation:** Watson and Crick's success was achieved by perserverance. They wanted to prove their theory.

9. **Significance of discovery:** The single most important development in biology of the 20th century. DNA determines our physical make up. DNA carries our genetic code.

10. **How was this discovery helpful or harmful to society?** It led to the mapping of the human genome, discovering of the structure of viruses and retroviruses, AIDS, cancer and genetic engineering and embryology. DNA helps the police identify criminals. This knowledge can bring up ethical issues regarding genetic engineering of human beings and animals.

11. **New word and meaning:** Answers will vary.

12. **Questions prompted through this study?** Answers will vary.

13. **Interesting bit of trivia:** Crick and Watson shared the 1962 Nobel Prize in Physiology or Medicine with Maurice Wilkins.

Cite your sources:

Inventions Questionnaire

1. **What invention:** USS Nautilus SSN-571 First nuclear powered submarine

2. **When:** 1954 (1951 Congress authorized construction) She put to sea in January, 1955

3. **Who is the inventor:** (person or country) Ship design by John Burnham, built by General Dynamics, and supervised by Admiral Hyman G. Rickover "Father of the Nuclear Navy"

4. **Motivation:** To create a submarine that could run on its own nuclear reactor. Extend the underwater time to 6 months. Serve as the main striking power of the Navy.

5. **How did this invention change life as it was then?** Submarine crews could stay underwater longer. Nautilus made the first complete submerged transit beneath the North Pole in 1958. The success of Operation Sunshine opens possibilities for new commercial seaway cargo sumarines.

6. **What have been the ethical consequences?** (if any) The crew lives with a nuclear reactor, an added danger. The submarine carries nuclear warheads for defense and attack situations. It has been copied by other countries that are considered enemies of the United States.

7. **Diagram or draw the invention**

Cite your sources:

Inventions Questionnaire

1. **What invention:** Sputnik I, artificial satellite

2. **When:** April, 1957

3. **Who is the inventor (person or country):** Chief Designer Sergei Korolyov of the USSR

4. **Motivation:** To see if a rocket could launch a satellite. The satellite is used for upper-atmosphere research. It sends out radio transmissions as it orbits the earth.

5. **How did this invention change life as it was then?** It began the great Space Race between the USSR and the Americans.

6. **What have been the ethical consequences (if any)?** We now have improved global communications, but also have increased incidences of spying and other illegal tracking.

7. **Diagram or draw the invention:**

Cite your sources:

Inventions Questionnaire

1. What invention: Explorer 1 Satellite

2. When: 1958

3. Who is the inventor (person or country): The U.S. responded to Sputnik 1 by launching Explorer I in July of 1958.

4. Motivation: Scientific space exploration. The race was on!

5. How did this invention change life as it was then? Satellites accomplish many tasks. Communication satellites relay radio and TV signals. They provide telephone links for business and government. The Van Allen radiation belts were discovered and now information and pictures can be transferred around the earth by satellite. Weather can be tracked and reported more quickly; allowing people to prepare. Navigation satellites help pilots and sailors keep track of plane and ship positions.

6. What have been the ethical consequences (if any)? Military satellites have been used to get secret information from other countries. They can transmit clear and detailed pictures and can warn against military attacks.

7. Diagram or draw the invention:

Cite your sources: http://www.jpl.nasa.gov/explorer/history/ 4/14/2012

Explorers Questionnaire

1. Who: Sir Edmund Hillary

2. Nationality: New Zealand

3. When: 1951

4. Point of departure: New Zealand to Katmandu, Nepal, and on to the Himalayas
or
Sponsoring country: Britain, the Royal British Geographical Society and British Alpine Club sponsored the British Everest Expedition.

5. Was this place the explorer's home country? Yes
Explain: New Zealand was an independent nation within the British Commonwealth.

6. Biblical or church history personality of the time: David Wilkerson works with the gangs in New York.

7. What was discovered or explored? They ascended the south summit of Mount Everest.

8. How? 15 mountaineers and 150 porters worked their way up the mountain, establishing base camps and moving up supplies.

9. What was their motivation? They wanted to be the first to climb Mt. Everest, the highest mountain in the world.

10. Topography: Himalayas Mountain Range in Nepal with fertile valleys

11. Climate: cool summers and severe winters

12. Natural resources: spring water

13. Crops: grain

14. Exports: None, subsistence farmers and Yak herders

15. Trivia: Nepalese Tenzing Norgay climbed the summit with Hillary.

Cite your sources: http://www.achievement.org/autodoc/page/hil0bio-1 /14/20121

S-31

What is DNA? DNA stands for deoxyribonucleic acid, which is a thin, chainlike molecule found in every living cell on earth. It is the building block of life and directs the formation, growth, and reproduction of cells and organisms. Short sections of DNA called genes determine heredity. DNA is found mainly within a cell's nucleus, in threadlike structures called chromosomes. DNA even occurs in bacterial cells, which do not have a nucleus, and in some viruses. The DNA molecule consists of two polynucleotide chains arranged in a double helix (spiral) that resembles a twisted rope ladder. Polynucleotide chains of phosphates and sugars form the sides of the ladder. Each rung represents two matching bases, called base pairs. Weak chemical bonds between specific base pairs hold the chains together.

No language worksheets in Lesson 31

Lesson 32

1960 - 1965

Lesson 32

Day	SCIENTISTS	INVENTIONS	EXPLORERS
Mon		**Space Vocabulary**	1961 Yuri Gagarin, first to travel in space
		astronaut	**Questionnaire**
		gyroscope	*outer space
		zero gravity	
		friction	
		atmosphere	
Tue	**S-32**		1961 Alan Shepard, first American to
	Earth's atmostphere		travel in space
			Questionnaire
			*outer space
Wed			1962 John Glenn, first American to orbit
			the earth
			Questionnaire
			*orbit
Thu			1963 Valentina Terishkova, first woman
			to travel in space
			Questionnaire
			*orbit
Fri			
			*indicates present-day location

LANGUAGE ARTS	READING SELECTIONS
Personal Pronouns	**Historical Fiction (read one per lesson)**
L-32a Worksheet 27	Journey Home - Yoshika Uchida
	Rebels - 1960's - Dorothy & Tom Hoobler
Sci-Fi Story	Before We Were Free - Julia Alvarez
L-32b	Escape to West Berlin - Maurine F. Dahlberg
* Optional IEW inclusion	Durango Street - Frank Bonham
Ψ **IEW Essay Writing**	The Starplace - Vicki Grove
Read the article *Between Two Worlds* and outline your five	Just Like Martin - Ossie Davis
paragraph essay. You may need additional resources.	A Journal of Seamus Flaterty - Ellen Emerson White
Demonstrative Pronouns	**Biographies (an alternate for a historical fiction)**
L-32c Worksheet 28	Through My Eyes - Ruby Bridges
	The Last Train North - Clifton Taulbert
Ψ **IEW Rough Draft**	
Create a rough draft of your essay.	
Antecedents	**Other Books for Research**
L-32d Worksheet 29	The 1960's: From the Vietnam War to Flower Power - Stephen Feinstein
	Silent Spring - Rachel Carson
	Vietnam Antiwar Movement in American History - Anita McCormick
	Launch Day - Peter A. Campbell
Indefinite Pronouns	**Historical Events for Timeline**
L-32e Worksheet 30	1960 Belgian Congo granted independence
	1960 Communists build the Berlin Wall
Ψ **IEW Final Paper**	1961 Bay of Pigs - unsuccessful invasion of Cuba
Include 3 openers, 3 dress-ups, and a decoration or triple	1962 Uganda and Tanganyika become independent
extension in each paragraph. Don't forget topic/clincher rule	1963 Kenya becomes an independent republic
and to double space.	1964 Zanzibar and Tanganyika join as Tanzania
	1964 Civil Rights Movement
	1965 President Johnson's "Great Society" address
Recognizing different kinds of pronouns	**Other Areas of Interest during this Lesson**
L-32f Worksheet 31	Lasers
	John F. Kennedy
	Space probes
	European Free Trade Association
	John Birch Society
	Pearl S. Buck
	Rachel Carson
	Freedom Schools in the South
Optional Movie: *When We Were Colored*	

Explorers Questionnaire

1. **Who:** Yuri Gagarin

2. **Nationality:** Russian

3. **When:** 1961

4. **Point of departure:** Baikonur, USSR
   or
   Sponsoring country: USSR

5. **Was this place the explorer's home country?** Yes
   Explain: Russian cosmonaut

6. **Biblical or church history personality of the time:** Religious persecution in Cuba

7. **What was discovered or explored?** He was the first man in space. His 108 minute flight orbited the earth.

8. **How?** He traveled in a Soviet spaceship/satellite, *Vostok 1*. Basically, Gagarin was sitting in a tin can on top of a bomb. To return to earth, Gagarin ejected at an altitude of approximately 7 kilometers and landed safely. The *Vostok* capsule impact made it impossible for a person to remain inside during a landing.

9. **What was their motivation?** USSR wanted Yuri to be the first man in space.

10. **Topography:** outer space   altitude 327,000 meters

11. **Climate:** subzero

12. **Natural resources:** none

13. **Crops:** none

14. **Exports:** none

15. **Trivia:** An old woman, her granddaughter, and a cow were the first to see him return to the planet. He was killed in a test pilot plane crash in 1968 at 34 years old.

Cite your sources:

Explorers Questionnaire

1. **Who:** Alan B. Shepard

2. **Nationality:** American

3. **When:** 1961

4. **Point of departure:** Cape Canaveral, Florida United States
   or
   Sponsoring country: United States

5. **Was this place the explorer's home country?** Yes
   Explain: NASA astronaut

6. **Biblical or church history personality of the time:** Brother Andrew, "God's Bible smuggler"

7. **What was discovered or explored?** He was the first American to travel in space. On May 5, 1961, astronaut Shepard rocketed 117 miles into space from Cape Canaveral, Florida.

8. **How?** *Freedom 7* spacecraft

9. **What was their motivation?** To travel in space (to compete with the Soviet Union in the Space Race)

10. **Topography:** outer space

11. **Climate:** subzero

12. **Natural resources:** none

13. **Crops:** none

14. **Exports:** none

15. **Trivia:** In 1963, he was designated Chief of the Astronaut Office with responsibility for monitoring the coordination, scheduling, and control of all activities involving NASA astronauts.

Cite your sources: http://www.jsc.nasa.gov/Bios/htmlbios/shepard-alan.html 4/14/2012

Explorers Questionnaire

1. **Who:** John Herschel Glenn Jr.

2. **Nationality:** American

3. **When:** 1962

4. **Point of departure:** United States
   or
   Sponsoring country: United States

5. **Was this place the explorer's home country?** Yes
   Explain: NASA

6. **Biblical or church history personality of the time:** The Pope presents Vatican II.

7. **What was discovered or explored?** He was the first man to orbit the earth.

8. **How?** *Mercury-6* spaceship

9. **What was their motivation?** The United States wanted to be the first country to put a man in orbit around the earth.

10. **Topography:** orbits earth

11. **Climate:** thermosphere 1,500 C or higher

12. **Natural resources:** none

13. **Crops:** none

14. **Exports:** none

15. **Trivia:** Glenn was assigned to the NASA Space Task Group at Langley Research Center, Hampton, Virginia, in April 1959 after his selection as a Project Mercury Astronaut. The Space Task Group was moved to Houston and became part of the NASA Manned Spacecraft Center in 1962. Glenn returned to space in 1998 at the age of 77 and became the oldest astronaut to ever engage in space travel.

Cite your sources:

Explorers Questionnaire

1. **Who:** Valentina Tereshkova

2. **Nationality:** Russian

3. **When:** 1963

4. **Point of departure:** Russia
   or
   Sponsoring country: Russia

5. **Was this place the explorer's home country?** Yes
   Explain: USSR cosmonaut   Soviet Space Program under the Soviet Air Force

6. **Biblical or church history personality of the time:** Brother Andrew, Bible smuggler to Communist countries

7. **What was discovered or explored?** She was the first woman and civilian in space. She spent three days in space and orbited earth 48 times.

8. **How?** Spacecraft *Vostok VI*

9. **What was their motivation?** The Soviets wanted another "first" to beat the United States. She wanted to be the first woman in space and proved women could withstand the physical and emotional stresses of a space flight.

10. **Topography:** orbits the earth

11. **Climate:** thermosphere 1,500 C or higher

12. **Natural resources:** none

13. **Crops:** none

14. **Exports:** none

15. **Trivia:** She was the first woman in space. Yuri Gagarin headed the selection committee for the female cosmonauts. This was her only space flight. She continued in the space program and married a cosmonaut.

Cite your sources: http://starchild.gsfc.nasa.gov/docs/StarChild/whos_who_level2/tereshkova.html 4/14/2012

S-32

Diagram and label the layers of the earth's atmosphere. What takes place or can take place in each layer? The atmosphere is divided into five layers as follows (from lowest to highest altitude) 1) troposphere, (2)stratosphere, (3)mesosphere, (4)thermosphere, and (5)exosphere.

The troposphere contains more than 75 percent of Earth's atmosphere and is nearest to earth. Almost all of Earth's weather conditions occur in this layer and weather forecasts are based on the study of this level.

The stratosphere extends from the tropopause to about 30 miles (48 kilometers) above Earth's surface. Very little moisture enters the stratosphere, and pilots prefer flying in this layer in order to stay above weather disturbances.

The mesosphere extends from the stratopause to about 50 miles (80 kilometers) above Earth. The temperature of the mesosphere decreases with altitude. The lowest temperatures in Earth's atmosphere occur at the top of the mesosphere, called the mesopause. Trails of hot gases left by meteors can be seen in the mesosphere. Extremely strong winds blow in this layer. These winds blow from west to east during the winter and from east to west during the summer.

The thermosphere begins at the mesopause and extends to about 300 miles (480 kilometers) above Earth. The air in the thermosphere is extremely thin. More than 99.99 percent of the atmosphere lies below it. The chemical composition of the thermosphere differs from that of the lower layers.
The exosphere begins at the thermopause and eventually merges with the solar wind. The exosphere contains so little air that satellites and spacecraft orbiting Earth in the region encounter almost no resistance. The atoms and molecules of the air in the exosphere move extremely fast and have been known to overcome gravity and escape into space. Satellites orbit in this layer of the atmosphere.

Worksheet 27

Pronouns
Fill in each blank with a personal pronoun from the box.

1. _They_ were almost ready.

2. _He_ needs to put on _his_ space suit.

3. _We_ watched _him_ prepare.

4. Do not try to talk to _me_ now.

5. _I_ can't hear _you_ through this helmet.

6. _You_ should use the microphone.

7. _It's_ wired into my helmet.

8. Thanks, now _we_ can communicate.

Worksheet 28

Demonstrative Pronouns
Fill in each blank with a demonstrative pronoun. (*this* and *those*)

1. Did *these* come today?

2. Have you read *this*?

3. *This* is exciting!

4. *These* will get us into NASA.

5. *This* is the launch day.

Fill in the blanks using that and those.

1. Did you hear *that*?

2. Are *those* real?

3. Who bought *those*?

4. Are *those* yours?

5. *Those* will get us into the launch.

Worksheet 29

Antecedents
An antecedent is the word or group of words to which a pronoun refers.

Underline the antecedent in sentence A to which the pronoun in sentence B refers.

A. 1. Robert Goddard was a scientist.
    2. He suggested reaching the moon by rockets.

B. 1. People thought this was absurd.
    2. They called him "moon man".

C. 1. In 1926, the first rocket to use liquid fuel was launched.
    2. It reached 60 mph and traveled 200 feet.

D. 1. People from his state complained about the rockets.
    2. They called the police.

E. 1. Goddard continued his work in New Mexico.
    2. He received funds to set up the test station.

F. 1. Robert Goddard died in 1945.
    2. He led the way to the exploration of space.

Worksheet 30

Indefinite Pronouns
Fill in the blank with an indefinite pronoun.

1. *Everyone* will be watching the launch.

2. *Everything* must function correctly.

3. *Nothing* must be questionable.

4. Safety is important for *everybody* here.

5. Has *anyone* seen the astronauts yet?

6. Will they carry *anything* for cargo?

7. *Many* cargo items are in the hold already.

8. *No one* has seen this ship's cargo.

9. *Few* know its contents.

10. The astronauts know *something* about this mission and its cargo.

Worksheet 31

Recognizing Different Kinds of Pronouns
Identify the pronoun by labeling it P for personal, D for demonstrative or I for indefinite.

I – nobody	P – my	I – no one	I – something
P – their	I – everybody	P – us	I – few
P – she	D – those	P – they	P – his
D – these	P – we	D – this	P – your
P – hers	P – me	P – our	D – that

Lesson 33

1965 - 1975

History's Masterminds - *TRISMS*©

Lesson 33

Day	SCIENTISTS	INVENTIONS	EXPLORERS
Mon	1967 Christiaan Barnard performed the first human heart transplant.		
	Questionnaire		
	S-33		
Tue	**Science Vocabulary**	1969 Microprocessor	
	prevent	**Questionnaire**	
	reject		
	transplant		
	organ		
	muscle		
Wed			1969 Neil Armstrong, first person to walk on the moon
			Questionnaire
			*moon
Thu		1973 Cellular phone	7/20/1969 "That's one small step for a man, one giant leap for mankind."
		Questionnaire	--Neil Armstrong
Fri		1975 Digital camera	
		Questionnaire	
			*indicates present-day location

LANGUAGE ARTS	READING SELECTIONS
Prepositions and phrases	**Historical Fiction (read one per lesson)**
L-33a	The Return of Gabriel - John Armistead
	Flying South - Laura Malone Elliot
Ψ **IEW Expanded Essay***	Till Tomorrow - John Donahue
*This assignment may take an additional week to	Red Scarf Girl: A Memoir of the Cultural Revolution - Ji Li Jiang
complete.	Where Have all the Flowers Gone? - Ji Li Jiang
Read the source text, choose your topics, and locate	
additional resources.	
Prepositions and adverbs	**Biographies (an alternate for a historical fiction)**
L-33b	Jessie De La Cruz - Gary Soto
	Freedom's Children - Ellen Levine
	Martin Luther King Jr. - Patricia McKissack
Ψ **IEW Key Word Outline**	Christiaan Barnard - John Bankston
Create a key word outline for each source on your five	
chosen topics.	
Coordinating conjunctions	**Other Books for Research**
L-33c	Sami and the Time of the Troubles - Florence Heide
	Freedom School, Yes! Amy Littlesugar
Ψ **IEW Fused Outline**	Who Shot the President? - Judy Donnelly
Fuse your key word outlines together into one outline for your	Human Body Revealed - Sue Davidson & Ben Morgan
paper.	The Healthy Body Cookbook - Joan D'Amico
Correlative conjunctions	**Historical Events for Timeline**
L-33d	1965 Gambia becomes independent
	1965 Revolution in Algeria
Ψ **IEW Rough Draft**	1966 Indira Gandhi becomes Prime Minister of India
Create a rough draft from your fused outline.	1967 Six Day War between Israel and Arab nations
	1969 Fighting in North Ireland between Protestants and Catholics
	1974 Israel & Egypt sign weapons accord
	1975 Israel signs an agreement with European Economic Market
	1975 Ethiopia ends monarchy after 3000 years
Interjections	**Other Areas of Interest during this Lesson**
L-33e	Richard Nixon
	Solar energy
Ψ **IEW Final Essay**	Malcolm X
Write your final essay including all required styles.	Al Fatah - Arafat
	Charles de Gaulle
	Nuclear powered submarines
Write your mini book report.	Indira Gandhi
6 Week Quiz	
	1973 GM research team create air bags
	1975 first personal computer, the Altair F

Scientist Questionnaire

1. **Who:** Christiaan Neethling Barnard   Pioneered Organ Transplants

2. **Nationality:** South African

3. **Life span:** 1922-2001

4. **Span of research:** He was trained to be a cardiothoracic surgeon in America and returned to South Africa. In 1958, he established the first heart unit at the Cape Town hospital.

5. **Biblical or church history event of the time:** Jim Elliot, Christian martyr in Ecuador, 1956

6. **Noted achievement & field of interest:** In 1967, he performed the first open heart surgery. The drug used to prevent the body from rejecting the new heart weakened his resistance to infection. Louis Washkansky died after 18 days.

7. **Secondary achievement & field of interest:** He also pioneered new and risky techniques as well as bypass sugery. He performed double transplants (1974), artificial valves and using animal hearts for emergency treatment (1977). He performed 10 orthotopic transplants (1967 – 1973), and Barnard or his group performed 48 heterotopic transplants (abnormal anatomic location) between 1975 and 1983.

8. **Motivation:** He had a passion for the heart, the human pump.

9. **Significance of discovery:** Heart surgery and transplants have saved and extended hundreds of lives.

10. **How was this discovery helpful or harmful to society?** Heart surgery is now a common practice. Many people's lives are saved. Other organs can be safely transplanted today. There is always a risk of the value of a human life being determined by what organs they can give to someone deemed "more worthy" or life than another.

11. **New word and meaning:** Answers will vary.

12. **Questions prompted through this study?** Answers will vary.

13. **Interesting bit of trivia:** He practiced on animals before attempting his surgery on Mr. Washkansky. In 1967, Dr. Barnard put a woman's heart in a man. Vital to the Barnard team was Hamilton Naki -- a man of incredible skill, entirely self-taught, who overcame a complete lack of education to be appointed Barnard's principal surgical assistant. Naki himself remains modest about his achievements. "I was blessed by God who gave me his teachings from heaven." He retired due to arthritis in his hands in 1983. Christiaan died of a severe asthma attack.

Cite your sources:

Inventions Questionnaire

1. What invention: Microprocessor

2. When: 1969

3. Who is the inventor (person or country): United States Intel engineers, led by Frederico Faggin built Ted Hoff's idea 4004 into hardware for the Japanese business Busicom. Gary Boone of Texas Instrument received the patent.

4. Motivation: To create a chip that would carry out all arithmetical calculations plus control the memory and the program of the calculator.

5. How did this invention change life as it was then? Computers have many uses. They aid greatly in complicated mathematical equations. They are ideal for quickly repeating jobs that need exact detail and precision. They can process and locate information quickly.

6. What have been the ethical consequences (if any)? Personal computers can be used for good or for bad. We find computers in our appliances, vehicles, and places of business. Programs are used to dictate the use and skills of the computer.

7. Diagram or draw the invention:

Cite your sources: http://www.ideafinder.com/history/inventions/microprocessor.htm 4/14/2012

Inventions Questionnaire

1. **What invention:** Cellular telephone

2. **When:** 1973 (First U.S. analog mobile phone call)
   1977 Cell phones available to the public
   1990's second generation – digital networks
   2001 third generation – high speed IP data networks & mobile broadband
   2009 fourth generation – all – IP networks
   Satellite mobile

3. **Who is the inventor:** Dr. Martin Cooper - Motorola

4. **Motivation:** It was the product of Cooper's vision for personal wireless handheld telephone communications, distinct from mobile car phones. Cooper has stated that watching Captain Kirk using his communicator on the television show *Star Trek* inspired him to develop the handheld mobile phone.

5. **How did this invention change life as it was then?** Instant communication. It is useful in emergencies. Parents can keep in touch with their children.

6. **What have been the ethical consequences?** (if any) The phone can become a distraction when driving or other tasks. Obsessive behavior and using the telephone for text messaging and conversation rather than face to face interaction can affect the ability to relate to others. For some there is the compulsion to answer phone or call someone immediately. The cell phone does allow for easier communication between families and for less expensive communication from remote locations and internationally.

7. **Diagram or draw the invention**

Cite your sources:

Inventions Questionnaire

1. **What invention:** Digital Camera

2. **When:** Deccember 1975

3. **Who is the inventor:** (person or country) Steven Sasson for Eastman Kodak

4. **Motivation:** To create a camera that used a digital format to record images by electronic sensor instead of film.

5. **How did this invention change life as it was then?** The first Kodak used an anolog cassette tape to store images. Change was slow but progressed with the memory chip. The chip allowed the camera to become smaller. Digital cameras allow you to see your pictures immediately and the memory sticks allow for mass storage. Pictures can be viewed on computer, shared on the Internet, edited with software programs, printed, or stored. Film photography is becoming history.

6. **What have been the ethical consequences?** (if any) Cameras are now a part of many devices; cell phones, PDAs, video cameras, even the Hubble Space Telescope. Satellites can send digital images from space. Google maps can be helpful or seen as intrusive. Pictures can be taken and posted on the Internet without the knowledge of the person.

7. **Diagram or draw the invention**

Cite your sources http://www.ehow.com/about_5071042_history-kodak-digital-cameras.html 4/14/2012

Explorers Questionnaire

1. **Who:** Neil Alden Armstrong

2. **Nationality:** American

3. **When:** July 20, 1969

4. **Point of departure:** Kennedy Space Center, Cape Canaveral, Florida
   or
   Sponsoring country: United States

5. **Was this place the explorer's home country?** yes
   Explain:

6. **Biblical or church history personality of the time?** Pope John Paul II visits his homeland, Poland.

7. **What was discovered or explored?** moon (earth's satellite)

8. **How?** *Apollo 11* lunar craft launched from earth by a Saturn rocket. The main capsule orbited the moon, while astronauts Neil Armstrong and Edwin Aldrin flew down in a small landing craft into the Sea of Tranquility.

9. **What was their motivation?** They wanted to be the first to walk on the moon.

10. **Topography:** mountains, craters, valleys, and plains

11. **Climate:** between-180c to 110c The moon has no atmosphere.

12. **Natural resources:** none

13. **Crops:** none

14. **Exports:** none Forty-seven pounds of lunar surface material was collected and brought back to earth for analysis.

15. **Trivia:** After Armstrong stepped off the spaceship, he uttered the famous words, "That's one small step for [a] man, one giant leap for mankind." Armstrong and Aldrin were on the moon for only a little over two hours. Armstrong took some of the ground powder and put it in a plastic bag, put up an American flag, and talked to President Nixon. Armstrong was only 16 years old when he received his student pilot's license. In order for Neil to take flying lessons, he got a job because his parents wouldn't pay. Neil Armstrong does not have a city named after him. However, he does have a crater on the moon named after him.

Cite your sources: http://www.jsc.nasa.gov/Bios/htmlbios/armstrong-na.html 4/14/2012

S-33

How long did the first heart transplant patient live?
The patient lived 18 days before dying of a lung infection.

Are heart transplants successful today?
For the most part, heart transplants are successful today. This is due to a drug called cyclosporine which helps to fight rejection. The greatest barrier to successful transplants today is the shortage of donor hearts.

What other transplants are successfully being performed today?
There are many successful transplants today including heart, lung, liver, and kidney. Not only are organs transplanted, but skin, corneas, and bone marrow are common tissues that are transplanted.

What causes a transplant not to work?
The main reason a transplant does not work is the way the body's disease-fighting immune system responds to them. The body recognizes the transplanted organs as coming from outside the body and "rejects" or attacks them as it would a diseases-causing invader. Special methods and drugs are used to protect the new organs and tissues.

Diagram and label the organs of the human body.
See diagram in the test answer key for the fourth quarter six week quiz.

No language worksheet in Lesson 33

Teacher's Notes

_____

_____

_____

_____

_____

_____

_____

_____

_____

_____

_____

_____

_____

_____

_____

_____

_____

_____

_____

_____

_____

_____

_____

_____

FOURTH QUARTER SIX WEEK QUIZ

MATCH: Match the names on the left with their description on the right by writing the letter of the correct description in the space provided.

C   1.   Jonas Salk   a. first to climb Mt. Everest

A   2.   Sir Edmund Hillary   b. performed the first heart transplant

D   3.   Francis Crick & James Watson   c. developed polio vaccine

B   4.   Christiaan Barnard   d. discovered DNA

H   5.   John Glenn   e. first American space traveler

I   6.   Valentina Terishkova   f. first space traveler

E   7.   Alan Shepard   g. first to set foot on the moon

G   8.   Neil Armstrong   h. first American to orbit the earth

F   9.   Yuri Gagarin   i. first woman in space

MULTIPLE CHOICE: Circle the letter of the word or phrase that correctly completes each sentence.

1. The prefix bio means _____.
   a. from under, below   b. little, small   c. of living things

2. The Russians landed their space craft _____.
   a. on land   b. in the sea   c. at an airport

3. The Americans landed their space craft _____.
   a. on land   b. in the sea   c. at an airport

TRUE OR FALSE: Mark each statement T for true or F for false in the space provided.

F   1.   Jonas Salk had a disease called polio.

T   2.   Polio can result in death.

T   3.   Polio vaccines are given routinely now.

T   4.   DNA consists of the genetic code that makes us unique.

F   5.   Heart transplants are always successful.

F   6.   The astronauts we've studied could reuse their spacecraft.

MATCH: Match the names on the left with their description on the right by writing the letter of the correct description in the space provided.

F   1.   paralysis   a. one not in the military

D   2.   helix   b. to keep from occurring

A   3.   civilian   c. to refuse to receive

E   4.   transplant   d. a spiral line

C   5.   reject   e. to remove from one place and replace it in another

G   6.   polio   f. partial or complete loss of the power of voluntary motion

B   7.   prevent   g. acute virus disease marked by inflammation of the nerve cells of the spinal cord, causing
                            paralysis and sometimes lasting disability

BONUS: Label the organs of this body. Transplant organs are the lungs, kidneys, liver and heart.

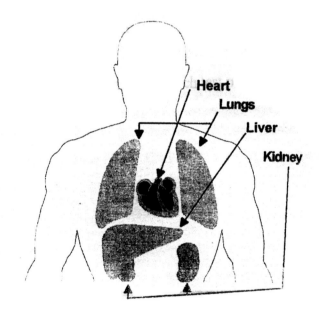

Lesson 34

1975 - 1981

Day	SCIENTISTS	INVENTIONS	EXPLORERS
Mon	Dr. Edward Stone, Voyager	1979 Sony Walkman	
	project leader	**Questionnaire**	
	Questionnaire		
	Twin probes		
	Voyager 1		
	Voyager 2		
Tue	**S-34**	**Space Vocabulary**	1981 John Young, commander of the
		shuttle	first reusable spacecraft
	Periodical	payload	**Questionnaire**
	"His Head in the Stars"	solar wind	*orbit
	by Michael Norman	lox	Space Shuttle Columbia
	New York Times Magazine	heliopause	
	20-May-90	interstellar	
Wed	**Science Vocabulary**	1981 Reusable Spacecraft	
	womb	**Questionnaire**	
	fertilize		
Thu	1978 Robert Edwards and		
	Patrick Steptoe, first test tube baby		
	Questionnaire		
Fri	**S-34**		
			*indicates present-day location

LANGUAGE ARTS	READING SELECTIONS
Direct objects	**Historical Fiction (read one per lesson)**
L-34a	Boat to Nowhere - Maureen Wartski
	The 1970's, The Arguments - Dorothy & Tom Hoobler
Ψ IEW Critique	Assassins in the Cathedral - Dave & Neta Jackson
View IEW DVD Disc 9	Stand Against the Wind - Ann Nolan Clark
Read Seminar & Practicum Workbook pp. 147- 158	
Choose a movie or program to view.	
Indirect objects	**Biographies (an alternate for a historical fiction)**
L-34b	The Importance of Anwar Sadat - Arthur Diamond
	Jimmy Carter: Thirty-ninth President - Mike Venezia
Ψ IEW Critique Outline	Henry Kissinger - Fred L. Israel
Outline your review following the Critique Model.	
(see pp. 149, 152 Seminar & Practicum Workbook)	
Appositives	**Other Books for Research**
L-34c	The 70's, From Watergate to Disco - Stephen Feinstein
	Crisis in Space-Apollo 13 - Mark Beyer
Ψ IEW Rough Draft	Three Mile Island-Nuclear Disaster - Michael Cole
Write a rough draft of your critique.	The History of Invention - Trevor I. Williams
	Extraordinary Explorers and Adventurers - Judy Alter
	The Space Shuttle - Frank Ross Jr.
	Cosmic Science - Jim Wiese
Negatives	**Historical Events for Timeline**
L-34d	1977 Egyptian President Anwar Sadat visits Israel
	1978 Military junta takes control of Honduras
Ψ IEW Final Critique	1979 Soviet Union invades Afghanistan
Write a final critique using words from p.150 Seminar	1979 Iranian terrorists seize US Embassy in Tehran
and Practicum Workbook and required styles.	1980 Smallpox eradicated
	1980-1988 Iraq and Iran at war
	1981 AIDS identified
	1981 US ends grain embargo with USSR
Using this, that, these, and those	**Other Areas of Interest during this Lesson**
L-34e	Jimmy and Rosalyn Carter
	Watergate
Ψ *IEW Optional Assignment	Oil embargo and the energy crisis
Write a 3 paragraph paper on the *Endangered Species*	Skylab
source text.	Henry Kissinger
	Godfrey Hounsfield invents the CT scanner
Write your mini book report	Baby Brown
	1979 Gordon Matthews invents voice mail
Optional Movie: *Remember the Titans*	

Scientist Questionnaire

1. **Who:** Edward C. Stone

2. **Nationality:** American

3. **Life span:** 1936-

4. **Span of research:** His studies centered on Physics, Mathematics, and Astronomy. In 1961, he became principal investigator for NASA.

5. **Biblical or church history event of the time:** Christian Coalition participates in politics by providing legislative scorecard, political reports, polling information, and details on voter registration in the states.

6. **Noted achievement & field of interest:** Dr. Stone was the project scientist for the Voyager Mission at the Jet Propulsion Laboratory. In 1977, two *Voyager* crafts revealed Jupiter, Saturn, Uranus and Neptune plus their moons.

7. **Secondary achievement & field of interest:** In 1989, *Voyager* left the planets behind. *Voyager 1* is now the most distant man-made object, with *Voyager 2* a close second. Even now *Voyager* is collecting useful information.

8. **Motivation:** NASA has 11 investigations for the *Voyager* to complete.

9. **Significance of discovery:** Both *Voyager 1 and 2* are headed towards the outer boundary of the solar system in search of the heliopause, the region where the Sun's influence wanes and the beginning of interstellar space can be sensed.

10. **How was this discovery helpful or harmful to society?** *Voyager* has revealed how little scientists really know about the solar system.

11. **New word and meaning:** Answers will vary.

12. **Questions prompted through this study?** Answers will vary.

13. **Interesting bit of trivia:** The *Voyagers* have enough electrical power and thruster fuel to operate until at least 2020. *Voyager* has exceeded expectations from NASA. In 1996, an asteroid was named after Dr. Stone.

Cite your sources:

Scientist Questionnaire

1. **Who:** Robert Edwards and Patrick Christopher Steptoe

2. **Nationality:** British

3. **Life span:** 1915-1989 Edwards physiologist   1913-1988 Steptoe gynecologist

4. **Span of research:** In 1968, Edwards, who had developed the method for in-vitro fertilization of eggs, contacted Steptoe, who had pioneered the technique of harvesting and re-implanting embryos into the womb. They combined 12 years of research with their specialties.

5. **Biblical or church history event of the time:** New English Bible published

6. **Noted achievement & field of interest:** They perfected in vitro fertilization of the human egg. Louise Joy Brown was conceived in a lab dish or in vitro, from the egg and sperm of a couple who tried for years to have a child. The first test tube baby was born in 1978 in Oldham, England. These advances are in the fields of obstetrics and gynecology.

7. **Secondary achievement & field of interest:** In 1951, Dr. Steptoe perfected the use of the laparoscope. He published his paper on laparoscopic surgery in 1965.

8. **Motivation:** Steptoe credited his mother for his perseverance. "She would say opposition, obstructions and setbacks are really challenges and that you should see them as opportunities for progress and development." He wanted to give hope to the childless.

9. **Significance of discovery:** Many infertile couples have had children by this method.

10. **How was this discovery helpful or harmful to society?** It has also been very successful with the endangered species program. There is controversy about whether or not the eggs that are discarded and are fertilized are a form of abortion. The Catholic Church opposes this method.

11. **New word and meaning:** Answers will vary.

12. **Questions prompted through this study?** Answers will vary.

13. **Interesting bit of trivia:** James Watson denounced their work, as did clergymen, scientists, and others who attacked them for degrading the procreative process.
In June 1980, an Australian team led by Alan Trounson, produced that country's first (and the world's third) IVF baby. In the United States, Howard and Georgianna Jones' IVF program in Norfolk, VA produced this country's first IVF baby, born December 28, 1981. This also marked the return of injectable fertility drug usage for IVF. Since the introduction of IVF, it is estimated that there have been one million IVF babies born worldwide. Some of these children, now grown, have begun to have their own children; IVF's second generation.

*IVF in-vitro fertilization

Cite your sources: http://www.faqs.org/health/bios/45/Patrick-Steptoe.html 4/14/2012

Inventions Questionnaire

1. What invention: Sony Walkman

2. When: 1979

3. Who is the inventor: Kazo Ohsone

4. Motivation: to create a portable playback stereo for cassette tapes and lightweight headphones

5. How did this invention change life as it was then? One can enjoy your music without bothering anyone and can take it with them easily.

6. What have been the ethical consequences? (if any) It inspired a whole industry of throw away electronics. The headphones allow a person to escape into the music and ignore people but also make themselves vulnerable to attack when exercising outside. It does allow for individualized, inexpensive entertainment.

7. Diagram or draw the invention

The cassette tape was invented by Philips Electronics in 1963.

Cite your sources:

Inventions Questionnaire

1. **What invention:** Re-useable Spacecraft (Columbia)

2. **When:** 1981

3. **Who is the inventor (person or country):** NASA, United States

4. **Motivation:** To launch like a rocket but land like a plane. To build a vehicle large enough to carry seven astronauts and 65,000 pounds of equipment, allowing for missions to last seven to eight days.

5. **How did this invention change life as it was then?** It put us ahead of the Soviets in the great Space Race. It allows scientists to conduct experiments in medicine, industry and astronomy. The shuttle can deliver satellites and other items between the earth and space. The space station can be serviced by the shuttle.

6. **What have been the ethical consequences (if any)?** A terrible cost has been paid in lives and money. So far there has been co-operation between the nations.

7. **Diagram or draw the invention:**

Cite your sources: http://www.astronomytoday.com/exploration/shuttle.html 3/7/2012

Explorers Questionnaire

1. Who: John Watts Young

2. Nationality: American

3. When: 1981

4. Point of departure: Kennedy Space Center   Cape Canaveral, Florida
or
Sponsoring country: United States

5. Was this place the explorer's home country? Yes

6. Biblical or church history personality of the time? Moral Majority: U.S. political action group composed of conservative, fundamentalist Christians. Founded (1979) and led (1979-87) by evangelist Rev. Jerry Falwell. The group played a significant role in the 1980 elections through its strong support of conservative candidates. The Moral Majority was dissolved in 1989.

7. What was discovered or explored? The 54 1/2 hour, 36-orbit mission verified Space Shuttle systems performance during launch, orbit, and on re-entry. Tests of the orbiter *Columbia* included evaluation of mechanical systems including the payload bay doors, the attitude and maneuvering rocket thrusters, guidance and navigation systems, and orbiter/crew compatibility.

8. How? Young's fifth space flight, *Columbia,* was also the first winged re-entry vehicle to return from space to a runway landing. It weighed about 98 tons as Young landed it on the dry lakebed at Edwards Air Force Base, California.

9. What was their motivation? It was the maiden flight of the space shuttle with a manned crew, John Young and Bob Crippen as pilots.

10. Topography: orbit earth 36 times

11. Climate: Thermosphere 1,500 C or higher

12. Natural resources: none

13. Crops: none

14. Exports: none

15. Trivia: Astronaut John Young has a staggering number of historic spaceflight firsts and NASA records included in his service record. Young flew on board the first manned Gemini mission, operated the first computer on a manned spacecraft, flew on two Apollo moon missions, and was mission commander on the very first flight of the Space Shuttle. His six spaceflights (seven, if you count his lift off from the moon on Apollo 16) tie a NASA record. He continues to advocate the development of the technologies that will allow us to live and work on the moon and, possibly on Mars.

Cite your sources:

S-34

What was the mission of *Voyager*?

The original mission for *Voyager* outlined visits only to Jupiter and <u>Saturn</u>. The plan was added to in 1981 to include a visit to <u>Uranus,</u> and again in 1985 to include a visit to <u>Neptune</u>. *Voyager* completed both of those missions and is currently performing scientific experiments in interstellar space.

Optional assignment:

Artificial Insemination: How does this process work?

Artificial insemination was developed due to infertility problems. In the procedure, a doctor places sperm from a woman's partner or a donor directly into her reproductive system. The most common treatment is called in-vitro fertilization in which eggs and sperm are combined in a laboratory dish and then inserted into a woman's fallopian tubes.

The eggs and sperm may come from the couple being treated or from donors. The woman who produces the eggs takes fertility drugs to make several eggs mature at once. Using several eggs increases the likelihood of successful pregnancy. When a man has an exceptionally low sperm count, doctors sometimes achieve fertilization by using tiny instruments to insert individual sperm into eggs. This delicate technique is called intracytoplasmic sperm injection, often shortened to ICSI.

Discuss the ethical and moral questions this procedure raises.

Answers will vary. Sometimes, many fertilized eggs occur and not all are implanted. Some see those that are discarded as unborn children being thrown away.

How is it being used in the endangered species program?

Many breeders use a process called artificial insemination to improve the quality of their stock, and it is also used to improve endangered species or to produce a pregnancy among endangered animals in captivity. It permits the best males to have many more offspring than would be possible by natural mating.

No language worksheet in Lesson 34

Teacher's Notes

_____

_____

_____

_____

_____

_____

_____

_____

_____

_____

_____

_____

_____

_____

_____

_____

_____

_____

_____

_____

_____

_____

_____

Lesson 35

1982 - 1990

Day	SCIENTISTS	INVENTIONS	EXPLORERS
Mon	1982 Robert Jarvic and William DeVries		
	implanted the first artificial heart. Jarvik 7		
	Questionnaire		
Tue	Science Vocabulary	1983 Video Camera	
	terminal	**Questionnaire**	
	artificial		
	S-35		
Wed	1982 Vinton Gray Cerf and Bob Kahn		1983 Sally Ride first American woman
	Internet		in space
	Questionnaire		**Questionnaire**
			*orbit
	Vocabulary		
	modem		
	router		
	servers		
	network		
Thu			**Vocabulary**
			civilian
			simulator
			1986 Christa McAuliffe, first civilian in
			a Space Shuttle
			Questionnaire
			*none
Fri			
			*indicates present-day location

LANGUAGE ARTS	READING SELECTIONS
English punctuation and capitalization	**Historical Fiction (read one per lesson)**
L-35a	When I Left My Village - Maxine Rose Schur
	Lupita Manana - Patricia Beatty
Ψ IEW Critique Writing	The Clay Marble - Minfong Ho
Write a critique on the Historical Fiction or Biography	Homeless Bird - Gloria Whelam
you chose for this lesson or a previous lesson.	The 1980's-Earth Song - Dorothy & Tom Hoobler
	Lost in the War - Nancy Antle
Commas	**Biographies (an alternate for a historical fiction)**
L-35b	Sacred Honor, Colin Powell - David Roth
	If You Could Be My Friend - Lisa Boudaka
Ψ IEW Outline	50 American Heroes Every Kid Should Meet - Dennis Denenberg
Create an outline for your critique.	Ben Carson - Ben Carson
	Sally Ride - Carolyn Blacknall
	The Importance of Simon Wiesenthal - Linda Jacobs Altnam
	Christa McAuliffe - Charlene Billings
	Ronald McNair - Dena Shaw
Semi-colons and colons	**Other Books for Research**
L-35c	The 1980's: From Ronald Reagan to MTV - Stephen Feinstein
	The Chernobyl Catastrophe - Graham Richard
Ψ IEW Rough Draft	Dust of Life-The 1980's - Mary Z. Holmes
Write the rough draft of your critique.	Extraordinary Explorers and Adventurers - Judy Alter
	The Fall of the Berlin Wall - Pat Levy
	The Iran-Contra Scandal - Christine Peterson
	Germany - Things to Make, Activites & Facts - Franklin Watts
	The Look-It Book of Explorers - Elizabeth Cody Kimmel
Apostrophes and quotation marks	**Historical Events for Timeline**
L-35d	1982 Israel drives out the PLO
	1983 First cell phone network
Ψ IEW Final Critique	1984 Syria frees US pilot after appeal from Jesse Jackson
Write your final critique, including words from the lists	1985 Jordan King Hussein & PLO leader Arafat sign accord
on page 150.	1986 Government of the Philippines overthrown
	1987 Portugal signs agreement to return Macau to China
	1988 Anti-Armenian pogrom in Azerbaijan
	1989 Akhito becomes emperor of Japan
Underlining, hyphens, and dashes	**Other Areas of Interest during this Lesson**
L-35e	Terrorism
Ψ IEW Response to Literature	US President Ronald Reagan
Read pp. 159-168 Seminar & Practicum Workbook	Prime Minister Margaret Thatcher
Create Stage One Response to Literature from critique	Astronaut Judith Recnik
See pp. 162-163 for topics and models	former US President Jimmy Carter
	AIDS identified
Write your mini book report	Scanning Tunneling Microscope STM
	Atomic Force Microscope
	1985 Nanoballs discovered

Scientist Questionnaire

1. **Who:** Robert Koffler Jarvik and Dr. William DeVries

2. **Nationality:** Americans

3. **Life span:** Jarvik 1946-   DeVries 1943-

4. **Span of research:** Jarvik's father was a physician and helped him. While still in his teens, he designed surgical tools. He graduated in occupational biomechanics in 1971.

5. **Biblical or church history event of the time:** The Pope is shot, but survives.

6. **Noted achievement & field of interest:** In 1971, Jarvik joined Dr. Willem Kolff's artificial organ team at the Institute. They worked on constructing a manmade heart. During this time, Jarvik got his medical degree from the University of Utah.

7. **Secondary achievement & field of interest:** In 1982, Dr. William DeVries performed the surgery. He was the only doctor approved by the FDA to perform a transplant and Jarvik assisted in the operation. They implanted the first artificial heart, called the Jarvik 7, in a human being. Barney B. Clark survived for 112 days. The Jarvik-7 performed perfectly. More implants followed, but on terminally ill patients.

8. **Motivation:** Jarvik's father had heart problems. He wanted to use his skill as an inventor to solve a problem.
    DeVries never knew his father, who was a surgeon that died during WWII. DeVries tried to enlist but was informed that he was a military "sole surviving son". They told him the best way he could serve his country was to get his medical degree. He became a cardiovascular surgeon.

9. **Significance of discovery:** The artificial heart keeps people alive until a new heart can be found for a transplant.

10. **How was this discovery helpful or harmful to society?** It was helpful because it saved and prolonged lives.

11. **New word and meaning:** Answers will vary.

12. **Questions prompted through this study?** Answers will vary.

13. **Interesting bit of trivia:** As a teenager, Javik invented the automatic surgical stapler. In 1976, he became a prime associate in an artificial-organs firm, a venture that was started by Dr. Kolff. Jarvik became the president of Kolff's company and changed its name to Symbion, Inc., a company that manufactures the prosthetic heart and other artificial organs. In 1983, he received the Inventor of the Year award by the National Inventors Hall of Fame.
    Dr. William DeVries went on to serve at Walter Reed Hospital and then in the Army Reserve.

Cite your sources:

Scientist Questionnaire

1. **Who: (Name)** Vinton Gray Cerf and Bob Kahn
   U.S. Government Research & Development Team: Robert Elliot, Jon Postel, Steve Crocker

2. **(Nationality)** American

3. **Life span:** Cerf 1943 - & Kahn 1938 -

4. **Span of research:** They worked at the Dept. of Defense to develop TCP/IP technology

5. **Biblical event of the time:**

6. **Noted achievement & field of interest:** 1982 Internet

7. **Secondary achievement & field of interest:** 1983 email

8. **Motivation:** system to allow all computers within a network to share information

9. **Significance of discovery:** Immediate communication with access to articles, books, blogs, maps, videos, music and websites. The Internet is available 24/7.

10. **How was this discovery helpful or harmful to society?** Access to up-to-date information and the ability to keep in touch with friends and relatives around the world quickly through email and video chats has revolutionized the way we communicate. It allows parents to have daily access to their students grades. Doctors can communicate with a pharmacy, radiology, etc. immediately.
    Danger can lurk in chat rooms for children. Your identity can remain anonymous so a child doesn't realize they aren't talking with another child. Children are starting to spend more time typing than talking (carpal tunnel). Children spend less time outdoors with physical exercise and more on the computer. Computer games have become addictive to some individuals, causing loss of jobs and wages. Identity theft has become a major problem for society. Information "overload" has increased and causes depression and other maladies.

11. **New word and meaning:** Answers will vary.
    Internet – a network that links computers worldwide

12. **Questions prompted through this study?** Answers will vary.

13. **Interesting bit of trivia:** The Internet was commercialized in 1995.
    In 2006 Cerf and Kahn were inducted into the National Inventors Hall of Fame.

Cite your sources: Swanson, Jennifer. *How the Internet Works.* MN: Child's World, 2012.

Inventions Questionnaire

1. What invention: Video Camera

2. When: 1983

3. Who is the inventor (person or country): Japan, Sony Beta Camcorder (records on video tape). In 1951, Charles Paulson Ginsburg, known as the "father of the video cassette recorder"

4. Motivation: Sony slogan, "Inside this camera is a VCR".

5. How did this invention change life as it was then? The smaller camera made home movies possible and people could record motion instead of still shots.

6. What have been the ethical consequences (if any)? Overall it is used for good. It records family and historical events. It aids speakers as they prepare for presentations. Citizens have filmed events that make the police accountable. They are used as a form of security. Most stores and banks have cameras to reduce theft. Cameras are placed at intersections and toll gates to record traffic violations, which many consider an infringement on their right. Cameras are also used to produce pornography.

7. Diagram or draw the invention:

Cite your sources:

Explorers Questionnaire

1. **Who:** Dr. Sally Ride

2. **Nationality:** American

3. **When:** 1983

4. **Point of departure:** Kennedy Space Center in Florida
   or
   Sponsoring country: USA

5. **Was this place the explorer's home country?** yes
   Explain:

6. **Biblical or church history personality of the time:** Ron Luce, head of Teen Mania Ministries

7. **What was discovered or explored?** 174 hours in orbit

8. **How?** *Challenger* Space Shuttle launched from Florida and landed on a lakebed runway at Edwards Air Force Base, California

9. **What was their motivation?** *Challenger* launched on her maiden voyage, STS-6, on April 4, 1983. That mission saw the first spacewalk of the Space Shuttle program, as well as the deployment of the first satellite in the Tracking and Data Relay System constellation.

10. **Topography:** orbit of the Earth

11. **Climate:** The space shuttle orbits in the thermosphere of the Earth. 1,500 C or higher

12. **Natural resources:** none

13. **Crops:** none

14. **Exports:** none

15. **Trivia:** First American woman in space. She entered the corps in 1978 and completed her training in 1979. Her first and second flights were aboard the Space Shuttle *Challenger*. Dr. Ride has also written a children's book, *To Space and Back*, describing her experiences in space. She has received the Jefferson Award for Public Service, and has twice been awarded the National Spaceflight Medal. Her latest books include *Voyager: An Adventure to the Edge of the Solar System* and *The Third Planet: Exploring the Earth from Space*. She was also a member of the Columbia Accident Investigation Board (CAIB), which investigated the February 1, 2003 loss of Space Shuttle *Columbia*. She left NASA in 1987 to teach at Stanford University. Since 1989, she has been at the University of California at San Diego as a professor and as head of the California Space Institute.

Cite your sources: www.**jsc.nasa.gov**/Bios/htmlbios/ride-sk.html 4/14/2012

Explorers Questionnaire

1. **Who:** Christa Corrigan McAuliffe

2. **Nationality:** American

3. **When:** 1986

4. **Point of departure:** Kennedy Space Center, Florida
   or
   Sponsoring country: USA

5. **Was this place the explorer's home country?** yes
   Explain:

6. **Biblical or church history personality of the time:** Bishop Barbara Harris; the first female bishop of the Episcopal Church.

7. **What was discovered or explored?** Just 73 seconds into mission STS 51-L, a booster failure caused an explosion that resulted in the loss of seven astronauts, as well as the vehicle. The crew on board the orbiter *Challenger* included the pilot, Commander M. J. Smith (USN) (pilot), three mission specialists, Dr. R. E. McNair, Lieutenant Colonel E. S. Onizuka (USAF), and Dr. J. A. Resnik, as well as two civilian payload specialists, Mr. G. B. Jarvis and Mrs. Christa McAuliffe.

8. **How?** Space Shuttle *Challenger* was built to serve as a test vehicle for the Space Shuttle program.

9. **What was their motivation?** McAuliffe was selected as the primary candidate for the "Teacher in Space" Project.

10. **Topography:** none

11. **Climate:** none

12. **Natural resources:** none

13. **Crops:** none

14. **Exports:** none

15. **Trivia:** The loss of *Challenger* does not overshadow its legacy in NASA's history. The discoveries made on *Challenger's* many successful missions continue to better mankind in space flight and in life on earth.

Cite your sources:

S-35
What has been the outcome of the artificial heart procedure?

In 1982, a surgical team led by William C. DeVries of the University of Utah implanted an air-powered device as the first permanent artificial heart. The device, called the Jarvik-7, was designed by the American physician Robert K. Jarvik. The recipient, Barney B. Clark, survived for 112 days. Several other patients also received Jarvik hearts, and one survived for 620 days.

Scientists have since worked to develop an artificial heart that can permanently replace a diseased human heart.
The Jarvik-7 had several features that limited the quality of life for patients. The device had a large, heavy, external power unit that hindered movement and air tubes that passed through the skin of the patient. Complications from the device, including bleeding and stroke in some patients, forced physicians to abandon it as a possible long-term heart replacement. But it is still used today for sustaining patients temporarily until a natural heart transplant can be performed.

In the 1990's, teams of scientists in the United States developed the AbioCor artificial heart. This device is made up of an electric pump implanted within the patient. With the AbioCor heart, patients can participate in most activities of daily living without being connected to a large power supply. The longest a patient has survived with this artificial heart is 512 days.

Scientists continue working to refine and improve the design and function of artificial hearts so that the devices can eventually be used as true replacement hearts.

What is a heart attack, what causes one, and what are some preventative measures?

A heart attack normally occurs because an artery to the heart becomes blocked. The result is a part of the heart is unable to receive oxygen-rich blood, which causes it to die. Many heart attacks are fatal, although many people survive if only a small portion of the heart is affected and it is caught in time. To prevent heart attack, people need to eat healthy, low-fat foods, exercise regularly, and avoid being over-stressed. Aspirin is also recommended as a preventative.

No language worksheet in Lesson 35

Teacher's Notes

Lesson 36

1990 - 1994

Day	SCIENTISTS	INVENTIONS	EXPLORERS
Mon		1990 Hubble Space Telescope	
		Questionnaire	
Tue		1991 Wind Farm	**Vocabulary**
		off shore wind farms	coalition
		Questionnaire	sanction
			embargo
			humanitarian
			catastrophic
			aggression
Wed	1991 Sumio Iijima discovers nanotubes.		1991 Persian Gulf War
	Questionnaire		**Worksheet**
Thu	1991 Tim-Berners-Lee and		Identify the countries that make up
	Robert Cailliau		the Middle East and mark them on
	World Wide Web free to public		**Map 13**
	Questionnaire		
Fri	**World Wide Web Vocabulary**	1992 Palm Pilot	Optional:
	hypertext	**Questionnaire**	CNN Movie: *Operation Desert Storm*
	URL - uniform resource locator		*The War Begins* and
	browser		*The Victory*
	search engine		

LANGUAGE ARTS	READING SELECTIONS
Parenthesis	**Historical Fiction (read one per lesson)**
L-36a	Habibi - Naomi Shihab Nye
	Parvana's Journey - Deborah Ellis
Ψ IEW Debate - Persuasive Essay	The Breadwinners - Deborah Ellis
Illegal Immigration in America	Adem's Cross - Alice Mead
	Indian Summer - Barbara Girion
	The Wall - Elizabeth Lutzeier
	Freya on the Wall - T. Degens
	Girl of Kosovo - Alice Mead
Homonyms	**Biographies (an alternate for a historical fiction)**
L-36b Worksheet 32	Zlata's Diary, A Child's Life in Sarajevo - Zlata Filipovic
	Teresa of Calcutta - Jeanene Watson
	Saddam Hussein - Charles J. Shields
Ψ IEW Key Word Outline	Boris Yeltsin: A Man of the People - Eleanor Ayer
Create a key word outline for your persuasive essay.	The Picture Life of Mikhail Gorbachev - Janet Caulkins
	Edwin Hubble: Discoverer of Galaxies - Margaret J. Anderson
	*Blinded by the Shining Path - Dave & Neta Jackson
Synonyms and antonyms	**Other Books for Research**
L-36c Worksheet 33	The 1990's: From the Persian Gulf War to Y2K - Stephen Feinstein
	When the Wall Came Down - Serge Schumemann
	United Nations - Linda Melvern
Ψ IEW Rough Draft	Middle East: A Background to the Conflicts - John Pimlott
Write a rough draft, be sure both sides are presented	Voyager: Exploring the Outer Planets - Joan Marie Verba
in each paragraph with your stance represented	Satellites and the GPS - Natalie M. Rosinsky
in the last paragraph.	Wind Energy Blown Away! - Amy S. Hanson
	The Great Voyager Adventure - Alan Harris and Paul Weissman
Abbreviations	**Historical Events for Timeline**
L-36d Worksheet 34	1990 Berlin Wall torn down
	1990 Iraq invades Kuwait
Ψ IEW Final Essay	1990 Sandanista government voted out of Nicarauga
Write your final essay and, if possible, use it to hold	1990 - 1901 Persian Gulf crisis
a debate with friends or family on the issue.	1991 Antarctica is designated as a world park
	1992 Soviet Union dissolves into 12 independent republics
	1993 US stops nuclear weapons testing
	1994 NAFTA North American Free Trade Agreement
Grammar quiz	**Other Areas of Interest during this Lesson**
L-36e	Shannon Lucid
	Mae Jemison
Optional Movie: *Stand and Deliver*	Saddam Hussein
	General Norman Schwartzkopf
	Philip Johnson - Intelligent Design
Write your mini book report	
9 Week Quiz	

Scientist Questionnaire

1. **Who:** Sumio Iijima

2. **Nationality:** Japanese

3. **Life span:** 1939--

4. **Span of research:** 1970—"the high resolution electron microscopy is my life-long research theme."

5. **Biblical event of the time:** In 1989, the New Revised Standard Version of the Bible was released.

6. **Noted achievement & field of interest:** condensed matter physics. **In 1991** he discovered carbon nanotubes. His previous work prepared him to recognize the tubes.

7. **Secondary achievement & field of interest:** His PhD thesis was the study of crystallography in silver. In 1982 he joined the government research project on "Ultra Fine Particles"

8. **Motivation:** To explore the new field of nanotechnology

9. **Significance of discovery:** Nanotubes are the first building block for nantechnology. They are light, flexible and very strong threads. They can carry an electric charge and function as a transitor.

10. **How was this discovery helpful or harmful to society?** By adding nanotubes of carbon the new mixture is stronger. By adding nanotubes to plastic, strong, lightweight, rustproof car bumpers have been created. Adding them to fabric can make it stain proof. Adding them to cement makes it waterproof. Scientists have many projections for the use of nanotubes. By attaching molecules that are attracted to cancer cells onto the nanotube, medicine can be applied directly to the affected cells. NASA is working with other materials to create a lightweight space ship. The application of electricity can change the shape of an object, giving the potential to morph airplane wings.

11. **New word and meaning** Answer will vary
    Nanoscale: A nano is a measurement for one billionth of something. And is unseen by the human eye.

12. **Questions prompted through this study?** Answers will vary

13. **Interesting bit of trivia:** Answers will vary
    Nanotubes are just a part of Nanotechnology.
    Nanomaterial: particles, crystals, quantum dots, fullerene (carbon balls), nanowhiskers

Cite your sources: Johnson, Rebecca L. Nanotechnology. MN: Lerner Publishing, 2006.
http://www.understandingnano.com/nanotubes-carbon.html 3/20/2012

Scientist Questionnaire

1. **Who:** (Name) Tim Berners-Lee and Robert Cailliau

2. **Nationality** British   Belgian

3. **Life span:** 1955 -   1947 -

4. **Span of research:** In 1980 they proposed a project based on hypertext

5. **Biblical event of the time:** In 1979, the *Jesus* film became the most watched movie of all time according to the *New York Times*

6. **Noted achievement & field of interest:** Computer science. The first website was initiated on August 6, 1991.

7. **Secondary achievement & field of interest:** 2009 - United Kingdom Government Project Making government more open and accountable

8. **Motivation:** To make it possible to share and update information among researchers by creating web pages - communication tool

9. **Significance of discovery:** On April 30, 1993, the World Wide Web was made free for anyone to use. You can access information from all over the world.

10. **How was this discovery helpful or harmful to society?** Information can be easily accessed. Unfortunately there are also evil websites, incorrect information, and a great deal of time can be wasted on the Internet.

11. **New word and meaning** Answers will vary
    Hypertext is text displayed on a computer or electronic device with references to other text, tables and images which readers can immediately access. The text is usually blue and underlined.

12. **Questions prompted through this study?** Answers will vary

13. **Interesting bit of trivia:** Answers will vary
    Tim Berners-Lee was knighted by Queen Elizabeth II for his pioneering work.

Cite your sources:

Inventions Questionnaire

1. **What invention:** Hubble Space Telescope

2. **When:** 1990

3. **Who is the inventor (person or country):** United States (it is named for the American astronomer Edwin Hubble)

4. **Motivation:** To build a satellite that will orbit the earth and transmit pictures so we can learn more about celestial objects and get a closer look at space

5. **How did this invention change life as it was then?** We are now able to see into the vast regions of space without the interference of the atmosphere and have color pictures sent home.

6. **What have been the ethical consequences (if any)?** Does the benefit justify the price of the project?

7. **Diagram or draw the invention:**

Cite your sources:

Inventions Questionnaire

1. **What invention:** Wind Farm utilizing wind turbines (a wind farm is a group of wind turbines in the same location)

2. **When:** 1991 The first wind farm was built off the coast of Denmark in the Baltic Sea.

3. **Who is the inventor:** In 1887 Charles F. Brush of Cleveland, OH built the first windmill that generated electricity. Danish Johannes Juul invented a wind turbine and named it as "Gidser wind turbine" in 1956. This 200kW, three-bladed turbine was the ancestor of the modern wind turbines.

4. **Motivation:** To create a renewable and nonpolluting energy source. Turbines convert kinetic energy from the wind into useable mechanical energy.

5. **How did this invention change life as it was then?** It costs a little more to generate electricity with a wind turbine than it does to use coal. However, it does not require men to work underground in the mines. It has brought a new source for energy, but will not be effective as a sole power source.

6. **What have been the ethical consequences?** (if any) It has limitations as an energy source; no wind, no power. The electricity can't be stored easily or moved over long distances. Birds and bats are killed by the huge blades. It prevents the spraying of crops in the area. Malfunctioning turbines can cause grass fires. Some people think they are noisy and ugly. Many of the wind farms built in the 1980's are no longer profitable because the turbines are technologically out of date, parts are not readily available, and the grants and subsidies used to build them are no longer available.

7. **Diagram or draw the invention**

Cite your sources: Hansen, Amy S. *Wind Energy Blown Away!.* NY: PowerKids Press, 2010.

Inventions Questionnaire

1. **What invention:** PDA (Palm Pilot) personal digital assistant

2. **When:** 1992, released in 1996

3. **Who is the inventor:** (person or country) Jeff Hawkins, Donna Dubinsky and Ed Colligan

4. **Motivation:** To create a hand held organizer that can store and access information while away from the office. This tool contains a calender, date book, address book, note taking function (for use with a stylus) and can transfer information to and from other computers. The PDA fits in the palm of the hand and weighs about four ounces.

5. **How did this invention change life as it was then?** You no longer had to be in the office to work or access your work. It was the presursor of the smart phone. It gives a great deal of flexibility to business owners and employees.

6. **What have been the ethical consequences?** (if any) It makes it difficult to be free from the concerns and work environment. It encourages a dependence on technology and the stress factors of work rather than encouraging time spent away with the family.

7. **Diagram or draw the invention**

Cite your sources:

Persian Gulf War Worksheet

1. **When and where did the Gulf War take place?** 1991, Kuwait & Iraq

2. **What act of aggression caused the Gulf War?** Invasion of Kuwait by Iraq in 1990

3. **List 5 of the allied countries involved.** 34 nation coalition mandated by the United Nations and led by the United States. Answers will vary.
   Examples: Saudi Arabia, France, United Kingdom, Kuwait, Egypt, Syria, Pakistan, United Arab Emirates, Spain, Norway, Greece, New Zealand, Belgium, Portugal, Italy, Poland, South Korea

4. **Who was the leader of Iraq?** Saddam Hussein

5. **What was the difference between *Desert Storm* and *Desert Shield*?**
   The United States came to the aid of Saudi Arabia under Desert Shield. They share a border with Iraq and Kuwait. They did not wish to fight Iraq alone. No one wanted Iraq to control the international oil supplies. Desert Storm was the liberation of Kuwait by the UN coalition.

6. **Tell 3 ways this war was different than any war fought before.** Answers will vary.
   Iraq took Western hostages and used them as human shields to deter attacks. UN Coalition against one country. Urban warfare.

7. **Why was the U.S. involved in this war?** Iraq was given a deadline to withdraw from Kuwait. The UN Security Council passed a resolution to allow member states to "use all necessary means" to force Iraq from Kuwait if they did not withdraw. The U.S. met directly with Iraq's foreign minister. Neither side offered to compromise. The UN resolution gave the U.S. authority to use military force. Congress authorized the president to use force. The U.S. led the U.N. forces.

8. **Name at least 5 important military leaders involved (from any country).** Answers will vary.
   Examples: Norman Schwarzkopf, Colin Powell, Khalid bin Sultan, Peter de la Billière, John Major

9. **Who won the war?** The Allies or UN

10. **Tell what kinds of losses were suffered in this war.** There were many civilian casualties and destruction of the major cities. Saddam caused an ecological disaster. Israel was attacked by Iraq. Coalition POW's were abused by Iraq.

To the allied soldiers: Many deaths were caused by friendly fire. Fervent journalists exposed troops and their movements to the enemy. Gulf War syndrome, a mysterious illness that also contributed to birth defects.

To the Iraqi soldiers and people: UN Sanctions against Iraq. The infrastructure was destroyed including the water treatment facilities. There were many civilian casualties. Sanctions resulted in a high mortality rate among children.

To the country of Kuwait: The country was plundered by Iraq. They took $2 billion in goods, and $25 billion in building and equipment. There were heavy casualties and destruction of Kuwaiti infrastructure. They stripped the hospitals of their equipment. They used the zoo animals for target practice. Oil wells were set afire, pipelines destroyed and oil dumped into the Persian Gulf.

*There are many possible answers to this questionnaire depending upon your available resources.

No science assignment in Lesson 36

Worksheet 32

Write the homonyms for the following words.

red	*read*	sale	*sail*
your	*you're*	maid	*made*
for*	*four, fore*	great	*grate*
sum	*some*	tied	*tide*
wait	*weight*	pair*	*pare, pear*
here	*hear*	to*	*too, two*
our	*hour*	write*	*right, rite*

*Words marked with a star have three words that make up the homonym.

Worksheet 33

Synonyms and Antonyms

If the group of words below shows a group of synonyms, write S. If they are antonyms, write A.

1. S
2. S
3. A
4. S
5. S
6. A
7. S
8. A
9. A
10. S

Replace the underlined words with synonyms. **

1. The idea of space travel started long ago.

2. In 1687 Sir Isaac Newton described the laws of motion.

3. In 1919 Robert Goddard explained the use of rockets in space travel.

4. In 1957 the Russians launched Sputnik I into orbit.

5. At that moment modern space exploration began.

6. Today American space vehicles visit other planets.

7. New information comes from these landings.

8. Before the year 2000 Americans explored several planets.

**Teacher's note: Answers will vary

Worksheet 34

Write each abbreviation next to the word or words it represents.

Mister	Mr.	inch	in.
Post Office	P. O.	volume	vol.
Misses	Mrs.	foot	ft.
Department	dept.	pages	pp.
Junior	Jr.	yard	yd.
apartment	apt.	edition	ed.
Doctor	Dr.	ounce	oz.
Street	St	Before Christ	B.C.
Mountain	Mt.	pound	lb.
Boulevard	Blvd.	Anno Domino	A.D.
for example	e.g.	Fahrenheit	F.
amount	amt.	Kilometer	km.
that is	i.e.	Liter	l.
weight	wt.	Gram	g. or gm.
and so forth	etc.	Meter	m.

FOURTH QUARTER NINE WEEK QUIZ

MATCH: Match the names on the left with their description on the right by writing the letter of the correct description in the space provided.

C   1.   John Young   a. made possible the first test tube baby

E   2.   Robert Jarvik   b. first American woman in space

A   3.   Robert Edwards & Patrick Steptoe   c. commander of the first space shuttle

F   4.   Christa McAuliffe   d. project scientist for Voyager 2

D   5.   Dr. Edward Stone   e. implanted the first artificial heart

B   6.   Sally Ride   f. first civilian in space

TRUE OR FALSE: Mark each statement T for true or F for false in the space provided.

F   1.   The test tube baby was a baby that grew until full term outside the mother's womb.

T   2.   The test tube process is still being used.

F   3.   The artificial heart is a successful treatment for heart disease.

F   4.   Your lifestyle (what you eat & drink) doesn't effect the condition of your heart.

T   5.   Blocked arteries can cause a heart attack.

F   6.   Voyager 2 was sent to explore Venus and Mars.

MATCH: Match the names on the left with their description on the right by writing the letter of the correct description in the space provided.

C   1.   fertilize   a. uterus, an organ in the female mammal that serves as a protective place for the fetus to develop

E   2.   artificial   b. system of tubes that convey the blood from the heart to all parts of the body

B   3.   artery   c. to make fruitful or productive

A   4.   womb   d. one not in the military

D   5.   civilian   e. imitation of something natural

BONUS: Mark in chronological order the following accomplishments in space exploration we've studied.

6_____1. Skylab

8_____2. Space shuttle program

3_____3. Explorer 1

1_____4. Sputnik 1

7_____5. International manned space flight

4_____6. Friendship 7 John Glenn orbits the earth

2_____7. NASA formed

5_____8. Apollo 11 Neil Armstrong walks on the moon

Lesson 37

1995 - 2000

Day	SCIENTISTS	INVENTIONS	EXPLORERS
Mon		1994 Global Positioning System	
		Questionnaire	
Tue		1994 Genetically Modified Organisms	
		Questionnaire	
Wed	1996 Ian Wilmut - Genetic Engineering		
	Questionnaire		
Thu	**Science Vocabulary**	1997 International Space Station	
	embryo	**Questionnaire**	
	cell		
	chromosome		
	gene		
	clone		
	Optional Movie: *Jurassic Park*		
Fri		1997 Hybrid Car	
		Toyota Prius	
		Questionnaire	
		Vocabulary	
		carbon footprint	
		greenhouse gases	
		generator	
		hybrid	

LANGUAGE ARTS	READING SELECTIONS
Apartheid	**Historical Fiction (read one per lesson)**
L-37a	Dream Freedom - Sonia Levitin
Write a paragraph on Apartheid	Figs and Fate - Elsa Marston
	The Color of My Words - Lynn Joseph
Ψ IEW Lesson 37 - Basic Essay	How Tia Lola Came to ~~Visit~~ Stay - Julia Alvarez
Research the United Nations & create a 5 paragraph essay	Any Small Kindness - Tony Johnston
Use assigned topics and create key word outline(s)	Iqbal - Francesco D'Adamo
	Brothers in Hope - Mary Williams
	Taste of Salt: A Story of Modern Haiti - Frances Temple
Ψ Basic Essay - Fuse Outlines & Create Rough Draft	**Biographies (an alternate for a historical fiction)**
	Osama bin Laden - Bill Loehfelm
	Nelson Mandela and Apartheid in World History - Ann Gaines
Ψ IEW Basic Essay - Final Paper	**Other Books for Research**
Include required styles	The United Nations from A to Z - Nancy Parker
	All About Electric and Hybrid Cars- Stephanie Bearce
	America's Leaders - Jill C. Wheeler
	Heroes of the Day - Nancy Louis
	9.11.01: Terrorists Attack the U. S. - Pat Lalley
	Superfoods: Genetic Modification of Foods - Sally Morgan
	Cloning Frontiers of Genetic Engineering - David Jefferis
	How Hybrid Cars Work - Jennifer Swanson
Ψ IEW Super Essay - You are a History Maker	**Historical Events for Timeline**
This is a two-lesson assingment	1995 Terrorist attack on the Federal Building in Oklahoma City
Begin by creating a topic outline (p. 133 Seminar & Practicum	1996 Czech Republic applies for membership of the European Union
Workbook)	1996 UK & US sign comprehensive Nuclear Test Ban Treaty
Find sources and begin key word outlines	1996 Congress passes Communications Decency Act
	1997 Hong Kong returned to China
	1999 Panama Canal returned to Panama
	2000 Israel withdraws from Lebanon
	2000 First inter-Korean summit
Write your mini book report	**Other Areas of Interest during this Lesson**
	Robotics
Ψ IEW Super Essay - You are a History Maker	Y2K bug
continue researching and finish your key word outlines	Euro currency of the European Commonwealth
	NAFTA North American Free Trade Agreement
	Kosmolyot - Soviet Space Shuttle
	Virtual Reality
	AIDS epidemic
Optional Movie: *Food Inc.*	
	1995 Digital Video Disc
	1996 Smart phone Nokia
	1998 Google Larry Page & Sergey Brin Web-based search engine
	1999 Napster Sean Parker musci sharing site
	1999 PayPal Elon Musk method of securely transferring money
	using a recipient's email address
	2000 eHarmony.com Neil Clark Warren & Geroge Forgatch
	online dating service

Scientist Questionnaire

1. **Who:** Ian Wilmut   Pioneer of Cloning

2. **Nationality:** British (Scottish)

3. **Life span:** 1944-

4. **Span of research:** He became interested in farming and animals around age 14. As a result, he pursued biology in school. He assisted in a lab for a summer project and that's where his interest in developmental biology and embryology came from.

5. **Biblical or church history event of the time:** A revival, known as the Toronto Blessing, breaks out in Canada.

6. **Noted achievement & field of interest:** July 5, 1996, Wilmut and his team were the first to clone an adult mammal, Dolly the sheep. Cloning of animals is a regular occurrence in this decade. Genetic engineering has been added to the cloning process. Genes are added to fetal cells to create certain characteristics in the offspring.

7. **Secondary achievement & field of interest:** In 1973, Chris Polge and Wilmut produced the first calf from a frozen embryo, named Frosty. The technical name for freezing cells is cryobiology, "cryo".

8. **Motivation:** He sought to improve reproduction in livestock.

9. **Significance of discovery:** Animal breeding through embryo transfer. Cloning had only been a dream until Wilmut and his team brought us Dolly the sheep.

10. **How was this discovery helpful or harmful to society?** Wilmut and his team have drawn a moral line against work towards or cloning human beings, even in infertility cases. Stem cell research could be the answer to curing many diseases; Parkinson's, diabetes, ALS, muscular dystrophy. The possibility of restoring the immune system could cure leukemia and AIDS.

11. **New word and meaning:** Answers will vary.

12. **Questions prompted through this study?** Answers will vary.

13. **Interesting bit of trivia:** It took nine years to prepare the lab and fund the project at Roslin Institute. In 1983, the institute changed its focus to molecular biology and modern genetics. In 1986, working with stem cells seemed to be the answer to the problem. Fifteen years later, Dolly was created. She is named after Dolly Parton.
    Before they produced Dolly, Wilmut's team tried about 275 times without success.
    Many people associate this kind of genetic research with science fiction.

    "In my own experience, I think a lot of ideas go on in your subconscious. I find myself saying something and almost seeing it go past and thinking, 'Hey, that's a good idea.' Apart from the social fun of a coffee break, this is also when scientific ideas get discussed. Somebody will develop a hypothesis in a conversation."   Dr. Ian Wilmut

Cite your sources:

Inventions Questionnaire

1. **What invention:** GPS Global Positioning System

2. **When:** Made available to the public in 1985. It began as a military tool for the U.S. Navy in 1978.

3. **Who is the inventor:** (person or country) U.S. Navy launched the GPS satellites that were managed by the Dept. of Defense.

4. **Motivation:** To locate people and things around the world.

5. **How did this invention change life as it was then?** GPS has many applications. American soldiers in the Gulf War used it to reach remote locations where there were no street signs or unique landmarks. Ships and airplanes navigate in bad weather using GPS. Police and firefighters can reach people in danger quicker. Scientists can locate minerals and track animals. Mapmakers use GPS to make maps on the computer. Companies use GPS to find shorter routes to send packages. Farmers use it to track crops, and the general public is growing increasingly familiar with using GPS for everyday travel.

6. **What have been the ethical consequences?** (if any) GPS has many benefits, but it can invade the privacy of individuals when the information is given to unauthorized individuals or companies. Many phones and cars are now equipped with GPS, making it possible to track individuals with or without their permission, imposing on their personal freedom.

7. **Diagram or draw the invention**

Cite your sources: Rosinsky, Natalie M., *Satellites and the GPS.* MN: Compass Point Books, 2004.

Inventions Questionnaire

1. **What invention:** Genetically Modified Organisms (GMO) The deliberate change of an organisms genes in order to give it new abilities.

2. **When:** 1994 (first plant successful, tomato)

3. **Who is the inventor:** United States

4. **Motivation:** To create a longer growing season and plants that can resist disease, pests and herbicides. To improve crops and livestock through artificial selection by changing the DNA and to develop crops that can feed more people.

5. **How did this invention change life as it was then?** There is still controversy over this science. In the United States GMO foods are on the grocery shelves. The four key ingredients in convenience foods contain GMO - soy beans, wheat, sugar beets and corn. Some countries ban GMO products.

6. **What have been the ethical consequences?** (if any) Scientist cannot predict what risk may be involved in eating modified foods. There is concern that the use of GMO is causing a rise in allergies to gluten and dairy and a rise in autism and ADHD (attention deficiet hyperactive disorder). None of these concerns can be verified. GMO foods allow more people to receive more food, which lowers prices, provides food for starving peoples, and modifies crops to grow in more environments.

7. **Diagram or draw the invention**

Cite your sources:

Inventions Questionnaire

1. **What invention:** International Space Station

2. **When:** 1997

3. **Who is the inventor (person or country):** 15 different nations including the USA, Canada, Russia, Japan, and Brazil

4. **Motivation:** To understand space and attempt to live in space for long periods of time

5. **How did this invention change life as it was then?** It has brought us closer to understanding the universe and our galaxy.

6. **What have been the ethical consequences (if any)?** We are learning how to more efficiently grow plants. Medical experiments are performed in the weightless atmosphere to study the effects of zero gravity on the body. Also, we are now closer to being able to establish long term living quarters in space.

7. **Diagram or draw the invention:**

Inventions Questionnaire

1. **What invention:** Hybrid car (Toyota Prius)

2. **When:** 1997

3. **Who is the inventor:** Japan

4. **Motivation:** To create an engine that can run on two or more fuel sources with the goal of cutting down on pollution and greenhouse gases and to design a lightweight, aerodynamic body.

5. **How did this invention change life as it was then?** Change is slow. There is an interest from the government and public which encourages car manufacturers to continue research and production of hybrid cars. Hybrid car technology and costs have kept them from becoming popular enough to have an impact on society as a whole and on the environment.

6. **What have been the ethical consequences?** (if any) Hybrid cars are more expensive than gas-powered vehicles and are not as reliable or as easy to repair. It will take time for people to choose hybrid cars over their wallet and the lack of perfected technology. Homes will need to be outfitted with special plug-ins for charging. As technology improves and the cars become more stable and available at a more reasonable cost, they will provide for a cleaner and healthier environment.

7. **Diagram or draw the invention**

Cite your sources:

No science assignment in Lesson 37

No language worksheet in Lesson 37

Teacher's Notes

Lesson 38

2001 - 2012

Day	SCIENTISTS	INVENTIONS	EXPLORERS
Mon		2004 Mars Rovers	
		Questionnaire	
		Mars Rovers - *Spirit & Opportunity*	
Tue	2004 Mark Zuckerberg	**Vocabulary**	
	Facebook creator	earthquake	
	social networking service	epicenter	
		richter scale	
	co-founders Dustin Moskovitz &	fault	
	Chris Hughes	tetonic plates	
		seismometers	
	Questionnaire on Zuckerberg	tidal bore	
		tsunami	
Wed		2005 Seismic Sea Wave Warning System	
		Questionnaire	
		Identify the countries effected by the	
		Indian Ocean Tsunami 12/2004	
		Map #15	
Thu		2007 Apple iPhone	
		Questionnaire	
Fri		2009 Kepler Telescope	
		Questionnaire	

LANGUAGE ARTS	READING SELECTIONS
Ψ IEW Super Essay - You are a History Maker	**Historical Fiction (read one per lesson)**
Fuse key word outlines and outline super introduction	Under the Persimmon Tree - Suzanne Fisher Staples
& conclusion	Among the Hidden - Margaret Peterson Haddix
	Shabanu Daughter of the Wind - Suzzane Fisher Staples
	The House of Djin - Suzzane Fisher Staples
	Thura's Diary - Thura Al-Windawi
	Beneath My Mother's Feet - Amjed Qamar
	Escaping the Tide - Peg Kehret
	Joseph and Chico - Jeanne Perego
Ψ IEW Super Essay - Rough Draft	**Biographies (an alternate for a historical fiction)**
Create your rough draft and bibliography	Mark Zuckerberg - Marcia Amiron Lusted
Create your title page	Steve Jobs - Think Different - Ann Brashares
Ψ Optional Five Paragraph Essay - Steve Jobs	**Other Books for Research**
Using the IEW Champlain Model (Seminar & Practicum Workbook	Tsunami Warning - Taylor Morrison
(pps. 125,130) create a five-paragraph biographical essay on this	Slammed by a Tsunami! - Miriam Aronin
incredible man who changed the world of technology.	Hurricane Katrina and the Devastation of New Orleans, 2005 -
Create your Key Word Outlines, Fused Outline, and Rough Draft	John A. Torres
*Alternatively, you may research and give an oral report on Steve	
Jobs	**Historical Events for Timeline**
	2001 September 11th attack on the United States
	2002 N. Korea admits developing nuclear bomb
	2002 US invasion of Afghanistan
Ψ Five Paragraph Essay - Final Essay	2003 World wide protest against war in Iraq
Create your final essay with all openers & dress-ups in each	2004 Osama bin Laden takes responsibility for 9/11
paragraph, as well as a decoration or triple extension	2005 China's manned spacecraft orbits earth
*Alternatively, give your oral report on Steve Jobs	2005 Hurricane Katrina flattens New Orleans, LA
	2009 Aids virus vaccine developed
	2010 Gulf of Mexico oil spill
	2011 Earthquake & tsunami in Japan
	2012 NASA discontinues Space Shuttle program
IEW Super Essay Final Paper	**Other Areas of Interest during this Lesson**
Complete your final paper	Homeland Security & the Patriot Act
	Wiki Leaks Julian Assange
Write your mini book report	War against Iraq and Al-Qaeda
	Occupy Wall Street Movement
Optional Movie: *The Social Network*	Tea Party Movement
	Nancy Pelosi becomes first woman Speaker of the House
	Pluto reclassified as a dwarf planet
	Fidel Castro steps down as leader of Cuba
2001 Wikipedia Jimmy Wales & Larry Sanger	
open source web-based free online encyclopedia	2006 Twitter Jack Dorsey microblogging service
2002 Friendster Jonathan Abrams pioneer social network	2007 Amazon Kindle e-reader
2002 LinkedIn Reid Hoffman Professional network	2007 Apple iPhone
2003 My Space Tom Anderson & Chris DeWolf	2010 iPad arrives in US
You could use different identities\youth based site	
2003 Skype Niklas Zennstrom-voice, video, instant messaging	
2004 TheFacebook Mark Zuckerberg social networking	
2005 YouTube Steve Chen, Chad Hurley, Jaued Karim	

Scientist Questionnaire

1. **Who:** Mark Elliot Zuckerberg   co-founders Chris Hughes, Billy Olson, Dustin Moskovitz

2. **Nationality:** American

3. **Life span:** May 14, 1984 -

4. **Span of research:** Began in 1995 and launched on February 4, 2004

5. **Biblical event of the time:** In 1999, the International House of Prayer in Kansas City began non-stop 24/7 continual prayer.

6. **Noted achievement & field of interest:** Facebook - social network

7. **Secondary achievement & field of interest:** Computer software development

8. **Motivation:** To connect people online through a profile page to share information, links and photographs. To stay in touch with popular culture and current events.

9. **Significance of discovery:** Provides web-based global communication for friends, families, and advertisers

10. **How was this discovery helpful or harmful to society?** Provides an opportunity to locate friends and family. Keeps a permanent record of communications in cyberspace and allows private information to get into the hands of possible information abusers.

11. **New word and meaning:** Answers will vary
    Prodigy – a person, especially a child, who has extraordinary talent or ability

12. **Questions prompted through this study?** Answers will vary

13. **Interesting bit of trivia:** Answers will vary
    Mark Zuckerberg became *Time* Magazine's Person of the Year in 2010.

Cite your sources: Lusted, Marcia Amidon. *Mark Zuckerberg–Facebook Creator.* MN: ABDO Publishing, 2012.

Inventions Questionnaire

1. **What invention:** Mars Rovers *Spirit* (2004-2010) and *Opportunity* (2004-)

2. **When:** 2004

3. **Who is the inventor:** (person or country) NASA National Aeronautics and Space Administration

4. **Motivation:** Explore the possibility of living on Mars.

5. **How did this invention change life as it was then?** *Spirit* found evidence that Mars once held a salty sea and hot springs. *Spirit* was designed to last three months. It last made contact March 2010. So far *Opportunity* has explored the Victoria crater and moved on to the rim of the Endeavour crater. There it discovered a rock that contained clay minerals and is different from any found on Mars.

6. **What have been the ethical consequences?** (if any) Scientists are very excited about the discoveries made by the Mars Rovers. They are preparing the *Curiosity*, Mars Science Laboratory Rover. Some people feel the space program is a waste of taxpayer money and would be better spent here on Earth for the American people.

7. **Diagram or draw the invention**

Cite your sources: marsrovers.jpl.nasa.gov 3/7/2012

Inventions Questionnaire

1. **What invention:** Seismic Sea Wave Warning System

2. **When:** 1948 In **2005 the system was applied globally**

3. **Who is the inventor:** (person or country) America Charles K. Green (Invented a system to detect the long wavelength waves created by tsunamis. It became the heart of the warning system.) Later, Congress funded a team organized by Commander Elliot Roberts to complete the system.

4. **Motivation:** To create a warning system to notify people in time to escape a tsunami.

5. **How did this invention change life as it was then?** In 1948, the system saved lives along the coast of North America and protected ships in the Pacific Ocean. Early warnings save lives and give ships the opportunity to move out to sea away from the shore.

6. **What have been the ethical consequences? (if any)** Without the system more lives are lost and there are extensive injuries to survivors. Homes and businesses, boats and ships are destroyed. The area hit by a tsunami is crippled for years.

7. **Diagram or draw the invention**

Cite your sources: Aronin, Miriam. *Slammed by a Tsunami.* NY: Bearport, 2010.

Inventions Questionnaire

1. **What invention:** Apple iPhone

2. **When:** 2007 (Time Invention of the Year)

3. **Who is the inventor:** Apple

4. **Motivation:** Create a hand held computer with touch screen phone, text messaging, camera, GPS and driving instructions, Internet access, QWERTY keyboard for texting, full feature operating system allowing for working on office documents.

5. **How did this invention change life as it was then?** The iPhone was designed to evolve. Each version is more powerful and has more features. 2012, the iPhone 4 uses Siri an artificial intelligence assistant that speaks.

6. **What have been the ethical consequences?** (if any) The phones make it possible to work outside the office. This speeds up many jobs that require quick responses to customers. Problems can be reported immediately - emergency services are a click away – 911
The phone can become a distraction when driving or other tasks. May create obsessive behavior, the person feels compelled to answer the phone or call someone immediately.
Such behavior can cause sleep deprivation and lower grades.

7. **Diagram or draw the invention**

Inventions Questionnaire

1. **What invention:** Kepler Telescope

2. **When:** Launched March 2009

3. **Who is the inventor:** Natalie Batalha – NASA engineers

4. **Motivation:** To locate habitable Earth-size planets

5. **How did this invention change life as it was then?** Earth is no longer a lone outpost in the Milky Way galaxy. The telescope uses a unique lightweight mirror with a honeycomb structure. It uses a photometer to track the changes in light that occur as planets pass in front of their stars.

6. **What have been the ethical consequences?** (if any) Not known. Who gets to live on this new planet? Will our energy go into finding a new home or into finding ways to renew the Earth?

7. **Diagram or draw the invention**

Cite your sources:

No science assignment in Lesson 38

No language worksheet in Lesson 38

Teacher's Notes

FOURTH QUARTER NINE WEEK TEST

MATCH: Match the names on the left with the descriptions on the right. Write the letter of the correct description in the space provided.

H	1. Robert Goddard	a.	ocean explorer
J	2. Jonas Salk	b.	first space traveler
F	3. John Young	c.	first civilian in space
G	4. Mark Zuckerberg	d.	artificial heart
E	5. Ian Wilmut	e.	genetic engineering
A	6. Jacques Cousteau	f.	commander of first space shuttle
I	7. Thor Heyerdahl	g.	creator of Facebook
K	8. John Glenn	h.	invented multi-stage rocket
B	9. Yuri Gagarin	i.	sailed from Peru to Polynesia by raft
C	10. Christa McAuliffe	j.	developed the polio vaccine
D	11. Robert Jarvic	k.	first American to orbit the earth
L	12. Enrico Fermi	l.	first controlled nuclear chain reaction
O	13. Edwards & Steptoe	m.	Voyager project leader
M	14. Dr. Edward Stone	n.	heart transplant
N	15. Christiaan Barnard	o.	test tube baby

ANSWER THE QUESTIONS:

1. **What act of aggression caused the Gulf War?** Invasion of Kuwait by Iran

2. **What is the International Space Station?** It is an orbiting laboratory developed by a league of nations that will support a crew of six astronauts.

3. **List two discoveries that have occurred because of the Hubble space telescope.** *Possible answers*
   Star birth, irregular galaxies, evolving galaxies, close-ups of Pluto's face, confirmation of the existence of black holes

ESSAY:

On a separate sheet of paper write a paragraph covering four points in favor of, or against genetic modification of organisms. *Possible answers*

Cross species modification	Create a longer growing season
Food companies own seeds not farmers	Develop plants that can resist disease, herbicides and pesticides
Scientists cannot predict the risks from eating GMO	Create a bumper crop to feed the world
GMO crops banned in some countries	Create super foods
GMO already in our convenience foods	
Food labels do not reflect GMO content	

MATCH: Match the words on the left with their definitions on the right. Write the letter of the correct definition in the space provided.

J   1. coalition   a. living creatures made from a single cell without sexual reproduction

K   2. embargo   b. one not in the military

E   3. virus   c. disease producing organism

I   4. sanction   d. partial or complete loss of voluntary motion

B   5. civilian   e. one celled living organism that brings fermentation, putrefaction, and produces disease

C   6. bacteria   f. the rays sent out; nuclear particles

L   7. catastrophic   g. a man-made object orbiting earth or another heavenly body

D   8. paralysis   h. a wheel mounted to spin rapidly about an axis and free to turn in various directions

F   9. radiation   i. an action taken to enforce a law or rule

H   10. gyroscope   j. temporary union of countries for a common purpose

O   11. cosmology   k. legal prohibition or restriction of trade

A   12. clone   l. complete failure or sudden disaster

G   13. satellite   m. the angular height of a celestial object above the horizon

M   14. altitude   n. a splitting or breaking up into parts

N   15. fission   o. a branch of astronomy that deals with the beginning, structure, and space-time relationships of the universe

MATCH: Match the words on the left with their definitions on the right. Write the letter of the correct definition in the space provided.

F 1. Nautilus SSN 571   a. science conducted at the nano level

E 2. Global Positioning System   b. car engine that can run on more than one type of fuel

J 3. Genetically Modified Organisms   c. allows computers within a network to share information

H 4. Wind turbine   d. use of a digital format to record images by electronic sensor

B 5. Hybrid car   e. satellites are used to transmit signals to equipment on the ground to pinpoint a location

A 6. Nanotechnology   f. nuclear powered submarine

C 7. Internet   g. hand held computer with operating system, Internet, telephone, camera, GPS, keyboard, text messaging and artificial intelligence

I 8. World Wide Web   h. converts kinetic energy from the wind into mechanical energy generating electricity

D 9. Digital camera   i. ability to share information by creating web pages based on html

G 10. iPhone   j. deliberate change of an organisms genes to give it new abilities

GRAMMAR QUIZ

Select the correct letter:

1. A common noun names ___B____ person, place or thing.
   a. specific   b. any   c. singular

2. A proper noun names a ___A____ person, place or thing.
   a. particular   b. any   c. plural

3. A noun that is singular in form but plural in meaning is called ___C___.
   a. concrete   b. abstract   c. collective

4. A noun that names ideas or qualities is called ___B___.
   a. concrete   b. abstract   c. collective

5. Words that show ownership are called __C___ nouns.
   a. concrete   b. plural   c. possessive

6. A ___A____ is a word that expresses action or being.
   a. verb   b. adverb   c. noun

7. Physical or mental action is expressed by a ___B____ verb.
   a. linking   b. action   c. predicate

8. ___B___ verbs help the main verb express its meaning.
   a. linking   b. auxiliary   c. phrase

9. A transitive verb requires a ___B___.
   a. indirect object b. direct object   c. auxiliary helper

10. Linking verbs are always ___B____.
    a. transitive   b. intransitive   c. plural

11. Adjectives usually come before a ___C___.
    a. verb   b. predicate   c. noun

12. An ___C____ is a word that tells when, where, why and how.
    a. adjective   b. verb   c. adverb

13. A pronoun is a word that takes the place of a ___C____.
    a. verb   b. adjective   c. noun

14. This, that, these and those are called ___B____ pronouns.
    a. singular   b. demonstrative   c. personal

15. An ___C____pronoun does not refer to anyone or anything in particular.
    a. personal   b. demonstrative   c. indefinite

16. A preposition is a word that shows __A____ or direction.
    a. location   b. possession   c. relationships

17. A ___B____ joins words or groups of words.
    a. preposition   b. conjunction   c. adverb

18. A word or phrase that expresses emotion or excitement is an ___C___.
    a. action verb   b. appositive   c. interjection

19. A direct object follows a ___A____ verb to complete its meaning.
    a. transitive   b. linking   c. intransitive

20. An indirect object tells to whom or for whom the action of the ___A____ is done.
    a. verb   b. noun   c. direct object

21. When this, that, these and those modify nouns they are called ___B____.
    a. subject   b. adjectives   c. pronouns

Label each quote as directed:

    Adj sn   v   do
1. "All men by nature desire knowledge."   Aristotle

Label the subject noun, adjective, verb, and direct object.

    Sn   adv   v
2. "Men willingly believe what they wish."   Julius Caesar

Label the subject noun, verb, and adverb.

    Sn neg v   adj   c   pronoun
3. "I never met a man so ignorant but that something might be learned from him."   Galileo

Label the subject noun, verb, negative, conjunction, pronoun, and adjective.

    Sn   v   c
4. "Genius is <u>one percent inspiration</u> and <u>ninety-nine percent perspiration</u>." Thomas Edison

Label the subject noun, verb, conjunction, and compound predicate.

    Sn v   v   adj   prep   prep
5. "If I have seen further, it is only <u>by standing</u> <u>upon the shoulders</u> of Giants." Sir Isaac Newton

Label the subject noun, verb, adverb, and prepositional phrases.

Name the eight parts of speech:

1. noun   2. pronoun

3. preposition   4. Conjunction

5. verb   6. interjection

7. adjective   8. adverb